sential GCSE ICT

AQA

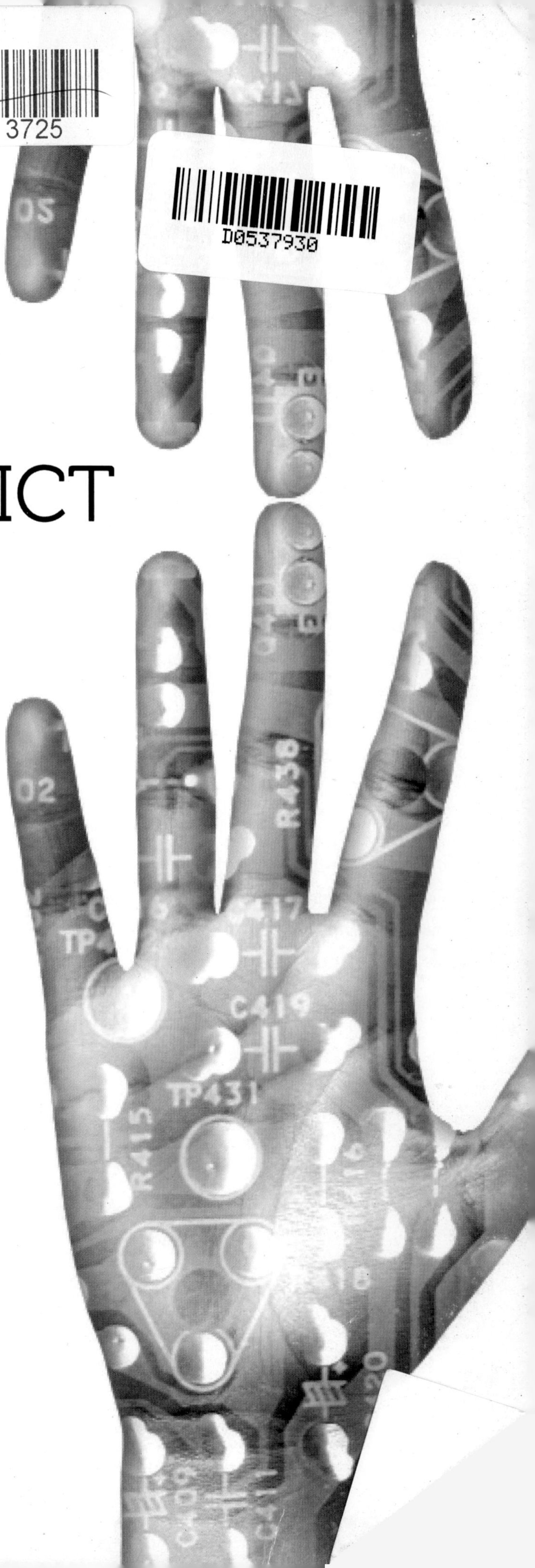

Stephen Doyle

© 2010 Folens Limited, on behalf of the author.

United Kingdom: Folens Publishers, Waterslade House, Thame Rd, Haddenham, Buckinghamshire HP17 8NT.

www.folens.com

Ireland: Folens Publishers, Greenhills Road, Tallaght, Dublin 24.

Email: info@folens.ie

Editor:	Geoff Tuttle
Project development:	Adrian Moss (Instructional Design Ltd) with Rick Jackman (Jackman Publishing Solutions Ltd)
Concept design:	Patricia Briggs
Layout artist:	GreenGate Publishing Services
Illustrations:	GreenGate Publishing Services
Cover design:	Jumpto! www.jumpto.co.uk
Cover image:	Courtesy of Chris Harvey/Fotolia.com

First published 2010 by Folens Limited

Every effort has been made to contact copyright holders of material used in this publication. If any copyright holder has been overlooked, we should be pleased to make any necessary arrangements.

British Library Cataloguing in Publication Data.

A catalogue record for this publication is available from the British Library.

ISBN 978-1-85008-543-0

Contents

Introduction to AQA GCSE

What the book covers

This book covers the AQA GCSE in Information and Communication Technology for the specification which starts for first teaching in September 2010.

Units

The specification for GCSE ICT is arranged in Units. There are three units:

Unit 1: Systems and Applications in ICT

Unit 2: Practical Problem Solving in ICT

Unit 3: The Assignment: Applying ICT

The way the book is organized

The book covers the content needed for Units 1 to 3. This means that if you are taking the AQA GCSE ICT you will need to cover all the material in this book.

Unit 1: Systems and Applications in ICT (120 marks)

1 hour 30 minutes
40% of total marks

Externally assessed

- Section A: very short and multiple-choice answer questions
- Section B: short and extended answer questions
- All questions will be compulsory for Sections A and B
- Section C: 1 essay question from a choice of 2
- Systems and Applications in ICT is available as an on-screen examination and on paper

Unit 2: Practical Problem Solving in ICT (60 marks)

15 hours approximately
20% of total marks

Internally assessed, externally moderated

- Centres choose one or more tasks set by AQA
- Candidates work individually to solve a problem and present a portfolio of evidence
- Controlled assessment conditions apply
- Many Level 1 and 2 Functional Skills Standards are embedded in this unit

Unit 3: The Assignment: Applying ICT (120 marks)

30 hours approximately
40% of total marks

Internally assessed, externally moderated

- AQA sets the scene in which candidates work independently to solve two tasks
- Controlled assessment conditions apply

The organization of the book

The material for the course is divided into Sections that are broken down into topics that are further divided into spreads.

Section 1: Current and emerging technologies and their impact on individuals, organizations and society

Topic 1   Computer systems and mobile technologies
Topic 2   Current input and output devices
Topic 3   Storage devices and media
Topic 4   Communications and entertainment

Section 2: A range of ICT tools and techniques and the ways in which they are used in different contexts to develop ideas and solve problems

Topic 5   Systems life cycle
Topic 6   Working with information to solve problems
Topic 7   Operating systems and user interfaces
Topic 8   Applications software
Topic 9   Word-processing, DTP, web design and other presentation software
Topic 10 Graphics production and image manipulation
Topic 11 Spreadsheets and modelling software
Topic 12 Databases
Topic 13 Web browsing and email
Topic 14 Web logs and social networking
Topic 15 Data logging and control software

Section 3: Legal, social, economic, ethical and environmental implications of the use of ICT for individuals, organizations and society

Topic 16 Legal issues relating to the use of ICT, including issues of safety and security
Topic 17 Social and economic issues relating to the use of ICT, including responsible use
Topic 18 Political, ethical and environmental issues relating to the use of ICT

Section 4: Collaborative working

Topic 19 Collaborative working

Section 5: ICT systems and applications used to put things into context

Topic 20 Case studies

Unit 2: Practical Problem Solving in ICT

Topic 21 Advice about Unit 2

Unit 3: Assignment: Applying ICT

Topic 22 Advice about Unit 3

Introduction to the features in the student book

The philosophy behind the student book

This student book has been based on extensive research from schools and colleges on the different ways ICT is taught, and this book has been developed with all the findings in mind. As this is a new specification, many students and teachers/lecturers will be finding their way and the aim of the book is to provide a depth of coverage for the material for Units 1, 2 and 3.

This book builds on the material your students will have covered at Key Stage 3 and seeks to build on this to cover the material needed for the AQA GCSE in ICT.

This book should be used by the teacher/lecturer in conjunction with the Teacher's Resource Guide. Of course this book can be used stand-alone, but if you are a teacher then there are many resources in the Teacher's Resource Guide to help your students succeed and maximize their marks. The Teacher's Resource Guide contains the following non-digital resources: Answers to the Questions, Worksheets, Activities, Multiple-choice questions and Case studies.

The Teacher's Resource Guide also includes a wealth of digital materials such as PowerPoint presentations, multiple-choice questions, matching questions and so on. These will all help your students consolidate their understanding of the topics.

The structure of the student book

There are three units for the GCSE and the student book covers all three units.

Unit 1 is assessed by examination and Units 2 and 3 are assessed by controlled assessment.

The material is divided into topics with each topic being further divided up into double-page spreads. This allows division of each topic into bite-size easily digested chunks of material. For consistency and to make the student book easy to use, all topics are structured in the same way.

Material for Units 2 and 3 use some of the material in Unit 1 but this time in a practical context. Students will have used many of the tools and techniques in their Key Stage 3 work and their work in other subjects.

Topic introduction pages

The first page of each topic consists of an introduction to the material in the topic and includes the following features:

- **Topic introduction**: just a couple of paragraphs introducing students to the subject matter in the topic.
- **Key concepts**: this lists the key concepts covered in the topic. These key concepts are identical to those in the GCSE AQA specification.
- **Contents**: lists the spreads used to cover the topic and each spread covers key concepts.

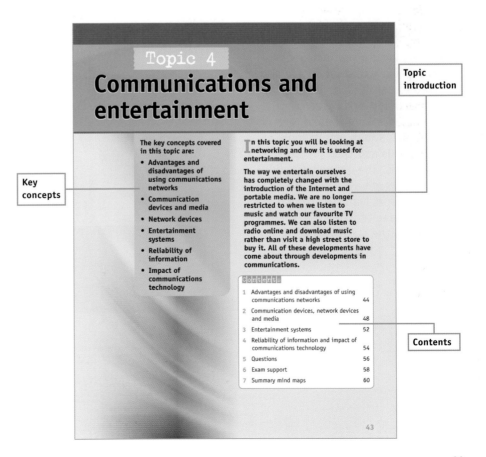

Topic introduction

Topic 4
Communications and entertainment

Key concepts

The key concepts covered in this topic are:
- Advantages and disadvantages of using communications networks
- Communication devices and media
- Network devices
- Entertainment systems
- Reliability of information
- Impact of communications technology

In this topic you will be looking at networking and how it is used for entertainment.

The way we entertain ourselves has completely changed with the introduction of the Internet and portable media. We are no longer restricted to when we listen to music and watch our favourite TV programmes. We can also listen to radio online and download music rather than visit a high street store to buy it. All of these developments have come about through developments in communications.

Contents

Contents

43

Topic spreads

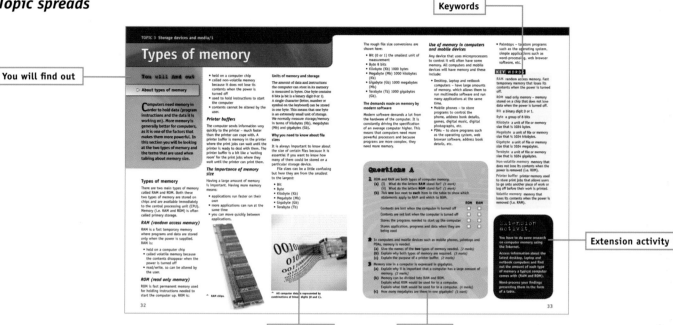

You will find out

Keywords

Photographs

Questions

Extension activity

Questions and Extension activities

Questions are usually included at the end of each content spread and are used to consolidate learning. Some **Extension activities** are also included within the content spreads. This allows you to look at the spreads and then practise the questions. The answers to all the questions are available in the teacher support materials, which are available separately on CD-ROM and complement the student text.

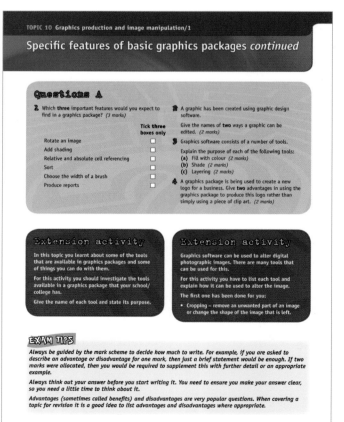

Questions spreads

Examination style questions: are designed to be similar to GCSE examination questions and have marks to give you the opportunity to understand how answers are marked. The answers to the questions are included on the Teacher Resource Guide CD-ROM.

Test yourself: consists of a series of statements with a blank space in which to insert the missing word or words that appear in a list. Students can either write the missing words as a list or they can write the complete sentence with the missing word inserted. The answers to these are available on the Teacher Resource Guide CD-ROM.

Activities: offer interesting things for you to do that will help add to and reinforce the material in the spreads and give you practice with ICT skills.

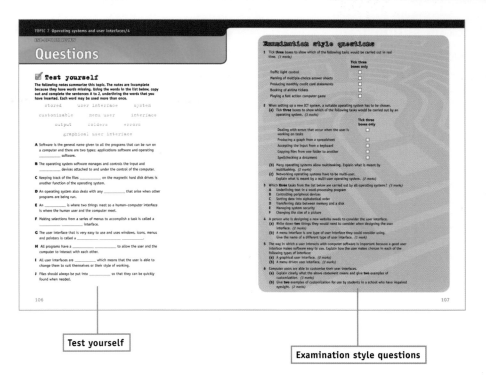

Test yourself

Examination style questions

Case study spreads

Case studies: real-life case studies are included in some of the topics that relate directly to the material in the topic. Case studies give a context in which you can answer the examination questions. Often examination questions on ICT ask not only for a definition or explanation but also an example. Case studies build up your knowledge of how the theory you learn about is used in practice.

Case study questions: will give you practice at answering questions that relate to real-life situations. The questions have been carefully constructed to be similar to the examination questions you could be asked and relate directly to the case study and other material contained in the content spreads. If your teacher has the Teacher Resource Guide, they will have the answers to these case study questions.

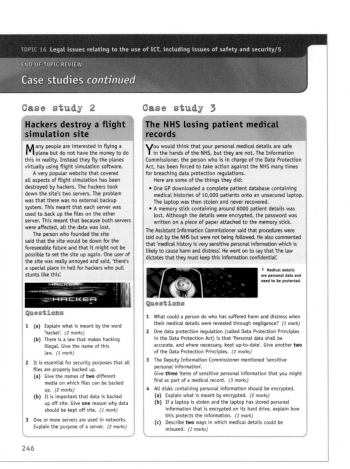

Exam support

Worked example: is an important feature because it gives you an insight into how the examination questions are marked. At GCSE, you can have the knowledge but still fail to get a good mark because you have failed to communicate what you know effectively. It is essential that you understand just what is expected of you when answering questions for GCSE.

Student answers: you can see an examination question with examples of two different student answers. For each student answer there is a corresponding sample Examiner's comment.

Examiner's comment: offers you an insight into how examiners mark student answers. The main thing here is to be able to see the mistakes that can be made and ensure that you do not make similar mistakes. By analysing the way answers are marked, you will soon be able to get more marks for the questions that you answer by not making common mistakes.

Examiner's answers: offers some of the many possible answers and an indication of how the marks are distributed between the answers. It should be borne in mind that there are many possible correct answers to some questions and that any mark scheme relies on the experience of the markers to interpret the mark scheme and to give credit for answers that do not appear in the mark scheme.

Summary mind maps

Mind maps are great fun to produce and a very good way of revising. They are included at the end of each topic to summarize the material contained in the topic. Sometimes there will be only one mind map and other times there will be several – it all depends on how the material in the topic is broken down.

As well as using these mind maps to help you revise, you should produce your own.

Why not produce them using the computer? There are many good pieces of mind-mapping software.

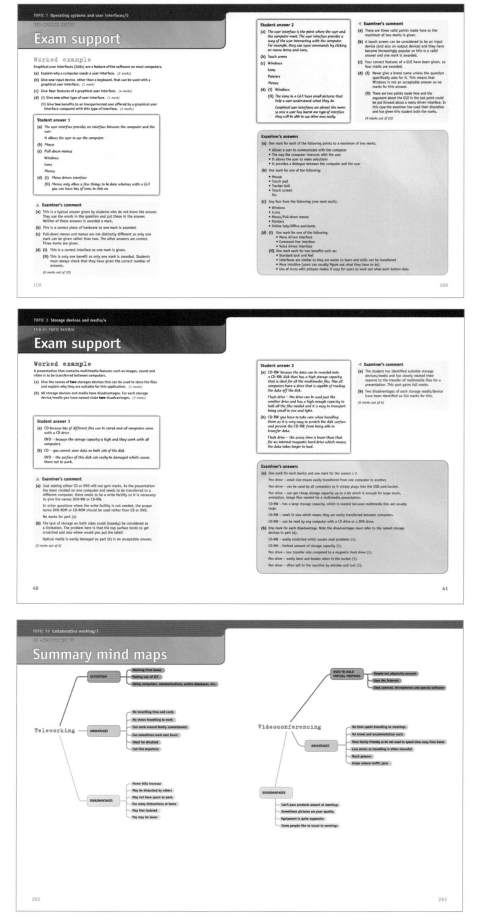

Computer systems and mobile technologies

The key concepts covered in this topic are:

- Hardware
- Types of hardware
- Software
- Personal and commercial computer systems
- Mobile technologies
- Using computer systems
- Identifying ICT problems and solve errors

All ICT systems consist of two main parts: the hardware and the software.

Hardware refers to those items of an ICT system that you can touch. This means that they are components such as printers, keyboards, memory, storage devices, etc. Even the storage media is classed as hardware. This means that a CD is hardware but if it has a program on it then the program itself is classed as software. It is hard to separate the program (i.e., the software) from the hardware that is used to store it.

In this topic you will be looking at the computer systems, their components and the mobile technologies that enable people to work and keep in contact whilst on the move.

Contents

Hardware and software

▷ **About what hardware is and the types of hardware**

▷ **About what software is and the types of software**

Hardware and software are used together to create computer systems. All computer systems consist of microprocessors, which are the brains of the system, but microprocessors are also present in other devices such as washing machines, cameras, children's toys, etc. In fact most of the electrical or battery-controlled devices you use in the home have microprocessors in them to help control their operation.

What is hardware?

Hardware are the physical components that make up the ICT system. If you can touch it, then it is hardware. Hardware includes input devices (keyboards, mouse, scanner, etc.), storage (memory, hard drive, etc.), the processor and the output devices (screen, printer, plotter, etc.). Also included in hardware are the communication devices needed to send data across networks.

▶ Mouse.

Examples of hardware

▲ Storage (e.g. hard drive).

▲ Keyboard.

▲ Memory chips.

Microprocessor technology

Modern computer systems consist of many different pieces of hardware but the most important is the microprocessor.

Microprocessors are computers, usually on a single chip, that are put into electronic devices to check, regulate and control something. A microprocessor performs all the processing that is needed. It does all the calculations and decides what to do next. You can find microprocessors in washing machines, cars, sewing machines, central heating controls, children toys, etc.

Applications for microprocessors

Microprocessors are the brains of many devices and make them more intelligent. Any device that can be controlled can have a microprocessor in it. Microprocessor technology can be used in many different places for lots of different things such as:

- Microprocessors in the home:
  - Washing machines – used to control valves to let the water in, motors to turn the drum, pumps to pump the water out, heaters to heat the water up and so on.
  - Children's toys – use microprocessors to control lights, motors, speakers, etc.
  - Heating systems – control the time the heating comes on, keeps the temperature constant by turning the heating on/off, etc. Modern heating systems can control the individual temperatures of each room from a central place.
  - Alarm systems – can detect the presence of an intruder and some systems will even contact the police.

- Microprocessors in everyday life:
  - Traffic lights – keep the traffic moving freely and they can adjust the time the lights are on green depending on the traffic flow from each direction.
  - Mobile phones – use microprocessors to control their many functions. For example, they control messages coming into the phone.
  - Used in cars – many parts of cars are microprocessor controlled. Examples include airbags, ABS braking systems, which help stop the car skidding when braking hard.

▲ A microprocessor.

- Microprocessors in the workplace:
  - Computers, communications and videoconferencing, which all contain microprocessors, enable many people to work from home.
  - Robots in factories and warehouses all contain microprocessors and are used for assembling components, spray painting, packing, etc.
  - Process control – microprocessors control valves to allow liquids into large vessels for fermenting, reacting, cooking, etc.

Software

Computer hardware is useless without the software as it is the software that instructs the hardware what to do. Software is the general name given to all the programs that can be run on computer hardware. They all give the hardware instruction and can be divided into two main categories: operating systems and applications software.

Operating systems software will be looked at in detail in Topic 7 and applications software will be looked at in detail in Topic 8.

Examples of software include:

- Operating system software (e.g. Windows, Linux, Mac OS)
- Word-processing
- Database
- Spreadsheet
- Presentation
- Web design
- Web browser
- Graphics
- Photo editing.

KEY WORDS

Hardware the parts of the computer that you can touch and handle.

Microprocessor the brain of the computer consisting of millions of tiny circuits on a silicon chip. It processes the input data to produce information.

Software the actual programs (i.e. instructions) that allow the hardware to do a useful job.

Questions A

1. A computer system consists of hardware and software. Explain the differences between hardware and software. *(2 marks)*

2. Here are some examples of items and you have to decide whether they are hardware, software or neither. *(10 marks)*

	Name of item	Hardware	Software	Neither
1	LCD screen			
2	Keyboard			
3	Operating system			
4	Word-processing program			
5	Printer			
6	Blank DVD			
7	Game for a Sony Playstation			
8	Toaster			
9	Web browser			
10	Web design program			

Personal and commercial computer systems and mobile technologies

You will find out

▷ **About personal and commercial computer systems**

▷ **About mobile technologies**

There are many different types of computer but the most popular by far is the general purpose computer, which is the one you are most likely to use at home and at school or college. Businesses and other organizations mainly use desktop computers and often these are networked together in order to share resources. In this topic you will be looking at the main components of a desktop computer and what their purpose is. Later on in the topic you will be looking at portable computers that enable their users to work in any place at any time.

Personal and commercial computer systems

There is no real difference between the personal computers you use at home and the type that are used in businesses. The main difference is the way in which they are used, because computers used in organizations and businesses tend to be networked together (other than connected to the Internet).

Desktop computers/personal computers (PCs)

A desktop computer (or PC as they are sometimes called) is the type of computer that you are most likely to encounter at home or at school and in most organizations. In many cases desktop computers are connected, either with wires/cables or wirelessly, to form networks.

Desktop computers are full-sized computers with a full-sized keyboard and screen and are designed to be used in one place.

▶ Desktop computers have full-sized keyboards and are designed to be used in one place.

The main components of a desktop computer

- Central Processing Unit (CPU) – microprocessor (one or more) processes the raw data and turns it into information.
- Main/internal memory – are chips inside the computer where data is held and can be accessed immediately by the computer. Some program instructions are stored here along with the data the computer is currently working on.
- Motherboard – is the central circuit board of the computer that contains all the electronic components such as the CPU and memory chips. It also contains connectors so that other devices can be controlled by the computer.
- Sound card – this is an electronic circuit board containing chips and other components that enables high quality sound signals to be produced. These sound signals can be played using loudspeakers or headphones.
- Video card – an electronic circuit board that allows the production of graphics on the screen. Some cards allow the production of realistic 3D graphics or allow the computer to receive ordinary TV signals.
- Input devices – these are those devices that are under the control of the computer (either wired or wireless) and are used to input data (e.g., commands/ instructions, raw data) for processing. Input devices can include a keyboard, mouse, joystick, stylus, etc.

- Output devices – these are the devices that give the results of processing the data by the computer. Output devices can range from screens and printers to motors and robot arms.
- Secondary/backing storage – this is any storage that is not classed as memory. It is used to hold programs and data. Secondary/backing storage devices include magnetic hard drives, optical drives (CD or DVD), flash/pen drives, etc.

▲ A netbook computer is smaller and lighter than a laptop.

▲ Motherboard. Notice the slots where the memory cards can be slotted in.

Mobile technologies

Laptop computers

Laptop computers (often simply called laptops) are designed to be portable, i.e. carried and used in different places. They are smaller than desktop computers and have a built-in screen and are much lighter and are designed to be used away from the power source. Laptop computers contain a rechargeable battery that can limit their use.

Netbook computers

Netbooks are smaller, lighter and less expensive compared to laptop computers.

Here are the main features of netbooks:

- much lighter than laptops (smaller screen and no CD/DVD drive reduces the weight)
- smaller keyboard
- smaller magnetic hard drive
- longer battery life (owing to the use of less powerful devices such as low power chips)
- cheaper – because some of the more expensive components are left out
- suited for general computing and Internet access.

▲ Laptops are light and have rechargeable batteries.

Palmtops

Palmtop computers are small hand-held computers that are used by occasional computer users to send and receive email, surf the Internet, record deliveries, record meter readings or record orders taken.

PDAs

Personal digital assistants (PDAs) are hand-held computers that enable the user to:

- keep track of meetings, appointments, birthdays, etc.
- store details of names, addresses, telephone numbers, email addresses, etc.
- synchronize details with those stored on a desktop or laptop computer
- browse the Internet
- send and receive email.

▲ Many mobile phones now have many of the features of palmtops.

Personal and commercial computer systems and mobile technologies *continued*

WAP

WAP stands for wireless application protocol and offers a way for users of mobile phones to access the Internet. Because of their smaller screen, the software to access the Internet has to be trimmed down.

Smart mobile phones

Smart mobile phones are those mobile phones that offer a lot more than just phone calls and text messaging. All new mobile phones can be considered to be smart mobile phones.

New services for mobile phones are being thought up all the time and who knows what they might do in the future. When mobile phones were first developed they were the equivalent of a telephone that could be used on the move. Nowadays they offer all sorts of new services and have started to blur the difference between a computer or PDA and a mobile phone. Many mobile phones also act as portable MP3 players, enabling you to play your music on the move.

Here are some of the services available through mobile phones:

- send and receive text messages
- make phone calls
- take digital photographs
- take short video clips
- surf the internet
- watch live TV
- send and receive email
- download and listen to music
- download and play games
- send picture messages
- play videos
- GPS (use your mobile phone as a satellite navigation system).

▲ **Many services are available through smart mobile phones.**

Questions B

1 Besides making voice phone calls, describe **three** tasks a mobile phone can perform. *(3 marks)*

2 Explain **two** differences between a desktop computer and a laptop computer. *(2 marks)*

3 Desktop computers consist of a number of components.
Explain the purpose of each of the following components.
(a) Central Processing Unit (CPU) *(1 mark)*
(b) Main memory *(1 mark)*
(c) Sound card *(1 mark)*
(d) Backing storage *(1 mark)*

4 Give the names of:
(a) **Two** input devices. *(2 marks)*
(b) **Two** output devices. *(2 marks)*
(c) **Two** backing storage devices. *(2 marks)*

Extension activity

Research the features of the latest mobile phones using the Internet.

Produce a list of your three most desirable mobile phones and their features.

Using computer systems and identifying ICT problems and errors

You will find out

▷ **About using computer systems**

▷ **About identifying problems and solving errors**

In order to prevent problems with ICT systems it is important to shut down the computer properly when you have finished your work rather than simply turn the power off. Also when using networks there are set procedures to follow to log-on to the network and to log-off from it. By adopting these procedures, the network facilities can be used by everyone who has permission to use them.

Starting the computer

As more than one person often uses the same computer, it is necessary for each user to have their own name and password. To start the computer you turn it on and then tell the computer which user you are from the list that has been created by the person who initially set up the computer. You are then asked for a password, which you then enter. On entering the correct password you are given access to the computer.

You can only use the computer as a stand-alone computer as you will need to supply more details to log-on to a network.

Log-on and log-off (also called log-in and log-out)

In order to use a network you have to log-on/log-in. To do this you have to supply two things:

- your username or user-ID
- a password.

The username or user-ID identifies you to the network. This means that the network will allocate storage space for you and allow you to use certain files.

The password, which you should always keep private, ensures that you are who you say you are and not someone trying to access the network without permission.

Using the shut down menu

You should always shut your computer down properly otherwise the following can happen:

- You can lose data.
- Programs can be corrupted (i.e. damaged).

To exit the computer properly you should follow these instructions:

- Click on the Start button (bottom left of your screen).
- From the menu that appears click on the arrow pointing to the right (bottom right menu item).
- Click on Shut Down.
- The computer has now been correctly shut down.

▶ Log-on/log-in means gaining access to the network after correctly giving your username and password.

7

Using computer systems and identifying ICT problems and errors *continued*

Identifying ICT problems and solving errors

ICT systems are complex and they can cause a lot of problems to the user. Users of computers need to know what to do when certain problems and errors occur.

Software freeze

Have you met the problem where the software just freezes and you cannot do anything? When this happens you have to press Ctrl + Alt + Del keys together and this gets you to the task manager where you can end the program. When this happens you may lose some of your work.

▲ The blue screen all computer users dread – it means you have probably lost the work you have done since the last time it was saved.

Error dialogues

These are error messages that appear when something is wrong such as:

- The computer memory is running low.
- You need the batteries changing for your wireless mouse or keyboard.
- There is a printer jam.
- The printer ink or paper is running low.

▲ Error dialogues.

Usually all you have to do is click on the OK button to acknowledge that you have seen the message and are doing something about it.

Storage full

When you try to save your work and the computer informs you that the storage media is full, there are a number of things you can do:

- Delete some old files and free up some space. Most people have a lot of files that they no longer need, which simply clog up space on the storage media.

- Save your files on a friend's storage media.

Paper jam

A paper jam occurs when printer paper gets stuck in the printer. In many cases it is because the printer paper has not been put into the paper tray properly.

To remove a paper jam you may need to first turn the power off and then follow the instructions in the manual, which may be paper based or online.

Uninstalling software

When you install new software on your computer there is a program that installs the software for you. If there is software on your computer that you no longer need, you can remove it to free up some space. Deleting the software is possible using 'delete' but the trouble is that it can leave parts of the program undeleted and this can cause future problems. The best way is to access the Control Panel.

You can see under the heading 'Programs' that there is a program that will uninstall a program properly. To uninstall a program you simply click on this and then tell the computer which program you want to remove.

Getting help to fix problems

There are a number of ways to get help:

- For help with usernames, passwords and storage space on the network ask the network manager.
- For general advice about software – simply ask the person next to you. Many problems are solved like this.
- Use the online help provided by the software.
- Ask your teacher/lecturer.
- Access the help-desk of the supplier of the hardware/ software/communications service. This can be done using email or over the phone.

▲ There are a number of ways to get help if you can't solve the problem yourself.

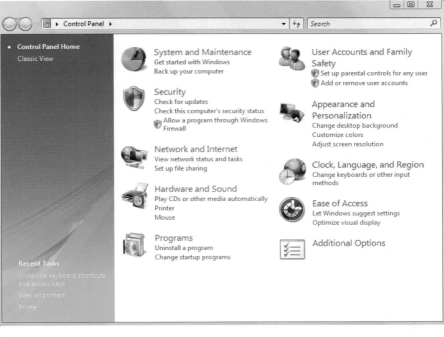

▲ Vista Control Panel.

Questions C

1 You are using some software when suddenly the software freezes, which prevents you doing anything with the computer.

Give the correct instructions that will enable you to start using the computer again. *(2 marks)*

2 A user is in a hurry to get out of the computer room and instead of logging off and shutting down their computer properly, they simply turn the power off.

Give one reason why computers should be shut down properly. *(1 mark)*

3 A computer user is having a problem with a printer.
   (a) Explain **two** sources of help they could use to solve this problem. *(2 marks)*
   (b) Another user wants to remove a program and simply right clicks on the program name and selects 'delete'. Give **one** reason why doing this is not a good idea and explain how it should be done. *(2 marks)*

Extension activity

Use the online help provided by Windows to find out what to do in each of the following situations:

- software freeze
- when the screen resolution has been changed and you want to alter it to what you are used to.

Questions

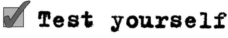 **Test yourself**

The following notes summarize this topic. The notes are incomplete because they have words missing. Using the words in the list below, copy out and complete the sentences A to J, underlining the words that you have inserted. Each word may be used more than once.

software	information	hardware	desktop
output	microprocessor	input	backing
	washing	applications	

A Computer systems consist of two main parts, hardware and _____.

B If you can physically touch it then it is _____.

C A _____ is a piece of hardware that is the brains of the computer and it turns data into _____.

D Microprocessors can be found in many electrical appliances such as _____ machines, toasters, dryers and dishwashers.

E Computer hardware is useless without the _____, which is used to give it instructions as to what to do.

F There are two types of software called operating system software and _____ software.

G A computer that has a full-sized keyboard and full-sized screen and is normally used in one place is called a _____ computer.

H _____ devices such as the keyboard and mouse are used to input data into the computer for processing.

I After data has been processed, the results of processing are passed to an _____ device.

J Storage which is not memory is called _____ storage.

Examination style questions

1 People often have problems when using ICT. Explain how each of the following will affect a computer user and describe what can be done to remedy the situation:
   (a) Paper jam *(2 marks)*
   (b) Software freeze *(2 marks)*
   (c) Storage full *(2 marks)*

2 (a) Define computer hardware. *(1 mark)*
   (b) Define computer software. *(1 mark)*
   (c) The following table shows items of hardware and software.

   Classify each item by ticking the correct box. *(5 marks)*

Item	Hardware	Software
Printer		
Operating system		
Database		
Microprocessor		
Web browser		

3 A user is having difficulty with a piece of hardware they have just bought.

   Describe **two** different ways they can get help with this problem. *(2 marks)*

4 Computers come in all sizes and can be used in different situations.
   (a) Describe what is meant by a desktop computer and explain how it differs from a laptop computer. *(3 marks)*
   (b) Netbook computers are becoming very popular. Give **two** ways in which a netbook computer differs from a laptop computer. *(2 marks)*

5 A salesperson who travels to newsagents taking orders for sweets uses a PDA.
   (a) Give the meaning of the abbreviation PDA. *(1 mark)*
   (b) Give **one** advantage of using a PDA rather than a laptop computer. *(1 mark)*

Exam support

Worked example

Microprocessors are used to control many devices (e.g. washing machines).

(a) What is a microprocessor? *(1 mark)*

(b) Name **two** devices other than 'washing machine' that can be controlled by a microprocessor. *(2 marks)*

(c) Microprocessors are included in computers. The microprocessors can be seen on the motherboard. Describe what a motherboard is. *(2 marks)*

(d) Computers make use of input devices, storage devices and output devices. Complete the following table putting a tick in the appropriate box for each item. *(10 marks)*

Item	Input device	Storage device	Output device
Printer			
Hard disk drive			
DVD drive			
Keyboard			
Touch screen			
Mouse			
Screen			
Loudspeaker			
Joystick			
Touch pad			

Student answer 1

(a) A microprocessor is a small processor.

(b) You can control a washing machine and a dishwasher.

(c) A motherboard is the main board on the computer and you put things into it.

(d)

Item	Input device	Storage device	Output device
Printer			✓
Hard disk drive		✓	
DVD drive		✓	
Keyboard	✓		
Memory card		✓	
Mouse	✓		
Screen	✓		
Loudspeaker			✓
Joystick	✓		
Touch pad			✓

◄ Examiner's comment

(a) Students often give this kind of answer. They use the word microprocessor and they know that micro means small so they just say it is a small processor. They have said nothing about that it is a chip or its purpose. No marks are given for this answer.

(b) Despite being told not to, the student has used the example given in the question as one of their answers. This is probably caused by the student not reading the question properly. This has cost them a mark. The other answer about the dishwasher is correct and worth a mark.

(c) This answer is far too vague. They needed to say that it is a circuit board and that there are connectors, CPUs, memory cards, etc., on it. No marks for this.

(d) Two of these answers are incorrect. Touch pad is an input device and Screen is an output device.

(9 marks out of 15)

Student answer 2

(a) A microprocessor is a chip that is the brains of the device and it does all the processing needed.

(b) A toaster and a burglar alarm.

(c) It is the main circuit board of the computer and all the other devices such as processors, memory chips, fans, sockets, etc., are connected.

(d)

Item	Input device	Storage device	Output device
Printer			✓
Hard disk drive		✓	
DVD drive		✓	
Keyboard	✓		
Memory card		✓	
Mouse	✓		
Screen			✓
Loudspeaker			✓
Joystick	✓		
Touch pad	✓		

◀ **Examiner's comment**

(a) This is a good answer as it states that it is a chip and that it performs the processing needed to control the device. Full marks here.

(b) Two uses that are correct so two marks.

(c) This is a very good answer as it makes it clear that it is the main circuit board and gives a range of components that would be connected to it.

(d) All these ticks are in the right places so another perfect answer.

(15 marks out of 15)

Examiner's answers

(a) One mark for one of the following points:

A chip

Performs all the processing

Turns data into information.

(b) One mark for each sensible device that can be controlled in some way to a maximum of two marks.

Dishwasher

Central heating

Mobile phone

Burglar alarm

Toaster

Etc.

(c) One mark for each point to a maximum of two marks.

Main circuit board

CPU and memory are attached to it

Connectors on the board allow input/output/storage devices to be attached.

(d) One mark for each correctly place tick.

Item	Input device	Storage device	Output device
Printer			✓
Hard disk drive		✓	
DVD drive		✓	
Keyboard	✓		
Memory card		✓	
Mouse	✓		
Screen			✓
Loudspeaker			✓
Joystick	✓		
Touch pad	✓		

Summary mind map

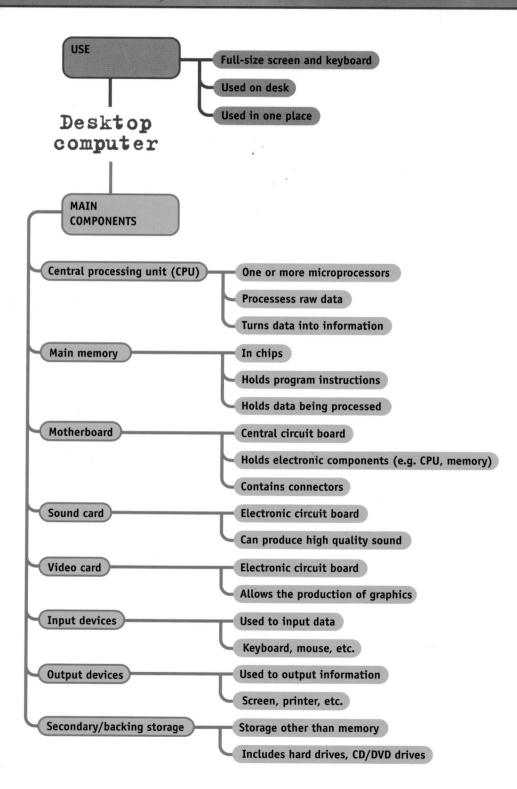

USE
- Full-size screen and keyboard
- Used on desk
- Used in one place

Desktop computer

MAIN COMPONENTS

- **Central processing unit (CPU)**
  - One or more microprocessors
  - Processess raw data
  - Turns data into information
- **Main memory**
  - In chips
  - Holds program instructions
  - Holds data being processed
- **Motherboard**
  - Central circuit board
  - Holds electronic components (e.g. CPU, memory)
  - Contains connectors
- **Sound card**
  - Electronic circuit board
  - Can produce high quality sound
- **Video card**
  - Electronic circuit board
  - Allows the production of graphics
- **Input devices**
  - Used to input data
  - Keyboard, mouse, etc.
- **Output devices**
  - Used to output information
  - Screen, printer, etc.
- **Secondary/backing storage**
  - Storage other than memory
  - Includes hard drives, CD/DVD drives

Current input and output devices

The key concepts covered in this topic are:

- **Input devices (common and specialist)**

- **Advantages and disadvantages of different types of input device**

- **Output devices (common and specialist)**

- **Advantages and disadvantages of different types of output device**

Data needs to get into the computer ready for processing. Input devices are those devices that are used to input the raw data. After processing, information is produced that needs to be output in some way. This is the job of output devices.

In this topic you will look at the range of input and output devices along with their advantages and disadvantages.

Contents

Input devices and their advantages and disadvantages

Input devices are used to enter data into the computer ready for processing. Some input devices such as a mouse and joystick supply data in the form of instructions. Other input devices such as the keyboard enable the entry of text. In this topic you will learn about a whole range of input devices, each suitable for entering a certain type of data.

Output devices are used to output information after the input data has been processed.

Input devices (common and specialist)

In this section you will be looking at the huge range of input devices, each with their advantages and disadvantages.

Keyboard

Keyboards are the most popular input device. Keyboarding:

- is the most popular way of inputting data as most computer systems come with one
- is a slow method of input for large amounts of data
- is inaccurate as it is easy to make mistakes
- needs typing skills so it is hard for beginners to use.

▲ This keyboard for a cash dispenser has raised dots on the keys so that it can be used by blind or partially sighted users as well as other users.

Special keyboards for the disabled

Braille keyboards make it easy for blind users to input data into the computer.

▲ A Braille keyboard.

For those users who have failing vision, there are also keyboards that have large coloured keys that are easier to see. Each key is about one inch square.

▲ A large-keyed, colour-coded keyboard for the visually impaired.

Mouse

This is called a mouse because its shape looks like a mouse and it has a tail in the form of the wire. Many mice do not have wires as they are used wirelessly. The main points about a mouse are:

- Mice are input devices because they are used to issue instructions by making selections.
- When the mouse is moved, a pointer or cursor moves on the screen mirroring the movement of the mouse.
- Selections can be made by pressing the mouse buttons.
- A scroll wheel can be used for scrolling through long documents.
- A mouse may also be used for drawing lines, sizing graphic objects such as pictures or clip art.

Joystick/video game controller

Most of you have used a joystick or video game controller. Here are some facts about them:

- They are ideal for quick movement and selection.

- This means they are an ideal input peripheral for playing games.
- They can be used to move a cursor on the screen.
- Joysticks are useful for the disabled because they can be operated by the foot, mouth, etc.

Tracker ball

This is a bit like an upside down mouse. The 'mouse' part is stationary and you move the 'ball' part with your fingers and this moves the cursor on the screen in the same way as a mouse does. Their main use is for people who are disabled or very young children who find it hard to use a mouse.

▲ A tracker ball is an alternative to a mouse.

Touch pad

Touch pads are seen on most laptop computers and are used where there is no smooth surface on which to use a mouse or where there is no space.

Most people would prefer to use a mouse if there is room as it takes longer to do tasks using a touch pad.

▼ Touch pads are used as an alternative to a mouse where there is not much space for a mouse to be used.

Microphone

A microphone allows sound to be converted into data. Special software called voice recognition software is used to interpret the sounds into words.

Here is what a microphone allows you to do:

- You can tell the computer what to do (i.e. you can issue instructions).
- You can dictate letters and other documents directly into your word-processor or email package. This is called voice recognition.
- You will need a microphone if you want to send voice mail or take part in videoconferencing.
- You can issue instructions verbally to your computer instead of typing them in.
- You can use the Internet for Internet phone calls, which are much cheaper than normal calls.

Remote controls

Remote controls are input devices as they issue instructions to ICT systems.

▷ Remote controls are input devices and are used to issue commands as well as allow characters to be typed.

Scanners

Here are some important points about scanners:

- They are used to scan in photographs and other images to put into documents or webpages.
- They can also be used to scan text into a word-processing or other package. This saves having to re-type the text. To be able to recognize the characters, special software called optical character recognition software is needed.

▷ Scanners are useful for converting old photographs so that they can be stored on the computer and used for websites, presentations, documents, etc.

Digital still camera

A digital camera looks like an ordinary camera except there is no film and there is usually a screen on which to view the picture (called an image) when taken.

Here are some facts about digital cameras:

- Digital cameras have memory cards where they store the image.
- The more memory a camera has, the more pictures you can store.
- There are no developing fees like an ordinary camera.
- If the picture is not suitable (as viewed on the screen) then it can be taken again.
- You can transfer the pictures to your computer where you can store and edit them.

Digital cameras produce an image made up of millions of dots called pixels. The greater the number of dots in the same space, the clearer the picture will appear. This is called the resolution of the image. High resolution images use more dots and take up more storage space on the storage media.

Most mobile phones are capable of taking digital photographs.

Input devices and their advantages and disadvantages *continued*

"I HAVE TO STAY HOME TONIGHT AND HELP MY DAD WITH HIS NEW CAMERA PHONE. WE NEED TO DELETE 750 PICTURES OF HIS HAND."

Digital video camera

Digital video cameras look the same as ordinary video cameras except that they store the image digitally. Here are some other facts:

- Most digital video cameras can capture still as well as moving images.
- Images may be stored and edited on the computer.
- You can use video in websites.

Web cameras (webcams)

A web camera (webcam) is simply a digital camera that is used to capture still images and video images (i.e. moving images). These images can then be transmitted to a computer where they are stored in a suitable graphics format. If required, pictures can be used on a website.

▶ **Webcams are good fun because you can see the person you are talking to.**

Webcams are often included with complete computer set ups with the camera in these systems placed on top of the screen. Such a system allows videoconferencing.

Webcams are not, however, restricted to the tops of computers. There are webcams everywhere. Here are some uses:

- To check the weather in ski resorts and other holiday destinations.
- To allow parents to check on their children in nurseries.
- To allow bar owners to check that staff are not giving free drinks to friends.
- To allow people to check on their home while they are away.

KEY WORDS

Digital camera a camera that takes a picture and stores it digitally.

Web camera (webcam) a digital camera used to capture still and video images.

Sensors devices that measure physical quantities such as temperature, pressure, etc.

Touch screen a special type of screen that is sensitive to touch. A selection is made from a menu on the screen by touching part of it.

Sensors

Sensors are able to sense quantities such as temperature, pressure and amount of light. The signals picked up by the sensors can be sent to and then analysed by the computer.

Here is some information about sensors:

- Sensors can be connected to the computer directly.
- Sensors can record data over time and then the data can be transferred to the computer (this is called data logging).
- Sensors can be found in lots of devices such as burglar alarms, central heating systems, washing machines, etc. As well as sensing, they are also used to control the device in some way.

Touch screen (touch sensitive screen)

To operate a touch screen you simply touch the item on the screen to make a selection. Touch screens are ideal input devices in some situations. Here are some facts about touch screens:

- Touch screens are easy for the general public to use.
- They are used in restaurants and shops because the staff need little training to use them.
- They are ideal for public information systems such as tourism displays, timetable information, etc.

▲ **Many mobile phones have touch screen interfaces.**

▲ Computerised ticket dispensers at train stations make use of touch screens.

Magnetic strip readers

Magnetic strip readers are able to read data stored in magnetic strips on plastic cards.

Magnetic strip readers are used for:

- reading data off credit/debit cards (as an alternative to chip and pin)
- reading loyalty card details
- access control to rooms
- access to computers.

MIDI (Musical Instrument Digital Interface) instruments

MIDI is an interface, which means a way of connecting and getting two devices to communicate with each other. MIDI can send signals to electronic devices such as keyboards, music synthesizers, guitars and drum machines. These devices can also send the signals back to the computer hardware so that the signals can be stored and modified in some way. For example, the sound from a drum might be too loud in a recording. Using MIDI you could save the sound from the drum and make it softer whilst keeping the loudness of the other instruments the same.

Interactive whiteboards

You will have seen these being used in your school or college. They consist of a large interactive display connected to a projector and computer that can be viewed by a whole class. Users can use a finger or a pen to make selections on the screen. The interactive whiteboard is able to detect the presence of a finger or pen on the screen and is therefore an input device.

▲ Sat navs use touch screens.

▲ Data is stored as a magnetic pattern in the strip on the card.

Input devices and their advantages and disadvantages *continued*

Bar code readers

Bar code reading involves using a series of light and dark bars of differing widths to enter a code that is usually printed underneath the bar code. Using the code, the system can determine from a product database the country of origin, the manufacturer, the name of the product, the price and other information about the product.

ISBN 978-1-85008-280-4

9 781850 082804

▲ Bar code.

Suitable applications for bar code recognition include:

- recording of goods in supermarkets
- warehouse stock control systems
- parcel tracking systems
- linking books to borrowers in libraries
- luggage labelling at airports.

Advantages of bar code input

- Faster – scanners are sophisticated and can read bar codes at different angles.
- More accurate – compared to typing in long codes manually.
- Low printing costs – can be printed on labels.

Disadvantages of bar code input

- Can only be used for the input of numbers.
- Expensive – the laser scanners in supermarkets are expensive, although hand-held scanners are relatively cheap.

Optical mark recognition/reader (OMR)

Optical mark recognition works by the user shading in marks on a form. The forms are then batched together and read in one go very quickly by an optical mark reader.

Optical mark recognition can be used for:

- reading lottery tickets
- automatically marking multiple-choice answer sheets
- reading questionnaires and analysing the results
- recording student attendance in a school or college.

Optical character recognition/ reader (OCR)

A scanner is used to scan an image of the characters (i.e. letters, numbers and punctuation marks) on a document. The special OCR software is then able to recognize the shape of the individual characters. The text can then be used with software such as word-processing or database software. OCR has the advantage that it is a fast alternative to typing text provided that the text is already available in printed form. OCR is not good at recognizing people's handwriting.

Graphics tablet

A graphics tablet consists of pen-like device that you use to draw or write on a tablet (it looks a bit like a flat board) and it then appears on the computer screen. You can use a graphics tablet to design your own graphics. Some graphics tablets contain special buttons to select shapes or special pictures.

▲ A graphics tablet.

▼ Numbers are marked by shading on a lottery ticket.

Questions A

1 Here is a diagram showing some devices used with a computer:

(a) Give the name of an input device shown in the diagram. *(1 mark)*

(b) Give the name of an output device shown in the diagram. *(1 mark)*

2 A large amount of text needs to be entered into a computer from a typed document.

The user is considering two methods for entering this data: keyboard entry and the use of voice input (voice recognition). Explain which method they should use and give a reason why. *(2 marks)*

3 (a) Explain the purpose of an input device. *(1 mark)*

(b) Give the names of **two** input devices that would be used by a desktop computer. *(2 marks)*

(c) Give the name of an input device that would be found on a laptop computer that you would not find on a desktop computer. *(1 mark)*

4 Here is a list of input devices:
Optical mark reader
Magnetic strip reader
Keyboard
Scanner
Microphone

Write down the name of the input device that is most suited for each of these tasks:

(a) For inputting a short email message. *(1 mark)*

(b) For reading the numbers on a large number of lottery tickets at high speed. *(1 mark)*

(c) For inputting an old photograph. *(1 mark)*

(d) For inputting loyalty card details when a customer makes purchases in a supermarket. *(1 mark)*

(e) For dictating a novel into a word-processing package. *(1 mark)*

(f) For reading lots of multiple-choice answer sheets. *(1 mark)*

5 Laptop computers enable people to do work or keep in touch when they are travelling.

Give the name of **two** input devices normally used with a laptop computer. *(2 marks)*

Extension activity

You are required to use the Internet and any other sources to find out about suitable applications that use the following input devices:

- Bar code readers
- Optical character readers
- Optical mark readers
- Touch screens.

Write a couple of sentences explaining why that input device is suited for the application.

Output devices and their advantages and disadvantages

You will find out

▷ **About output devices (common and specialist)**

▷ **About the advantages and disadvantages of different types of output device**

Once data has been entered into the computer and has been processed, the resulting information is output. Output devices are those parts of an ICT system that produce the information in the most appropriate form for the user. There are many output devices with a screen/VDU and a printer being the most popular.

In this topic you will cover the main output devices and learn about their advantages and disadvantages.

"I spent a fortune for a 60-inch plasma TV and *now* you'd rather watch programs on a 2-inch iPod screen?!"

Screen or monitor

Screens are sometimes called monitors. Here are some facts about screens:

- They come in lots of sizes.
- They are usually in colour.
- They are useful for enquiries (when is the next train to...?, do you have a holiday on this date....?).

TFT/LCD screens

Both desktop and laptop computers use TFT/LCD (thin film transistor/ liquid crystal display) flat panel display screens. The advantages of TFT/LCD screens are:

- They are light – hence their use in laptop computers.
- They are cheaper to run – because they consume less power.
- In the case of desktop computer systems – they do not take up very much desk space.

Plasma screens

Plasma screens are large flat panel screens and are generally available in larger sizes compared to TFT/LCD screens. They have the following uses in ICT:

- in reception areas
- in videoconferencing systems
- for presentations to a large audience.

Printers

There are many different types of printer but the main ones are laser printers and ink-jet printers. Both types of printer produce hard copy. This means they produce output on paper.

Laser printers

Laser printers are the type of printer mostly used by businesses and organizations mainly because of their high speed. Most laser printers print in black and white, although you can buy colour laser printers but they are relatively expensive.

Advantages of laser printers:

- Supplies last longer – the toner cartridge lasts longer than ink-jet cartridges.
- High printing speed – essential to have high speed if lots of people on a network are using the one printer.
- Very reliable – fewer problems compared to ink-jet printers.

- No wet pages that smudge – ink-jet pages can smudge but there is no such problem with a laser printer.

Disadvantages of laser printers:

- More expensive to buy – but they are cheaper to run.
- Colour lasers are very expensive to buy.
- Power consumption is high.

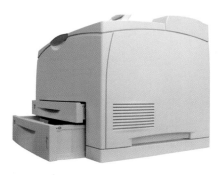

▲ Laser printers are ideal for use in offices.

Ink-jet printers

Ink-jet printers are popular with home users because they are cheap to buy. There are expensive to run, because of the high cost of the ink cartridges. They work by spraying ink onto the paper and can produce very high quality colour or black and white printouts.

Advantages of ink-jet printers:

- High quality print – ideal for printing photographs, brochures or just simple text.
- Quietness of operation – this is important in an office as telephone calls or conversations with colleagues can be conducted while it is printing.
- Cheap to buy – ink-jet printers are very cheap.

Disadvantages of ink-jet printers:

- High cost of the ink cartridges – this is ok for low volume work but for large volume it is much cheaper to use a colour laser printer.
- Ink smudges – when the printouts are removed the paper can get damp, which tends to smudge the ink.
- Need special paper – thick glossy paper is needed for high quality printouts.

▲ Ink-jet cartridge refills can be expensive.

Other output devices

Speakers

Speakers are used to output sound and are an important component of multimedia systems.

Digital projectors

Digital projectors are used to project what is on a computer screen onto a large screen. They are used when there is an audience that needs to view what is on the screen and are therefore used with presentations. They are also used with electronic whiteboards in classrooms.

Plotters

Plotters are used to output diagrams such as maps and plans. They produce accurately scaled diagrams and can print on much larger paper than a printer can print on. They use pens to draw lines with each pen drawing a different colour.

Control devices

Computers can issue signals to control devices based on the data they receive from sensors. They can, for example, turn a motor on or off, they can turn a heater on or off, etc.

▲ Large plans can be printed out using a plotter.

Devices that respond to a signal from a computer are called actuators. Examples of things that can be controlled by a computer include:

- lights
- motors
- pumps
- buzzers
- heaters.

Output devices and their advantages and disadvantages *continued*

Robotic arms

A robot arm is a device that can be programmed to perform a sequence of actions. Robot arms can be re-programmed with a new set of instructions so that they are able to carry out a completely different task. For example, a robot arm can be programmed to hold equipment for welding and the same robot arm holding a different tool can be reprogrammed to spray cars with paint.

Robots are often seen in factories doing routine jobs such as assembling, welding and paint spraying.

Advantages of using robots include:

- No time taken off sick and robots do not take holidays.
- Possibility of robots working 24/7.

- Ensures consistency in the quality of the job.
- Robots do not need paying (although the start-up costs are high).
- Robots are able to carry out boring or dangerous jobs.

Robots are used in hazardous situations. Here are some situations where they might be used:

- Using them to investigate bombs to make them safe.
- Using them to search for wreckage of aircraft that have crashed into the sea.
- Using them to investigate underwater structures such as the feet on drilling platforms.

Robots in factories do replace people. However, people are needed to build, program and repair them.

Robots are used in car factories.

Questions B

1 Robots are used in car manufacturing as they speed up the production process.

Give **two** other advantages of using robots in car manufacturing. *(2 marks)*

2 (a) Robots are used in industry for assembly work, paint spraying and picking and packing goods into boxes. Define the word robot. *(2 marks)*

(b) Describe **one** disadvantage of using robots to pack goods in factories. *(2 marks)*

3 The manager of an office is buying a printer for the office. They are looking to buy one of the following types of printer:
Laser printer
Ink-jet printer

Discuss the relative advantages and disadvantages of each of these types of printer. *(4 marks)*

Extension activity

Robots can be seen packing goods in warehouses, assembling components, paint spraying and so on. How far are we away from seeing robots being used in the home?

For this activity you are required to research whether there are any robots available for the home.

Write a short essay explaining what you have found. You can use photographs to help explain.

Questions

✓ Test yourself

The following notes summarize this topic. The notes are incomplete because they have words missing. Using the words in the list below, copy out and complete the sentences A to N, underlining the words that you have inserted. Each word may be used more than once.

input   touch pad   keyboard   microphone   scanner

optical character recognition   laser   joysticks   output

mouse   stylus   ink-jet   digital   sensors

A Devices used to get data from the outside world into the computer are called _____ devices.

B The commonest input device, which comes with all computers, is the _____.

C A _____ is used to move a pointer or cursor around the screen and to make selections.

D Where space is restricted, such as when a laptop is being used on your knee, a _____ _____ is used instead of a mouse.

E _____ are used primarily with games software.

F In voice recognition systems a _____ is used as the input device.

G The input device used to scan in text and images is called a _____.

H Special software can be used to recognize the individual letters in a scanned piece of text and this is called _____ _____ _____.

I Cameras that do not use film and can transfer an image to the computer are called _____ cameras.

J A pen-like device used to draw or write on a tablet is called a _____.

K Quantities such as temperature and pressure can be detected and measured using _____.

L Printers and plotters are examples of _____ devices.

M The type of printer that produces the highest print quality print and uses a toner cartridge is called a _____ printer.

N A cheaper printer that squirts a jet of ink at the paper is called an _____-_____ printer.

Questions *continued*

Examination style questions

1 Here is a list of devices that may be attached to a computer system:

LCD screen
keyboard
portable hard drive
mouse
touchpad
laser printer

flash/pen drive
microphone
digital camera
speakers
web camera
CD-ROM drive

(a) Write down all the names of the output devices in the list above. *(3 marks)*

(b) List **two** other output devices not in the above list. *(2 marks)*

(c) Give the name of **one** input device that is not included in the list above. *(1 mark)*

(d) Give the name of **one** device in the list above that could be used to back up data and programs. *(1 mark)*

2 (a) Give **two** uses for each of the following input devices in a personal computer *(6 marks)*:
(i) mouse
(ii) microphone
(iii) digital camera

(b) Give the names of **four** output devices and give **one** use for each of them. *(8 marks)*

3 Copy and complete the table below *(10 marks)*:

Application	Most suitable output device
Alerting the user that an error has occurred by making a beep	
Printing a poster in colour	
Listening to a radio station using the Internet	
Producing a large plan of a house	
Producing a hard copy of a spreadsheet	
Producing a colour picture on paper taken with a digital camera	
Producing a series of invoices with several copies that can be sent to different departments	
Producing a warning when a bar code is read incorrectly	
For listening to messages from a voicemail system	
Displaying the results of a quick search on the availability of a holiday	

4 Touch screens can often be seen at tourist information offices.
(a) Describe what a touch screen is and how it works. *(2 marks)*
(b) Give **one** advantage of using a touch screen as an input device for use by the general public. *(1 mark)*

5 There are two different types of printer each with their own advantages and disadvantages. The names of these printers are:
Laser printer   Ink-jet printer
Identify the name of the printer being described for each one of the following:
(a) A printer that is used in offices for printing lots of documents in a short period of time. *(1 mark)*
(b) A cheap printer that is ideal for the home that can print in colour as well as black and white. *(1 mark)*
(c) A printer that sprays the ink onto the page. *(1 mark)*
(d) The type of printer where you have to be careful not to smudge the damp printouts as they come out of the printer. *(1 mark)*
(e) The type of printer that uses a toner cartridge. *(1 mark)*
(f) The printer that is cheap to buy but that has high running costs owing to the high cost of the ink cartridges. *(1 mark)*

END-OF-TOPIC REVIEW

Exam support

Worked example

Web cameras can take live video that can be transferred using the Internet to a computer in the home.

(a) Tick the three applications that are possible using a webcam. *(3 marks)*

	Tick **three** boxes
Watching the evolution of dinosaurs	☐
A parent checking up on their children in a nursery when they are at work	☐
Looking at live video of an erupting volcano in a geography lesson	☐
Watching a movie star constantly wherever they go	☐
Watching the space shuttle taking off as it happens	☐

(b) Give **two** advantages of using a webcam. *(2 marks)*

(c) Give **two** disadvantages of using a webcam. *(2 marks)*

Student answer 1

(a)

	Tick **three** boxes
Watching the evolution of dinosaurs	☑
A parent checking up on their children in a nursery when they are at work	☐
Looking at live video of an erupting volcano in a geography lesson	☐
Watching a movie star constantly wherever they go	☑
Watching the space shuttle taking off as it happens	☑

(b) You can use it to spy on other people.

They are very cheap to buy and many computers have them built into the screen.

(c) They do not produce a very good image.

You cannot store the image produced.

▲ **Examiner's comment**

(a) Webcams produce live images so you obviously cannot watch the evolution of dinosaurs.

Watching a movie star wherever they go would require a webcam to be present all the time. Clearly this is false.

The last tick is in the correct box.

(b) The first answer is a bit vague and needed further amplification to get the mark. The second answer is ok and gains a mark.

(c) The first answer is correct and gains a mark.

It is possible to save an image produced by a webcam and this is how they are used for security purposes.

(3 marks out of 7)

Exam support *continued*

Student answer 2

(a)

	Tick **three** boxes
Watching the evolution of dinosaurs	☐
A parent checking up on their children in a nursery when they are at work	☑
Looking at live video of an erupting volcano in a geography lesson	☑
Watching a movie star constantly wherever they go	☐
Watching the space shuttle taking off as it happens	☑

(b) You can look at famous sites throughout the world using live or almost live pictures.

They can be used for surveillance by the police and MI5 as they are extremely small.

(c) They can be used to make secret films of people without their knowledge which is morally wrong.

Webcams can encourage online flirting with people who are married, which could destroy a marriage.

▲ Examiner's comment

(a) All the ticks are in the correct places so all three marks are given here.

(b) Both of these are advantages of webcams, so full marks for this part.

(c) Both of these are valid answers and so full marks are awarded.

(7 marks out of 7)

Examiner's answers

(a) One mark for each correctly placed tick.

	Tick **three** boxes
Watching the evolution of dinosaurs	☐
A parent checking up on their children in a nursery when they are at work	☑
Looking at live video of an erupting volcano in a geography lesson	☑
Watching a movie star constantly wherever they go	☐
Watching the space shuttle taking off as it happens	☑

(b) One mark for each of two advantages such as:

A webcam can watch a bar to check that staff are not stealing money or drinks.

They can record criminals and be used as evidence.

You can see what the weather is like in a resort you are soon to visit.

They are very cheap to buy.

You can chat with people and see them at the same time.

They are small and so can be hidden easily so people do not know you are looking at them.

Webcams mean that you can have a simple meeting without the need to travel.

People can view things in distant places that it would be hard for them to visit in person.

(c) One mark for each of two disadvantages such as:

The images from webcams are often poor quality.

It can make it easy for others to spy on you without you knowing.

It can invade people's privacy.

Summary mind maps

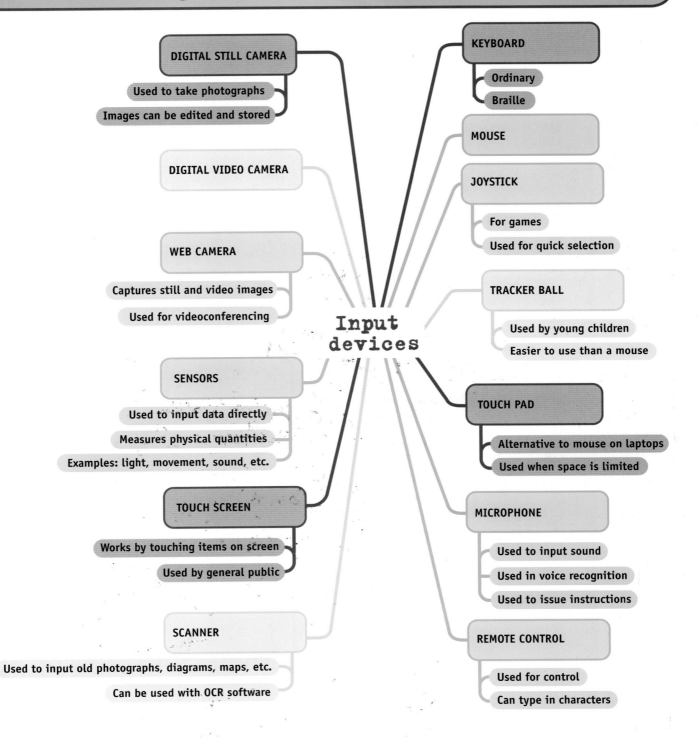

DIGITAL STILL CAMERA
- Used to take photographs
- Images can be edited and stored

DIGITAL VIDEO CAMERA

WEB CAMERA
- Captures still and video images
- Used for videoconferencing

SENSORS
- Used to input data directly
- Measures physical quantities
- Examples: light, movement, sound, etc.

TOUCH SCREEN
- Works by touching items on screen
- Used by general public

SCANNER
- Used to input old photographs, diagrams, maps, etc.
- Can be used with OCR software

Input devices

KEYBOARD
- Ordinary
- Braille

MOUSE

JOYSTICK
- For games
- Used for quick selection

TRACKER BALL
- Used by young children
- Easier to use than a mouse

TOUCH PAD
- Alternative to mouse on laptops
- Used when space is limited

MICROPHONE
- Used to input sound
- Used in voice recognition
- Used to issue instructions

REMOTE CONTROL
- Used for control
- Can type in characters

Summary mind maps *continued*

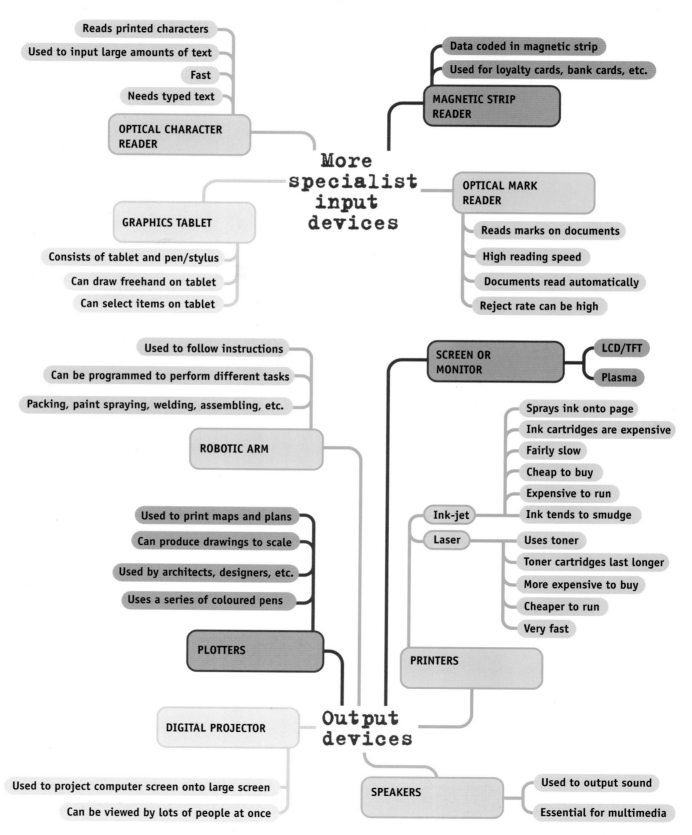

Reads printed characters
Used to input large amounts of text
Fast
Needs typed text

OPTICAL CHARACTER READER

Data coded in magnetic strip
Used for loyalty cards, bank cards, etc.

MAGNETIC STRIP READER

More specialist input devices

GRAPHICS TABLET

Consists of tablet and pen/stylus
Can draw freehand on tablet
Can select items on tablet

OPTICAL MARK READER

Reads marks on documents
High reading speed
Documents read automatically
Reject rate can be high

Used to follow instructions
Can be programmed to perform different tasks
Packing, paint spraying, welding, assembling, etc.

ROBOTIC ARM

SCREEN OR MONITOR

LCD/TFT

Plasma

Sprays ink onto page
Ink cartridges are expensive
Fairly slow
Cheap to buy
Expensive to run
Ink tends to smudge

Ink-jet

Laser

Uses toner
Toner cartridges last longer
More expensive to buy
Cheaper to run
Very fast

Used to print maps and plans
Can produce drawings to scale
Used by architects, designers, etc.
Uses a series of coloured pens

PLOTTERS

PRINTERS

Output devices

DIGITAL PROJECTOR

Used to project computer screen onto large screen
Can be viewed by lots of people at once

SPEAKERS

Used to output sound
Essential for multimedia

Topic 3

Storage devices and media

The key concepts covered in this topic are:

- Types of memory
- Backing/secondary storage devices and their media
- The advantages and disadvantages of backing/storage devices and media
- Impact of using storage devices

Computers need to have memory where data and some program instructions are stored temporarily when the computer is processing data. The memory is stored in chips. Other storage is needed where programs are stored such as the operating system software and the applications software and this is called backing storage. Files of data that are not needed immediately are also stored here.

In this topic you will learn about the types of memory and their purpose. You will also learn about the different types of backing storage and the need to keep backup copies of programs and data should the originals be damaged or lost.

Contents

Types of memory

▷ **About types of memory**

Computers need memory in order to hold data (program instructions and the data it is working on). More memory is generally better for computers, as it is one of the factors that makes them more powerful. In this section you will be looking at the two types of memory and the terms that are used when talking about memory size.

Types of memory

There are two main types of memory called RAM and ROM. Both these two types of memory are stored on chips and are available immediately to the central processing unit (CPU). Memory (i.e. RAM and ROM) is often called primary storage.

RAM (random access memory)

RAM is a fast temporary memory where programs and data are stored only when the power is supplied. RAM is:

- held on a computer chip
- called volatile memory because the contents disappear when the power is turned off
- read/write, so can be altered by the user.

ROM (read only memory)

ROM is fast permanent memory used for holding instructions needed to start the computer up. ROM is:

- held on a computer chip
- called non-volatile memory because it does not lose its contents when the power is turned off
- used to hold instructions to start the computer
- contents cannot be altered by the user.

Printer buffers

The computer sends information very quickly to the printer – much faster than the printer can cope with. A printer buffer is memory in the printer where the print jobs can wait until the printer is ready to deal with them. The printer buffer is a bit like a 'waiting room' for the print jobs where they wait until the printer can print them.

The importance of memory size

Having a large amount of memory is important. Having more memory means:

- applications run faster on their own
- more applications can run at the same time
- you can move quickly between applications.

▲ RAM chips.

Units of memory and storage

The amount of data and instructions the computer can store in its memory is measured in bytes. One byte contains 8 bits (a bit is a binary digit 0 or 1). A single character (letter, number or symbol on the keyboard) can be stored in one byte. This means that one byte is an extremely small unit of storage. We normally measure storage/memory in terms of kilobytes (Kb), megabytes (Mb) and gigabytes (Gb).

Why you need to know about file sizes

It is always important to know about the size of certain files because it is essential if you want to know how many of them could be stored on a particular storage device.

File sizes can be a little confusing but here they are from the smallest to the largest:

- Bit
- Byte
- Kilobyte (Kb)
- Megabyte (Mb)
- Gigabyte (Gb)
- Terabyte (Tb)

▲ All computer data is represented by combinations of binary digits (0 and 1).

The rough file size conversions are shown here:

- Bit (0 or 1) the smallest unit of measurement
- Byte 8 bits
- Kilobyte (Kb) 1000 bytes
- Megabyte (Mb) 1000 kilobytes (Kb)
- Gigabyte (Gb) 1000 megabytes (Mb)
- Terabyte (Tb) 1000 gigabytes (Gb).

The demands made on memory by modern software

Modern software demands a lot from the hardware of the computer. It is constantly driving the specification of an average computer higher. This means that computers need more powerful processors and because programs are more complex, they need more memory.

Use of memory in computers and mobile devices

Any device that uses microprocessors to control it will often have some memory. All computers and mobile devices will have memory and these include:

- Desktop, laptop and netbook computers – have large amounts of memory, which allows them to run multimedia software and run many applications at the same time.
- Mobile phones – to store programs to control the phone, address book details, games, digital music, digital photographs, etc.
- PDAs – to store programs such as the operating system, web browser software, address book details, etc.

- Palmtops – to store programs such as the operating system, simple applications such as word-processing, web browser software, etc.

KEY WORDS

RAM random access memory. Fast temporary memory that loses its contents when the power is turned off.

ROM read only memory – memory stored on a chip that does not lose data when the power is turned off.

Bit a binary digit 0 or 1.

Byte a group of 8 bits

Kilobyte a unit of file or memory size that is 1024 bytes.

Megabyte a unit of file or memory size that is 1024 kilobytes.

Gigabyte a unit of file or memory size that is 1024 megabytes.

Terabyte a unit of file or memory size that is 1024 gigabytes.

Non-volatile memory memory that does not lose its contents when the power is removed (i.e. ROM).

Printer buffer printer memory used to store print jobs that allows users to go onto another piece of work or log off before their work is printed.

Volatile memory memory that loses its contents when the power is removed (i.e. RAM).

Questions A

1 ROM and RAM are both types of computer memory.
- **(a)** (i) What do the letters **RAM** stand for? *(1 mark)*
  - (ii) What do the letters **ROM** stand for? *(1 mark)*
- **(b)** Tick **one** box next to **each** item in the table to show which statements apply to RAM and which to ROM.

	ROM	RAM
Contents are lost when the computer is turned off	☐	☐
Contents are not lost when the computer is turned off	☐	☐
Stores the programs needed to start up the computer	☐	☐
Stores application, programs and data when they are being used	☐	☐

2 In computers and mobile devices such as mobile phones, palmtops and PDAs, memory is needed.
- **(a)** Give the names of the **two** types of memory needed. *(2 marks)*
- **(b)** Explain why both types of memory are required. *(3 marks)*
- **(c)** Explain the purpose of a printer buffer. *(2 marks)*

3 Memory size in a computer is expressed in gigabytes.
- **(a)** Explain why it is important that a computer has a large amount of memory. *(2 marks)*
- **(b)** Memory can be divided into RAM and ROM.
  Explain what ROM would be used for in a computer.
  Explain what RAM would be used for in a computer. *(4 marks)*
- **(c)** How many megabytes are there in one gigabyte? *(1 mark)*

Extension activity

You have to do some research on computer memory using the Internet.

Access information about the latest desktop, laptop and netbook computers and find out the amount of each type of memory a typical computer comes with (RAM and ROM).

Word-process your findings presenting them in the form of a table.

Backing/secondary storage devices and media

You will find out

▷ **About backing/secondary storage devices**

▷ **About backing/secondary storage media**

▷ **About the advantages and disadvantages of devices and media**

▷ **About the advantages and disadvantages of using storage devices for individuals and organizations**

Memory (ROM and RAM) is an expensive component of a computer and the RAM loses its contents when the power is switched off. Backing or secondary storage is used for the storage of programs and data that are not needed immediately by the computer. They are also used for storing backups of programs and data in case the originals are damaged or destroyed.

Backups and the reasons for taking them

Backups are copies of data and program files kept for security reasons. Should the originals be destroyed then the backups can be used. Using a file server and storing both programs and data on it, means that backups can be taken in one place. Backups should be held on removable devices or media that are taken off site each day. The individual users do not need to take their own backups. The person in charge of the network (i.e., usually the network manager) will take the backups needed. Many systems now take backups automatically at a certain time of the day and send the data using the Internet to a company that specializes in storing backups.

Backing/secondary storage devices

Backing/secondary storage is needed for the storage of data and programs. The devices are the hardware that take the data and store it on the storage media. For example, a DVD drive is the storage device and a DVD is the storage media. As well as storing the original sets of data and programs, backing/secondary storage devices are also used for the taking of backup copies.

Memory stick/pen drive/USB drive

Memory sticks, pen drives and USB drives are all names for the same things and are ideal storage for photographs, music and other data files. These are the portable small stick-like devices that you insert into the USB port/slot and use for storing work on. These are a very useful backing storage device and probably the way you transfer your work between home and school or college. They consist of printed circuit boards enclosed in a plastic case.

The main advantages are:

- small and lightweight – easy to put on your key ring or in your pocket and can be used with any computer
- large storage capacity (up to 30 Gb)
- no moving parts, so they are very reliable
- not subject to scratches like optical media.

Flash/pen drives are the most popular portable storage media. Their portability is their main advantage and you simply plug them into the USB port where they are recognized automatically.

The main disadvantages are:

- their small size means they are easily stolen
- they are often left in the computer by mistake and lost
- they do not have as high a transfer rate as magnetic hard disk drives.

◀ Flash/pen drive.

Magnetic hard disk drives

Magnetic disk drives are the main form of backing/secondary storage on a computer. Hard drives consist of a series of disks with a magnetic coating and a series of read/write heads that put the data onto or record it off each surface.

Magnetic hard drives have the advantages of:

- a very high transfer rate (quick to put data on and to read it off)
- a very high storage capacity.

You can buy additional hard drives for backup purposes. These hard drives are called portable hard drives and may be removed each night and stored safely.

▲ Hard disks store data as a magnetic pattern.

Magnetic cartridges

Magnetic cartridges usually use reels of magnetic tape in a hard plastic case. They are used for backing up large amount of data for security purposes. They have huge storage capacities and are ideal for taking daily and weekly backups.

▲ Magnetic cartridges can store backups taken daily.

Optical drives

Optical disks are flat circular disks on which data is stored as a series of bumps. The way the bumps reflect laser beam light is used to read the data off the disk. CD/DVD drives read the data off the disk or in some cases store the data onto the disk.

▲ Optical disks include CDs and DVDs and are used to store digital data as a binary pattern on the disks.

CD-ROM (Compact Disk-Read Only Memory)

CD-ROMs are used mainly for the distribution of software. Although most home computers are equipped with DVD drives, a lot more computers, especially those used in businesses, still only have CD drives. You can read a CD using a DVD drive but you cannot read a DVD with a CD drive. This is why software is still being sold on CD rather than DVD.

With CD-ROM:

- data is read only
- data is stored as an optical pattern
- there is a large storage capacity (600 Mb)
- they are used for the distribution of software.

DVD-ROM (Digital Versatile Disk-Read Only Memory)

DVDs have a much higher storage capacity than CDs and are ideal for the storage of multimedia files such as MP3, digital images and video clips.

DVD-ROM is used for the distribution of movies where you can only read the data off the disk. A DVD-ROM drive can also be used for the reading of data off a CD.

CD-R (CD-Recordable)

CD-R allows data to be stored on a CD, but only once. It is ideal for the backing up of data or for storing digital music.

▲ A CD-R disk being used with a laptop.

CD-RW (CD-Rewriteable)

A CD-RW disk allows data to be stored on the disk over and over again – just like a hard disk. You can treat a CD-RW like a hard drive but the transfer rate is less and the time taken to locate a file is greater. The media is not as robust as a hard drive.

DVD-RAM (Digital Versatile Disk – Random Access Memory)

DVD-RAM drives allow repeated storage and erasure of data so they act a bit like a hard drive but the disks cannot be used with all DVD drives.

DVD-R (DVD-Recordable)

DVD-R allows data to be stored on a DVD, but only once. It is ideal for the backing up of data, for storing digital music or for storing a film.

DVD+RW (Digital Versatile Disk+Read/Write)

A DVD+RW drive can be used to write to as well as read data from a DVD. DVD–RW are sometimes called DVD burners because they are able to be written to and not just read from.

Typical storage capacities are:

- 4.7 Gb for the older DVD drives
- 8.5 Gb for the latest DVD drives.

Backing/secondary storage devices and media *continued*

Flash memory, card drives and memory cards

Memory cards are the thin cards you see in digital cameras. They are ideal storage media for photographs but can also be used for storing other types of data.

▲ Memory cards in cameras have a capacity measured in gigabytes.

▲ Flash memory is also used in MP3 players for the storage of digital music.

Solid state drives

A solid state drive is use to store data and it is used in a similar way to a hard drive except unlike a hard drive, there are no moving parts. They have the advantage over a hard drive that they are very robust so not easily damaged. Data is also transferred between the drive and computer and vice versa faster compared to a hard drive.

Virtual memory

This is where applications software such as word-processing software, database software, etc., is given the impression it has lots more memory available to it. This is because it is using some of the storage on a disk drive as well as the memory and the computer thinks it is just using memory.

Online storage

Online backup companies, for a fee, will allow you to store your backup data on their computers. The Internet is used to transfer the files to and from their storage devices.

Online imaging/photographic management and sharing sites

Photographs of family and friends are stored on most people's computers and are irreplaceable if the computer were damaged or stolen. Of course people should always take backups of this data. One way to ensure that the photographs are not lost is to use online imaging or photographic management. This is where you copy all your photographs onto a site and they keep them safe for you in case the originals are ever lost. Some of the sites may allow the public to see and use your photographs but you can choose which ones are for public viewing. The most popular site for this is called flickr. Take a look at the site on:

http://www.flickr.com/

Looking after media

Media can be delicate and easily damaged so it is important that you take care when handling it and putting it into and removing it from drives.

Here are a few tips on looking after media:

- Avoid putting your fingers on the reading surface of the disk.
- Ensure that the disks are flat in the drive before closing the drive door.
- Always put the disks back in their cases after use to avoid dust settling on them, which can scratch them.
- Store disks away from sources of heat such as radiators and window sills.
- Label disks so that they can be found easily.

▲ Hold disks like this to avoid touching the reading surface.

The impact of using storage devices

One of the main developments in ICT that has influenced the way we work and play has been the development of storage devices and media that can store huge amounts of data in a small space.

This has led to the following:

- Portable music players that can store thousands of music tracks.
- Computers that can store lots of full length movies.
- Small cameras capable of storing thousands of photographs.
- Mobile phones with music players and digital cameras.
- Small netbook computers.

The advantages of being able to store large amounts of data include:

- Makes it possible for new applications (e.g., camera phones, portable music players, etc.).
- It is much cheaper to store data than in the past.
- You are not restricted as much with how many photographs you can take with a camera.
- You have a greater choice of music and video on your player.

The disadvantages of being able to store huge amounts of data include:

- It is much easier for the government to store all sorts of personal data about us.
- Large amounts of personal data can be stored on portable storage media.
- It encourages organizations to collect more data than they actually need.
- It encourages people to copy copyrighted works such as music and video.

▲ Netbooks provide portable and low cost access to the Internet.

Questions B

1 Which **three** of the following are backing storage devices? *(3 marks)*
- RAM
- Hard drive
- CD-RW drive
- ROM
- Plotter
- Speaker
- Keyboard
- Pen drive

2 Give the meaning of the following abbreviations.
- **(a)** DVD-R *(1 mark)*
- **(b)** DVD-RW *(1 mark)*

3 Explain what is meant by virtual memory. *(2 marks)*

4 Backups of programs and data should be taken on a regular basis.
- **(a)** Explain what is meant by a backup. *(2 marks)*
- **(b)** Give **one** reason why backups should be taken on a regular basis. *(1 mark)*
- **(c)** Give **one** example of backing storage suitable for the taking of backup copies and explain why it is suitable. *(3 marks)*

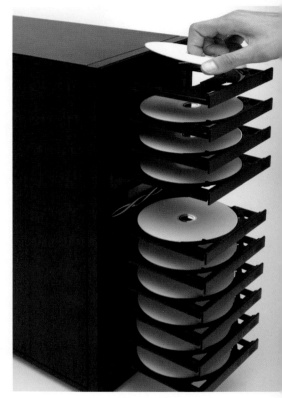

▲ Copyrighted work is illegally copied and sold.

Extension activity

Everyone who uses a computer needs to store their data and programs somewhere.

For this activity you have to find out about the backing storage devices that are available for computer users. Use the Internet to find out:

- Types of storage devices and their storage capacity.
- The main advantages and disadvantages of each device.

- The cost of the storage device.
- The media they need if applicable.

A good place to look for information is the website of the large online stores who sell computer equipment such as PC World.

END-OF-TOPIC REVIEW

Questions

✔ Test yourself

The following notes summarize this topic. The notes are incomplete because they have words missing. Using the words in the list below, copy out and complete the sentences A to K, underlining the words that you have inserted. Each word may be used more than once.

RAM   cartridges   off   power

portable   DVD   ROM   secondary

hard   programs   backups

A _____ is a fast temporary memory where programs and data are stored only when the power is supplied.

B _____ is fast permanent memory used for holding instructions needed to start the computer up.

C _____ is held on a computer chip and is called non-volatile memory because it does not lose its contents when the _____ is turned off

D _____ is held on a computer chip and is called volatile memory because the contents disappear when the power is turned _____.

E _____ are copies of data and program files kept for security reasons.

F Backing or _____ storage is used for the storage of programs and data that are not needed immediately by the computer.

G They are also used for storing backups of _____ and data in case the originals are damaged or destroyed.

H Flash/pen drives are the most popular _____ storage media.

I _____ drives consist of a series of disks with a magnetic coating and a series of read/write heads that put the data onto or record it off each surface.

J Magnetic _____ usually use reels of magnetic tape in a hard plastic case.

K Optical drives include CD and _____ drives.

Examination style questions

1 **(a)** Give **two** uses for each of the following devices in a personal computer.
   (i)   Hard disk drive *(2 marks)*
   (ii) Floppy disk drive *(2 marks)*
   (iii) CD-ROM drive *(2 marks)*
   (b) Give **two** ways small high-storage devices have influenced the development of portable equipment that can be used for work and play. *(2 marks)*

2 Many people use online sites in order to store their collections of family photographs.
   (a) Explain how online imaging/photographic management and sharing sites can be used to store family photographs. *(2 marks)*
   (b) Give **one** advantage in using an online site for storing your photographs. *(1 mark)*

3 There are two types of memory used by a computer: ROM and RAM.
   (a) Give the meaning of ROM. *(1 mark)*
   (b) Give the meaning of RAM. *(1 mark)*
   (c) Explain why the two types of memory are needed in a computer. *(2 marks)*

4 Computers need memory and backing storage.
   (a) Give **one** difference between memory and backing storage. *(1 mark)*
   (b) Give **one** example of what would be stored in memory. *(1 mark)*
   (c) Give **one** example of what would be stored in backing storage. *(1 mark)*

5 Data needs to be stored for future use. Here are a number of storage devices/media. For each of these, explain a suitable use and explain clearly why the storage device/media is suited to the application.
   (a) Memory card *(2 marks)*
   (b) CD-ROM *(2 marks)*
   (c) Magnetic hard drive *(2 marks)*
   (d) Flash/pen drive *(2 marks)*

END-OF-TOPIC REVIEW

Exam support

Worked example

A presentation that contains multimedia features such as images, sound and video is to be transferred between computers.

(a) Give the names of **two** storages devices that can be used to store the files and explain why they are suitable for this application. *(4 marks)*

(b) All storage devices and media have disadvantages. For each storage device/media you have named state **two** disadvantages. *(2 marks)*

Student answer 1

(a) CD because lots of different files can be stored and all computers come with a CD drive.

DVD – because the storage capacity is high and they work with all computers.

(b) CD – you cannot store data on both side of the disk

DVD – the surface of this disk can easily be damaged which causes them not to work.

▲ **Examiner's comment**

(a) Just stating either CD or DVD will not gain marks. As the presentation has been created on one computer and needs to be transferred to a different computer, there needs to be a write facility so it is necessary to give the names DVD-RW or CD-RW.

In other questions where the write facility is not needed, the proper terms DVD-ROM or CD-ROM should be used rather than CD or DVD.

No marks for part (a)

(b) The lack of storage on both sides could (loosely) be considered as a limitation. The problem here is that the top surface tends to get scratched and also where would you put the label!

Optical media is easily damaged so part (b) is an acceptable answer.

(2 marks out of 6)

Student answer 2

(a) CD-RW because the data can be recorded onto a CD-RW disk that has a high storage capacity that is ideal for all the multimedia files. Also all computers have a drive that is capable of reading the data off the disk.

Flash drive – the drive can be used just like another drive and has a high enough capacity to hold all the files needed and it is easy to transport being small in size and light.

(b) CD-RW you have to take care when handling them as it is very easy to scratch the disk surface and prevent the CD-RW from being able to transfer data.

Flash drive – the access time is lower than that for an internal magnetic hard drive which means the data takes longer to load.

◀ Examiner's comment

(a) The student has identified suitable storage devices/media and has clearly related their reasons to the transfer of multimedia files for a presentation. This part gains full marks.

(b) Two disadvantages of each storage media/device have been identified so full marks for this.

(6 marks out of 6)

Examiner's answers

(a) One mark for each device and one mark for the reason × 2.

Pen drive – small size means easily transferred from one computer to another.

Pen drive – can be used by all computers as it simply plugs into the USB port/socket.

Pen drive – can get cheap storage capacity up to 4 Gb which is enough for large music, animation, image files needed for a multimedia presentation.

CD-RW – has a large storage capacity, which is needed because multimedia files are usually large.

CD-RW – small in size which means they are easily transferred between computers.

CD-RW – can be read by any computer with a CD drive or a DVD drive.

(b) One mark for each disadvantage. Note the disadvantages must refer to the named storage devices in part (a).

CD-RW – easily scratched which causes read problems (1).

CD-RW – limited amount of storage capacity (1).

Pen drive – low transfer rate compared to a magnetic hard drive (1).

Pen drive – easily bent and broken when in the socket (1).

Pen drive – often left in the machine by mistake and lost (1).

Summary mind map

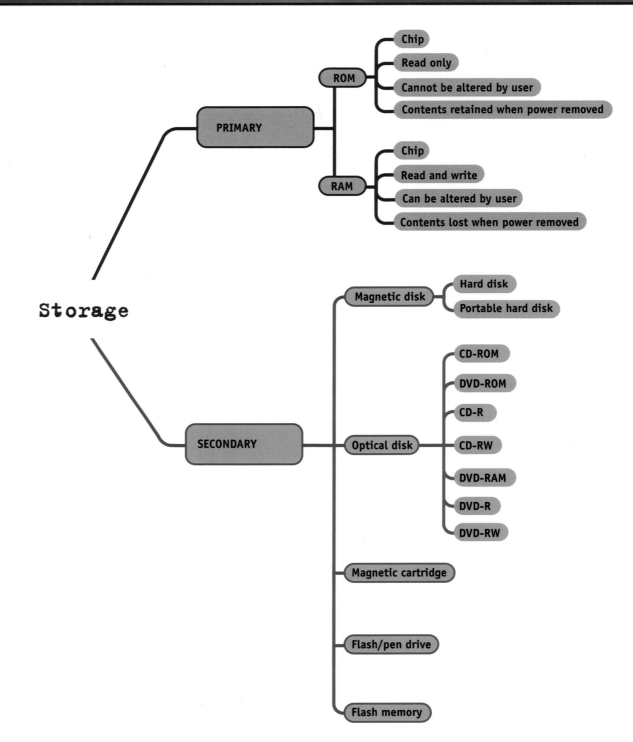

Topic 4

Communications and entertainment

The key concepts covered in this topic are:

- Advantages and disadvantages of using communications networks
- Communication devices and media
- Network devices
- Entertainment systems
- Reliability of information
- Impact of communications technology

In this topic you will be looking at networking and how it is used for entertainment.

The way we entertain ourselves has completely changed with the introduction of the Internet and portable media. We are no longer restricted to when we listen to music and watch our favourite TV programmes. We can also listen to radio online and download music rather than visit a high street store to buy it. All of these developments have come about through developments in communications.

Contents

43

Advantages and disadvantages of using communications networks

If more than one computer is used in the home or in a business, then it makes sense to network them. Networking means that devices such as printers and scanners can be shared between all the computers on the network. It also means that all the computers can share an Internet link that will allow all computers access at the same time. There is also the ability to share programs and data.

What is a network?

A network is two or more computers that are linked together so that they are able to share resources. These resources could be a printer, scanner, software or even a connection to the Internet. You can also share data using a network. For example, a pupil database in a school could be accessed from any of the computers connected to the network.

Peer-to-peer and client–server networks

There are two ways of operating a network: peer-to-peer and client–server. Large organizations would use a client–server network because it is more powerful and can do a lot more.

Peer-to-peer networking is fine for home networks or small businesses where a simple inexpensive network is all that is needed.

Whether an organization chooses peer-to-peer or client–server is mainly determined by the size of the network.

Peer-to-peer networks

Here are the main features of peer-to-peer networks:

- Each computer on the network has equal status.
- All computers can share each other's resources (e.g., data, an Internet connection, printers, scanners, etc.).
- They are only suitable for small networks with fewer than ten users.

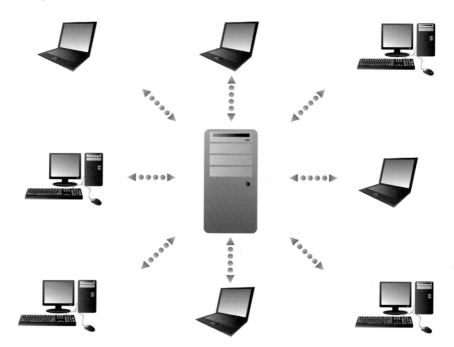

The server in a client–server network is in control of the network.

- Only very basic knowledge is needed to set one up and use it.
- As more people use the network, the whole network slows down considerably.

Client–server networks

Here are the main features of client–server networks:

- One more powerful computer, called the server, is used to store the data and the programs needed by the whole network. The server is in control of the network.
- Software and data is stored on the server, so it can be accessed by all the computers on the network.
- The network is totally dependent on the server. If the server breaks down, the network cannot be used.
- They are the popular choice for networks that need lots of computers.

The two types of network: LAN and WAN

There are two types of network: a local area network (LAN) and a wide area network (WAN).

Basically a WAN is much bigger than a LAN and spread over a much wider area. The table below gives you the main features of each type of network.

Internet

The Internet is a huge group of networks joined together. Each of these networks consists of lots of smaller networks. This means that the Internet consists of hardware.

The advantages and disadvantages in using the Internet

The advantages of the Internet

- Huge amounts of information can be accessed almost anywhere.
- Improved communication systems – this includes the use of text messages, emails, instant messaging, etc.
- Changes in the way we shop – many people prefer to shop online.
- VoIP (Voice over Internet Protocol) – enables cheap international phone calls to be made using the Internet.
- Can help people with disabilities be more independent – because they can order goods and services online.

The disadvantages of the Internet

- Cyber crime – we have to be much more careful about revealing personal information such as bank and credit card details.
- Addiction to gambling, as there are many casino, bingo, horse racing, etc., betting sites.
- Addiction to pornography.
- Deserted city centres as shops close down as they cannot compete with Internet shopping.
- Paedophiles look for children using the Internet.

- Addiction to games, chat rooms, social networking sites, etc.
- Starting rumours on the Internet. You only have to start a rumour in a chat room, a blog or on a social networking site and it soon spreads.
- Misinformation. Many sites have been set up containing wrong information.

Authentication techniques

Authentication techniques are those techniques that are used to check that a person accessing a network or communications system is the genuine person. They can also be used to ensure that an email sent by a person is genuinely from them and not somebody pretending to be them.

The two main authentication techniques are:

- usernames and passwords
- digital signatures.

LAN (local area network)	WAN (wide area network)
Confined to a small area	Covers a wide geographical area (e.g., between cities, countries and even continents)
Usually located in a single building	In lots of different buildings, cities, countries, etc.
Uses cable, wireless, infra-red and microwave links that are usually owned by the organization	Uses more expensive telecommunication links that are supplied by telecommunication companies
Cheap to build	Expensive to build
Cheap to run	Expensive to run

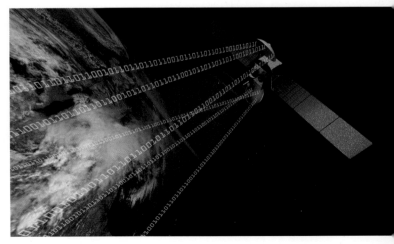

Wide area networks often make use of satellite links.

Advantages and disadvantages of using communications networks *continued*

Identifying the user to the system: usernames

A username is series of characters that is used to identify a certain user to the network. The person who looks after the network will use this to allocate space on the network for the user. It is also used by the network to give the user access to certain files.

The network manager can also keep track of what files each user is accessing for security reasons.

Preventing unauthorized access to the system: the use of passwords

A password is a string of characters (letters, numbers and punctuation marks) that the user selects. Only the user will know what the password is. When the user enters the password, it will not be shown on the screen. Only on entry of the correct password will the user be allowed access to the network.

Digital signatures

Ordinary signatures can be used to check the authenticity of a document. By comparing a signature you can determine whether a document is authentic.

When conducting business over the Internet you also need to be sure that emails and electronic documents are authentic. Digital signatures are a method used with emails to ensure that they are actually from the person they say they are from and not from someone pretending to be them.

If you are sent a signed letter, you can check that it is authentic by comparing the signature on the letter with a stored one. Digital signatures are used in a similar way.

Encryption

Because so many people use a network it is important to ensure that the system is secure. If there is access to the Internet via the network, then there needs to be protection against hackers. These hackers could simply intercept and read email or they could alter data or collect personal details and credit card numbers to commit fraud.

Encryption is used to protect data from prying eyes by scrambling data as it travels over the Internet. Encryption is also used when saving personal data onto laptops or removable storage devices. If any of these gets lost or stolen then the data cannot be read.

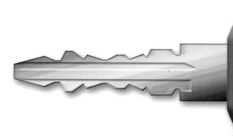

When encrypted data is sent to a person, they need a key/password to read it.

Encryption should be used for:

- sending credit card details such as card numbers, expiry dates, etc., over the Internet
- online banking
- sending payment details (bank details such as sort code numbers, account numbers, etc.)
- confidential emails
- sending data between computers on a network where confidentiality is essential
- storing sensitive personal information on laptops and portable devices and media.

GLASBERGEN

"I'm sure there are better ways to disguise sensitive information, but we don't have a big budget."

Questions A

1. LAN and WAN are both types of computer network.
   (a) (i) What do the letters LAN stand for? *(1 mark)*
       (ii) What do the letters WAN stand for? *(1 mark)*
   (b) Give **two** differences between a LAN and a WAN. *(2 marks)*
   (c) Give **three** advantages to computer users of a LAN, rather than working on stand-alone machines. *(3 marks)*
   (d) Give **one** method that can be used to prevent data from being misused when it is being transferred between computers. *(1 mark)*

2. When goods are ordered over the Internet payment has to be made.
   (a) Give **one** method of payment used over the Internet. *(1 mark)*
   (b) Describe why some people may not want to put their payment details into a website. *(2 marks)*
   (c) Describe **one** way the online store can make sure that payment details are safe. *(2 marks)*

3. Explain briefly how each one of the following helps improve the security of a network.
   (a) User-ID *(2 marks)*
   (b) Password *(2 marks)*
   (c) Encryption *(2 marks)*

4. (a) Give **two** advantages of using the Internet. *(2 marks)*
   (b) Give **two** disadvantages of using the Internet. *(2 marks)*

▲ Passwords ensure the user is who they say they are.

▲ Encryption is used to help prevent fraud.

Extension activity

Investigate how to set up digital signatures using the email service you use at school or college. See if you can set them up between you and a friend.

Communication devices, network devices and media

You will find out

▷ **About telephones and SMS (texting)**

▷ **About instant messaging (e.g. MSN)**

▷ **About fax**

▷ **About email, chat rooms, forums and bulletin boards**

▷ **About VoIP (Internet telephone)**

▷ **About sat nav (satellite navigation)**

▷ **About network devices**

There are many different ways of communicating using communication devices such as telephones, computers, etc. In this section you will be looking at those devices that make use of communications systems and the communication services they offer. You will be looking at the network devices including those devices that allow access to the Internet.

I'm still discovering cool stuff I can do with my smartphone. Today I sent a photo to my mom, bought some music, trimmed my sideburns, blended a smoothie, and neutered my cat!"

Telephones

Telephones are one of the most popular communication devices and, although the land-line phone is still very popular, the growth in the use of mobile phones has meant that these have many more services available.

New services for mobile phones are being thought up all the time and who knows what they might do in the future. When they were first developed, they were the equivalent of a telephone that could be used on the move. Nowadays they offer all sorts of new services and have started to blur the difference between a computer or PDA and a mobile phone. Many mobile phones also act as portable MP3 players, enabling you to play your music on the move.

Advantages and disadvantages of mobile phones

Advantages

- You can be contacted in case of an emergency.
- Plans can be changed at the last minute.
- Parents like children to have a mobile phone as they feel it is safer.

Disadvantages

- Many people use their phones when walking along and this has caused accidents.
- Calls can disturb other people in the cinema, theatre, cafes, etc.
- Many people still use hand-held phones when driving, which is dangerous and illegal.
- Long-term use may cause health problems.

"I decided to have the surgery because I need the extra thumb for text messaging."

SMS (texting)

SMS (short messaging service) or, as most people know it, texting, allows short low-cost messages to be sent between phones. It is also possible to send text messages to phones using a computer or mobile device such as a PDA or palmtop.

Instant messaging (IM)

Instant messaging is a method of two people using real-time text to conduct a conversation. Some instant message services can make use of webcams that allow the people conducting the text conversation to see each other.

Fax

Fax is like a long distance photocopier. You put the document in the fax machine at one end and then enter the telephone number of the fax machine to which it is to be sent. The page is scanned, passed along the telephone line and it is printed out on the recipient's fax machine. Documents as well as diagrams/drawings can be sent by fax.

It is possible to use a computer with a scanner and a printer as a fax machine.

Online communications

Chat rooms

Chat rooms are virtual meeting places where you can meet and hold conversations with others. They are not without their dangers. Paedophiles have been known to use chat rooms to make contact with children.

Forums

Forums are often called message boards and they allow people to post and respond to messages posted on them. Usually the forum is about a particular subject or interest.

KEY WORD

Fax A machine capable of sending and receiving text and pictures along telephone lines.

Bulletin boards

A bulletin board is a computer with special software that users can log into. Once logged in, they can upload and download files, read bulletins and messages, etc.

VoIP (Voice over Internet Protocol)/Internet telephone

VoIP enables cheap phone calls to be made using the Internet. It is a technology that allows voice signals to be transferred over the Internet but it can sometimes be unreliable and the quality of the sound can be poor.

Sat nav

Satellite navigation systems, commonly just called sat navs, enable maps to be displayed and show a location and guide the person to their destination.

Advantages of satellite navigation systems

There are many different advantages in using satellite navigation systems and here are just some of them:

- They reduce fuel consumption, which is therefore greener because you do not get lost.
- You can arrive at your destination without delay, as you can be warned in advance of roadworks.
- You can save money by choosing the shortest route.

▶ A fax machine.

Communication devices, network devices and media *continued*

Disadvantages of satellite navigation systems

Some of the disadvantages of satellite navigation systems include:

- Satellite navigation systems can send you down very small and windy roads.
- Satellite navigation systems are sometimes difficult to use.
- Sometimes the information is out-of-date.
- Satellite navigation systems can cause accidents if people start inputting information into them whilst driving.

Using communications systems to access the Internet

There are a number of devices and systems that can be used to access the Internet.

Modem

Modems are devices that enable a communication link to be set up between the computer and a medium such as a wire or cable that is used to carry the data. There are two types of modem.

Dialup modem

This is a slower more old-fashioned modem. When you log onto the Internet using a dialup modem it dials the number of your Internet service provider. You are then asked for your user-ID or screen name and a password. On providing this, you are connected to the Internet.

Broadband modem

Broadband modems are the latest modems and offer connection to the Internet using a broadband link.

Broadband is much faster than dialup and allows you to:

- download files at high speed
- watch online video
- use web cameras
- listen to online radio
- watch TV programmes
- surf the Internet very quickly.

Satellite communication

Satellites are used to beam data signals from one continent to another where the terrain makes it difficult to lay cables. It is interesting to note that communication between Britain and America is via a cable laid on the ocean bed. Because of the importance of this cable, its whereabouts are kept secret to protect it from a terrorist attack.

Data signals from one continent are beamed up to the satellite in orbit and then beamed back down to a satellite dish in another continent.

Wireless

Many computers and other devices are now able to connect to the Internet or communicate with other computers in a local area network wirelessly. With wireless communication, the data travels through the air rather through cables.

Wireless networks enable people to connect wirelessly to the Internet or to a network set up in a home. This means they can work anywhere they can get a radio signal for their network. Many people, especially people who travel a lot, need to access the Internet regularly. There are many public places where the Internet can be accessed wirelessly using a laptop computer or other portable device such as mobile phone or PDA. These places where you can access the Internet using Wi-Fi are called hot spots.

KEY WORDS

Hotspot a region where the Internet can be accessed wirelessly.

Wi-Fi a trademark for products that meet certain standards for transmitting data over wireless networks.

Internet service provider (ISP) a company that provides users with an Internet connection.

▲ Satellites allow communication across continents.

Advantages of wireless communication

- You are not restricted to where you can work.
- You can work whilst on the move.
- Fewer/no trailing wires to trip over.
- It is easier to keep a working area clean if there are not as many wires in the way.
- No costs associated with sinking wires.

Disadvantages of wireless communication

- The danger of hackers reading messages.
- There are areas where you cannot get a wireless network.
- There may be a danger to your health.

Bluetooth

Bluetooth is a method used to transfer data over short distances from fixed and mobile devices. For example, you could print a document using a laptop and printer even though there were no wires between them. Other applications for Bluetooth include:

- Wireless keyboards and mice avoid clutter on your desk and make the desk easier to clean.
- Wireless headsets allowing you to use a mobile phone legally when driving.
- Sharing data such as voice, music and video wirelessly with others.
- Printing a picture from your camera phone.
- Listening to music using wireless earphones.
- Children's games, e.g. Wii, PlayStation and Lego Mindstorms.

Servers

In a client–server network a more powerful computer is needed to act as the server. A server is responsible for the storage and the moving of the data around the network.

Most desktop computers are capable of acting as servers, but it is better to use one specifically designed for the task.

Specialist servers are available for large networks with each server performing a particular task in the network.

File server

A file server is a high-speed computer in a network that stores programs and data files shared by users. It deals with the requests made by the users on each networked computer for programs and data.

Print server

A print server is a computer in a network that controls one or more printers. It feeds the print jobs to the printer one at a time. Each print job goes into a printer queue where it waits until the printer is ready to deal with it. On very small networks, the printer server and the file server may be the same computer.

Email server

When you send an email, the organization that supplies you with your Internet connection receives your email and distributes it to the correct email address. The ISP (Internet service provider) has a server called an email server that is devoted to dealing with email.

Questions B

1. (a) What do the initials ISP stand for? *(1 mark)*
   (b) Give **one** purpose of an ISP. *(1 mark)*

2. A person uses VoIP.
   (a) Explain what VoIP is. *(2 marks)*
   (b) Give **one** advantage in using VoIP. *(1 mark)*

3. Copy and complete the sentences by filling in the missing word in each case.
   (a) _____ is a slow connection to the Internet and connection is made by the computer dialling a number.
   (b) _____ provides high speed Internet access and no time is wasted dialling a number to make a connection. *(2 marks)*

4. An office is thinking of introducing a wireless network with a wireless connection to the Internet.
   Give **two** advantages in using a wireless network rather than a wired one. *(2 marks)*

5. Describe **two** tasks that can be performed using broadband access to the Internet that would be very difficult or frustrating to do using dialup access. *(2 marks)*

Extension activity

Some older people get a bit lost with the latest communications technology.

Many older people would like to learn a bit more so that they are less ignorant when people start talking about communications devices and media.

For this activity you have to produce a short guide to the technology. Your guide should at least cover the following:

- Texting
- Instant messaging
- Chat rooms
- Forums
- Bulletin boards
- VoIP.

Entertainment systems

You will find out

▷ **About TV (terrestrial, digital, cable and broadband)**

▷ **About radio, video, film and music streaming**

▷ **About integrated entertainment systems**

▷ **About digital TV recording**

▷ **About the advantages and disadvantages of media downloads/streaming**

Entertainment systems are more flexible than they used to be. You do not have to watch television programmes at a certain time nor do you need to view them on a TV set. The development of high speed broadband has meant that it is feasible to download entire films in a reasonable time. It is also possible to stream video over the Internet, which means you watch the video as the signal arrives and do not have to download it first. In this section you will look at the developments in entertainment systems.

TV (terrestrial, digital, cable and broadband)

Digital TV offers a host of services that allow many interactive services other than just watching the programmes. TV used to be watched only on a television but now many people are watching it using the Internet.

Terrestrial TV

These are the TV services that come from a signal received from the TV aerial and not from a satellite or an underground cable.

Digital TV

Digital TV may be free or it may be offered as a pay-to-view service. Either way digital TV offers many interactive features that were not possible before. These include being able to:

- join in with programmes by sending in comments
- see extra new stories and sports coverage
- book cinema and holiday tickets
- play games
- shop
- place bets
- use email
- place votes for programmes – there are plans to use this service for voting in parliamentary elections
- see interactive advertisements.

Some problems caused by interactive services:

- May encourage young children to play games on their TV rather than play more energetic games.
- Could cause addiction to checking and sending email, playing games, etc.
- Gambling services could cause addiction to gambling.

Cable TV

Cable TV is sent along an underground cable and offers more or less the same services as satellite TV. It is a digital service and offers all the interactive features.

Broadband TV

Some TV programmes can be viewed over the Internet in real time. Many programmes can be watched after they have been transmitted by using the Internet. This means you can watch programmes you have missed on the Internet.

Radio

Digital radio has become very popular owing to the improved sound quality. As well as radio being sent and picked up by aerials, radio can be sent along cables. You can also listen to the radio using the Internet and many people like to listen to the radio on the Internet when working on their computer.

Film and music streaming

In the past, if you wanted to use your computer and the Internet to listen to music or watch video/film, you would have had to download the file first and then listen to or watch it. This caused copyright problems as you would have had a copy stored on your computer.

▼ **Internet gambling sites can cause addiction to gambling.**

With a fast broadband Internet connection film and music can be streamed, which means the data is sent to your computer as you are watching the video/film or listening to the music. Video sharing sites like YouTube use streaming.

streaming

Streaming data involves sending data exactly at the time it is used. This means you can watch films, video, listen to music, etc., without downloading the files first.

Integrated music systems

Rather than have lots of different devices such as CD players, DVD players and recorders, MP3 players and computers, it makes sense to combine these to produce one device. This device is called an integrated music system.

Digital TV recording

Many people want to simply record a TV programme in the easiest way possible and without the need for a blank DVD. Many systems use hard drives that enable large numbers of programmes to be recorded on the hard drive.

Many systems for watching programmes allow you to pause and then restart the programme. This is great for when you are watching a programme and someone calls you. Some systems allow you to restart the program another time.

Advantages of media downloads/streaming

- With streaming you do not have to save anything to your hard drive, so there is no problem about clogging up your hard drive with media.
- With streaming you do not have to wait while all the video, music, etc., is downloaded to your computer before you can start watching.
- There is a huge amount of material freely available on sites such as YouTube.
- With music downloads you can just pay for the tracks you like rather than have to pay for the whole CD.
- It is very easy to download files straight to a portable media device.

Disadvantages of media downloads/streaming

- With radio and TV programmes you can only watch them for a certain time before they are removed from the system.
- Musicians, artists, etc., may not be happy about having their work distributed in this way, as they may lose out on their royalties.
- The system is not completely reliable. When there is a lot of network traffic, the system sometimes cannot cope.
- Many people use file sharing sites to avoid having to pay for downloaded media.
- You need fast broadband in order to stream video, radio, music, etc.

Questions C

1. Integrated music systems are very popular.
   (a) Explain what is meant by an integrated music system. *(1 mark)*
   (b) Describe **two** features of an integrated music system. *(2 marks)*

2. Films or video can be downloaded or streamed.
   (a) Explain the difference between downloading a film and streaming the film. *(2 marks)*
   (b) Give **one** advantage in streaming a movie rather than downloading it. *(1 mark)*

3. Digital TV offers many features other than simply watching the TV.

   Explain **two** different features of digital TV. *(2 marks)*

4. A person wants to watch a programme on TV but they need to go out when it is on.

   Give **two** ways of watching the programme at a later date. *(2 marks)*

Extension activity

For this activity you need to form a small group and work with each other (i.e. collaboratively) to produce a list of the features of digital TV. You are free to use the Internet if you have difficulty.

Reliability of information and impact of communications technology

You will find out

▷ **About unreliability and undesirability of information on the Internet**

▷ **About how to evaluate information for relevance, accuracy, bias and currency**

▷ **About how to consider the intention and authority of the information provider**

▷ **About the impact that communications and entertainment technology has on individuals, organizations and society**

Just because it is on the Internet does not make it true. Any information you get off the Internet needs to be treated with caution. In this section you will be looking at how you might assess the worth of the information and how you can check its accuracy. Also, when collecting material off the Internet you need to ensure that the information is relevant for your purpose.

Unreliability of information on the Internet

Many people think that because it is published on the Internet it must be true. This is far from the truth, as there are many examples of sites that contain material that is completely untrue. Some sites deliberately set out to misinform or deceive.

It is important to remember that anyone is able to produce a website and publish it on the Internet. They do not have to be an authority on the subject the site is about. In some cases the person creating the site has not checked the information on the site.

How can you make sure that information you use is accurate? Here are a few steps you can take:

- Check the date that the site was last updated. Bogus sites are not updated very often. Also sites go out-of-date, so you need to be sure that the site you use has been updated recently.
- Only use sites produced by organizations you have heard of (e.g., newspapers, BBC, etc.).
- Use several sites to get the information and check that the sites are giving the same information.
- Follow the links to see if they work. Many bogus sites have links that do not work.

Undesirability of information on the Internet

It is impossible to censor what is on the Internet. This is because much of the information on the Internet comes from other countries.

Unfortunately the Internet contains pornography, violent videos, sites that promote racial hatred and so on. Schools and parents are able to use parental controls that restrict the sites and information that can be viewed on the Internet.

Searching for information using the Internet

When searching the Internet you enter a series of key words into a search engine. The search engine then searches the Internet for sites with matches to your words. By using precise key words you can usually find the information you need quickly. There are usually lots of sites that contain the information you need but you do need to discriminate between them.

Here are some methods you can use when selecting the sites to use to collect your information.

Fitness for purpose

This is whether or not the information (text, images, video, etc.) is suitable for what you are using it for. For example, if you want a large image of a sports car for a background to a poster and you found some pictures but as you enlarged them they became blurred, then they are not fit for purpose. Fitness for purpose can be assessed in terms of the following:

- relevance
- accuracy
- currency
- bias
- intention and authority of provider.

Relevance – Relevance means how near the information matches your requirements. For example, if you search for details on sites in Rome and the site only contains details of hotels, then this information is not relevant to your needs.

Accuracy – It is hard to assess the accuracy of unfamiliar information supplied by an unknown organization. It is best to check the information against other sources.

Currency of information – This refers to the timeliness of the information. You need to ask if the information on the site is up-to-date. Some sites are created and then forgotten about, so the information on them quickly becomes out-of-date.

Bias – Some information is slanted to favour one particular viewpoint. There is no point in going to a site of a toothpaste manufacturer to find out which is the best toothpaste to use. They are bound to say it is theirs. Many sites are biased but if you know this then you can find other sites that put forward other points of view.

Intention and authority of the provider – Some sites are produced by experts in their field. For example, the NHS Direct site is more likely to have correct information about medical problems than a site created by someone who sells complementary medicines. The intention of the NHS site is to inform and help you, whereas the other site may simply want to sell you complementary medicines.

The impact of communications and entertainment technology

There are lots of ways in which communications technology impacts on individuals, organizations and society and here are some of them:

- Teleworking is possible – this allows many people to work from home. This reduces the amount of traffic on the road and can help with family life. It also enables disabled people to work from home.
- Videoconferencing – allows people to conduct virtual meetings rather than have to waste time and money travelling to them.
- Chat rooms, instant messaging, text messaging and low cost Internet phone calls – allow people who may feel isolated to keep in touch with friends and family.

- The use of social networking sites – these enable people to make friends and meet people with interests similar to their own.
- You no longer have to be present when some TV programmes are shown – you can watch them using the Internet or the services provided by cable and satellite providers.
- You can purchase and download music instantly – using music downloads you can just purchase the tracks you like and you have access to a huge choice of music and films.
- You can listen to the radio whilst working on the computer – if you have access to the Internet then you can get hundreds of radio channels.
- Access to information about almost anything – the Internet is the largest store of information in the world and you can access it without leaving your home.
- Mobile phones – allow arrangements to be made at the last minute and people to be contacted while away from home.
- Satellite navigation systems – these save people from getting lost and therefore wasting time and fuel.
- Use of webcams – allow people to view sites, see their children in nurseries, view friends and family whilst talking to them using the Internet, etc.

Problems of confidentiality of data and of respecting confidentiality

Using communications systems allows data to be transferred easily from one place to another. Some of this data is personal data and contains details such as credit card numbers, bank account details, medical information, etc.

The Internet is not normally secure, so special measures need to be taken to ensure that there is no unauthorized access to these details. The methods used include:

- usernames/user-IDs and passwords
- encryption
- access levels – this means that only certain staff can access certain data
- training of staff – to ensure they understand the risks to personal data.

The use of cookies

Cookies are pieces of text that websites put onto your hard drive when you visit them.

Without you knowing, Internet 'cookies' record details of the websites you have visited and how long you spent on them, what pages were looked at, whether you have visited the site before, etc. Many people consider this to be an invasion of their privacy.

Questions D

1. Explain what parents can do to prevent their children accessing undesirable information using the Internet. *(3 marks)*

2. A student is doing a history project at school. This project will involve them doing a lot of research for information (i.e. text and images) using the Internet.
   (a) Explain how this student could check the accuracy of a fact that appears on a particular website. *(2 marks)*
   (b) Explain what is meant by 'fitness for purpose' of information searched for on websites. *(2 marks)*

3. Information obtained from the Internet should be checked for accuracy and bias.
   (a) Explain what bias in information means. *(1 mark)*
   (b) It is important that the information you use off the Internet is accurate. Explain what accuracy means and explain **one** way you can determine the accuracy of a piece of information. *(2 marks)*

END-OF-TOPIC REVIEW

Questions

☑ Test yourself

The following notes summarize this topic. The notes are incomplete because they have words missing. Using the words in the list below, copy out and complete the sentences A to I, underlining the words that you have inserted. Each word may be used more than once.

Internet   dialup   local   hackers

wireless   encrypted   modems

wide   broadband

A With _____ communication, the data travels through the air rather through cables.

B When making online payments, the card details are _____, which means if they are intercepted by hackers, then details will be meaningless and useless.

C _____ are devices that enable a communication link to be set up between the computer and a medium such as a wire or cable that is used to carry the data.

D _____ modems make a connection with the Internet by automatically dialling a number.

E _____ is always on, so the connection to the Internet is made almost instantly.

F _____ area networks are those networks that are restricted to a single building or site.

G _____ area networks are situated across a wide geographical area.

H E-commerce systems use the _____ for the purchase of goods and services.

I In order to pay for online purchases, a customer must enter their credit or debit card details and many customers worry that this information could be accessed by _____.

Examination style questions

1 Lots of people use the Internet and other communications technologies for entertainment.

Discuss the ways in which the Internet has changed the way people entertain themselves. *(5 marks)*

2 The use of the Internet has opened up a whole new source for films and music downloads.
   (a) Explain why downloads are so popular for the purchase of media. *(2 marks)*
   (b) Give **one** example of a problem caused by media downloads. *(1 mark)*

3 Give **two** differences between a local area network (LAN) and a wide area network (WAN). *(2 marks)*

4 Many people keep in touch by using VoIP.
   (a) Explain what VoIP is. *(2 marks)*
   (b) Give **one** advantage that VoIP gives a user. *(1 mark)*

5 Explain **two** disadvantages of using satellite navigation systems in cars. *(2 marks)*

6 (a) A user who has broadband access to the Internet notices that the speed of access to the Internet appears slow. Give **two** possible reasons why this might be. *(2 marks)*
   (b) Describe **two** things that can be done using high speed broadband access to the Internet that would be difficult or impossible to do using a very slow link. *(4 marks)*

7 Internet connections may be 'broadband' or 'dialup'. Explain the differences a user would notice in using each of these connections. *(2 marks)*

Exam support

Worked example

There has been a huge increase in people's use of ICT in the home, particularly in the area of entertainment. Many traditional activities such as sport and reading have been replaced by new forms of entertainment making use of ICT.

(a) Discuss, by giving **four** distinctly different examples, the benefits that ICT developments have brought to home entertainment. *(8 marks)*

(b) There are a number of disadvantages in using ICT for entertainment. Discuss, by giving **two** distinctly different examples, **two** such disadvantages. *(4 marks)*

Student answer 1

(a) One benefit is downloads where you can select which tracks you want, instead of having to buy the whole CD. This saves you money and using play-lists you can choose to listen to all your favourite tracks together.

Another benefit is Internet shopping where for a small fee you can select all the goods that you want from the comfort of your own home and get them delivered to your house at a certain time.

Word-processing is useful at home because you can type in all your letters, school work, CVs, etc., and print them out on your home printer.

Cable TV is ideal because you can watch films by paying a small fee which means you do not have to visit a video shop any more as the film data is sent along a cable. You can also watch repeats of old series or even programmes that you wanted to watch the previous week.

(b) You can become lazy just watching TV all day and you can end up not making friends or communicating with other people.

There are dangers in meeting strangers from chat rooms, especially for young children who may meet without their parents knowing. They could meet a paedophile who pretends to be a child when online.

◀ Examiner's comment

(a) The first two benefits are well explained and the examples given are sensible and relate to the benefit.

The third answer gives a benefit of word-processing, as a form of entertainment. This is stretching the word entertainment a bit too far, so credit is not given for this answer.

The fourth answer is correct as it describes a pay-to-view service provided by a satellite or cable TV service.

(b) Just because people watch TV does not make them lazy and this is far too general to be given any marks. The Examiner should not have to read anything into an answer in order to award it marks.

The second part of the answer is good as it clearly identifies the disadvantage and the problems it creates. *(8 marks out of 12)*

Student answer 2

(a) Many people use their home ICT equipment for digital photography. Digital photography, allows them to experiment by taking pictures, which they would not have been able to do with traditional film owing to the expense of getting them developed. They can edit these pictures, attach them to emails and send them to friends and family and print them in colour using ink-jet printers.

Some use the interactive facilities of their TV service or the Internet to gamble from their own home, using a credit card. It makes it more interesting when watching a football match to put some money on your favourite team. Using the Internet to do this is much easier than having to go to a high street betting shop.

You can use the Internet to play computer games. It is possible, for example, to play a game of chess over the Internet with your opponent in a different country. The good thing about this is that there is always someone to play with.

Mobile phones are great because you can do so much with them. For example, you can send and receive text messages, send and receive email, surf the Internet, use your phone as an MP3 player, take digital photographs and even have a telephone conversation!

(b) You have to be careful when using the Internet, as there is a tendency to slouch in your chair. This is likely to cause you back ache in the future.

Also, the repeated use of the mouse, joystick and keyboard could lead to repetitive strain injury (RSI).

Computer games can cause a problem because young children cannot seem to leave them alone so their school work suffers as a result.

◀ **Examiner's comment**

(a) This is a good set of answers which are all different and are clearly explained. Full marks were given for this part of the question.

(b) The first answer was more comprehensive than the second, and therefore deserves two marks. The second answer could have been explained in more detail, so only one mark is given for this part. *(11 marks out of 12)*

Examiner's answers

(a) Any four from the following list. (One mark for the name of the item and the second mark for further amplification by describing the hardware or explaining what it has allowed the user to do.)

- MP3 player – allowing people to listen to a choice of thousands of tracks on a small portable player.
- Music downloads – allows users to pick only the tracks they want rather than have to buy the entire CD.
- Digital photography – allows users to become much more proficient at taking photographs by allowing them to immediately see the results.
- Interactive TV – allows people to shop, check email, book holidays, bet, etc.
- Chat rooms – allows people to make new friends with people all around the world.
- Mobile phones – can communicate with friends in a large number of ways such as text message, voice and email.
- Betting – can place bets without leaving your home and also you do not need to pick up your winnings as they are put back on your card.
- Dating – meeting new dates is made easy by viewing the online pictures and profiles.
- Games – can play computer games on long journeys to help relieve boredom.
- Editing digital images – bad digital photographs can be improved by making use of image/photograph editing software.

- Online shopping – people are able to pick up bargains at many of the online stores that offer special discounts to online shoppers.
- Online booking – many people now choose to book flights, hotels and car hire separately as it is more flexible and often cheaper.
- Voting – you can place votes for TV shows using the Internet and this will eventually mean that you will be able to vote in local and general elections in this way.
- Improved hardware – home users are by far the biggest users of computers, so their demands are used to produce new improved hardware such as sound cards, video cards, etc.
- Speakers – the demand for high quality sound from gamers and watchers of TV has led to the design of surround sound systems.

(b) Any two from the following list. (One mark for the name of the item and the second mark for further amplification by describing the resulting problems.)

- Computer games – can be addictive and this can affect schoolwork.
- Computer games – playing computer games is often a sedentary activity and so can lead to obesity.
- Health problems – incorrect posture can lead to back ache; repeatedly using joysticks can lead to RSI.
- Chat rooms – young children could be groomed in order to meet undesirable people.

Summary mind maps

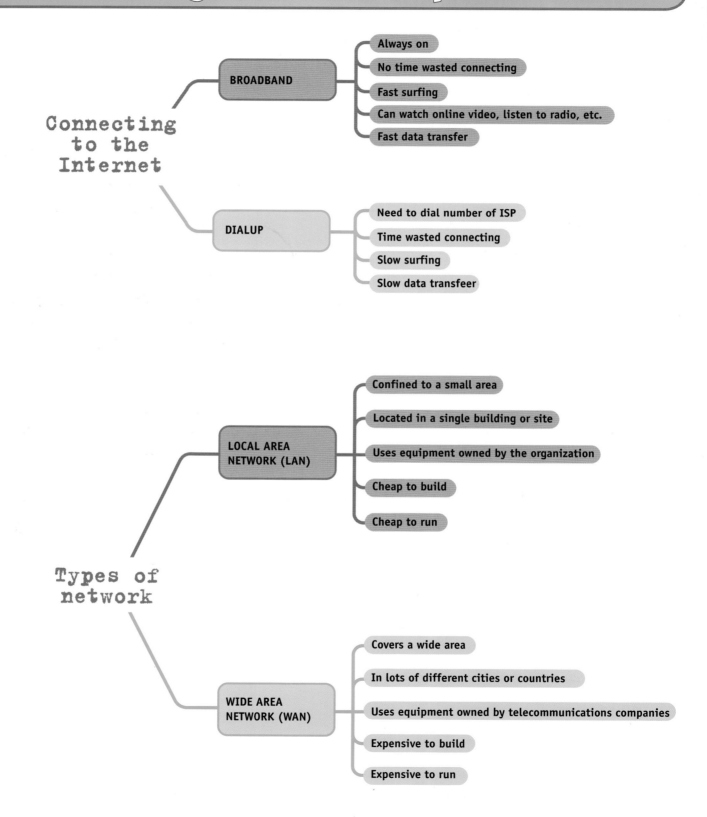

Connecting to the Internet

BROADBAND
- Always on
- No time wasted connecting
- Fast surfing
- Can watch online video, listen to radio, etc.
- Fast data transfer

DIALUP
- Need to dial number of ISP
- Time wasted connecting
- Slow surfing
- Slow data transfeer

Types of network

LOCAL AREA NETWORK (LAN)
- Confined to a small area
- Located in a single building or site
- Uses equipment owned by the organization
- Cheap to build
- Cheap to run

WIDE AREA NETWORK (WAN)
- Covers a wide area
- In lots of different cities or countries
- Uses equipment owned by telecommunications companies
- Expensive to build
- Expensive to run

Topic 5

Systems life cycle

The key concepts covered in this topic are:

- **The systems life cycle**

The systems life cycle is the series of stages that are completed when developing a new system or improving an old one. The stages of the systems life cycle are carried out in order and this ensures that the system being developed is developed properly.

In this section you will learn about the systems life cycle and the tasks that are completed for each stage.

Contents

The feasibility study and evaluation criteria

You will find out

▷ **About the purpose of the feasibility study**

▷ **About the fact finding methods that can be used**

▷ **About the purpose, nature and use of evaluation criteria**

▷ **About desired outcomes and performance criteria**

When a new system is being thought about, a feasibility study is conducted to collect some facts about what it is the new system has to do. If there is already a system being used, the feasibility study will look to see how this system might be improved. The feasibility study is the first part of the analysis and attempts to see if it is feasible to develop a new or improved system.

When designing a solution to a problem, you should give some thought to the desired outcomes. These are what the system must do. These can be expressed as a list of desired items, which are what the system must be capable of doing. Another thing to consider is the performance criteria, which is a way of measuring the success of a project. In this section you will learn the importance of establishing the evaluation criteria in the design stage.

The purpose of the feasibility study

The feasibility study seeks to find out whether a new system can be developed at a reasonable cost and in a sensible amount of time. It looks to see if it is worth going to the effort of creating a new system. It checks that the benefits of the new system will outweigh the costs in producing it.

At the end of the feasibility study a decision will be made whether or not to create the new system (or improve an old system).

Fact finding and the methods that can be used

Fact finding involves finding out what people want from the new proposed system or looking at an existing system to find out how it works and might be improved. There are several ways that fact finding can be done.

Questionnaires – A questionnaire could be given to each user. The questions on the questionnaire should be about how the job is

done now and not about the overall running of the business. It could also be about the information the new system needs to give them.

Interviews – Interviews take longer than questionnaires, so this method is good if there are only a few users of the system. People at the different levels in the organization who will use the new system should be interviewed. At these interviews you can find out how the existing system works and what things are required from the new system.

Observation – Here you sit with someone who is actually doing the job the new system is designed to do. You then see the problems encountered with the old system as well as chat to the user about what the new system must be able to do.

Inspection of records – This involves looking at any of the paperwork involved with the current system. This would include documents such as order forms, application forms, lists of stock and so on. You can also look at the records that are kept in filing cabinets.

▼ Questionnaires can be used to collect information about the new system from lots of people.

QUESTIONNAIRE

Very often ☐

Often ☑

Sometimes ☐

Rarely ☐

◀ Interviews can be used to find out about existing or proposed new systems.

Evaluation criteria

Evaluation criteria are those things that will determine at the end of the project whether it has been a success or not. They are those things by which the project will be judged. It is important to establish these criteria at the design stage of the project, as it reinforces what the system must do and how it must perform.

When the project is complete, the evaluation criteria can be used to see how the actual project that was developed met the criteria. Evaluation criteria can be expressed in two sections:

- desired outcomes
- performance criteria.

Desired outcomes

These are a list of what the systems must be able to do expressed in general terms. For example, the desired outcomes for an ICT department website in a school might be:

- A website that can be used by all students in the school.
- Contains up-to-date material on what material students will cover for each year in ICT.
- It must allow students to add messages to a message board.
- It must provide links to examination board materials and links to useful revision sites.
- It must make use of the full range of multimedia features.
- It must allow students to access files of presentations given to their class that they may have missed.

KEY WORD

Fact finding the investigation of a system to understand how it works or should work.

Performance criteria

Performance criteria are those criteria that can be measured and they also give some thought to how the desired outcomes can be measured. For example, performance criteria for a school website might be:

- Does the new website attract more users than the previous one?
- Do the people using the website find the content better?
- Can they find the information they want by using the search facility?
- Do all the pages load in a reasonable time?
- Can all the students understand the material on the website?

Questions A

1. Feasibility studies are carried out as part of the analysis phase of the system development life cycle.
   (a) Explain why a feasibility study is carried out. *(1 mark)*
   (b) Give **two** things that would be looked at as part of the feasibility study. *(2 marks)*

2. During the development of a new system it is important to find out how the existing system works if there is one. The usual way to do this is to perform a fact find.
   (a) Name and describe **three** different ways of collecting facts about an existing system. *(6 marks)*
   (b) Fact finding is carried out as part of a feasibility study.
   Give **one** reason why it is important to conduct a feasibility study at the start of the development of a new system. *(2 marks)*

3. When developing a new system it is essential that evaluation criteria are listed.

   Explain what is meant by evaluation criteria. *(1 mark)*

4. Evaluation criteria can be divided into desired outcomes and performance criteria.
   (a) Explain what is meant by desired outcomes. *(1 mark)*
   (b) Explain what is meant by performance criteria. *(1 mark)*

Extension activity

You have been asked to develop a database system for a small sports club with around 300 members. Using word-processing software, produce a questionnaire that could be sent to the club officials to enable you to get a better idea of what they require from the new system.

The stages of the systems life cycle

You will find out

▷ **About the stages of the systems life cycle**

▷ **About what is carried out as part of each stage**

To ensure ICT systems live up to user expectations, it is important that they are developed in a series of stages. The systems life cycle is the series of stages that are carried out in order to develop a new system or alter an existing system.

In this section you will learn about the stages of the systems life cycle and the sorts of things that are completed in each stage.

▲ Analysis looks in detail at the current system or the requirements for a task that has never been performed before.

The stages involved in producing a new ICT system

The following diagram shows the stages that are worked through when a new computer system is being developed. These stages are known as the systems life cycle.

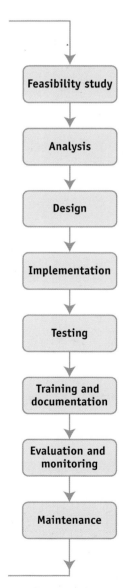

Feasibility study

Analysis

Design

Implementation

Testing

Training and documentation

Evaluation and monitoring

Maintenance

▲ The eight stages involved in the development of a system.

Analysis

Analysis looks in detail at the current system or the requirements for a task that has never been performed before. The person performing the analysis is called a systems analyst, or just analyst for short.

Analysis will normally involve the following:

- Identifying the problem that needs solving.
- Understanding the existing system.
- Understanding the proposed system, if there is no existing system.
- Identifying desired outcomes.
- Setting up performance criteria.

The feasibility study is often conducted as the first part of the analysis.

Design

During the design stage the systems analyst will take the desired outcomes and start to plan how best to create the system.

Design will normally involve the following:

- Designing the system in line with the desired outcomes.
- Choosing methods for input, storage and output.
- Deciding on what processing needs to be performed on the data.
- Producing designs of input screens, output screens/ reports, layouts of spreadsheets, databases, etc.
- Designing validation tests.
- Designing test plans.

Test plans

A test plan is a detailed list of the tests that are to be conducted on the system when it has been developed to check it is working properly.

Because of the importance of testing a system, a test plan is produced during the design stage. These test plans should be comprehensive. A good way of making sure that they are is to make sure that:

- tests are numbered
- each test has the data to be used in the test clearly specified
- the reason for the test is stated
- the expected result is stated.

Space should be left for:

- the actual result and/or comment on the result
- a page number reference to where the hard copy evidence can be found.

Testing using typical data, extreme data and erroneous data

Testing should always be performed with the following three types of data:

- Typical data – is normal data that should pass the validation checks.
- Extreme data – is data on the borderline of what the system will accept. For example, if a range check specifies that a number from one to five is entered (including one and five) then extreme data used would be the numbers one and five.
- Erroneous data – is data that is unacceptable and that should be rejected by the validation check.

Here is a test plan to test a spreadsheet for analysing the marks in an examination. A mark is input next to each candidate's name. The mark is a percentage and can be in the range 0% to 100%. In this exam, half marks are possible.

Test no	Test mark entered	Purpose of test	Expected result	Actual result
1	45.5	Test typical data	Accept	
2	100	Test extreme data	Accept	
3	0	Test extreme data	Accept	
4	123	Test erroneous data	Error message	
5	–3	Test erroneous data	Error message	
6	45D	Test erroneous data	Error message	

The 'actual result' column would be filled in when the test mark was entered. If the expected result and the actual results are all the same then the validation checks are doing their job. If the two do not agree, then the validation checks will need to be modified and re-tested.

Implementation

This is the stage where the system is actually built according to the design produced in the previous stage. All the different staff in the project team will bring their particular expertise to the project and work together to produce the working system.

Implementation will normally involve the following:

- Using the design produced in the previous stage to produce a working system.
- Programmers producing any programming code needed for the working solution.
- Producing the framework needed for databases.
- Using software tools to produce the working version.
- Modifying existing software.
- Producing the working system according to the desired outcomes.

Testing

Once the system has been implemented it should be thoroughly tested. The test plan that was created during the design stage is now used to test the system. Testing may involve the following:

- Entering the test data as specified in the test plan created during the design stage.
- Comparing the results with what should have happened and making changes to validation checks if needed.
- If a website is being produced, testing it to ensure the content is correct, the links work and the navigation is easy to use.
- Comparing results of calculations with those produced manually.
- Checking that the validation checks work with typical, extreme and erroneous data.

User training and documentation

When new ICT systems are created, users need to be trained on how to use them.

User documentation is documentation that the user can turn to for learning a new procedure or for dealing with a problem that has cropped up.

Evaluation and monitoring

Evaluation and monitoring takes place soon after the implementation. It is only then that the users and others involved in the development of the system will find out about any problems with the new system.

Evaluation and monitoring normally involves the following:

- Checking that the original user requirements and performance criteria have been fully met by the new system.
- Assessment of how happy the clients are with the development of the new system.
- Setting up a review cycle so that the system is checked periodically to make sure that it is still meeting requirements.

The stages of the systems life cycle *continued*

Maintenance

Once they are developed, systems cannot be left until a new system is developed to replace them. Changes in the way the business or organization operates will need alterations in the system. Programs may need to be written or altered. For example, the rate of VAT could change, or changes in income tax could trigger the need for changes. Businesses change direction or get involved in new ventures.

▲ **Maintenance is the final stage of the systems life cycle.**

Maintenance can involve:

- Setting up help-desk facilities to help users who experience problems with the new system.
- Extra functions that need to be added to the existing system are identified at the review meetings.
- Maintenance teams will alter existing programs or create additional ones.
- Any operational issues such as poor performance or software bugs will be identified at the review meeting and corrected by the appropriate staff.
- Any system crashes to be investigated to find out the reasons for their occurrence.

Questions B

1 Here is a list of the steps that are stages of the systems life cycle. At present these are in the wrong order. Put the steps in the correct order. *(5 marks)*
>   Evaluation
>   Analysis
>   Testing
>   Implementation
>   Design

2 Here are some of the steps that are stages in the systems life cycle.
>   Testing
>   Implementation
>   Design
>   Analysis
>   Evaluation

Write down the name of a step in the list above where the following tasks would be carried out:
- **(a)** Planning the construction of the new system. *(1 mark)*
- **(b)** Planning the testing of the new system. *(1 mark)*
- **(c)** Getting the user to answer a questionnaire to find out what is required from the new system. *(1 mark)*
- **(d)** Asking users what they think of the new system that has been developed. *(1 mark)*
- **(e)** Putting data into the computer to check if the output is what was expected. *(1 mark)*

3 A new computer system is to be used to handle bookings in a theatre.
- **(a)** Finding out about the existing system is important if a new system is being developed.
  - (i)   Give the names of **two** different ways used for finding out about the existing system. *(2 marks)*
  - (ii) For each way named in (i), describe how the method is used to find out about the existing system. *(2 marks)*
- **(b)** After the analysis stage, the following stages are performed:
  >   Design
  >   Implementation
  >   Maintenance
  >   Training and documentation

  In which stage does each of the following tasks take place? *(5 marks)*
  - (i)   Keeping the new system up-to-date and error free.
  - (ii) Installing the hardware and software.
  - (iii) Training users to use the new system.
  - (iv) Setting up the ticket sales database.
  - (v)   Identifying suitable output reports.

Questions

☑ Test yourself

The following notes summarize this topic. The notes are incomplete because they have words missing. Using the words in the list below, copy out and complete the sentences A to J, underlining the words that you have inserted. Each word may be used more than once.

```
systems life cycle        performance          implementation

     testing        evaluation        feasibility study

   test plan        input        training        fact find
```

A The series of stages worked through when a new system is introduced is called the _____ _____ _____.

B To assess the project's feasibility, a _____ _____ is performed.

C During the analysis stage, the person developing the system will perform a _____ _____ in order to find out a variety of facts about the new system.

D _____ criteria are established in the design stage so as to establish the criteria by which the new system can be judged.

E During the design stage the _____, processes and output will be designed.

F With the design stage complete, the working version of the solution can be produced. This is called the _____ stage.

G Testing uses the _____ _____ created in the design stage to ensure that all parts of the system are working correctly.

H Thorough testing is then undertaken to make sure that the solution works properly. This is called the _____ stage.

I Users need to know how to use the new system. The process of helping them to understand the new system is called user _____.

J _____ gives a brief overview of the development and sees how closely the developed system matched the performance criteria.

Questions *continued*

Examination style questions

1 Five stages of the systems life cycle have been labelled A to E in the following table:

Label	Stage
A	Evaluation
B	Design
C	Testing
D	Analysis
E	Implementation

(a) Write down the labels in their correct order by completing the following table. The first one has been done for you. *(4 marks)*

Label
D

(b) Give the names of **two** of the stages of the systems life cycle that are not included in the above table. *(2 marks)*

2 Here are some of the steps that should be completed when creating a new computer system:
Analysis
Design
Implementation
Maintenance
Write down the name of the stage from the above list in which the following tasks would be carried out: *(7 marks)*
(a) Preparing a test plan for the new system.
(b) Getting the user to answer a questionnaire to find out what is required from the new system.
(c) Working out accurate costs for the new system.
(d) Deciding what outputs are needed from the new system.
(e) Typing the details from the paper records into the new system.
(f) Keeping the system up-to-date by making small changes to it.
(g) Designing suitable security systems.

3 Match the letters A, B, C, D and E below with the stage of the systems life cycle during which the following tasks would take place: *(12 marks)*
A Analysis
B Design
C Implementation
D Testing
E Evaluation

Description of task	Letter
Checking that all the parts of the system work	
Carrying out a feasibility study	
Setting up performance criteria	
Checking that any values outside a certain range are not accepted for processing	
Collecting information about the new system	
Planning screen and report layouts	
Entering all the records into a database	
Creating a website according to the design	
Preparing a test plan	
Suggesting future improvements to the system	
Reviewing how well the system works	
Setting up criteria that will judge how successful the system is	

END-OF-TOPIC REVIEW

Exam support

Worked example

When a new system is produced it should be thoroughly tested. A testing plan is produced that uses typical, extreme and erroneous data. This test plan is carried out during the testing stage.

(a) Give **one** reason why a system should be tested. *(1 mark)*

(b) A test plan is created in the design stage of the systems life cycle.

Explain what is meant by a test plan. *(1 mark)*

(c) Explain what is meant by each of the following:

(i) Typical data *(1 mark)*
(ii) Extreme data *(1 mark)*
(iii) Erroneous data *(1 mark)*

Student answer 1

(a) To make sure it works.

(b) It is a plan that tests all the parts of the system.

(c) (i) This is just ordinary data that you input. It is not too big or small and will not be rejected by the system.

(ii) This is data that is too big or small and should be rejected by the system.

(iii) This is data that is just on the border of what is acceptable.

◀ Examiner's comment

(a) This is far too vague for a mark. Most systems will 'probably work' but a user wants a system to work without any errors. No marks for this answer.

(b) This is a typical answer where the student simply gives an answer based on what is in the question. No marks here.

(c) (i) This is just about OK for a mark.

(ii) This is an incorrect definition so no mark here.

(iii) The student is getting mixed up here with extreme data. No marks for this answer.

(1 mark out of 5)

Student answer 2

(a) To make sure that the system works as expected by performing a number of tests.

(b) The test plan includes lists of which tests are to be carried out with data to test and what should happen to the data when it is entered.

(c) (i) This is data that should be accepted by the system for processing.

(ii) This is data that is on the borderline of what is acceptable.

(iii) This is data that is completely incorrect and should be rejected by the system.

◀ Examiner's comment

(a) This is a good answer and gains one mark.

(b) This is a very good description of a test plan and gains one mark.

(c) (i) This is an acceptable answer so one mark is awarded.

(ii) This is a good answer so one mark.

(iii) Another good answer so one mark.

(5 marks out of 5)

Exam support *continued*

Examiner's answers

(a) One mark for an answer such as:

Testing involves performing a series of checks to ensure that the system works as expected.

(b) One mark for an answer such as:

A detailed list of checks to be performed to test the system.

(c) (i) One mark for answer similar to the following:

This is normal data that will pass all the validation rules and will be accepted for processing.

Alternatively an example can be given:

Mark greater than or equal to 0 and also less than or equal to 100 so a typical piece of data would lie in this range.

(ii) One mark for an answer similar to the following:

It is a piece of data on the borderline of what is accepted.

Or a clear example such as:

For example, if an exam mark can be from 0 to 100 then 0 and 100 are examples of extreme data.

(iii) One mark for an answer similar to the following:

Data that is outside the validation checks and should be rejected by the system.

EXAM TIP

If you are asked to explain something then giving a one-word or a couple of words example is not sufficient. You must include a sentence.

If you are asked to 'give' an answer then a one-word or a couple of words answer is ok.

The word 'describe' means that you must give your answer in sentences. Be guided by the mark scheme as to how much you need to write. If there are two marks then the minimum you need is two clearly different points. It is important to note that you are never penalized for writing too much, although you may waste some time.

Be careful about being too creative in your English. You are always limited by the number of lines given for your answer on the paper. Most students get to the end of the number of lines and stop. You need to work out your answer and try to convey it with the minimum number of words. This gives you plenty of room for making more points.

Summary mind maps

8 MAINTENANCE
- Alter solution
- To include new functions
- Changes in tax, VAT, etc.

1 FEASIBILITY STUDY
- Initial analysis
- Is it feasible to develop system?
- Fact finding

7 EVALUATION AND MONITORING
- Check match of solution
- To desired outcomes and performance criteria
- Check system still meets requirements

2 ANALYSIS
- Identification of problem
- Understand problem
- Identify desired outcomes
- Set up performance criteria

Systems life cycle

6 USER TRAINING AND DOCUMENTATION
- Train how to use new system
- Produce user guide

3 DESIGN
- Design methods for input, process and output
- Design of input screen
- Design of output reports
- Design validation
- Design test plan

5 TESTING
- According to test plan
- Enter test data and compare results
- Correct errors
- Check calculations manually
- Check content

4 IMPLEMENTATION
- Creating working versions
- According to designs
- Uses software to create solution

Summary mind maps *continued*

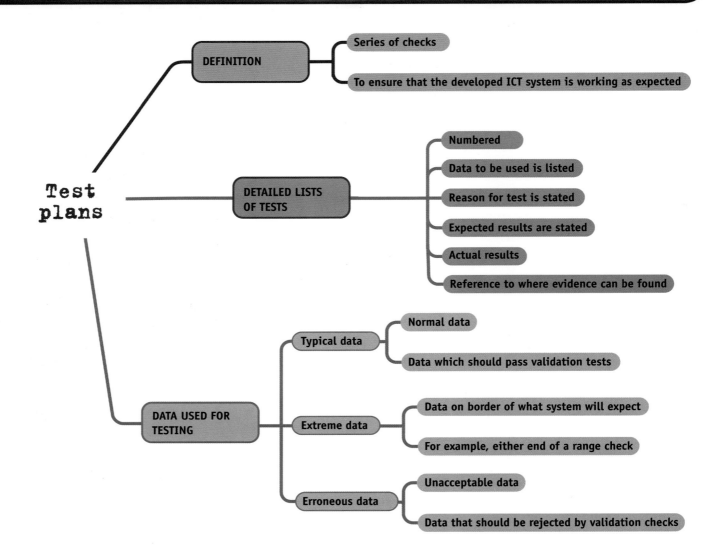

Topic 6

Working with information to solve problems

The key concepts covered in this topic are:

- Information and data
- Finding, selecting and using information
- Quality of information and data
- Data collection/capture methods
- Reviewing and modifying work
- Presenting information in ways that are fit for purpose and audience
- Sharing and exchanging information electronically
- Evaluating the effectiveness of ICT tools to meet needs

ICT systems are created to supply information from raw data and in this topic you will be looking at the distinction between data and information. When you create material for yourself you will need information, some of which will come from ICT sources such as databases and the Internet. You will learn that you need to question information sources, before you use them, to check that the information being used is accurate and fit for purpose.

This topic also looks at how information can be searched for and the need for specifying search conditions so that the information can be found in the least amount of time.

Raw data has to be collected for processing and put into the computer, which is called data capture. In this topic you will look at a series of different methods of data capture and the applications for which they are suited.

Contents

Information and data

▷ **About the distinction between information and data**

▷ **About the link between input, storage, output, processing and feedback needed by an ICT system**

In this section you will learn that data is the raw material for any ICT system and how data is processed to give information. It is important to distinguish between these two important terms and this section will make their definitions clear. You will also be looking at the terms: input, storage, output, processing and feedback and how they are connected.

What exactly is data?

There are a number of forms that data can take. Data can be:

- numbers
- words
- images
- sound
- video.

Data consists of raw facts and figures (e.g., readings from sensors, survey facts, etc.). These raw facts and figures are meaningless because they lack relevance. If you look at data, it is either no use to you or not in a form that you can use.

Take a look at the following figures:

£72,000, £110,000, £128,000

The above set of numbers is data. It tells us nothing because there is no context. We do not know if they are a Premiership player's weekly wage, the price of a car or the value of sales of own brand baked beans sold in a week.

If we are told that these three numbers are a Premiership footballer's average weekly wage for the years 2008, 2009 and 2010, we now have information.

The raw data (i.e. the numbers) can be processed in many ways:

- A graph could be drawn to show the trend.
- We could work out the percentage by which the average increased for each year.
- We could work out the average wage over the three years.

All this processing will produce information and will give us knowledge.

▼ Raw data can be processed by producing graphs and charts.

GIGO (garbage in garbage out)

ICT people often use the term GIGO, meaning garbage in garbage out. This means that if the data is inaccurate then no amount of processing will produce any useful information. The output from the computer will be incorrect. It is therefore essential that the data put into a computer system is good quality data.

Ways in which data can arise

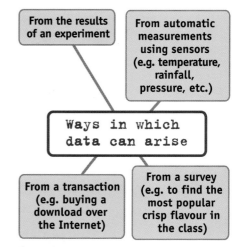

Data can arise in the above ways.

Information

Information is data that has been processed by the computer. Processed can mean:

- Having calculations performed on it.
- Converting it to give it meaning.
- Organizing it in some way (putting it into numerical order, alphabetical order, into a database structure, etc.).

Input, processing, output, storage and feedback in ICT systems

- **Input** – is the raw data from the outside world that is entered into a computer for processing.
- **Processing** – means doing something with the raw data such as putting it into a certain order or structure, performing calculations on it, compressing it so that it does not take as much space, etc.
- **Output** – these are the results after the processing of raw data.

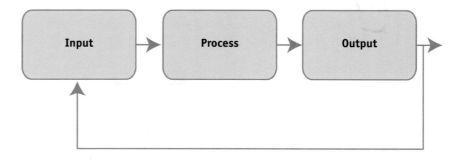

▲ Input, process and output also showing the feedback loop.

- **Storage** – is used for holding the data temporarily while processing takes place. It is also needed to store programs such as the operating system and the applications software.
- **Feedback** – this is where the output from a system directly affects the input. It is used in systems that use control, for example showers are usually controlled by a small microprocessor. If you are having a shower and you would like the water hotter you adjust the temperature setting. You are supplying an input to the system telling the control you would like hotter water. The shower then heats the water more and at the same time it measures the temperature of the water coming out and feeds the information back to the control. It compares the actual temperature of the water with the setting you would like, to see if it has to increase or decrease the temperature. Thus the output (i.e. the hot water) is fed back as an input to the system which in turn affects the output.

▲ Feedback is used in showers to help keep the water at a constant temperature.

KEY WORDS

GIGO abbreviation for garbage in garbage out. It means that if you put rubbish into the computer then you get rubbish out.

Data raw facts and figures, e.g. readings from sensors, survey facts, etc.

Processing performing calculations or arranging the data into a meaningful order.

Transaction a piece of business, e.g. an order, purchase, return, delivery, transfer of money, etc.

Information data that has been processed by the computer.

Questions A

1. Complete the sentences below by filling in the missing word in each case.
   (a) Raw facts and figures such as readings from sensors are called _____.
   (b) Data that has been processed by the computer is called _____.
   (2 marks)

2. (a) Give **three** different types of data. *(3 marks)*
   (b) By giving a suitable example, explain how data is processed to produce information. *(3 marks)*

Finding, selecting and using information

You will find out

▷ **About using discrimination when selecting and using sources of information**

▷ **About searching using search engines**

▷ **About using and refining search conditions**

We all use information on a day-to-day basis and we usually have a choice of the source for the information. We may need the information for a task we are completing. For example, we might want to book a holiday and want to find out what there is at the hotel/resort when we get there. There are huge amounts of information available, so we need to be selective about the information that we use. Sometimes the information is not that easy to find, so we have to create careful search conditions to find it. Maybe there is too much information and you need to narrow it down.

In this section you will get advice on sources of information and the need to be precise in the searches you make.

Sources of information

Organizations need information in order to function and this information can come from a variety of different sources such as:

- Newspapers/magazines – many of these are online, which makes it much easier to find the information you want.
- Books/e-books – these are good sources of information as they are usually written by experts and are more likely to be correct than some other sources of information.
- Images – can be obtained off the Internet, and many search engines allow for just searches of images. There are also images available in photo-sharing sites.
- Alternatively, you can create your own images using graphics packages or by taking photographs.
- Maps – many of these are online but for old maps and charts it may be necessary to scan them in using the originals.
- Conversation – these can be stored digitally using a microphone and then incorporated into a multimedia product such as a presentation or website. The Internet is a good source of famous speeches.
- CD-ROMs or DVDs – these are used to hold large video and music files but they can hold large databases. For example, there is a CD-ROM produced by the Royal Mail that contains the address details that go with all the postcodes in the country. This means that an organization can type in the postcode and the full address will appear, which saves them a lot of typing time.

There are examples of other searchable databases such as encyclopaedias and medical dictionaries that are available on CD-ROM.

- Online databases – these are searchable stores of data, usually on the Internet. For example, when you are searching for a holiday or a particular book or other product using an Internet shopping site, you are using an online database.
- The Internet – this is the biggest store of information and the most popular source of data, as you can access it using so many different devices such as computers, PDAs, mobile phones, etc. Software called a search engine is used to find information by putting in search criteria. The Internet can be used for finding sounds, music, clip art, photographic images, animations, text and so on.
- Podcasts – are digital media files that can be audio or video that are released in episodes so that you can be fed them automatically when you connect to the service. This method is called web syndication. They are useful sources of current affairs information.
- Web logs (blogs) – are websites that are created by an individual with information about events in their life, videos, photographs, etc. They can be useful sources of information about celebrities.
- Wiki (Wikipedia) – the online encyclopaedia that is created by ordinary people is a huge store of information on almost every subject. Because the information

has been put up by ordinary people you do have to be careful about the information you use. Luckily, as it is viewed by so many people, if there is wrong information posted, it is usually quickly corrected.

Using discrimination when using sources of information

Always question any information you get. Information is not always correct unless it is obtained from a very reliable source. If you are not sure about the information then try to find the information from two completely different sources and see if they agree.

Searching using search engines

Search engines are programs for finding information on the Internet. They work by you typing in a word or a series of words. Most search engines allow you to type in sentences such as 'What is the capital of Greece?' but some work better if you stick to a series of key words.

Using and refining search conditions

You can search using search engines for information on the Internet or you could be using search criteria to extract information from a database. The principles are the same.

You can search for information in a database using a single field or a number of fields.

You can also add operators chosen from the following table to your search criteria.

Operator	Meaning
=	Equal to
>	Greater than
<	Less than
<=	Less than or equal to
>=	Greater than or equal to
<>	Is not equal to

▲ **There are many sources of information.**

Complex searches

Don't be put off by the name. Complex searches help you save time searching for information, so they are worth knowing about.

When you do a simple search, you may be overwhelmed by all the information. Complex searches help you narrow down a search.

AND

If you type in the search **USA AND flag** you will get all those documents that contain both words.

If you just type in **USA Flag** you will still get all those documents that contain both words. With most search engines you do not need to type the 'and' between the words.

AND means: 'I want **only** documents that contain **both** words.'

OR

If you type in the search **USA OR flag** then you will get all the documents containing the word **USA**, all the documents containing the word **flag** and all those documents that contain both words.

OR means: 'I want documents that contain either word. I don't care which word.'

Searching for an exact match

If you want an exact match of words (i.e. the words side-by-side and in the same order), then put quotation marks around the words like this:

'Recipe for a chocolate chip cookie'

NOT

Suppose you want to search for information about different pets but you can't stand cats. You can exclude cats like this:

Pets NOT cats

Searching for a quotation

If you know the exact wording of the quotation, you can type it into the search engine. To get the exact match you need to put quotation marks around the words like this:

'I have a dream'

Activity

Fact detective

How good are you at tracking down information? Here are some things you are going to find out using the Internet and the search engine of your choice. Good luck!

1 The name of the animal with the Latin name Buffo Buffo.
2 The name of the plant that the drug called digitalis comes from.
3 Another name for the bone in the human body called the patella.
4 The names of all the football clubs that the footballer David Beckham has played for.
5 The name of any five of the British Prime Ministers since 1900.
6 The year when the National Health Service was first introduced.
7 The names of any four actors who have played the part of Doctor Who on TV.

Quality of information and data

Data is the raw material for computer systems. The way that it is collected is important, because it determines the accuracy of the information produced by the system. If the data is incorrect, then no amount of processing by the computer will turn it into correct information. In this section you will be looking at the reasons why you must be wary of any data you have not collected yourself and also why you must always question information supplied to you by others.

This section will also look at the methods that can be used to ensure that incorrect data is not processed by the computer.

Evaluation of data for fitness for purpose, accuracy and bias

Evaluating data for fitness for purpose

Fitness for purpose means that the data is suitable for doing the job for which it was collected.

Here are two ways data may not be fit for purpose:

- Too few items of data – for example, data could be collected to determine which polystyrene cup was the best at keeping a cup of coffee hot. If the person took only two readings, the data would be unfit for purpose as you cannot plot a graph using so few readings.
- Not collecting the right data – another example would be if you wanted to find out what 16–18 year olds did in their free time. If some of the people you interviewed were not in this age group the data would not be fit for purpose. It would be pointless using this data to produce any meaningful information.

Evaluating data for accuracy

The data collected may not be accurate. For example, temperature readings taken by a person reading a thermometer rely on them being able to read the thermometer properly.

Here are some ways that data could be inaccurate:

- Making data up – a person recording traffic flow manually may get fed up after a few hours and decide to make up some of the readings. This data will no longer be accurate.

- Some data missing – for example, a company that sells trainers might want to know who the best salesperson is for each month. The data they would need would be the value of each order a particular salesperson has made. There will be lots of these orders so totals need to be worked out. If some of the orders had not been included in the figures then it would be impossible to rank the sales staff and the data. The data used is inaccurate.
- Mistakes when collecting data – numbers could be written down incorrectly.

Evaluating data for bias

It is so easy to bias data in some way. Bias means that there is a tendency or preference towards a particular result. Here are some ways you can bias data:

- Not taking a representative sample – for example, going along to the local Labour club to collect data that can be used to find out how the whole population is likely to vote in the next election is not a good idea. Clearly the majority of people will vote Labour. By collecting the data in this way the person has biased the data.
- Prompting a certain answer – asking the questions in a way that you might be prompting a person to give a certain answer. For example, 'You don't like Manchester United football team do you?' clearly tells the person that you don't like them. They are more likely to agree with you, so an argument does not develop.

Evaluating and questioning the accuracy and plausibility of information

Information obtained from a computer is not always right. This means you have to be careful about the information you use. You have to be particularly careful when you are using information off the Internet.

Here are some things you should consider:

- Can the source be relied upon? – Well-known sources such as NASA, the BBC, NHS direct, etc., have material produced by experts.
- Are there spelling mistakes and mistakes in the grammar – if so, it may lead you to think that the accuracy of the information may be suspect.
- Does it sound reasonable – for example, a website tells you that the tallest man in the world is 10 feet tall. Have you ever seen anyone anywhere near that height? You could check this by finding sites that agree or disagree.
- Ask how the data that provided the information was collected – if it was a survey, they might have biased the data without realizing it.

Ensuring the accuracy and plausibility of information

When you create your own websites, blogs, multimedia presentations, posters, letters, etc., you need to ensure that the material is accurate. Here are some ways you can do this:

- The more people who look at your work, the more likely they are to spot your mistakes. So use friends and family to read through your material and ask for their comments.
- If you present facts, you should always check these using several reliable sources.
- Use the spelling and grammar checkers provided in the software you are using. Be aware that although text has been spelling and grammar checked, it could still be incorrect.

- Proof read your work carefully by reading through it slowly to check it makes sense and there is nothing missing.

Limitations of spelling and grammar checkers

Spellcheckers are provided with most software packages used to produce text. The spellchecker checks to see if each word in the document is in its dictionary. If you used the word 'care' instead of 'core', then as both are spelt correctly, the spellchecker will not pick it up. If a word is not spelt correctly, the spellchecker alerts the user and offers some corrections for the user to choose from. Spellcheckers are also able to spot if the same word has been typed in twice.

Grammar checkers can be used to check that:

- sentences end with only one full stop
- there is a capital letter at the beginning of a sentence
- common errors like writing 'you and I' rather than 'you and me' have been avoided.

Here is some text that someone has typed. Can you spot what is wrong?

```
I no their are mistakes
in my spelling but I will
use the spell cheque to
cheque them.
```

If you look at this sentence, you will see that the words are all spelt correctly. You will also notice that some of the words are the wrong ones. The spellchecker will not pick this up because there are no spelling mistakes. Using the grammar check may pick up some mistakes such as the word 'their'. This should read 'there'.

Type this sentence, then use the spellchecker and then the grammar checker.

Spellchecking and grammar checking will not ensure that your document makes sense. It is therefore important to proof read your document. It is a good idea to get someone else to read through your work, as they might spot mistakes that you have missed.

▲ Spellcheckers won't pick up everything.

Activity

Obtain some text for an article off the Internet and copy and paste the text into a word-processed document. Hopefully this document will be accurately spelt and the grammar will be correct.

Make some changes to the spelling and grammar (making a note of what changes you have made). Run the spellchecker first and then the grammar checker. See if both of these can find the errors.

Quality of information and data *continued*

How errors can occur

Errors in data can occur during:

- transcription (using the wrong form, mishearing words, etc.)
- input (e.g., keyboarding errors, etc.)
- processing (e.g., mistakes in formulae in spreadsheets, programming errors, etc.)
- transmission (e.g., data is corrupted as it travels through wires, cable, air, etc.).

Types of error

When inputting data using a keyboard there are two types of error:

- **Transcription errors** – errors introduced when transferring data from a form (e.g., application form, order form, etc.) to a computer. They can also be caused by mishearing what a person says over the telephone and entering it into the computer.
- **Transposition errors** – easily made when typing quickly and involves typing letters or numbers in the wrong order.

Here are some examples:

- 'fro' instead of 'for'
- the account number 100065 instead of the correct account number 100056
- the flight number AB376 instead of BA376.

Data validation

Validation is a check performed by a computer program during data entry. Validation is the process that ensures that data accepted for processing is sensible and reasonable. For example, a living person's date of birth could not be before 1890 as in 2010 this would make them 120 years old (the current oldest person is 115). Validation is performed by the computer program being used and

consists of a series of checks called **validation checks**.

When a developer develops a solution to an ICT problem, they must create checks to reduce the likelihood of the user entering incorrect information. This is done by restricting the user as to what they can enter, or checking that the data obeys certain rules.

Types of validation check

Validation checks are used to restrict the user as to the data they can enter. There are many different validation checks, each with their own special use including:

- **Data type checks** – these check that data being entered is the same type as the data type specified for the field. This would check to make sure that only numbers are entered into fields specified as numeric.
- **Presence checks** – some database fields have to be filled in, whilst others can be left empty. A presence check would check to make sure that data had been entered into a field. Unless the user fills in data for these fields, the data will not be processed.
- **Range checks** – are performed on numbers. They check that a number being entered is within a certain range. For example, all the students in a college are aged over 14, so a date of birth being entered which would give an age less than this would not be allowed by the range check.
- **Look-up lists** – are very useful and work in the following way. When you enter data, the software looks through a list of data until it finds a match along with other important data. For example, if each product in a shop is given a number, this number can be stored along with the description of the product and

its price. If you then input the product number, all the other details for that product are displayed.

- **Format checks** – are performed on codes to make sure that they conform to the correct combinations of characters. For example, a code for car parts may consist of three numbers followed by a single letter. This can be specified for a field to restrict entered data to this format.
- **Check digits** – are added to important numbers such as account numbers, International Standard Book Numbers (ISBNs), Article numbers (the numbers under the bar code), etc. These numbers are placed at the end of the block of numbers and are used to check that the numbers have been entered correctly into the computer.

When the large number is entered, the computer performs a calculation using all the numbers to work out this extra number. If the calculation reveals that the extra number (called the check digit) is the same as that calculated by the other numbers, it means that all the numbers have been entered correctly.

Restricting the user to a list

One way of helping a user enter correct data is to supply them with a list of items to choose from. Using a list prevents the user from entering data that is not on a list. The only problem with lists is that they are

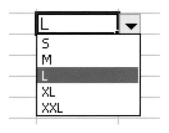

▲ Here the sizes of a shirt are shown as a list from which the user can select.

only appropriate when there are only a small number of choices, for a field such as M or F, ranking of 1 to 5, etc.

Data verification

Verification means checking that the data being entered into the ICT system perfectly matches the source of the data. For example, if details from an order form were being typed in using a keyboard, then when the user has finished, the data on the form on the screen should be identical to that on the paper form (i.e., the data source). Also if data was sent over a network, the data needs to be checked when it arrives to make sure no errors have been introduced.

Here are some methods of verification:

- **Visual check/proof reading** – involves one user carefully reading what they have typed in and comparing it with what is on the data source (order forms, application forms, invoices, etc.) for any errors, which can then be corrected.

- **Double entry of data** – involves using the same data source to enter the details into the ICT system twice and only if the two sets of data are identical will they be accepted for processing. The disadvantage of this is that the cost of data entry is doubled.

Double entry of data is often used when creating accounts over the Internet. They may ask you to create a password and enter it twice. This ensures there are no mistakes that would prevent you from accessing the account.

Questions B

1. (a) What is meant by a check digit? *(3 marks)*
   (b) Give **two** different examples where check digits are used. *(2 marks)*

2. Here are some dates of birth that are to be entered into an ICT system:
   (a) 12/01/3010
   (b) 01/13/2000
   (c) 30/02/1999

   Assume that all the dates are in the British format dd/mm/yyyy. For each one, explain why they cannot be valid dates of birth. *(3 marks)*

3. When an employee joins a company they are given an employee code.
   (a) Here is an example of an employee code:
   LLLNNNNNN   where L is a letter of the alphabet and N is a number.
   Explain **one** type of validation that could be used with this field. *(2 marks)*
   (b) Employees are given an annual salary.
   Explain **one** type of validation that could be used with this field. *(2 marks)*

4. A computer manager says, 'data can be valid yet be incorrect'. By giving **one** suitable example, explain what this statement means. *(3 marks)*

5. An online form for ordering DVDs uses a presence check for some of the fields.
   (a) Explain what a presence check is and why some fields have them whilst others don't. *(3 marks)*
   (b) Give **one** field that might have a presence check and **one** field that would not need a presence check. *(2 marks)*

6. (a) Explain the use of a spellchecker. *(2 marks)*
   (b) Explain why despite the use of a spellchecker a document will still need to be proof read or visually checked. *(1 mark)*

7. Explain the difference between a grammar checker and a spellchecker. *(2 marks)*

8. Information can be biased. By giving a suitable example, explain what is meant by biased information. *(2 marks)*

9. When using the Internet as a source of information you have to be careful about the information you use.

   Explain **two** things you can do in order to ensure the accuracy and plausibility of the information. *(2 marks)*

Data collection/capture methods

Data collection can involve documents being filled in or the data being collected automatically using sensors. Data capture involves preparing the data so that it is in a form that the computer can process. You can also think of data capture as the way of getting the data from the outside world into the computer system.

Data collection

Data from the outside world is often obtained from forms or by speaking to a person over the telephone. These forms, called data capture forms, need to contain the data that has to be input.

Examples of data capture forms include:

- application forms
- forms for supplying change of details (e.g., contact details, name, employer, etc.)
- filled-in questionnaires
- multiple-choice answer sheets
- order forms

- requests for further information
- booking forms
- online forms for the ordering of goods from online stores.

Data can also be collected automatically from the outside world using sensors.

Data capture

In order for data to be processed it needs to be in a form that the computer can use. Data capture is the term for the various methods by which data can be entered into the computer so that it can be processed. The most common way to capture data is to use the keyboard, but this is not appropriate in many instances. For example, how do you capture a piece of music using a keyboard or obtain a digital version of an old photograph? The choice of data capture method depends on the type of ICT problem being solved.

Chip and pin

Most credit/debit cards are chip and pin, which means there is a small chip on the card containing encrypted data that only the reader in the store can read. This means that when you enter your PIN (personal identification number), the store can be sure that you are the correct owner of the card. Credit/debit cards are used to make purchases either over the phone or using the Internet. In both these cases the customer is not present when they pay for their goods Instead they give certain details such as name, address and their card details.

Chip and pin has reduced card fraud when a card is being used in

ordinary stores but owing to the rise in transactions where the customer is not present (e.g., when buying goods or services over the Internet) there has been a total increase in credit/debit card fraud.

▲ **Most credit/debit cards are chip and pin to help prevent fraud.**

▲ **A chip and pin reader: the customer inserts their card then enters their PIN**

OMR (optical mark recognition)

Many schools use a system making use of optical mark recognition for student registration, where the teacher or lecturer marks a student's attendance by shading in boxes using a pencil. The forms are passed to the administration office, where they are collected and batched together and processed automatically using an optical mark reader. As the forms are read automatically, it removes the problems of making mistakes when the marks are typed in using a keyboard. Once input, the data about attendance is processed and reports can be generated highlighting students for whom attendance is a problem.

Optical mark recognition can also be used for marking multiple-choice answer sheets and reading survey documents.

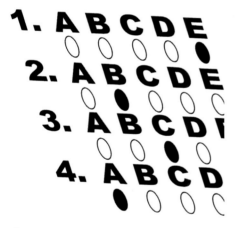

▲ OMR is used to mark multiple-choice tests.

Advantages of OMR

- OMR readers are cheap.
- The forms can be read at high speed.
- It saves a lot of time compared to typing the data in.

Disadvantages of OMR

- Many of the forms will not be filled in correctly unless training is given.
- Forms can be folded or crumpled, which causes them to be rejected.
- Special forms need to be created, which takes time.

Bar code reading

You came across bar codes in Topic 2. Their main use is for recording goods sold at the checkout in supermarkets. There are also portable scanners that are used in supermarkets and warehouses for the recording of stock on the shelves.

Bar code readers are fast and accurate at recording item details and the operator only has to scan the bar code and then enter the number of items on the shelf after counting them.

▲ A bar code reader being used for stock taking.

Magnetic strip cards

Magnetic strips can be seen on credit and debit cards and can be used to read information about the card when paying for goods. Nowadays chip and pin is being used to input the same information and is a better way of inputting the information and preventing fraud. Magnetic strips are still included on the cards because in some countries they do not yet have chip and pin.

▼ Credit and debit cards contain a magnetic strip.

◄ The details on a credit card being swiped (i.e. read).

Voice recognition

Voice/speech recognition systems allow you to enter data directly into a computer via a microphone. Basically you dictate the data into the computer. The input device in this system is a microphone. Voice recognition is ideal for entry of data into word-processing software or into a structure such as a database by people such as lawyers, doctors, etc., who only use ICT systems as part of their job. Voice recognition can also be used to dictate and send emails as well as enter commands into the operating system. Voice recognition software turns voice into text.

Advantages of voice recognition

- Faster than typing – (up to 160 words per minute, which is three times the average typing speed).
- Accuracy of 99% – provided time has been spent teaching the computer about your voice.
- Cheap – many computers come with a microphone, so the only cost is the cost of the software.

Disadvantages of voice recognition

- Takes a while to get used to – can be frustrating for beginners to use.
- Not accurate at first – you may need to train the system about your voice. This is done by entering data and then correcting the mistakes the system has made.
- Errors due to background noise – few people have their own offices. Usually there is lots of background noise (people talking, telephones ringing, etc.). This can cause errors as the system tries to interpret these sounds.

Data collection/capture methods *continued*

Voice recognition security entry systems

These systems used a system where a person speaks into a microphone and the system is able to recognize their voice pattern and allow them access. People whose voice they do not recognize will not be allowed access.

Biometrics

Biometric methods provide a fast and easy way of recognizing a person by using a feature of the human body that is unique to a particular person in order to identify them. It saves the person having to use other forms of identification such as swipe cards, passwords, etc.

Biometric methods include:

- voice/speech recognition
- fingerprint recognition
- retinal scanning.

Biometrics have the following advantages:

- They are not easily abused.
- Unlike swipe cards there is nothing to forget.

Biometrics have the following disadvantages:

- They use expensive technology.
- They are often vandalized (e.g., when used in schools).

RFID tags

RFID (radio frequency identification) obtains data stored on a tag (a small chip) using radio signals, which means that the reading device and tag do not have to come into contact with each other. This means that the data on the tag, which is usually attached to a credit card sized plastic card, can be read from a distance. This system is therefore a wireless system.

The main advantage of using this system is that there is no need for the reader and tag to come into

contact with each other. This system can be used in schools to record attendance where students have to have their card with them for their attendance to be automatically recorded. All this comes at a price and the main disadvantage with the system is the cost.

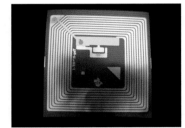
▲ **An RFID tag.**

Questions C

1 (a) Give the name of a biometric method used for the registration of students in a school. *(1 mark)*
(b) Describe **one** advantage the biometric method has over non-biometric methods. *(2 marks)*

2 OMR is frequently used in schools for school registration systems and also for marking multiple-choice answer sheets.
(a) Give the meaning of the abbreviation OMR. *(1 mark)*
(b) Explain how data is captured using OMR. *(2 marks)*
(c) Give **one** advantage OMR has compared to typing the data in using a keyboard. *(1 mark)*
(d) Give **one** disadvantage OMR has. *(1 mark)*

3 (a) Explain how RFID is used to capture data. *(1 mark)*
(b) Give **one** advantage RFID has as a method of data capture. *(1 mark)*

4 Biometric methods are often used for capturing data.
(a) Explain what the term biometric means. *(1 mark)*
(b) Give an example of an application that uses a biometric method. *(2 marks)*

5 Voice recognition systems are becoming a popular method of inputting data.
(a) Give the name of the input device used with a voice recognition system. *(1 mark)*
(b) Explain how the data is captured using a voice recognition system. *(3 marks)*
(c) Give **one** advantage of voice recognition. *(1 mark)*
(d) Give **one** disadvantage of voice recognition. *(1 mark)*

Extension activity

Use the Internet to research biometric methods and their applications.

Produce a document on their advantages and disadvantages and also some of the non-school uses.

Reviewing and modifying work and presenting information

You will find out

▷ **About reviewing and modifying your work**

▷ **About presenting information in ways that are fit for purpose and audience**

When work has been produced using ICT it is important to check that the work is accurate and is fit for purpose. As you have produced the work, you may be biased, so it is always better to allow others to look over your work. They will be able to offer comments and ways of improving it. They will also be able to spot errors that you have missed yourself. Reviewing and modifying your work is an important part of producing work that is as good as it can be.

In this section you will be looking at those things that are part of reviewing and modifying your work as well as how to present information in ways that are fit for purpose and audience.

Reviewing and modifying your work

Reviewing your work means you and others looking at your work critically with a view to making comments so that you can make improvements if they are needed.

When you are asked to produce something such as a website, a document (e.g., letter, brochure, poster, booklet, etc.) or a presentation, you will usually have an initial plan of what you intend to do. If you are producing the work for someone else, then the initial plan will be agreed with them.

When producing your own work by making use of ICT you should:

- Work accurately by taking steps not to introduce any errors.
- Check that what you have produced is the same as that outlined in the initial plan.
- Proof read your work to ensure that the text makes sense and that you have not missed any text out.
- Check any diagrams to ensure that they are of an appropriate quality.
- Use the facilities provided by the software (i.e., spellcheckers and grammar checkers) to help eliminate spelling and grammatical errors.
- Check any calculations by performing the calculations manually and comparing the results.
- Check the consistency from one page to another. This means that all the pages in a document or website or slides in a presentation should have a similar design. They should look as though they belong together.
- Seek the opinions of others.

Using drafts

A draft is a piece of work that is not considered to be the final version. It is a working version and it is given to others for their comments. The comments are acted upon and changes are made to give a second draft. The second draft is then given to the same people who reviewed the first draft for their comments. By using a series of drafts all the problems with the first draft are eliminated and the piece of work is completed.

By using drafts you can ensure:

- That the work you have produced is 'fit for purpose'. This means it does what it is supposed to do.
- The meaning is clear. The reviewers will point out things that are not clear.
- The work matches the initial plan. This means that you have done what you set out to do.
- That enough 'eyes' have seen the work to check for accuracy, appearance, ease of use, etc.
- It is suitable for the intended audience. It is a good idea to get some reviews from people who will be your typical audience. So, if you produced a website for young children, it should be shown to them for their comments.

Reviewing and modifying work and presenting information *continued*

▲ The material you produce must meet the audience's needs.

Presenting information in ways that are fit for purpose and audience

Presenting material for others is one of the uses of ICT. Presentations can be produced using presentation software or you could present material in a similar way using a website.

Visual (on screen) presentations

– You will have sat through many of these during your time at school – some good and some bad. Basically slides are prepared that are then projected onto a large screen so that all the audience can see them. There is another way to show a presentation. You can create a multimedia presentation that allows the user to be in control of which slide or section of the material they would like to view.

▲ Many presentations use a data projector as the output device so that a large audience can view the slides.

Hard copy – You can print out the slides and give them to the audience. Usually these printouts show the slide contents and some space for the viewer to make their own notes.

Multi-sensory – These are those presentations that make use of multimedia. For example, you can incorporate text, sound, images, video and interactivity into presentations. This helps people who learn in different ways, learn using the material in the presentation.

Bringing together and organizing information

To present information successfully it needs to come from a number of sources. With paper-based documents you are restricted to text and images but with multimedia material, such as presentations and websites, you can use the full range of multimedia features.

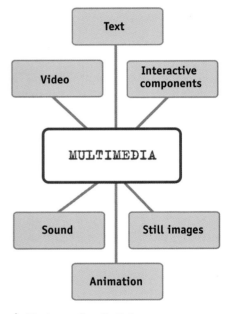

▲ The types of media that can be used in multimedia.

Here are some sources of information.

Text

- From websites – remember the copyright restrictions. You should always put the material into your own words. You can use copy and paste to obtain text from websites or type it in or even use voice recognition software to dictate it in.
- From books – again because of copyright you need to put text into your own words. But it is OK to quote small amounts of text provided you acknowledge the author.

Images

- From websites – it is easy to search for images and then copy and paste them into documents. In some cases you may need to actually download the image file and save it into a folder.
- By scanning – old photographs, maps, photographs from books may be scanned in using a scanner.
- From clip art/image collections – these are often provided as part of the software you are using. There is usually a way of searching for a suitable image.

Sounds

- Record your own – to do this you will need a microphone. Often presentations include narration, which means you pre-record what you are going to say and save it with the presentation.
- Use sound clips – these can be obtained from websites or clip art libraries.

Video

- You can take your own video – this can take time but it is quite rewarding and you do not have to worry about copyright.
- You can link to a website that contains the video, such as YouTube, but your access may be restricted by your network manager at school or college.

Presenting information to suit the needs of the audience

You will have used lots of websites and also seen and maybe used presentations other people have produced. You will also have used material produced in posters, brochures, etc. You will have realized that there are good ones and bad ones.

In this section you will be looking at the things you can do to ensure that the information you produce is fun to use and appropriately aimed at the audience. You will also learn about the need to consider that your users may have certain disabilities and that there are things that you can do to help them.

Target audience

The target audience are the people your document is aimed at.

Finding out about your target audience

Once you have identified who your audience is, you still need to find out more about them. You must ask yourself questions such as:

- **What are their needs?**
  Your audience will look at your document for a reason. Think about what this reason is and what the audience will need from your document. For example, if you have designed a poster advertising a school/college night out, think about what information they will need. Satisfying your audience's needs is an important part in creating any document.

- **How much do they know already?**
  It is essential to assess how much your audience knows about the subject of your document. If they have a good knowledge of the subject, you will not have to start at the beginning.

- **What is the knowledge of the reader about the subject?**
  If you were writing an article on a subject such as the Data Protection Act 1998 for computer users, then it would need to be different from the same article aimed at lawyers, who are able to untangle the intricacies of the law.

- **What level of literacy do they have?**
  Not everyone is good at English. Any document aimed at the whole of the adult population will need to be written simply. Generally, to make a document as readable as possible, you would need to make sure that:
  - only well-known words are used
  - the sentence length is kept short
  - as few punctuation marks as possible are used.

- **How much specialist vocabulary can they handle?**
  Most subjects have a series of words that tend to be used only within that subject. The subject is said to have a specialist vocabulary. For example, medical staff, doctors, nurses, etc., have special medical terms for illnesses. You need to make sure that if you are using any specialist words to people not knowledgeable in the area, then you will need to carefully explain them.

- **How interested are they likely to be in the subject?**
  Some topics or subjects are more interesting than others. Also different people find different things interesting. If the information you have to present is uninteresting to the audience then you will need to try to make it as interesting as you can.

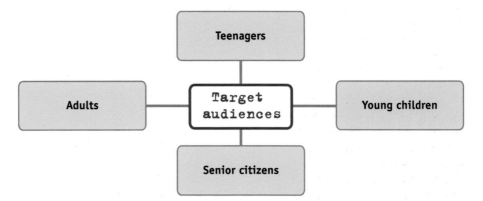

▲ It is common to classify a target audience according to their age.

Reviewing and modifying work and presenting information *continued*

Thinking about the target audience

The target audience is the people your document is aimed at. You need to make sure that the design of the document is appropriate for the people who will be reading it. For example, a poster advertising a school disco for 14–16 year olds would need a different design compared to a poster advertising a drink driving campaign. If you are talking about ICT to others who also know about ICT then you can use technical terms without explaining them. They should know what they mean.

Who is your target audience?

The information you have will need to be presented. Before you present the information you need to think about who the intended audience for the information is. The data needs to be presented in a manner that the audience can use and understand. The way you would present the information to an adult audience would be totally different from the way you would present the same information to a young audience.

Presenting the same information to different audiences

It is possible to present the same item of information in different ways. For example, you could have a poster giving the key information and then a leaflet giving more details.

Presenting information sensitive to the needs of a particular audience

Disability considerations

When designing websites and presentations you must be aware that users with a range of disabilities will be using the products you produce.

You will need to consider people who are visually impaired (i.e., blind or partially sighted) by:

- having a facility to speak words on the screen
- having a facility to zoom in so that the page is magnified
- increasing the font size
- choosing those font types that are easy to read
- use plenty of contrast between the text and the background
- allowing the user to change the colour scheme.

You will need to consider people who have a hearing impairment (i.e., completely or partially deaf) by:

- using visual warnings rather than sound warnings
- using typed versions of any speech used
- using subtitles for any video used.

Producing information that is relevant and fit for purpose

When producing information for documents or for presentations/websites, it is important to consider the following:

- The information must be relevant – do not include any information that the reader/audience does not need.
- The information must be fit for purpose – it must give the reader/audience what they want and expect.

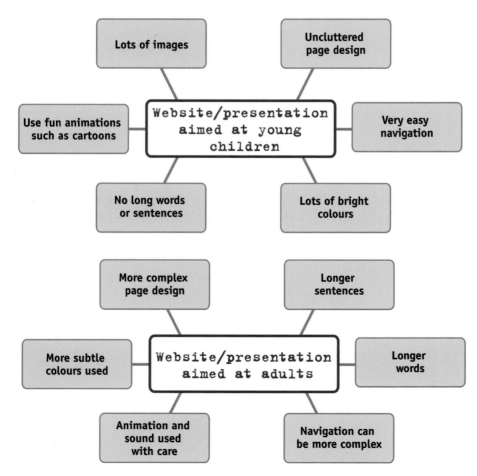

- The information must be fit for the audience – a document/website/presentation aimed at children would need to be totally different from one aimed at adults.
- That the material is readable. No matter how well arranged the document is and how professional it looks, if the intended audience cannot understand it, then it is useless.
- The material on the page must have visual impact. It must make people want to read it.
- It must contain enough detail and all the important detail must be included. It is no use spending hours on a poster for a school disco if you leave off the important information such as the date.
- The layout must be consistent. If there is more than one page to a document, then all the pages must look as though they belong together. They must therefore look as though they are all part of the same thing.
- The design must not be too complex. Adults will be able to cope with a more complex design than children.

Using accepted layouts and conventions

There are a variety of documents that people use and it is important that the layout for each document follows an accepted layout and convention.

If you are asked to produce these documents then you will need to check that you understand how the document should be laid out. Here are documents that have accepted layouts:

- letters
- essays
- memos
- reports
- posters
- newsletters
- flyers
- brochures
- webpages
- magazines
- business cards
- multimedia presentations.

◀ Business cards contain a logo, name of the organization and a person's name and contact details.

Questions D

1 Disabled people often use websites.
   (a) Describe **one** thing the website designer can do to help a user who is partially sighted. *(1 mark)*
   (b) Describe **one** thing the website designer can do to help a user who is deaf. *(1 mark)*

2 (a) Proof read the text below and make a note of three errors you find. *(3 marks)*

> ### Getting cash from your supermarket
>
> It is common to see cash dispensers in the walls of out-of-town supermarkts. It is possible to get cash at the same time as paying for the goods.
>
> The service is called 'Cashback' and to get cash, the customer needs to have a card called a SWITCH card or a similar debit card. Debit cards can be used as an alternative to paying by cheque. When the customer pays for their goods they will be asked if they want 'Cashback'. The customer details are red using a chip and pin reader.
>
> When a debit card is used, the money is transferred from the shopper's account to the store's bank account. This process takes plaice immediately.

   (b) Spellcheckers will sometimes not highlight a word as being spelt incorrectly.
   Tick the boxes that are correct reasons why this might happen. *(3 marks)*

	Tick 3 boxes only
The word might not be in the spellchecker dictionary	☐
The spellchecker only checks the hard words to spell	☐
Two words the same might be next to each other	☐
The spellchecker might be set to American spellings	☐
The spellchecker might be turned off	☐

3 To produce good documents that are fit for purpose it is important to produce a number of drafts. Each of these drafts should be reviewed by others.
   (a) Explain what is meant by 'fit for purpose'. *(1 mark)*
   (b) Explain what is meant by a draft. *(1 mark)*
   (c) Explain why draft versions should be reviewed by others. *(2 marks)*

Sharing and exchanging information electronically and evaluating ICT tools

You will find out

▷ **About sharing and exchanging information electronically**

▷ **About evaluating the effectiveness of ICT tools to meet needs**

Most computers are networked together, so this allows the sharing and exchanging of information. There are also many occasions when you are working using several pieces of applications software at the same time. This means it is also important to be able to transfer data between applications.

In this section you will look at the methods of exchanging data electronically and also how to evaluate the effectiveness of ICT tools.

Transferring data within and between applications

Software packages such as web design software or desktop publishing software use files created in lots of different packages. For example, most people would type the text using word-processing software first and then save it as a file. They

would then open up the DTP package and import the saved file containing the text into the DTP software.

Sometimes the image/text/sound/video file is not in a format that the other package can use. In cases like this you can usually save the file in a file format that is acceptable to the other package.

Exporting data means taking some of the data from one file and saving it separately so that it can be used in a completely different software package from the one in which it was created.

File attachments

A convenient way of sending data to someone else is to attach files to emails. If the file is large then the email software will automatically compress the file. When the receiver opens the file it will be decompressed.

Photo-sharing websites

Photo-sharing websites allow you to transfer your digital photographs online and this allows you to share them with others. You can then decide whether you want to share them with a selected group of friends or with the public (i.e., anyone who accesses the site). Transferring photograph files onto the site is an example of uploading, and saving photograph files from the site is an example of downloading.

File compression when transferring files

If images/sound/video are to be used on a website or a presentation, they can take time to load, so it is best to

use compressed images. Compressing files makes the file size smaller, which makes it quicker to load for the software and also to copy onto other media. If the presentation is to be provided as a download on a website, it will be quicker to upload (i.e., save onto the server) and to download by users.

Audio files, such as files containing speech or music, are extremely large and these are normally saved in MP3 format, which compresses the file and makes the file more manageable. Movie/video files are even bigger than audio files and so need to be compressed.

Advantages of data compression techniques

The advantages of data compression techniques include:

- More files can be stored on the storage medium (e.g., DVD, memory card, hard disk, pen drive, etc.).
- It is much faster to upload to put it on a webpage.
- It is much faster for others to download it from a webpage.
- It is faster to load when viewed with any software used to view or edit it.
- It is faster to transfer as an email attachment.

Disadvantages of data compression techniques

The disadvantages of data compression techniques include:

- Images/music/video are not as high quality compared to those without compression.

- Sound quality is not as high with compression such as that used with MP3 files, although not many people would notice the difference.
- Compression means it is much faster to transfer movie files and this causes problems with people illegally copying movies.

Bitmap image
1280 × 960 pixels
File size:
3150 KB (3.5 MB)

Compression

JPEG image
1280 × 960 pixels
File size:
292 KB

▲ Compression results in a much smaller file.

Zip and Unzip

Zip and Unzip is popular software for compression and decompression. It is used mainly for the transfer of data by attaching it to an email.

▲ This icon means a file that has been zipped (i.e. compressed).

Evaluating the effectiveness of ICT tools to meet needs

There are many different ICT tools that can be used to collect, process and present information. Selecting the best one is not always easy. For example, you could produce a poster in lots of different software, but some would be better than others.

When deciding which ICT tool to use, there are a lot of considerations such as:

- Time constraints – there is never enough time to complete work, so you often have to use the ICT tool that will produce the end result in the least amount of time. This may result in a compromise. For example, you may use a template for a slide design in a presentation because you don't have time to create your own.
- Convenience – usually means whatever is easiest. Usually the easiest piece of software is the one used the most. This may mean that you produce material using software that is not ideally suited for the job. For example, you may decide to produce a brochure using word-processing software rather than DTP software simply because you are more familiar with it.
- Quality of presentation – this often depends on the time you can spend on the material. The more versions and drafts you can produce and the more comments you can get from others, the better the final product will be. The only problem here is the time it takes to produce quality work.

- Range of facilities – these are often limited by the software you choose. The greater the number of facilities offered by the software, the more complex it is and the greater the amount of time to find out how to use it.
- Versatility – this is the ability of the software to cope with all the requirements that the developer may have.
- Transferability of information into other formats – this is very important, as you often have to create images, animations, text, sound, etc., in one package and then transfer it to another package such as DTP, web design or presentation software.
- Cost – this limits what you can do. For example, you may have to pay for images you use. You may not have the money to buy the ideal software and therefore have to create the product in less desirable software.
- Internet connection speed – this can vary a lot depending on whether you have dialup or broadband. There are many things that you cannot do with a dialup connection such as stream video.

◀ Time, or the lack of it, is an important consideration in choosing an ICT tool.

Sharing and exchanging information electronically and evaluating ICT tools *continued*

Questions E

1 Files are often compressed before being transferred over the Internet.
  (a) Explain what is meant by compressed. *(1 mark)*
  (b) Give **one** advantage in compressing a file. *(1 mark)*
  (c) Give **one** disadvantage in compressing a file. (1 mark)

2 Many people use photo-sharing websites.

  Explain the features of a photo-sharing website. *(3 marks)*

Extension activity

Use the Internet to find out which file formats use compression for each of the following:

- Images
- Music
- Video/movies.

Case study

Using fingerprinting in schools

Many schools are now using fingerprinting methods to help with pupil registration. One such school in South Wales has been using fingerprinting methods for a couple of years now. The system works by the pupils placing their finger on a scanner that is installed outside the classrooms. The scanner reads certain aspects of the print to identify the pupil and then records the attendance details on the computer.

The head teacher of the school has sung the praises of the system, saying how it has helped reduce truancy because pupils now know that it can be immediately identified by the system. Teachers at the school have welcomed the system because it frees them from having to do this important but time-consuming task.

If a pupil fails to register at the start of the day, a text message can be sent to the parent's mobile phone alerting them of the non-attendance of their child. This makes it virtually impossible for a pupil not to attend school without their parents knowing.

Many pupils like the system because it gives them more time to chat with friends and find out what is going on in the school with their form teacher.

Some parents and pupils were initially worried that fingerprints were being routinely taken and stored by the school and that this was personal data which could be misused. However, the company who supplied the system explained to parents that no full fingerprints are stored by the system. Instead the fingerprint is stored as a code and it is this code that is matched. They were reassured that a fingerprint cannot be re-created from this code and that it is only used by the school for identification purposes and not for some other sinister use.

Questions

1 Many schools use fingerprinting as a method for recording the presence of pupils at school.
  (a) Fingerprinting is an example of a biometric input device. Explain briefly what this sentence means. *(2 marks)*
  (b) Give **three** advantages of using fingerprinting to register attendance. *(3 marks)*
  (c) Many parents may be worried that the system stores their child's fingerprints. Write a sentence to explain how you might address this worry. *(2 marks)*

2 Describe **one** way in which the fingerprinting system helps prevent truancy in schools. *(2 marks)*

3 Give **one** example of how this fingerprinting attendance system could possibly be misused. *(1 mark)*

END-OF-TOPIC REVIEW

Questions

☑ Test yourself

The following notes summarize this topic. The notes are incomplete because they have words missing. Using the words in the list below, copy out and complete sentences A to J, underlining the words that you have inserted. Each word may be used more than once.

transcription   data   GIGO   information

transposition   validation

verification   optical mark recognition

biometric   processing

A _____ consists of raw facts and figures (e.g., readings from sensors, survey facts, etc.).

B Data processed by a computer is called _____.

C _____ is the term ICT people use to describe that if you put rubbish into an ICT system, you get rubbish out.

D _____ means performing calculations or organizing the data.

E An error made when typing in data using a document as a source is called a _____ error.

F Swapping characters around while typing is called a _____ error.

G _____ checks are used to restrict the data a user can enter.

H _____ means checking that the data being entered perfectly matches the source of the data.

I A registration system in a school that makes use of marks made on a form to record attendance, which is then processed by a computer, is called _____ _____ _____.

J A school registration system that makes use of a unique property of the human body is an example of a _____ method.

Questions *continued*

Examination style questions

1 When Year 7 students join the senior school, a form is filled in by their parents. The details on the form are then typed into a computer. The details are verified after typing.
Explain briefly, how the details may be verified. *(2 marks)*

2 A person's date of birth is entered into a database. State **three** things the validation program could check regarding this date as part of the validation. *(3 marks)*

3 When a new member joins a fitness club they are given a membership number. The membership number is made up in the following way:
  Customer date of birth as six numbers.
  The final two figures of the year in which the customer joins the fitness club.
  A letter which is either J or S depending on whether they are a junior or senior member.

(a) Write down the membership number for a junior member who joined the club in 2010 and was born on 21/05/98. *(1 mark)*

(b) When the membership number is entered into the database, it is validated.
Explain what is meant by data validation. *(2 marks)*

(c) Two examples of data validation are:
  range check
  format check.
Explain how these two methods could be used on the **membership number** field described above. *(2 marks)*

(d) It would be better if the membership number were unique to a particular member.
  (i) Explain why the method described might not result in a unique membership number. *(1 mark)*
  (ii) Explain **one** problem not having a unique membership number might cause. *(2 marks)*

4 There are lots of different sources of information that can be used.

Choose which source of information best matches each description in the following table. *(7 marks)*

Wiki   Podcast   Blog   Book
Newspaper   Text message

Description	The best source of information to match the description
An episode of a 10-part programme on the radio	
A note to your parents to say you have arrived safely	
An online diary of a celebrity on a website	
A series of video and audio files that are made available to download via web syndication	
Details of the latest news from around the world	
An authoritative account of a famous battle in history	
A collection of webpages designed so that people can add new content and add their corrections to the old content	

END-OF-TOPIC REVIEW

Exam support

Worked example

Here is a first draft of a poster used to advertise a Halloween party at a school.

Mount Hill School
Years 10 and 11
Halloween party
Friday 30ᵗʰ Oct 09
Starts 7:30 pm
Music Hall
Tickets £2.50

Some features of DTP have been used to improve the appearance of this poster.

(a) Describe **three** features of DTP software that have been used to improve the appearance of this poster. *(3 marks)*

(b) Give **one** other feature of DTP that they could use to improve the design. *(1 mark)*

(c) The person who produced the poster spellchecks it before printing.

State what is meant by spellchecking. *(2 marks)*

Student answer 1

(a) Graphics

Text

Centre.

(b) Use a different font type such as Gothic.

(c) The computer does this automatically. It spellchecks all the spelling.

◀ Examiner's comment

(a) The ability to import clip art/graphics would have been an acceptable answer to this but the answer given is not worth a mark.

Text is not a feature and it would have been too brief an answer anyway so no marks are given here.

Centre is a feature but there is no description of how it is used. Students must look at the question carefully: to any question that asks a user to 'give', a one-word answer is OK, but where they are asked to 'describe', a one-word answer is not sufficient.

(b) This is a correct answer. The student has clearly stated font type rather than font on its own. One mark is given here.

(c) This a typical answer from a weak student. Students must remember not to simply write down an answer that anyone could guess from the word 'spellchecking'. There needs to be detail about how the spellchecking is done. No marks are given for this answer.

(1 mark out of 6)

END-OF-TOPIC REVIEW

Exam support *continued*

Student answer 2

(a) All the text used has been centred to make it look more interesting.

The font size has been increased for some of the text to make it stand out.

Clip art images have been imported to improve the appearance.

(b) Use a border to go around the edge of the page. This can be obtained from clip art libraries.

(c) Checks all the words in a document against words that are in a stored dictionary to make sure they are spelt correctly. If they are not they can be corrected automatically or underlined in red so that the user can decide what to do.

◀ Examiner's comment

(a) These are all very good answers. The student has clearly identified the features and described how they are used. Three marks out of three for this answer.

(b) This is a good feature to include on a poster so one mark here.

(c) This is a very good answer and the student has clearly identified that the software uses a dictionary against which the words are compared. There are two marks here, so there must be two points made. The student has made two valid points in their two sentences so full marks are given for this answer.

(6 marks out of 6)

Examiner's answers

(a) One mark (up to a maximum of three marks) for each feature, which must have been used on the poster such as:

- Increase in font size to make more important text in the poster stand out.
- Centring of all the text so that it draws attention and looks like a poster.
- Use of coloured text to make the important text stand out the most.
- Importing clip art to add interest to the page.
- Use of bold to make the name of the school prominent.

(b) One mark for one feature similar to:

- Use different fonts.
- Use a page border.
- Use a watermark.
- Use a background colour.

(c) One mark for each point to a maximum of two marks.

- Checks the spelling of each word in a document.
- Against a pre-stored dictionary.
- Automatically changes the spelling as a user types.
- Highlights misspelt words for user action.
- Suggests correct spelling of words.

Summary mind maps

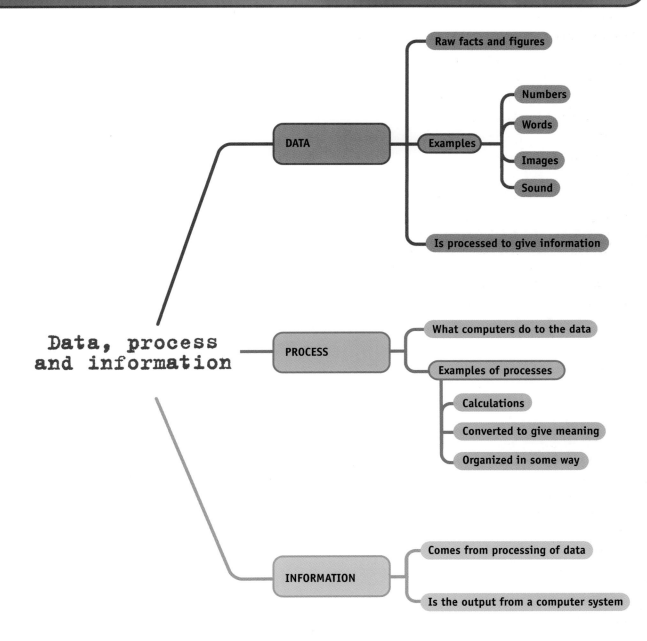

Data, process and information

- DATA
  - Raw facts and figures
  - Examples
    - Numbers
    - Words
    - Images
    - Sound
  - Is processed to give information
- PROCESS
  - What computers do to the data
  - Examples of processes
    - Calculations
    - Converted to give meaning
    - Organized in some way
- INFORMATION
  - Comes from processing of data
  - Is the output from a computer system

Summary mind maps *continued*

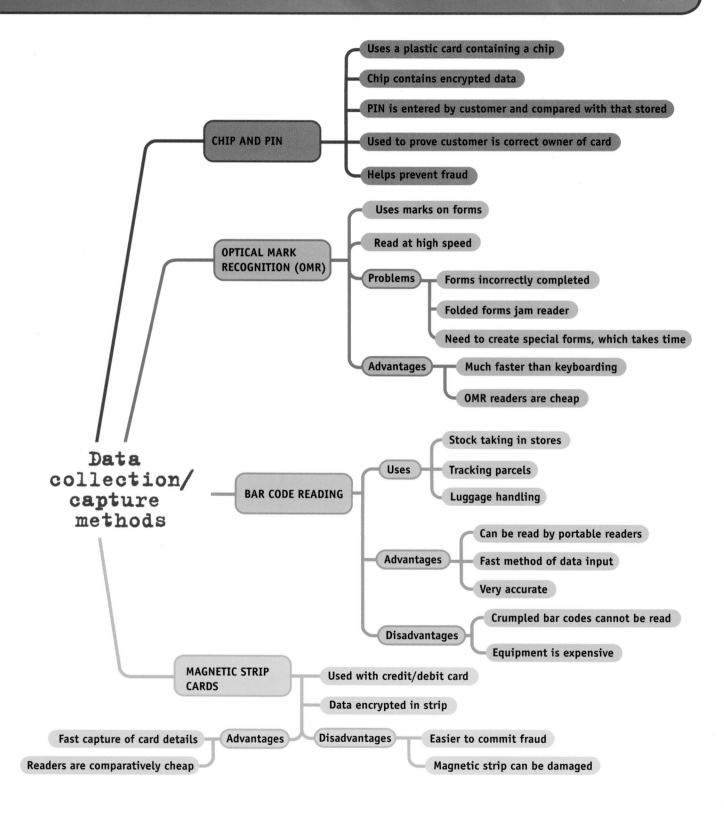

CHIP AND PIN
- Uses a plastic card containing a chip
- Chip contains encrypted data
- PIN is entered by customer and compared with that stored
- Used to prove customer is correct owner of card
- Helps prevent fraud

OPTICAL MARK RECOGNITION (OMR)
- Uses marks on forms
- Read at high speed
- Problems
  - Forms incorrectly completed
  - Folded forms jam reader
  - Need to create special forms, which takes time
- Advantages
  - Much faster than keyboarding
  - OMR readers are cheap

Data collection/ capture methods

BAR CODE READING
- Uses
  - Stock taking in stores
  - Tracking parcels
  - Luggage handling
- Advantages
  - Can be read by portable readers
  - Fast method of data input
  - Very accurate
- Disadvantages
  - Crumpled bar codes cannot be read
  - Equipment is expensive

MAGNETIC STRIP CARDS
- Used with credit/debit card
- Data encrypted in strip
- Advantages
  - Fast capture of card details
  - Readers are comparatively cheap
- Disadvantages
  - Easier to commit fraud
  - Magnetic strip can be damaged

Topic 7

Operating systems and user interfaces

The key concepts covered in this topic are:

- Operating systems
- User interfaces
- File/folder organization

Software is the general name given to all the programs that can be run on computer hardware. They all give the hardware instructions and can be divided into two main categories: operating systems and applications software. In this topic you will be looking at the function of an operating system and you will be looking at the different types of operating system.

User interfaces are important because having a good one means the computer is easier to use. User interfaces are being developed all the time and many of the new interfaces are making more use of touch screens and voice recognition. In this topic you will be learning about the function of the operating system as well as the range of user interfaces that are available.

Contents

Operating systems

You will find out

▷ **About the functions of an operating system**

▷ **About the need for different types of operating system**

In order for ICT hardware to do a useful job it needs two types of software: systems software and applications software. The applications software performs a particular job or application but the operating system software is needed to control the hardware directly. Both these two types of software are essential components of any ICT system.

Any software has to interact with the user and this is through the user interface. The main aim is to make this interface as easy to use as possible. In this section you will be looking at the functions of the operating system.

The functions of an operating system

Operating systems are programs that control the hardware directly. The operating system supplies the step-by-step instructions that tell the computer hardware what to do.

Operating systems have the following functions:

- Manage and control any devices such as printers, scanners, webcams, etc., that are attached to the computer.

- Provide a user interface that makes it easy for the user to load programs, search for files, copy files, etc.
- Hide the complexity of the hardware from the user.
- Deal with any errors that occur while the computer is working on tasks.
- Provide the interface between the application packages being run and the hardware.
- Allow new hardware or software to be installed using installation programs.
- Include various utilities such as disk formatter, virus checking, encryption, etc.
- Handle the storage of data by keeping track of all the files and directories/folders on the disk drives.
- Maximize the use of computer memory by the operating system deciding where in the memory the program instructions are placed.
- Recognize when new hardware such as a pen drive, camera, portable hard drive, etc., has been attached to the computer and load the software needed to control it.
- Organize resources (e.g., processing time and memory) when the computer user is running several programs at the same time.
- Handle the saving of data by keeping track of all the files and directories/folders on the disk drives.
- Allow the user to perform file operations such as delete, copy and rename.

Methods of operation that operating systems have to cope with

There are many different types of operating system and here are some of the methods of operation for some of them.

▲ Without an operating system the computer hardware is useless.

Interactive

Interactive means that there is a constant dialogue between the computer and the user. This means that the computer asks the user questions or highlights problems and the user has to acknowledge that they have read the message or make a response.

Multitasking

It is possible to have several windows open at the same time. For example, you might be printing a very long document and want to type in another document at the same time. Or you may be working on a DTP document and listening to the radio on the Internet at the same time. These are examples of multitasking.

▲ The operating system is used to install new hardware and software.

Multi-user

A multi-user operating system allows several users to access the same data at the same time. Multi-user operating systems are used with networks. Each person on the network appears to have sole use of the network. Each user on the network is allocated a slice of the computer's time. Once they have used up this time slice the next person is given a go and so on. Because the processor of the computer works so fast, each person does not notice that the computer's time is being shared. Multi-user operating systems have to deal with allocating usernames and authenticating passwords.

Online

An online operating system is an operating system that runs on a web server. The user of the operating system will use it through the web browser software. This means that applications that are stored on the web can be used rather than having them stored on the user's computer. This means that the operating system stored on the user's computer is not needed as much. This is becoming more popular especially with netbook computers.

Processing a bit at a time or doing it in one go: batch and real-time processing

Processing of data may be done a bit at a time (i.e. real-time processing) or the work may be saved up over a period of time and done in one go (i.e. batch processing).

Batch processing

Batch processing is used when a particular job needs to be done in one go rather than in a number of parts. All the relevant data is collected and processed together. It has the advantage that once all the inputs are ready and the program has been selected, the computer can just get on with the job without any human intervention.

Batch processing is ideal for:

- producing attendance statistics from attendances recorded on OMR forms
- producing bills for water, gas, telephone and electricity companies
- producing monthly bank or credit card statements
- marking multiple-choice examination papers.

Real-time processing

With real-time processing, the system is automatically updated when a change is made. This means that the system always contains up-to-date information. An airline booking system would use real-time processing because, as seats are sold, the number of seats available would need to be reduced to prevent double booking. Because terminals need to be connected to and under control of the computer all the time, a real-time system is also an online system.

Real-time processing is ideal for:

- flood warning systems
- booking systems (for airline, holiday, concert and theatre tickets)
- autopilots for aircraft
- computer games
- traffic light control
- process control in factories (i.e., making steel, chemical plants, etc.)
- controlling robots.

KEY WORDS

Batch processing all the inputs needed are batched together and processed in one go.

Real-time processing the input data is processed as it arrives. The results have a direct effect on the next set of available data.

Questions A

1. Choose **three** tasks from the list below that are carried out by all operating systems. *(3 marks)*
   renaming a file
   deciding where to store data on a hard disk drive
   underlining text in a word-processing package
   cropping a picture
   loading a file from the disk drive.

2. (a) Give **three** tasks (other than those in Q1) performed by an operating system. *(3 marks)*
   (b) Most operating systems are interactive.
   Explain the meaning of the term interactive. *(2 marks)*

3. The operating system Windows 7 is capable of multitasking.

   By giving a suitable example, explain what is meant by multitasking. *(2 marks)*

4. Online operating systems are becoming popular.

   Explain what an online operating system is. *(2 marks)*

Extension activity

Use the Internet to find out about the move towards online operating systems.

Write a short magazine article summarizing what you have found out.

User interfaces

You will find out

▷ **About the features and uses of different types of user interface**

▷ **About graphical user interfaces (GUIs)**

▷ **About selecting and adjusting the user interface to meet needs**

▷ **About menu user interfaces**

When you turn on your computer and the operating system loads, the first thing you will see is the user interface. The user interface provides a way of you communicating with your computer. You can inform the computer what you want to do and the computer can tell you about any problems it has, such as not being able to find a certain file, or not being able to print out a document because the printer is not switched on.

In this section you will be looking at user interfaces, what they consist of and how you can customize the interface to suit you.

The features and uses of different types of user interface

An interface is where two things meet, so a user interface in ICT is the point where the human user meets or interacts with the ICT system. This is commonly called the user interface. User interfaces have seen huge changes over the years and are being developed all the time so that ICT systems are made as easy to use as possible.

In this section you will be looking at the range of user interfaces used by ICT systems and their relative strengths and weaknesses.

When you turn on the computer you see a user interface. The cursors, prompts, icons, menus, etc., allow you to get things done with your computer. They are all part of the user interface. A user interface can make your computer either harder or easier to use.

Graphical user interfaces (GUI) and WIMP

Graphical user interfaces (GUIs) are very popular because they are easy to use. Instead of typing in commands, you enter them by pointing at and clicking on objects on the screen. Microsoft Windows and Macintosh operating systems use graphical user interfaces. The main features of a GUI include:

Windows – the screen is divided into areas called windows. Windows are useful if you need to work on several tasks.

Icons – these are small pictures used to represent commands, files or windows. By moving the pointer and clicking, you can carry out a command or open a window. You can also position any icon anywhere on your desktop.

Menus – menus allow a user to make selections from a list. Menus can be pop-up or pull-down and this means they do not clutter the desktop whilst they are not being used.

Pointers – this is the little arrow that appears when using Windows. The pointer changes shape in different applications. It changes to an 'I' shape when using word-processing software. A mouse can be used to move the pointer around the screen.

Notice that the first letter of each feature in the above list spells out the term WIMP (i.e., Windows, Icons, Menus, Pointers).

Customizing the user interface

When you start to use a computer you often use it without making any changes to the user interface. However, if someone has used the computer before you and has made changes to the user interface, then this might prevent you working effectively. It is therefore important to know about the settings and how you can alter them for yourself. If you use a networked computer, such as the ones at school, then the network will save any changes you make to the user interface. This means that the next time you log on using your username and password you will be presented with your own personalized user interface.

There are many ways you can customize the user interface and here are just some of them:

- You can alter the size of the icons.
- You can alter the way the mouse works.
- You can alter resolution, brightness and contrast on the computer screen.

Settings that can be changed in a user interface include the following: window size, mouse settings, icon size, screen resolution, etc. A user interface normally consists of:

- icons
- folders
- windows
- menus
- help
- toolbars.

Making changes

Adjusting window size – windows can be maximized, minimized and made any size in between.

- Maximizing a window makes the window occupy almost all the screen.
- Minimizing a window makes the window appear as just a title in the taskbar at the bottom of the screen.
- Re-sizing a window can be done by left clicking on one of the corners of the window and keeping the mouse button down, dragging the corner to the correct size.
- Restoring a window takes it back to its original size.

Mouse settings – you can change how the mouse buttons work, how the mouse pointer looks and how it works and alter the speed of the scroll wheel.

Icon size – if you right click the mouse button when on the desktop, you can adjust the size of the icons. You can have large, medium and classic (i.e., the smallest size). By making icons bigger you can improve the use by children and people with poor eyesight.

Screen resolution – this determines how sharp the icons, etc., appear on the screen. It also determines their size. Higher screen resolutions mean items on the screen are sharp but small. Screen resolution determines the number of pixels (i.e., dots of light) used on the screen (e.g., 1600 × 1200 pixels).

Desktop fonts – text and other items such as icons that appear on the screen can be made bigger or smaller. This can be done by increasing or decreasing the dpi (dots per inch).

Colour – you can change most of the colours used for the desktop. For example, you can change the colour of windows.

Position – you can alter the position of elements on the screen such as windows and toolbars.

Graphics – you can change the screensaver, background, customize icons and many other graphics elements.

Contrast – contrast determines the difference between the dark and light parts of the screen. Too much contrast can cause eye strain.

Volume – can be changed using the control panel. You can set the master volume and also change the volume for each of the programs you use.

Toolbars – these are the bars that appear across the top and sometimes the bottom of the interface you are using. There are many tools available and too many to put on the screen all in one go. You can customize toolbars by adding only those you require and you can add only those tools that you use regularly to the toolbar.

Set date and time – this can be done by double clicking on the time.

Hyperlinks and hotspots

Many user interfaces, such as those used by multimedia products and websites, use hyperlinks and hotspots. Hyperlinks allow you to jump from one part of a website to another or even to a completely different website. Links are fundamental to the Internet but they can be used with any multimedia product such as presentations.

Hotspots are an image or piece of text used as a link on a webpage. When you click on the image or text, you are taken to another part of the same page, a different page or a different site, or it may open a new file or a new window.

Menu/dialogue boxes

A dialogue box is a window used with a graphical user interface (GUI) that displays a message to the user or requests that a user types in some information it needs. It is called a dialogue box because there is a constant interaction between the user and the computer. Sometimes the dialogue box simply informs the user about something such as the printer running out of paper and the user only has to acknowledge they have seen the information and click on OK to get rid of the box.

Drag and drop

Many user interfaces offer drag and drop, which allows users to click on items such as pictures, blocks of text, files and then drag them into new positions or folders.

Scrollbars

Scrollbars are the vertical bars you see on the right of the screen and they allow you to move forward and backward through a document, picture, webpage, etc.

Questions B

1 Operating systems allow the user to customize them.

   Give **two** ways a user can customize their operating system. *(2 marks)*

2 All computers need an operating system.
   - **(a)** Explain what an operating system is. *(2 marks)*
   - **(b)** List **three** different functions of an operating system. *(3 marks)*
   - **(c)** Windows is one operating system. Give the name of **one** other operating system. *(1 mark)*

3 **(a)** Explain what is meant by screen resolution. *(1 mark)*
   - **(b)** Give **one** reason why a user might want to change the screen resolution. *(1 mark)*

File/folder organization

You will probably know quite a bit about this material already. After all, it is impossible to get much done on a computer without knowing a bit about folders and files. This section looks at the importance of managing and organizing files and the problems that occur when the file size is very large.

In this section you will also be looking at encoding and how it can be used to make the transfer of files easy and also reduce the size of a file.

The management and organization of files and folders

Because of the large number of files you store on a computer, over a period of time you need to be organized in the way you maintain them. You need to think carefully about filenames that give you some idea of their contents. Files should always be put into folders so that they can be found quickly when needed.

In order for you to use ICT successfully you need to be able to do the following with files and folders:

- move
- delete
- copy
- rename.

The implications of very large files

Graphic, music, photographic and video files can be extremely large. This creates the following problems:

- They take up a lot of space on the storage media.
- They take a long time to copy.
- Their download time when they are downloaded off the Internet is long.
- Their upload time, e.g. when put on a website, is long.
- Their file transfer time, e.g. when attached to emails and sent to others, is long.

Encoding data

Encoding is the process of putting information/data (e.g., text, numbers, symbols, images, sound and video) into a specified format that allows effective transmission or storage by an ICT system.

Encoding data in a suitable format is used to reduce the file size and make it easy to enter the data into other software packages. It also helps retrieve the data.

The opposite of encoding is decoding where the coded information is changed back into its original form.

Examples of encoding

ASCII encoding – here characters on the keyboard (i.e., letters, numbers, symbols and punctuation marks) are changed into a series of binary digits. For example, the letter A is stored as 01000001.

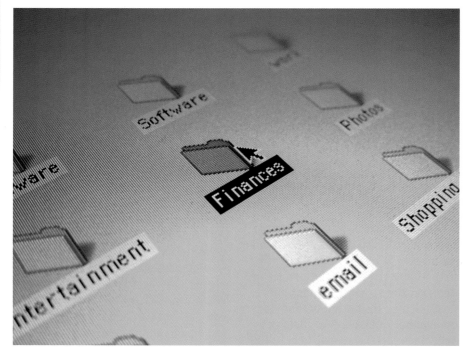

▲ **Use folders to store and organize files.**

▲ Encoded data.

There are a number of reasons for encoding:

- To compress data – this makes it occupy less space on a storage device and makes it faster to send to another computer over a network.
- To enable a file produced in one software package to be read by someone who does not have that software package available on their computer. For example, a user could save a file as a text file in ASCII, so that it can be read and used by other users.

Encoding image files

Image files are encoded, which means the image is represented in a certain way when it is stored. There are many different ways in which an image can be encoded and it depends on how the image is produced (e.g., by digital camera, scanned in, produced using paint/drawing software, etc.).

Encoding sound files

Sounds are not digital, so to save sounds on a computer requires the data to be encoded. Sound (i.e., speech and music) is quite complex and requires a lot of storage space, so to reduce the storage needed for sound files, a technique called compression is used during encoding.

There are many formats for sound files but the most popular one is MP3. MP3 format uses compression to reduce the file size considerably and this is why the MP3 file format is so popular with portable music playing devices such as iPods.

▲ Music, video and image files are often compressed. This reduces the time needed to download them.

Encoding video files

Video files are very large because they have to store information about moving images as well as sound. Video files are encoded and are compressed so that they do not take as long to download and take up less space when stored on a computer.

KEY WORDS

ASCII a code for representing characters in binary.

Encoding putting information/data (e.g., text, numbers, symbols, images, sound and video) into a specified format that allows effective transmission or storage by an ICT system. This normally involves digitizing the information.

Questions C

1. Here are some of the things you can do with files. For each one explain clearly what is being done to the file. *(4 marks)*

   Copy   Move   Rename   Delete.

2. The organization of files into folders and subfolders is extremely important.
   (a) Explain the difference between a folder and a subfolder. *(2 marks)*
   (b) Give **two** reasons why file organization is important. *(2 marks)*

3. Data is encoded.
   (a) By giving a suitable example, explain what encoding means. *(2 marks)*
   (b) Explain **one** advantage in encoding data. *(1 mark)*

4. Files are often compressed before they are saved or transferred over networks.
   (a) Give the name of a type of file that is usually compressed. *(1 mark)*
   (b) Explain why files are often compressed. *(1 mark)*

Extension activity

For this activity you are required to do some research on file formats.

Write down the names of the file formats that are used for each of the following:

- Graphics
- Photographs
- Music
- Video.

Questions

☑ Test yourself

The following notes summarize this topic. The notes are incomplete because they have words missing. Using the words in the list below, copy out and complete the sentences A to J, underlining the words that you have inserted. Each word may be used more than once.

stored   user interface   system

customizable   menu user   interface

output   folders   errors

graphical user interface

A Software is the general name given to all the programs that can be run on a computer and there are two types: applications software and operating _____ software.

B The operating system software manages and controls the input and _____ devices attached to and under the control of the computer.

C Keeping track of the files _____ on the magnetic hard disk drives is another function of the operating system.

D An operating system also deals with any _____ that arise when other programs are being run.

E An _____ is where two things meet so a human–computer interface is where the human user and the computer meet.

F Making selections from a series of menus to accomplish a task is called a _____ _____ interface.

G The user interface that is very easy to use and uses windows, icons, menus and pointers is called a _____ _____ _____.

H All programs have a _____ _____ to allow the user and the computer to interact with each other.

I All user interfaces are _____ which means that the user is able to change them to suit themselves or their style of working.

J Files should always be put into _____ so that they can be quickly found when needed.

1 Tick **three** boxes to show which of the following tasks would be carried out in real time. *(3 marks)*

	Tick three boxes only
Traffic light control	☐
Marking of multiple-choice answer sheets	☐
Producing monthly credit card statements	☐
Booking of airline tickets	☐
Playing a fast action computer game	☐

2 When setting up a new ICT system, a suitable operating system has to be chosen.
   (a) Tick **three** boxes to show which of the following tasks would be carried out by an operating system. *(3 marks)*

	Tick three boxes only
Dealing with errors that occur when the user is working on tasks	☐
Producing a graph from a spreadsheet	☐
Accepting the input from a keyboard	☐
Copying files from one folder to another	☐
Spellchecking a document	☐

   (b) Many operating systems allow multitasking. Explain what is meant by multitasking. *(2 marks)*
   (c) Networking operating systems have to be multi-user.
   Explain what is meant by a multi-user operating system. *(2 marks)*

3 Which **three** tasks from the list below are carried out by all operating systems? *(3 marks)*
   A   Underlining text in a word-processing program
   B   Controlling peripheral devices
   C   Sorting data into alphabetical order
   D   Transferring data between memory and a disk
   E   Managing system security
   F   Changing the size of a picture

4 A person who is designing a new website needs to consider the user interface.
   (a) Write down **two** things they would need to consider when designing the user interface. *(2 marks)*
   (b) A menu interface is one type of user interface they could consider using.
   Give the name of a different type of user interface. *(1 mark)*

5 The way in which a user interacts with computer software is important because a good user interface makes software easy to use. Explain how the user makes choices in each of the following types of interface:
   (a) A graphical user interface. *(2 marks)*
   (b) A menu driven user interface. *(2 marks)*

6 Computer users are able to customize their user interfaces.
   (a) Explain clearly what the above statement means and give **two** examples of customization. *(3 marks)*
   (b) Give **two** examples of customization for use by students in a school who have impaired eyesight. *(2 marks)*

END-OF-TOPIC REVIEW

Exam support

Worked example

Graphical user interfaces (GUIs) are a feature of the software on most computers.

(a) Explain why a computer needs a user interface. *(2 marks)*

(b) Give **one** input device, other than a keyboard, that can be used with a graphical user interface. *(1 mark)*

(c) Give **four** features of a graphical user interface. *(4 marks)*

(d) (i) Give **one** other type of user interface. *(1 mark)*

   (ii) Give **two** benefits to an inexperienced user offered by a graphical user interface compared with this type of interface. *(2 marks)*

Student answer 1

(a) The user interface provides an interface between the computer and the user.

It allows the user to use the computer.

(b) Mouse

(c) Pull-down menus

Windows

Icons

Menus

(d) **(i)** Menu driven interface

   (ii) Menus only allow a few things to be done whereas with a GUI you can have lots of icons to click on.

▲ **Examiner's comment**

(a) This is a typical answer given by students who do not know the answer. They use the words in the question and put these in the answer. Neither of these answers is awarded a mark.

(b) This is a correct piece of hardware so one mark is awarded.

(c) Pull-down menus and menus are not distinctly different so only one mark can be given rather than two. The other answers are correct. Three marks are given.

(d) **(i)** This is a correct interface so one mark is given.

   (ii) This is only one benefit so only one mark is awarded. Students must always check that they have given the correct number of answers.

(6 marks out of 10)

Student answer 2

(a) The user interface is the point where the user and the computer meet. The user interface provides a way of the user interacting with the computer. For example, they can issue commands by clicking on menu items and icons.

(b) Touch screen

(c) Windows

Icons

Pointers

Menus

(d) (i) Windows

(ii) The icons in a GUI have small pictures that help a user understand what they do.

Graphical user interfaces are almost the norm so once a user has learnt one type of interface they will be able to use other ones easily.

◄ **Examiner's comment**

(a) There are three valid points made here so the maximum of two marks is given.

(b) A touch screen can be considered to be an input device (and also an output device) and they have become increasingly popular so this is a valid answer and one mark is awarded.

(c) Four correct features of a GUI have been given, so four marks are awarded.

(d) (i) Never give a brand name unless the question specifically asks for it. This means that Windows is not an acceptable answer so no marks for this answer.

(ii) There are two points made here and the argument about the GUI in the last point could be put forward about a menu driven interface. In this case the examiner has used their discretion and has given this student both the marks.

(9 marks out of 10)

Examiner's answers

(a) One mark for each of the following points to a maximum of two marks.

- Allows a user to communicate with the computer
- The way the computer interacts with the user
- It allows the user to make selections
- It provides a dialogue between the computer and the user

(b) One mark for one of the following:

- Mouse
- Touch pad
- Tracker ball
- Touch screen
  Etc.

(c) Any four from the following (one mark each):

- Windows
- Icons
- Menus/Pull-down menus
- Pointers
- Online help/Office assistants

(d) (i) One mark for one of the following:
- Menu driven interface
- Command line interface
- Voice driven interface

(ii) One mark each for two benefits such as:
- Standard look and feel
- Interfaces are similar so they are easier to learn and skills can be transferred
- More intuitive (users can usually figure out what they have to do)
- Use of icons with pictures makes it easy for users to work out what each button does

Summary mind map

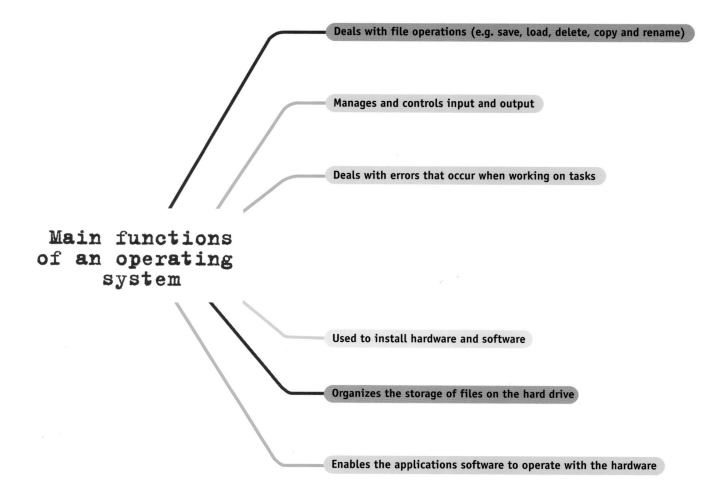

Deals with file operations (e.g. save, load, delete, copy and rename)

Manages and controls input and output

Deals with errors that occur when working on tasks

Main functions of an operating system

Used to install hardware and software

Organizes the storage of files on the hard drive

Enables the applications software to operate with the hardware

Applications software

The key concepts covered in this topic are:

- **Uses of applications software**
- **Generic features of software (appearing as reasonably common features in most software packages)**

Applications software is software that is capable of doing a specific job called an application. Software such as word-processing software, presentation software, desktop publishing software, etc., is not limited to doing one particular job and is therefore often called general purpose applications software.

In this topic you will be looking at applications software in general and how it is important to choose the best software for the job. For example, you could create a simple poster in word-processing software, but if you wanted an eye-catching one that used lots of features, then it would be better to produce it in desktop publishing (DTP) software.

Contents

Uses of applications software

▷ **About how to select and use software applications to meet needs and solve problems**

Applications software is software that is designed to carry out user-related tasks to solve problems. Much of the software you use on a day-to-day basis is general purpose software, which means it can be used for lots of different tasks rather than a single task.

In this section you will learn about the tasks that are suited for particular pieces of software.

How to select and use software applications to meet needs and solve problems

In order to select the right software you need to consider the requirements of the task. Generally the more complex the task is then the more likely you will need more specialist software. For example, a simple poster can easily be created in word-processing software but the graphic capabilities of the software are very limited. A better solution would be to use specialist DTP software.

Over the GCSE course you will be using a lot of different software and you will understand the strengths and weaknesses of each piece of software.

Word-processing software

Word-processing packages are used to produce documents containing text such as:

- letters
- reports
- memos
- essays.

Word-processing software is also used to prepare text for other packages such as DTP or web design software. The idea is that that the text is prepared and edited using the word-processing software and then saved and imported into the other package for further arrangement. Word-processing software is perfect for processing text but less good for creating posters, diagrams and complex newsletters.

Before starting to word-process a document you need to think about the layout of the page.

Once text has been entered, you can start thinking about adding structure to certain text and making some text stand out. This is called formatting text.

To add further structure to the document you can format blocks of text to make paragraphs, sections, etc.

KEY WORDS

Bullet point a block or paragraph of text that has a symbol placed in front to make the section of text stand out.

Footer text placed at the bottom of a page.

Header text placed at the top of a page.

Templates files that hold standardized document layouts. Templates hold the design of the document so that only the variable information needs to be added.

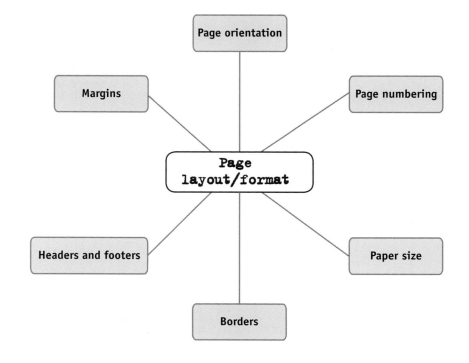

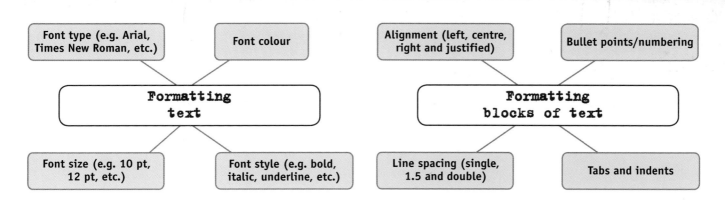

DTP software

Desktop publishing software, commonly called DTP software, is used to produce posters, brochures, magazines, newsletters, etc. It is ideal where the page design is quite complex and involves lots of graphics. For very simple documents it is possible to use word-processing software.

Spreadsheet software

Spreadsheet software is used to manipulate numbers and text arranged in cells. Formulae are used to relate one cell with other cells. Once a formula has been entered, then if one value of a cell, on which the formula is based, changes, then the formula will automatically perform the calculation with the new value.

Spreadsheets are ideal for:

- budgets
- cash flow forecasts
- accounts (e.g., profit and loss, end of year accounts, etc.)
- creating and using models

- performing statistical analysis on data
- producing graphs and charts from sets of data.

The basic functions of spreadsheet software are shown in the diagram below.

Database software

Database software is used where a store of data needs to be kept and where the information needs to be extracted from this store in lots of different ways.

Simple databases can be created using spreadsheet software but these have limited use. More complex and useful databases are created in specialist database software and these are called relational databases.

Web design software

You can create simple websites in lots of different software such as word-processing software. However, it is better to use specialist web design software because there are lots of effects you can use.

Presentation software

You will already be familiar with presentation software such as PowerPoint for producing slide presentations. Presentation software can also be used for:

- creating self-running presentations
- creating interactive presentations where the user can decide what to do next
- creating multimedia quizzes
- creating teaching material.

Proprietary and open source software

Open source software is software where the licence to use the software allows users to use, change and improve the software freely, if they so wish.

Proprietary software is software that is neither free nor open source. This means that the user pays for the software and is not free to alter it in any way. Most of the software you use is proprietary software.

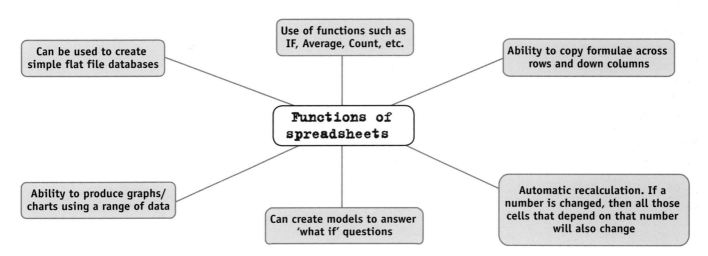

Uses of applications software *continued*

The advantages and disadvantages of proprietary software versus open source software

Here are the main advantages and disadvantages:

- Open source software is free, whereas you pay for proprietary software.
- A user can alter the program code legally for the open source software. The copyright restricts them from doing this with proprietary software.
- Proprietary software has a copyright owner who can control what can be done with the software. Open source software is open to the public and there is no control over how it is used.
- With proprietary software the software producer will often take steps to make it virtually impossible for a user to view the source code (i.e., the step-by-step program instructions).

Hosted applications

Most computers are connected to the Internet via fast and reliable broadband links that are immediately available and always on. Hosted applications are software applications where the software is hosted on servers connected to the Internet rather than on network servers or the individual computer hard drives. This means that to access and use the software you use the Internet.

The advantages and disadvantages of hosted applications

The advantages of hosted applications include:

- Reduced costs. It is not necessary to install and maintain the software, so there are reduced administration costs.
- Instantly available. You do not

need to download the software. You just log in and start using it.

- Lower risk. You can often access software freely for a certain period to see if you like it. You can also pay for the software using pay-as-you-go.
- Improved access. Anywhere you have access to the Internet, you can gain access to the software.
- Support. You do not have to download updates or new versions. The latest version and other older versions are available for you to choose.

The disadvantages of hosted applications include:

- May not have high speed access to the Internet. Some countries/ regions do not have the high speed Internet access that is

needed for hosted applications.

- Security. There are security issues when using the Internet with sensitive or personal data.
- May become expensive. Monthly subscriptions may rise and make the system expensive and it might be difficult to change to a different software provider.

Extension activity

Make a list of all the different types of applications software you use at school or college and produce lists of the tasks you have used them for.

Questions A

1 Which type of software, from the list, would be best used for the following tasks? *(7 marks)*

A	Database
B	Word-processing
C	Spreadsheet
D	Web design
E	DTP

(a) Creating a website.
(b) Creating a model showing the money coming into and going out of your bank account.
(c) Writing a letter to be posted.
(d) Creating bar charts to show the sales of goods in a sports shop.
(e) Adding up lots of columns of numbers.
(f) Producing a high quality glossy brochure.
(g) Storing the personal details of all the pupils in a school.

2 Which one of the following types of applications software is often used for creating financial models? *(1 mark)*

	Tick **one** box only
Desktop publishing	☐
Database	☐
Spreadsheet	☐

Generic features of software

▷ **About using generic features of software**

▷ **About entering and formatting text to maximize clarity of the material and improve its presentation**

You will now have experienced using a whole range of software from word-processing software to web design software. You may have noticed that this software contains many common features. For example, if as part of the task you have to enter text into the software, you expect to be able to change the font type and size. You will probably expect to be able to cut, copy and paste text. All these are features, that are common to most pieces of applications software, are called generic features of software. In this section you will be looking at these features.

Generic features of software

Most, but not all software has generic features. Generic features are those features of software that are not found in just one type of software but are common to most types of applications software. Most of these features are included as part of the software in order to help a user enter and format the text to maximize the clarity of the material and improve its presentation. In this section you will be looking

at those generic features of software that can be used to enter and format text in order to maximize clarity and enhance presentation.

Copy, cut and paste

To cut text or cells in a document or spreadsheet, select them (the selected cells will be highlighted) then right click on the mouse. A menu will appear with a number of options including the following:

- Cut
- Copy
- Paste.

If you click on Cut, the text or cells will now be placed in a temporary storage (called the clipboard) by the computer. You can now move the cursor to another part of your document or worksheet where you want the text or cells to be moved to. Right clicking on the position brings the menu up again where you can choose to paste the contents into position.

When we cut text or cells, they are taken out of the document or worksheet. Suppose we just wanted to use the same text or cells in a different document/worksheet without having to type them in. We can use Copy. Copy is similar to Cut, except that a *copy* of the text/cells is put onto the clipboard. The document from which the text/cells are copied remains unaltered.

Font type and font size

Changing the font type (e.g., Arial, Times New Roman, etc.) alters the appearance of the characters.

Font types are given names and you can change the font by selecting the text and then clicking on the correct part of the formatting toolbar. Notice also that there is a section for altering the font size (i.e., how big the characters appear).

Click here to alter the font size.

Click here to alter the font type (each font is given a name – in this case the font is called Times New Roman).

▲ Font type is the shape of the letters and can be chosen to suit the purpose of the document.

Font styles

Font styles include **bold** (text in heavy type), *italic* (text slanting to the right) and <u>underlining</u>. These can be used to highlight certain words or text in order to draw particular attention to them.

Font colour

The colour of text can be changed using the Font dialogue box, which is accessed by clicking on Format and then Font.

▲ The colour of text can be changed using the Font dialogue box.

Generic features of software *continued*

Drag and drop

Drag and drop means clicking on a virtual object such as a file, photograph, piece of clip art, etc., and dragging it into position. You can drag or drop an object onto a document or you can drag it into a folder or the recycle bin. Drag and drop is a quick way of moving objects.

Undo and redo

Undo is a feature of most software and it erases the last action taken. Redo is the opposite where the last action taken is re-applied. This is one of the most important features of software and most software is able to reverse a whole series of actions. Many people wish that life had an 'undo' button!

Find and replace

Find can be used to quickly find a certain word or phrase in a long document.

Find and replace can be used to search for all the occurrences of a certain word and replace them with a different word.

▲ Here 'find and replace' is looking for all the occurrences of 'email' and replacing them with 'e-mail'.

Zoom

Zoom is found in most software packages and can be used to display a document in more or less detail. This is usually done by altering the % view using the drop down menu.

`100%  ▾`

▲ Document size can be expressed as a percentage of the original size. By altering the percentage you can zoom in and out.

Some software has a small magnifying glass with either a + or − marked on it and when you click on it you either zoom in or zoom out.

▲ Zoom in and zoom out icons.

WordArt (or similar)

WordArt is decorative text that you can add to a document. You can create all sorts of text effects such as:

In some packages you can fit the text to certain shapes.

Wizards

Microsoft Office uses Wizards that help you through some of the more complex tasks. For example, you might want to perform a mail merge but you have forgotten the steps you have to take. The Wizard will take you through the steps guiding you through until you have completed the task.

Help

Everyone has been a beginner at using software at some time. It can be frustrating to know what you want to do but not be sure how to do it. This is where online help screens come in. Software packages usually have an online help facility where users can get help supplied by the package rather than have to look through manuals or user guides.

Print and print preview

Software nearly always has a print function so you can get a printout of your work on paper. To save printer and toner/ink most applications software has a print preview feature that is used to check how your work will appear on the page before printing. You should get into the habit of using print preview to save resources.

Page layout

It is very annoying if the headings are inconsistent and the font and font size are changed too often. Always think about what you want to achieve with your document and what will appeal to the readers.

When thinking about the page layout you will need to consider the following:

- position of common items
- page layout
- textual styles
- special features
- paragraph formats
- position of common items.

Page layout is also concerned with the arrangement of the following:

- margins
- headers and footers
- alignment
- page orientation (landscape and portrait)
- pagination
- paper size.

Margins

Margins mark the boundary of the text itself and therefore determine the amount of blank space left at the sides, top and bottom of the page. If you leave insufficient margins, the document will appear cluttered.

Headers and footers

Headers and footers are used to hold information that appears at the top of the page in the case of a header, and at the bottom of each page of the document in the case of a footer. Headers are placed in the top margin whilst footers are placed in the bottom. You can choose whether the text included in the header or footer is included on every page or just some of the pages.

Here are some types of information that is commonly put into headers and footers:

- page numbers
- today's date
- the title of the document
- a company logo (it can be a graphic image)
- the author's name
- the filename of the file that is used to hold the document.

Justifying (aligning) text

Justifying text means aligning (lining up) the text in some way:

- Align left (also called left justified) – this lines the text up with the left margin but leaves the right-hand side ragged. This alignment is the most common and is the one used by a word-processor unless we tell it to use another.
- Align right (also called right justified) – this lines the text up with the right margin but leaves the left-hand margin ragged.
- Centre – this lines text up with the centre of the page.
- Fully justified (also called justified) – this lines text up with both the right and left margins.

Orientation

There are two ways in which a page can be printed onto paper. With portrait orientation the height is greater than the width; with landscape orientation the page is turned sideways so that the width of the page is greater than its height. Portrait orientation is much more common and is used for most business documents such as letters, memos and reports; this book is portrait format. However, landscape format can be useful for charts, spreadsheets and notices.

▲ The Page Setup menu allows you to set the page orientation to portrait or landscape.

Page breaks

When you type a page of text/numbers into a document, as a page is filled the software inserts a page break and a new page is started. The software does this automatically. There is a problem with this. For example, you may find that a heading appears at the bottom of a page where the reader is least likely to look. It would be even worse if the heading appeared at the bottom of the page on its own with the text to which it refers over the page. It is therefore important during the proof reading process to look out for this and correct it. You can make the computer start a new page by inserting what is called a page break.

Page numbering

Pages in documents should always be numbered, as people need to refer to the content of the page by its number. Also if you have a load of unnumbered pages and you drop them, putting them back into order is a difficult task.

Templates

Creating documents from scratch takes time. You have to consider the design of the page as well as the content. Luckily templates help you with the design, leaving you to simply add your own content. A template is a blueprint for the text, graphics and formatting and it ensures that all documents of a particular type look the same. It is common for members of an organization to be given templates, one for each type of document, to ensure a common or corporate style. The template is an electronic file that holds the basic outline of the document. The user needs only to input the variable data, since formatting, font size, etc., will already be included. The main advantage of using templates is consistency of style, irrespective of author.

Most word-processing software has template facilities, so all you need do is 'fill in the blanks'. Each time you want a similar document, simply open the template, fill in the blanks, save the document (under a different name from that of the template) and then print it out.

Text/picture boxes

If you wanted to put some text that needs to stand out in the middle of a page then you can use a text box. Once the text box has been created you can add a border around it, or give it a colour background or shade the background.

If you want to create an effect like you see with newspapers where the text starts on one page and finishes on another, then you can put the text into two different text boxes and then link them.

Generic features of software *continued*

A simple text box

Once the text box has been created you can alter the text size and font. You can also make the text italic, bold, etc. You can then start to think about borders, etc.

Activity

Experimenting with background and text colours

Here is an activity to find out which background and text colours work best together.

Produce a text box, type in the text as shown in the box and alter the colours of the text and the background. Produce a table with the combinations of text and background along with a comment about the result for future reference.

This is a text box that has text of one colour and a background of another.

Obtaining, inserting, resizing, cropping and positioning images

When choosing or designing an image you need to consider the fitness for purpose. Certain images would be too shocking for children yet a shocking image may be needed to get the message across to adults. You will have seen such images in posters and adverts to stop people from drinking and driving. Always ask yourself if the image you intend to use is fit for purpose.

Is the image suitable for the purpose and will it be appropriate for the intended audience?

Obtaining images

When you research images you will often be using other people's images. It is important for you to understand the legislation (i.e. laws) that affects the way you can use other people's images.

There are many methods of obtaining images. For example, you can use:

- your own drawings (produced using software or created on paper and then scanned in)
- sketches (usually scanned in)
- photographs (usually created using a digital camera but could be scanned in from an old photograph)
- photographs on websites that you can copy and paste
- photographs in books, magazines, newspapers, etc.
- the clip art provided with Microsoft Office
- photographs in clip art collections on CD-ROM, the Internet, etc.

Inserting images

Images may be placed in a document such as DTP, word-processing, spreadsheet software, but in the case of web design software the images are usually linked to the document. Images may be inserted using copy/cut and paste or inserted by using Insert Picture.

Resizing images

Images usually need to be re-sized to fit the design of the document. Resizing can be done by clicking on the image and then using the handles (i.e., the small squares at the corners of the image) to alter the size.

Cropping

Cropping means only using part of an image. For example, you might just want a picture of a person's face rather than a picture of their whole body.

Positioning images

Images have to be moved into a suitable position and in some cases you have to work out how you want the text to move around the image. Images can usually be positioned by dragging them.

Manipulation of graphics

Once a graphic has been obtained, it may need adjusting in some way. Graphics software is available that allows you to alter (i.e., manipulate) images. Here are some of the ways that an image can be manipulated:

- It can be resized (i.e., made bigger or smaller).
- It can be rotated through a certain angle.
- It can be mirror imaged (i.e., like reflecting the image in a mirror).
- Part of the image can be cropped (this is just like cutting the part you want out of the picture).

AutoShapes

AutoShapes are shapes that are already stored by the software. You can select the shapes from the various menus and edit them (e.g., resize, rotate, reflect, coloured and combined to make more complex shapes). The AutoShapes can be seen on the Drawing toolbar and include the following:

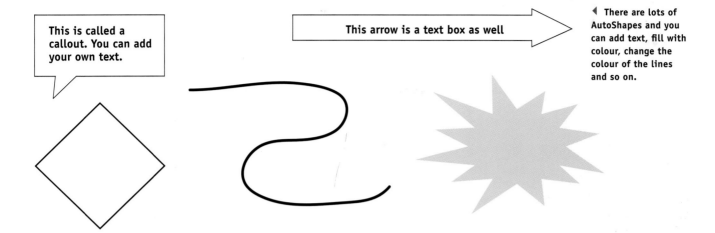

This is called a callout. You can add your own text.

This arrow is a text box as well

◀ There are lots of AutoShapes and you can add text, fill with colour, change the colour of the lines and so on.

- lines
- connectors
- basic shapes (e.g., squares, rectangles, triangles, etc.)
- block arrows
- flowchart symbols
- stars and banners.

You can turn any of the boxes used into text boxes, which means you can enter text inside the box. If you then apply a change to the box such as rotate, the text inside the box will also rotate.

Shading

Shading can be added to text to make it stand out and to images to make the image appear more realistic. Shading can also be added to backgrounds of tables.

Overlapping objects

An object is any piece of graphic, text, line, path, shape or fill that is present in an image. More than one object can be positioned on the canvas so that they overlap. The order the objects have been created determines how they appear.

◀ In this image two rectangles have been drawn but the pink vertical rectangle is in front of the other rectangle. The vertical rectangle is made slightly transparent so the colours combine.

Wrap text

If you enter text into a spreadsheet cell, the width of the cell will increase to fit in the text. You can instruct the software to wrap the text, which means that the cell width is kept constant and the text overflows automatically onto the next line. Text wrapping occurs in word-processing software where the margins offer a fixed width for the text.

	A	B	C	D
1	A spreadsheet to model the depreciation of a car's value			
2				
3	A spreadsheet to model the depreciation of a car's value			
4				

▲ In row 3 the text is wrapped.

Print screen

It is useful, when explaining to others how to use a piece of software or how you used software to solve a problem, to be able to produce a copy of what appears on the screen. The easiest way to produce a copy of the screen is by producing a screenshot. To produce a screenshot, first display the screen you want to capture and then: keeping the 'Alt' key on the keyboard

pressed down, press the 'Prt Scr' key on the keyboard. Nothing visible happens but a copy of the screen is pasted to the clipboard. You can then paste the image into a document. Print screen produces a copy of the current screen being displayed. If a dialogue box has been opened then when the print screen is performed, only the dialogue box will be pasted to the clipboard.

You can edit this diagram and add arrows and text boxes to explain things.

Activity

Fitness of images for purpose

There are lots of reasons why you may not be able to use an image in a document you are preparing. With some simple editing it might still be possible to use the image.

Write down a list of the things that can be wrong in an image. You should assume that the content of the image is suitable.

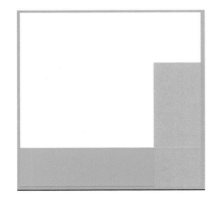

◀ Desktop printer.

Generic features of software *continued*

Questions B

1 (a) A designer says that it is important that any images you produce are 'fit for purpose'. Explain what 'fit for purpose' means. *(2 marks)*

   (b) Give **two** ways in which an image might not be 'fit for purpose'. *(2 marks)*

2 One generic feature common to most applications software is text formatting.

   (a) Give **two** examples of text formatting. *(2 marks)*

   (b) A document can be made more attractive by putting artwork (pictures, clip art, photographs, etc.) into it. Describe **two** ways in which artwork can be put into a document. *(2 marks)*

3 Many pieces of software use templates to allow the user to get things done in less time.

   (a) Explain what is meant by a template. *(2 marks)*

   (b) Give the name of a piece of software you have used where the use of the template made things easier for you. *(1 mark)*

Extension activity

Using AutoShapes, images and text boxes to create diagrams

For this activity you are required to produce a diagram that can be included in a book about ICT like this one. This diagram is to be produced using word-processing software.

The purpose of the diagram is to illustrate and explain the different ways of obtaining images for inclusion in a document.

You must use the following in your diagram:

- **AutoShapes** (for the production of boxes, arrows, etc.)
- **Text boxes** (you can turn boxes created using AutoShapes into text boxes)
- **Images** (you can use images to show places where you can get images from)

Your work needs to be printed out on A4-sized paper.

Be sensible in your choice of colour on your diagram.

Extension activity

Using print screen

Produce a screenshot of the screen in Microsoft Excel by pressing down the Alt key and keeping it down, press the Prt Scrn key. Nothing happens because the screenshot is stored in the clipboard. Now load the word-processing software, create a new document and then go to Edit and then Paste. The picture of the screen will now appear in the document.

Mark on your diagram (you can do this by hand or by using the drawing tools in the word-processor) the following:

(a) The active cell (sometimes called the cell pointer)

(b) The title bar

(c) The close button

(d) The minimize button

(e) The restore/maximize button

(f) A scroll bar

(g) The formatting toolbar

(h) The column headings

(i) The row headings

END-OF-TOPIC REVIEW

Questions

✔ Test yourself

The following notes summarize this topic. The notes are incomplete because they have words missing. Using the words in the list below, copy out and complete the sentences A to K, underlining the words that you have inserted. Each word may be used more than once.

copy and paste   font style   undo

font type   footers   drag and drop

print preview   WordArt   search and replace

page numbers   page breaks

A _____ _____ _____ copies text and then puts it into a different place in the same document or a completely different document.

B _____ _____ is the shape of the text. Examples include Times New Roman and Arial.

C _____ _____ includes bold, italics and underline.

D _____ _____ _____ means clicking on a virtual object such as a file, photograph, piece of clip art, etc., and dragging it into position.

E Most software has _____ which allows you to reverse an action.

F _____ _____ _____ is handy if you want to find all the occurrences of a certain word and replace them with a different word.

G _____ is decorative text that you can add to a document.

H Work should always be checked carefully before printing and _____ _____ allows you to see how the document looks when it is printed.

I Headers and _____ are used to hold information that appears at the top and the bottom of the page.

J _____ _____ determine where one page ends and a new page starts.

K Applications software can insert _____ _____ on multi-page documents.

Questions *continued*

Examination style questions

1 Some types of applications software are more suitable than others for carrying out a task.

(a) Here is a list of applications software. Choose the letter of the software that is best used for carrying out the task in the table. *(5 marks)*

A   Web design
B   Database
C   Presentation
D   Graphics

Task	Letter
Keeping an organized store of data about pupils in a school	
For developing an e-commerce site	
For creating a logo for a new business	
For editing a digital photograph	
To help explain the benefits of a new product to a group of sales staff in a room	

(b) A company uses a computer and software to model the amount of money coming into and going out of the business. A screenshot of this model is shown below.
Which type of applications software has been used to produce this model? *(1 mark)*

2 It is always best to choose the most suitable software for the job when carrying out a task. Match the best type of applications software A, B, C, D or E to carry out the tasks in the table below. *(4 marks)*

A   Database
B   DTP
C   Word-processing
D   Spreadsheet
E   Web design

Task	Letter
Producing a personal website	
Typing in, formatting and checking the text for a letter	
Producing a school magazine with lots of graphics and design elements	
A large collection of patient records to be typed in and kept for easy access in a medical practice	

3 By giving a suitable example, explain how each of these generic features of applications software could be used. *(6 marks)*

(a) Find and replace
(b) Drag and drop
(c) Orientation (portrait and landscape)

	A	B	C	D	E	F	G	H
1	**Cash Flow Forecast for ABC Products**							
2			Jan	Feb	Mar	Apr	May	June
3	Income							
4		Bank balance from last month	£1,000	£831	£794	£728	£361	£903
5		Sales	£720	£900	£1,115	£1,200	£2,010	£2,500
6		**Total Income**	£1,720	£1,731	£1,909	£1,928	£2,371	£3,403
7								
8	Expenditure							
9		Supplies of product	£240	£289	£304	£576	£476	£427
10		Postage	£48	£29	£34	£123	£78	£57
11		Packing	£25	£38	£51	£54	£65	£100
12		Fees	£12	£15	£21	£46	£76	£69
13		Electricity	£24	£26	£31	£28	£33	£32
14		Rent	£140	£140	£140	£140	£140	£140
15		Wages	£400	£400	£600	£600	£600	£600
16		**Total Expenditure**	£889	£937	£1,181	£1,567	£1,468	£1,425
17								
18								
19		**End of month balance**	£831	£794	£728	£361	£903	£1,978

END-OF-TOPIC REVIEW

Exam support

Worked example

Applications software has many generic features, such as copy and paste, and this helps users learn new software.

(a) Explain what is meant by applications software. *(2 marks)*

(b) Which **two** of the following are generic features you would find in lots of different applications software? *(2 marks)*

Tick **two** boxes only

The ability to change font type, size and style	☐
The ability to perform a mail merge	☐
The ability to undo and redo an action taken	☐
Being able to copy formulae across a row or down a column	☐
The ability to use functions	☐
The ability to remove red eye from a digital photograph	☐

(c) Many people use templates.

(i) Explain what is meant by a template. *(1 mark)*

(ii) Describe, by giving a suitable example, how a template is used. *(1 mark)*

(iii) Give **one** advantage in using a template to complete a task. *(1 mark)*

Student answer 1

(a) Applications software is software that you use to complete an application.

There are lots of different applications you can do using applications software.

(b)

Tick **two** boxes only

The ability to change font type, size and style	☑
The ability to perform a mail merge	☐
The ability to undo and redo an action taken	☐
Being able to copy formulae across a row or down a column	☑
The ability to use functions	☐
The ability to remove red eye from a digital photograph	☐

(c) (i) It is a grid into which you put your data so it is nice and neat.

(ii) You make it and then it is ready to put data in. You add your own data as only the structure is provided.

(iii) It is quicker.

◀ Examiner's comment

(a) This is the sort of answer given by lots of students who make up an explanation using the words given in the question. None of this answer is worth marks.

(b) The ability to change font type, size and style is a generic feature of software but the copying of formulae is not a generic feature as it mainly applies to spreadsheet software. One mark is given for the correct answer.

(c) (i) This sounds like they are describing a table rather than a template so no marks for this.

(ii) This sounds like they are still describing a table so no marks again.

(iii) This is true but this could be the answer to any advantage questions in ICT. You should always say 'in what way is it quicker'. No marks are given for this answer.

(1 mark out of 7)

END-OF-TOPIC REVIEW

Exam support *continued*

Student answer 2

(a) Applications software is software that is designed to do a particular job. For example, word-processing, spreadsheet, web design software, etc., are all examples of applications software.

(b)

	Tick **two** boxes only
The ability to change font type, size and style	☑
The ability to perform a mail merge	☐
The ability to undo and redo an action taken	☑
Being able to copy formulae across a row or down a column	☐
The ability to use functions	☐
The ability to remove red eye from a digital photograph	☐

(c) (i) A template is a framework that holds a standard document layout. All the formatting such as font types, font sizes and items such as graphics, text, links, etc., have their positions marked. You then only have to add your own content.

(ii) The template is used to supply the structure and you only have to enter the content and the document will look professional.

(iii) It is much faster to use a template as you do not have to worry about the design as this is already done. You can then concentrate on adding the content.

◀ Examiner's comment

(a) This is a good answer with a correct definition and some examples to clarify. Full marks for this answer.

(b) Both answers are correct, so two marks here.

(c) (i) This is a clear explanation of what a template is so one mark is given.

(ii) Here the student has made it clear that the structure is provided and the user only has to add their variable content. One mark is given.

(iii) Notice that, unlike the last student, this student has qualified their 'faster' answer by giving a clear reason why this is an advantage. Another mark is given here.

(7 marks out of 7)

Examiner's answers

(a) One mark for a definition similar to the following and another mark for further detail or an explanation.

Applications software is software that is capable of doing a specific job called an application (1). Applications software includes word-processing software, database software, DTP software, etc. (1).

(b) One mark each for the two correct answers as shown here:

	Tick **two** boxes only
The ability to change font type, size and style	☑
The ability to perform a mail merge	☐
The ability to undo and redo an action taken	☑
Being able to copy formulae across a row or down a column	☐
The ability to use functions	☐
The ability to remove red eye from a digital photograph	☐

(c) (i) One mark for an answer similar to the following:

A template is an electronic file that holds the basic outline of the document.

(ii) One mark for an answer similar to the following:

The user needs only to input the variable data, since formatting, font size, etc., will already be included.

(iii) One mark for an answer similar to the following:

Less time consuming as the user does not need to worry about the layout as this is determined by the template.

Summary mind maps

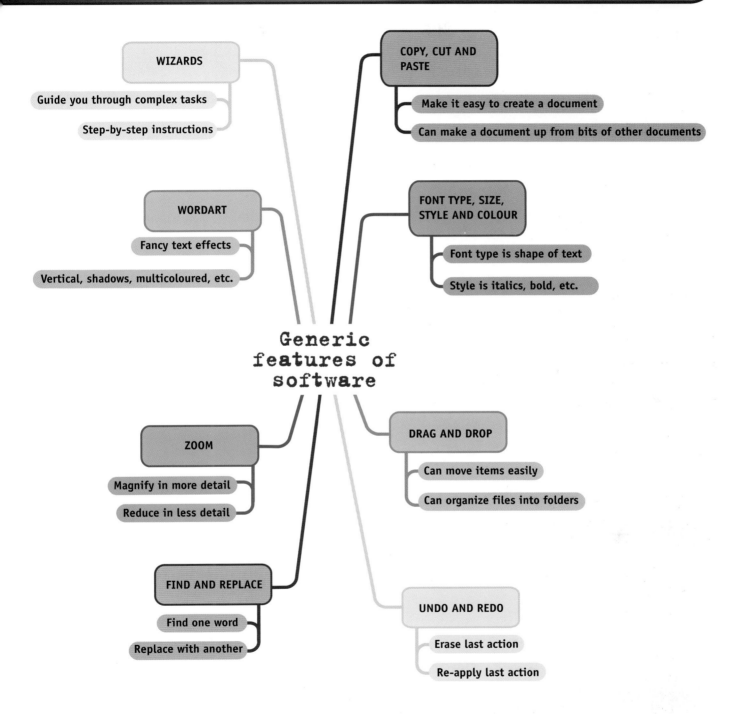

WIZARDS

Guide you through complex tasks

Step-by-step instructions

COPY, CUT AND PASTE

Make it easy to create a document

Can make a document up from bits of other documents

WORDART

Fancy text effects

Vertical, shadows, multicoloured, etc.

FONT TYPE, SIZE, STYLE AND COLOUR

Font type is shape of text

Style is italics, bold, etc.

Generic features of software

ZOOM

Magnify in more detail

Reduce in less detail

DRAG AND DROP

Can move items easily

Can organize files into folders

FIND AND REPLACE

Find one word

Replace with another

UNDO AND REDO

Erase last action

Re-apply last action

Summary mind maps *continued*

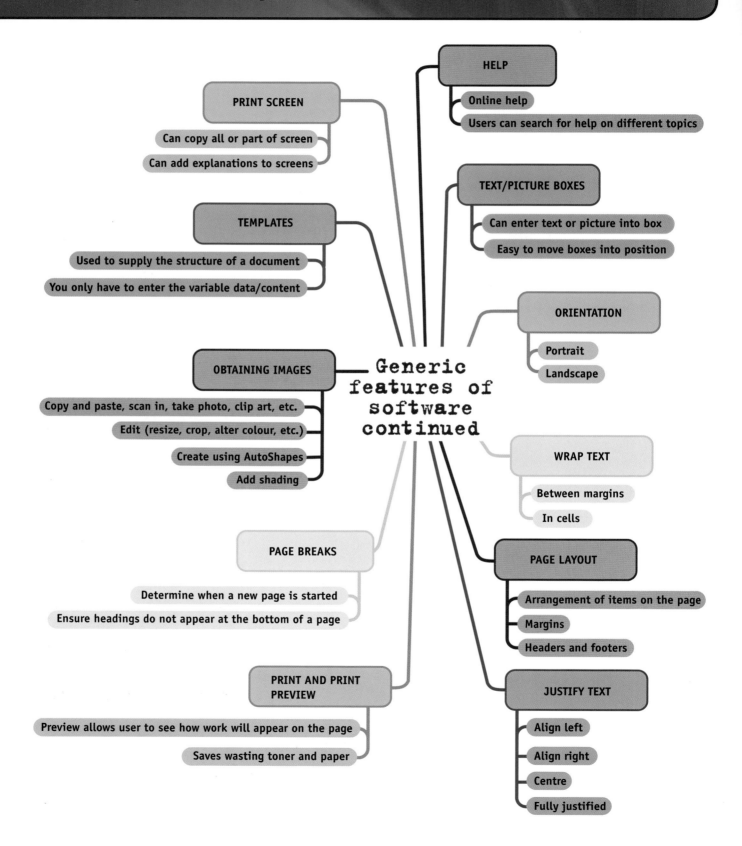

HELP
- Online help
- Users can search for help on different topics

PRINT SCREEN
- Can copy all or part of screen
- Can add explanations to screens

TEXT/PICTURE BOXES
- Can enter text or picture into box
- Easy to move boxes into position

TEMPLATES
- Used to supply the structure of a document
- You only have to enter the variable data/content

ORIENTATION
- Portrait
- Landscape

Generic features of software continued

OBTAINING IMAGES
- Copy and paste, scan in, take photo, clip art, etc.
- Edit (resize, crop, alter colour, etc.)
- Create using AutoShapes
- Add shading

WRAP TEXT
- Between margins
- In cells

PAGE BREAKS
- Determine when a new page is started
- Ensure headings do not appear at the bottom of a page

PAGE LAYOUT
- Arrangement of items on the page
- Margins
- Headers and footers

PRINT AND PRINT PREVIEW
- Preview allows user to see how work will appear on the page
- Saves wasting toner and paper

JUSTIFY TEXT
- Align left
- Align right
- Centre
- Fully justified

Word-processing, DTP, web design and other presentation software

The key concepts covered in this topic are:

- **Specific features of and differences between word-processing and DTP**

- **Using features of different software packages to organize and present information**

- **Presentation software**

- **Web design software**

- **Software for audio, DVD and video players**

- **Podcasts**

In the last topic you looked at the generic features of software. If you remember, these were those features of software that could be found in many different types of application software. In this topic you will be looking at the common features that are found in word-processing, DTP and other presentation software. These features are used to enter, organize, develop, refine and format information. You will have come across a few of these features already in the previous topic as some are present in most application software.

Contents

Features of and differences between word-processing and DTP

You will find out

▷ **About specific features of and differences between word-processing and DTP**

In the last topic you came across a lot of the generic features of software. In this section you will be looking at the features that are common to word-processing, DTP and presentation software.

Specific features common to word-processing and DTP software

Here are some of the common features found in word-processing, DTP and other presentation software to enter, organize, develop and format information.

Edit text – all word-processing, DTP and presentation software allows you to enter text and then go back and edit it. Editing text can include changing a sentence to make it clearer, formatting the text to make the headings stand out, correcting any mistakes, etc.

Auto wrap – this is the way the software automatically allows the text to flow and start new lines.

Lists – lists are often used to make points and these points can be numbered automatically.

Indentation – this is the gap left before the first word starts in a paragraph. This can be set automatically by the software.

Tabs – the Tab key on your keyboard is the one with two arrows pointing in different directions on it. If you press it, it moves the cursor to a new position to allow the entry of text. The place where the cursor moves to when the Tab key is pressed depends on the tab stops. There are default settings for the tab stops (usually every half inch) but you can also alter them using this screen.

▲ Setting the tabs.

Paragraphs – there are several ways you can mark paragraphs in a document. For example, you can indent the first letter and leave a blank line between paragraphs. This can all be set in the Format Paragraphs section of the software.

▲ Indentation can be altered in the Paragraph settings.

Bullets – are useful to draw the reader's attention to a list of points you would like to make. Rather than just write an ordinary list, you can put a bullet point (a dot, arrow, diamond, square or even a small picture) at the start of the point. The text for your points is then indented a small amount from the bullet.

KEY WORDS

Bullet point a block or paragraph of text that has a symbol placed in front to make the section of text stand out.

Footer text placed at the bottom of a page.

Header text placed at the top of a page.

Templates files that hold standardized document layouts. Templates hold the design of the document so that only the variable information needs to be added.

▲ Here is the general format for a bulleted list.

▲ There are lots of different bullets to choose from.

Headings and subheadings – these are best decided before you start a document.

Numbering and sub-numbering – these add structure to a document. As well as numbering each heading, you can number the subheading.

▲ This shows some numbering and sub-numbering you can use.

Borders – can be used to add more emphasis to a word, section of text, paragraph or table. A border can be just a line or you can have a picture border such as a row of Christmas trees around the edge of a page. If you look at the selection of clip art, then it usually includes a good selection of picture borders.

Page and line breaks – page breaks are where one page finishes and another starts. Line breaks are where the return is pressed so that a new line starts.

Line spacing – determines the amount of white space between the lines of text. Normally single line spacing is used but sometimes, when draft copies of documents are produced, it is useful to print them using one and a half or even double line spacing so that the readers can insert their comments in the white space between the lines.

Columns – you can format text into newspaper-style columns and you can choose how many columns are used. You can also control the way the text flows from one column to another.

Sections/chapters – the software can help you organize this. You can select an existing template or create your own. This means that the structure will be the same for each section or chapter. You can then just worry about the content.

Create and format tables – tables are made up of rows and columns that can be filled with text. Tables are used to organize and present information. They may also be used to align numbers in columns and once this is done you can perform calculations on them. There are many different ways of creating a table and one way in Word is to use the Table menu.

To make creating tables easy there are set formats already created and you can just select the table format that suits your needs.

This is the heading and you can see what happens if you type in too much			

▲ The Insert Table dialogue box is used to insert a table in a document. Notice that you can select the number of rows and columns in the table.

▲ You can select and see all the pre-stored table formats.

Merge and split table cells – if you create a table and then want to type in a heading in the first cell, this is what happens:

Features of and differences between word-processing and DTP *continued*

The text is wrapped in order to keep the width of the cell the same. This is not what you want to happen with a heading, so it is necessary to merge cells. When this is done the heading fits in like this:

This is the heading when the cells have been merged to fit the heading				

It is also possible to split cells like this				

Spelling and grammar checkers
– these have their limitations. Spellchecking is a facility offered by word-processing, DTP and presentation packages. They check that the words in the document are in the dictionary but not whether the words are correct for the context. Therefore it would not detect 'care' typed instead of 'core' or 'which' typed instead of 'witch' since neither is spelt incorrectly. If a word is not in the dictionary, it will be marked as incorrectly spelt. When a spelling mistake is recognized, the spellchecker will suggest possible corrections.

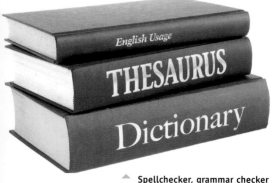

▲ Spellchecker, grammar checker and thesaurus are all provided with word-processing software.

Grammar checkers are used to check the grammar of a document against set rules, although they do not check the meaning. Mistakes, such as the subject and verb disagreeing, too long sentences or full stops not followed by capital letters will be detected; however, they do have their limitations due to the complexity of the English language.

Despite the use of spelling and grammar checkers there may still be mistakes, so there is no substitute for slowly proof reading a document.

Word count – is accessed from the Tools menu. Often when you write an essay, article or advert, there is a limit on the number of words you can write. By using word count you can get the software to count the number of words you have produced.

Grouping, ungrouping and layering
– when you make a drawing out of separate components such as lines, circles, rectangles, etc., you can group them together so that you can work on the whole drawing as a single object. If you want to work on part of the drawing, you will have to ungroup it.

Layering is the concept of working on diagrams in layers. Part of the diagram is drawn on a layer and the layers are combined to form the complete picture.

The differences between word-processing and DTP

The distinction between word-processing and desktop publishing is blurred because there are many desktop publishing features in word-processing software. Bringing lots of different files together to form a document is the main feature of a specialist desktop publishing package. In this section we will cover features that are either features of word-processing software or desktop publishing software.

▲ Magazines usually have a complex page design and need to be produced using DTP rather than word-processing software.

Word-processing and DTP

If the home user needs to produce a simple document such as an advertisement or a simple newsletter, they will probably decide to use the software that they are most familiar with. This is likely to be word-processing software, because they already understand most of it. Word-processing software does have many features that you would also find in DTP software such as:

- newspaper/magazine-type columns
- the ability to add vertical lines between newspaper-type columns
- the ability to create an index
- the use of templates.

Here are some of the main advantages in using DTP rather than word-processing software. DTP software is more suitable when:

- the page design is complex (as word-processing software would not cope with this)
- there are lots of images, as DTP is good at integrating files that have been created using other software
- a design uses lots of frames, which contain text and graphics that can be moved around the page and positioned more accurately than with word-processing software
- the file can be sent straight to a professional printer for the job to be professionally printed.

Simple newspaper columns can be produced in both word-processing and DTP software.

Questions A

1 (a) A spellchecker can sometimes highlight words that are correctly spelt. Tick **two** boxes that give sensible reasons why a word that is correctly spelt can still be highlighted as incorrectly spelt by the spellchecker. *(2 marks)*

Tick two boxes only

- The word might be a specialist term that is not in the dictionary ☐
- The word might be used in the wrong context ☐
- The spell checker might be set to American spellings ☐
- The spellchecker will only check easy spellings ☐
- The spellchecker can only check short words ☐

(b) Tick **one** box to show another feature of word-processing software that would highlight mistakes in text. *(1 mark)*

Tick one box only

- Check digit ☐
- Grammar check ☐
- Range check ☐
- Mail merge ☐

2 Word-processing software and DTP software can often be used to produce the same document.
  (a) What is meant by DTP? *(1 mark)*
  (b) Give **two** differences between DTP software and word-processing software. *(2 marks)*

3 Text is often formatted to make it clearer and to enhance the presentation of a document.
  (a) Describe **two** ways in which text can be formatted. *(2 marks)*
  (b) Spellcheckers are used to check the spelling in documents. Give **two** limitations of spellcheckers. *(2 marks)*

Extension activity

Investigate both word-processing and DTP software and write a list of the tasks you would typically perform using each piece of software.

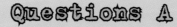

131

Using features of different software packages and presentation software

You will find out

▷ **About using features of different software packages to organize and present information**

▷ **About using presentation software**

You have already seen some of the features that are common to word-processing and DTP software. When you have both pieces of software and have the skills to use either you need to think hard about which piece of software to choose. This section will guide you through those particular pieces of software that you might consider using.

In this section you will also be looking at presentation software and some of the features it has and how it can be used to create multimedia products.

It is important to choose the best software and also choose the features of the software that can help you accomplish what you are doing. In this section you will be looking at the types of document and the features of the software you could use.

Using features of different software packages

Letters

Letters are best produced using word-processing software. Here are some of the features you can use:

- Mail merge – if you want to produce lots of individualized letters to different people.
- Templates – these are useful as you do not need to worry about the structure of the letter each time.
- Alignment/justification – used to position items.
- Spelling and grammar – to check your work in addition to carefully proof reading it.
- Paragraphs and indentation – to block certain text.

Memos

Memos are used to solve problems. They have a simple design and are best created using word-processing software. They solve problems by informing the reader about new information such as the release of a new product or price increase, or they persuade the reader to take an action such as attend a meeting or reduce the amount of paper used or keep the area around the photocopier tidier. Here are some of the features you can use:

- Templates – there are many templates already available in the word-processing software.
- Bullet points/lists – help you list the items that need to be brought to people's attention.

Essays

Essays are important because they are usually marked and are best created using word-processing software.

Here are some of the features you can use:

- Spelling and grammar – to check your work in addition to carefully proof reading it.
- Paragraphs and indentation – to block certain text.
- Headers and footers – title, author, date, page number and other information can be added automatically on each page.
- Word count – so that you do not go over the word limit.
- Line spacing – the tutor might ask for double spacing so they have room to mark your work and write in their comments.

Reports

Reports contain feedback from a 'finding out' exercise. For instance, a manager might ask you to look at the buildings and office equipment to make sure that your company is complying with the Health and Safety at Work Act. After completing your research you would provide your boss with a summary of the main points arising from your investigation in a document called a report.

Reports usually contain text with just a few diagrams or photographs and are best created using word-processing software. Here are some of the features you can use:

- Page breaks – so that headings are not at the bottom of a page.

- Headings and subheadings – so the report is structured and information can easily be found on the page.
- Bullets – list the important points.
- Spellchecking and grammar checking.

Posters

Simple posters can be created using word-processing software but the features of DTP make it better for more complex and interesting designs. Here are some of the features you can use:

- Grouping/layering – to manipulate images on the page.
- Columns – to position content on the page.
- Inserting images – these can be created in other packages such as graphics packages.

Leaflets and flyers

These could be prepared using word-processing software but DTP would be better as there are templates that you can use for leaflets that are folded in a variety of ways. Here are some of the features you can use:

- Inserting images.
- Spellchecking and grammar checking.
- Templates – specifically for leaflets.
- Columns – can use newspaper style columns which allow the text to flow from one column to another.

Brochures, catalogues and magazines

DTP software is essential for brochures, catalogues and magazines because DTP has a greater number of features that can be used to produce an interesting page layout. Here are some of the features you can use:

- Columns.
- Inserting images.
- Spell checking and grammar checking.
- Templates – to make sure that the design is consistent from one page to the next.

Business cards

Business cards can be produced in DTP software as there are many templates already created, which will save time.

You can produce business cards using word-processing software. Once the design of the card has been sorted, the variable information on the cards (e.g., name of the person, position in the organization) can be printed on each card using mail merge.

Webpages

Webpages are best created using web design software, although simple webpages can be created using word-processing and other types of software. More information on web design is included later in this topic.

Presentation software

You will already have used presentation software and this section looks at just some of the many features it has.

Colour schemes

You can create your own colour scheme for background, bullets, diagrams, etc., but it is easier to choose one already created. You do not have to waste time seeing which colours work well together.

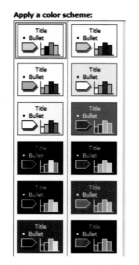

Some of the many colour schemes available.

Layouts

Layouts are designs of the items such as text and graphics on the slide.

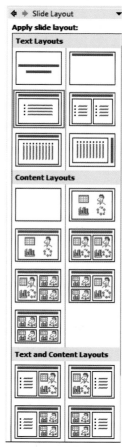

It is easy to choose one of the standard layouts.

Insert slide

Sometimes you need to insert a slide between two existing slides and you can do this using Insert Slide.

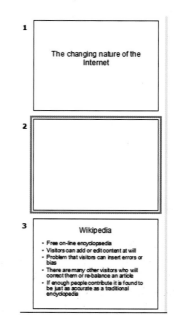

Here a new slide has been inserted between two existing slides.

133

Using features of different software packages and presentation software *continued*

Enter and edit slide content

Variable data such as text and graphics can be entered via the keyboard, copied and pasted from other documents, copied and pasted from websites and so on. Once the material has been entered it can be edited.

Navigation

Navigation is the way provided by the software for a user to choose which slide they want to view next. Remember that it is possible for a presentation to be interactive just like a website.

Hyperlinks

A hyperlink is an icon, graphic, or word on a document (slide or webpage) that, when clicked with the mouse, opens another slide or webpage.

Hotspots

As well as using text for hyperlinks, you can create images that contain links. Images containing links are called graphical hyperlinks, although you will often hear them

referred to as hotspots. You can create your own buttons and turn them into hotspots or you can use an image. It is important that you tell the user that the image is a hotspot. Sometimes you want to have an image that contains several hotspots. An example of this could be a map where the towns or main tourist areas on the map are the hotspots. When a user moves over a town or area, the cursor changes to a hand indicating a hotspot and when they click on it, they are taken to a different page containing information on that town or area.

Buttons

Buttons, called action buttons, can be added to slides to help a user navigate the slides.

▲ Backward, forward, beginning and end buttons can be added to slides so that the slides can be made interactive.

Slide transitions and timings

The movement from one slide to another is called a slide transition. To make your presentation more interesting you can:

- alter the way the slide appears on the screen
- alter the speed at which the slide appears
- get the computer to make a sound during the transition.

When a slide presentation is self-running it is important to leave enough time for your audience to read what is on each slide. Using the software, you can alter the timings for each slide.

Video and sound

If a picture paints a thousand words then video probably paints a whole book. There is sound and movement and you can add so much more interest than simply writing about the same thing or looking at a still picture. There are two main ways of obtaining video for use in presentations and websites:

- By creating the video yourself using a digital video recorder.
- By using video created by someone else.

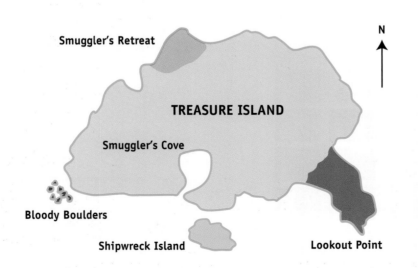

▲ This is graphic on a slide where there are several hotspots (i.e., the different coloured areas). When a user clicks on one of these areas they are taken to different slide about that area.

▲ Many mobile phones can be used to take short video clips.

You can use a search engine such as Yahoo to search for video in a similar way to the way you search for images. There are sites such as YouTube that are huge sources of video and it is possible to link to these sites from websites and presentations.

Sound effects

Most people think of clip art sites as just containing ready-made images but many of them contain sounds as well. Sounds and music can liven up a multimedia product but they need to be used with care as they can detract from the message or content being delivered.

As well as clip art libraries, you can use the following sites as sources of sound files:

- Sound files from the movies: http://www.moviesoundscentral.com/
- One of the best sound sites where you can search for sound effects is at: http://www.findsounds.com/

Animation

Animation involves getting some of the content that makes up the slides to move. The simplest way of including animation is to use animation provided by the presentation software. This allows you to select certain animations for the way the material, such as headings and bullet points, is added to a slide.

Animation is classified as follows:

- subtle
- moderate
- exciting.

Another way of including animation would be to include clip art that is animated or to produce a Flash animation and include it on the slide.

Print handouts

When presentations are given to an audience by a speaker it is usual for the speaker to give out handouts of the slides to the audience. This enables them to take notes and refer to the material in the future.

There are several different printing formats for slides:

- You can have 1, 2, 3, 4, 6 or 9 slides on each page.
- You can print an outline view that lists what is on each slide in the presentation.

▲ Here three slides are printed on each page and lines are left for the audience to add their own handwritten notes.

Multimedia presentations

As well as for making presentations to a group you can also use presentation software to create multimedia products that people can use on their own. For example, you can use presentation software to create information points where a user is able to determine their own path through the slides of information. In other words you can use links and action buttons so the user can choose what they see next. Presentation software can also be used to create quizzes. Presentations can be made much more interesting by using animation, video, slide transitions and other techniques such as interactivity.

KEY WORD

Multimedia making use of many media such as text, image, sound, animation and video.

© 2004 by Randy Glasbergen.
www.glasbergen.com

"I think I've put together the perfect presentation that's guaranteed to hold everyone's attention from start to finish...all 17 seconds of it!"

135

Using features of different software packages and presentation software *continued*

Questions B

1 Many presentations make use of multimedia features.
  (a) Explain what is meant by multimedia. *(1 mark)*
  (b) Explain why adding multimedia features can improve many presentations. *(2 marks)*

2 A PowerPoint presentation can make use of multimedia. Apart from text, write down **three** different multimedia effects that a presentation can have. *(3 marks)*

3 A business creates a presentation to advertise its products. The presentation allows users to decide which slides of the presentation they want to look at by making use of hyperlinks.
  (a) Describe what is meant by a hyperlink. *(1 mark)*
  (b) Hotspots can be used as hyperlinks. Explain what is meant by a hotspot. *(1 mark)*

4 The creator of a presentation for children aimed at helping them learn their times tables wants to make it interesting for them. They decide to use slide transitions and animation to help.
  (a) Explain what is meant by a slide transition. *(1 mark)*
  (b) Explain what is meant by an animation. *(1 mark)*

Extension activity

It is important to know where to look for multimedia content when you create multimedia products such as presentations and websites. For this extension activity you have to use the Internet to find three different sites where the following resources can be found:

- Images (still and moving)
- Sounds
- Video.

Either write down the web addresses for future reference, bookmark the pages, or add them to your favourites.

EXAM TIPS

Always be guided by the number of marks in the mark schemes. You need to think in terms of marks when you are writing the sentences for your answer. If a sentence does not make a point, then do not write it, as it simply wastes time (as well as space on the answer paper).

Avoid the use of slang in answers. Remember to use the correct terminology where appropriate. For example, rather than say 'you get music off the Internet' it would be better to say that music can be 'downloaded off the Internet'.

When answering questions about topics you know lots about, such as MP3 files and portable music players, it is wrong to make assumptions and produce answers as if the examiner knows what you are talking about.

Extension activity

You have produced some original work such as music, photographs, graphics, etc., on a website. This work took you a long time to produce and you hope to be able to sell some of the work to others.

Present a written argument to explain to others why they should not copy your work without your permission or without paying for it.

Web design software, software for audio, DVD and video players, and podcasts

In order to be able to create websites it is necessary to understand the components of websites such as links. You can then use the tools and techniques of web design software to create the components.

In this section you will also cover the software needed to play audio, DVD and video on websites and also the software used for the production and playing of podcasts.

Web design software

Master pages/templates

Master pages/templates provide a quick way of creating webpages. They supply the structure for the website and the navigation that is used to move around the site. They act as a framework for the website and all the developer has to do is fill in their own content.

They are ideal for people who need to develop websites quickly and have no design or website development skills.

Hyperlinks

Hyperlinks allow you to jump from one part of a website to another or even to a completely different website. Links are fundamental to the Internet but they can be used with any multimedia product such as presentations, as you will see in the next topic.

There are two types of hyperlink:

- Hypertext links – these are text that you can click on to activate the link and take you to somewhere else.
- Graphical links – these are graphical images that you click on to activate the link. You can tell whether an image is a hyperlink because when you move the cursor over the graphic, and the graphic is a hyperlink, the cursor changes to a hand shape.

Hotspots

Hotspots are an image or piece of text used as a link on a webpage. When you click on the image or text, you are taken to another part of the same page, a different page or a different site, or it may open a new file or a new window.

▼ The navigation bar for the ISP AOL.

Navigation bars

Web browsers contain a toolbar called a navigation bar containing buttons that you use to move around the site and perform certain actions. These buttons would typically include:

- Back – go back to the previous page.
- Forward – jump forward to the next page.
- Refresh – (also called Reload) refresh the contents of the page.
- Home – return to the page that you use as your home page (i.e., your starting point) or the page that your ISP uses as their home page.
- Stop – stop trying to load the page.
- Key word search – to search a site using one or more key words.

Templates and layout guides

You have already seen that there are ready-made templates for word-processed documents and presentations. There are also templates for creating webpages and websites. These offer a quick way of producing websites with little or no design skills.

Layout guides are guides that are produced in web design software that allow you to drop your content into place. In some cases the layout is like a table and you can insert objects such as text, diagrams, photographs, clip art, etc., into the cells in the table.

http://google.yahoo.com/bin/query?p=%22discount+cruises+UK%22   KEYWORD   SEARCH

Web design software, software for audio, DVD and video players, and podcasts *continued*

Forms

Forms are used to collect data from website users. For example, you might want users to comment about your site using a feedback form. The form containing the comments can be automatically sent to the owner of the website.

Marquee tool

The marquee tool is a selection tool that allows you to select rectangles, ellipses, lines and columns. For example, you could select an elliptical area of a photograph that you would like to use on a website.

Animation

Animations can bring the most boring subject to life and they are used extensively in websites and other products to help children learn. They are also used in websites to sell goods and services. Animation can be produced using special animation software such as Flash.

Flash tools

Flash is software that allows you to add interactivity and animations to webpages. It is often used to put advertisements into webpages and you will have seen the Flash Movie Player which is used to play video within webpages. Flash tools are all the software tools that Flash uses to make these interactive features and animations.

RSS feed

RSS feed is a web feed format that is used to publish frequently updated works such as news, radio programmes and video. The user does not have to visit the websites to get the content as it is sent to them automatically. Readers subscribe to these feeds and they can read, listen to or watch the material using reader software.

▲ RSS feeds are used for news.

Counters

These are added to webpages so that the website owner can see how many visitors there have been to that webpage or website.

HTML (HyperText Markup Language)

HTML is short for HyperText Markup Language and it the special code that is used for making webpages. HTML consists of special markers called tags that tell the computer what to do with the text that is entered. It could tell the computer to present the text in a certain way. For example, the tags could tell the computer that the text being entered is intended to be a heading or to make a certain block of text bold. HTML is a text file, just like Word, except that it contains the special markers called tags. Tags basically tell the computer how to display the text or format the page.

Software for audio, DVD and video players

There are many different players available for the playing of audio (sound and music), DVD and video. Such software has a number of features including:

- Volume adjustment – you can increase or decrease the volume.
- Mute – a button you press that stops the sound going through the speakers.

- Play – starts the music, video, etc.
- Pause – stops whatever it is from playing until you press play again.
- Forward/Fast forward – can move forward to a particular part of music, video, DVD, etc.
- Backwards/reverse – useful if you want to go back and listen to or watch something again.
- Start – starts the player.
- Stop – stops the player.
- End – goes to the end of the music/video, etc.
- Play list – you can build a list of music tracks so they are played one after another automatically.
- Subtitles – the spoken words are displayed as text on the screen. Useful if the person watching is deaf or if you want help to learn another language.
- Music downloads – some music players can connect to a website so that you can select and pay for downloads to be stored on your computer.
- Streaming – this is where you do not download the whole music track/CD or DVD. Instead the file is sent via the Internet so you are able to watch it as it is being sent.

▲ Windows Media Player is a multimedia player capable of playing music, video, animation, sound, etc.

HyperText Markup Language (HTML) a set of instructions used to create documents on the World Wide Web. You use it to specify the structure and layout of a web document.

Hotspot an image or piece of text used as a link. When you click on the image or text, you are taken to another part of the same page, a different page or a different site, or it may open a new file or a new window.

Hyperlink a feature of a website that allows a user to jump to another webpage, to jump to part of the same webpage or to send an email message.

Image map an image that contains more than one hotspot.

Rollover button/image a button/image that changes its appearance when a cursor is moved over it.

Podcast

A podcast is a series of digital files (usually radio-style programmes, news, interesting info about sports, politics, entertainment, etc.) that are released in episodes and are sent to your computer automatically each time one is released. You don't have to do anything other than say that you want to subscribe in the first place. They are then sent to your computer and you can then transfer them to your MP3 player to listen to them. It is also fairly easy to create your own podcast. You probably have all the equipment you need already and the podcast software is freely available on the Internet.

▲ Podcasts can be listened to on portable media players as well as computers.

Questions C

1. One quick way of developing webpages is to use a template. Explain what a template is and how one can be used to create a website. *(3 marks)*

2. Websites can be created using web design software.
   - **(a)** Describe **two** features of web design software. *(2 marks)*
   - **(b)** Websites often contain hotspots. Explain what is meant by a hotspot. *(3 marks)*

3. Podcasts are a good way of keeping abreast of the news.
   - **(a)** Explain what is meant by a podcast. *(2 marks)*
   - **(b)** Give **one** advantage of a podcast. *(1 mark)*

Extension activity

Viewing HTML code

In this activity you will look at how you can view the HTML code (i.e., the set of instructions) used to produce a website.

1. Log on to the Internet and access any website you like.

2. Rather than look at the content of this site we are going to look at the HTML code used to produce the website.
   To do this, position the cursor anywhere on the webpage.
   Right click the mouse button.
   The following window appears:

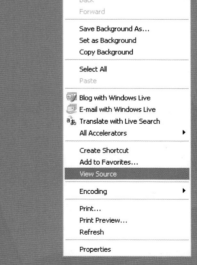

3. Select View Source by clicking on it.

4. You will now be able to see the HTML code for the webpage you have just viewed.

Questions

✓ Test yourself

The following notes summarize this topic. The notes are incomplete because they have words missing. Using the words in the list below, copy out and complete the sentences A to H, underlining the words that you have inserted. Each word may be used more than once.

transition   podcast   design template

navigation   button   hyperlink

animation   automatically   hotspots

A A _____ _____ is an outline design providing a basic colour scheme, font type, font size, etc.

B _____ involves getting some of the content that makes up the slides to move.

C Backward, forward, beginning and end _____ can be added to slides so that the slides can be made interactive.

D The movement from one slide to another is called a slide _____.

E The way a user can move from one slide to another is called the slide _____ .

F A _____ is an icon, graphic, or word on a document (slide or webpage) that, when clicked with the mouse, opens another slide or webpage.

G Images containing links are called graphical hyperlinks, although you will often hear them referred to as _____.

H A _____ is a series of digital files such as radio programmes that are released in episodes. Each episode is downloaded _____ to your computer.

Examination style questions

1 A person is to give an important presentation in front of a large audience. They have the choice of using a design template or creating the design of their slides themselves.
   (a) Explain what is meant by a design template. *(2 marks)*
   (b) Give **one** advantage to them in using a design template. *(1 mark)*
   (c) Give **one** disadvantage in using a design template. *(1 mark)*

2 A tourist information office decides to produce a self-running presentation of all the local attractions.
   (a) Define each of the following functions of the presentation software, and explain, using an appropriate example, how each function could be used in this situation. *(4 marks)*
   (i)   Templates
   (ii) Slide transitions
   (b) Animations can be added to a presentation. Describe **one** type of animation that is provided as part of the presentation software. *(2 marks)*

3 Choose which one of the following best matches the description in the left-hand column of the table below. *(5 marks)*

master pages   transition
podcast   HTML   hyperlink

Description	Source of information which best matches the description
A series of digital media files that is made available via web syndication	
Special code that is used for making webpages	
An icon, graphic, or word on a document (slide or webpage) that, when clicked with the mouse, opens another slide or webpage	
The movement from one slide to another	
They act as a framework for the website and all the developer has to do is fill in their own content	

Exam support

Worked example

A presentation is to be used by visitors to a castle. The idea is that users will be able to find out about the history of the castle and what it was like to live in a castle in that era.

Explain how each of the following could be used in the design of this presentation.

(a) Animations *(2 marks)*

(b) Links *(2 marks)*

(c) Slide transitions *(2 marks)*

Student answer 1

(a) Use moving things. Makes it better.

(b) You can move from one slide to another.

The user can click on a hotspot.

(c) The material on the slide can shoot in from the side of the slide. It makes it exciting for the user.

◀ Examiner's comment

(a) This is a vague and poor answer and no marks are awarded.

(b) Both of these are valid answers and two marks are awarded.

(c) Material such as bullet points shooting onto the slide is not really an example of slide transition as the slide is already on the screen. One mark (just) is given for the second answer.

(3 marks out of 6)

Student answer 2

(a) Use moving images showing what is in each room.

Have a heading showing the names of the castle which moves from left to right.

(b) Allow the user to decide what they want to see next by allowing them to click on links that take them to other pages.

Links could be used to allow the user to visit each of the rooms virtually and look around.

(c) These are pictures around the edge of a slide.

You can sometimes find these included with clip art.

◀ Examiner's comment

(a) These are both suitable examples so two marks are awarded.

(b) These two very good answers explaining how links might be used are awarded two marks.

(c) What the student has described here are borders. Slide transitions are the way one slide is removed and the next slide appears. No marks for this answer.

(4 marks out of 6)

Examiner's answers

(a) One mark for each point (NB must be a sensible use of animation) to a maximum of two marks.
- Have a cartoon showing what life was like.
- Use animation to show how certain parts of the castle were used.
- Etc.

(b) One mark for each point to a maximum of two marks.
- Link to an aerial view such as Google Earth.
- Link to other pages in the presentation.
- Link to the Internet so that they can access further information.
- Etc.

(c) One mark for each point to a maximum of two marks.
- Have one slide fading as another slide appears.
- Have one slide shooting in from the side.
- Etc.

EXAM TIPS

Make sure you refer to the scenario, if there is one

When a scenario is given, this sets a context for the answer you should give. For example, in this question you would need to tailor your answer to a presentation used to help people learn about the castle and what it was like to live in one.

One mistake that many students make is that they totally ignore the scenario and give a general answer. Usually when they do this, students fail to get all the marks as they have not exactly done what the question has asked.

Do not get confused between slide transitions and animations

It is easy to get confused here.

Slide transitions are the way one slide disappears and the next slide appears.

Animations are the movements of the content on the screen. This can be the way the content is added to the screen. For example, an image of a knight on a horse could be added to the slide by it moving in from the side of the slide.

Be specific

Most people know what the word animation means. As a student of ICT you need to make your answer specific to a presentation used to inform visitors to a castle. If you start mentioning about what an animation is, then you will not get any marks as this is not a question about the definition nor is it a question about the various ways that animations can be produced.

Summary mind map

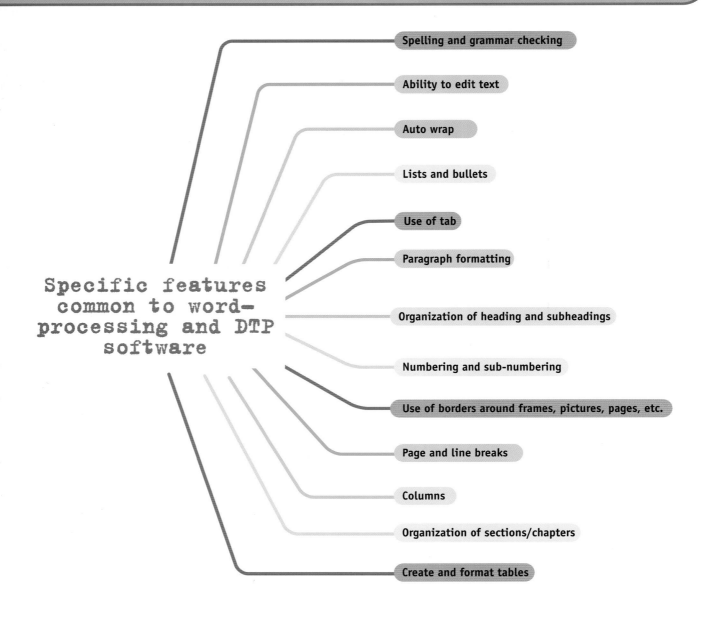

Specific features common to word-processing and DTP software

- Spelling and grammar checking
- Ability to edit text
- Auto wrap
- Lists and bullets
- Use of tab
- Paragraph formatting
- Organization of heading and subheadings
- Numbering and sub-numbering
- Use of borders around frames, pictures, pages, etc.
- Page and line breaks
- Columns
- Organization of sections/chapters
- Create and format tables

Topic 10

Graphics production and image manipulation

The key concepts covered in this topic are:

- The specific features of basic graphics packages
- The tasks that can be carried out using graphics packages

There are many pieces of software that allow the production of graphics. It all depends on how complex the graphics you want to produce are. For example, you may want a simple diagram showing text boxes and lines with arrows to put in a word-processed document. It is easy to create such a diagram using the word-processing software.

There are special packages that can produce graphics and in some packages you can produce animations and get the graphics to move. As well as producing graphics, most graphics packages allow the editing of images such as digital photographs.

In this topic you will be looking at the features of graphics packages and look at how graphics, including digital photographs, can be altered using this software.

Contents

Specific features of basic graphics packages

You will find out

▷ **About the specific features of basic graphics packages**

You will have used some graphics packages and will already have some idea of the sorts of features they have. There are many different graphics packages around and they usually differ in the range of features available. In this section you will be looking at the basic features of graphics packages.

Specific features of basic graphics packages

In this section you will look at these basic features.

Erase

If you have added a component to an image but you want to get rid of it, then there is the Undo option, which will remove the last thing you did. Another way is to use erase, which in some graphics packages is just like an eraser/rubber that you move just like a real rubber to erase part of the picture.

Fill with colour

In most graphics packages to fill an enclosed shape with colour you use the paint bucket/pot tool. The paint bucket/pot tool is used to:

• fill an enclosed shape with colour
• change the colour of an enclosed shape.

If there is a gap in what you think is a closed shape, the paint bucket/pot tool will not work.

Pick colour

Any element of a graphic can be produced in a colour using a palette of colours similar to the one shown below.

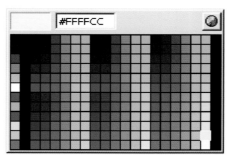

▲ **Colour palette**

Choose pencil

In most graphics software the pencil tool is used to draw lines (both straight and curved). It is quite hard to draw using the mouse and this tool tends to be used more for changing the colour of pixels in a photo. For example, if you have a photograph with a cloud in it, then you can remove the cloud by zooming in on the cloud so you can see the individual pixels. You can then take the colour of the blue sky and replace the white pixels of the cloud with this colour by clicking on the pixels with the pencil tool. In the graphics package Photoshop you can click on the screen and then click in a different position and the software will automatically add a line between the two points.

Choose brush

In most graphics editing packages there is a tool called the paintbrush and when you click on it you will see various options appear in the options section like this:

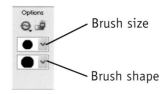

Controlling a paintbrush on a screen by moving a mouse is quite difficult and some professional artists prefer to use an alternative input device such as a light pen (where they draw directly onto the screen) or a graphics tablet.

Choose airbrush tool

The airbrush tool gives a soft-edge stroke similar to one you would get when using a can of spray paint. The longer you leave the airbrush tool in the one position then the greater the build up of paint on that area. You can alter the size of the area that the airbrush tool covers with a stroke by selecting a brush size.

▲ **Using the airbrush tool with different brush sizes.**

▲ The airbrush tool produces a paint effect like that produced by a can of spray paint.

Shade

To make pictures realistic, shade can be added to the diagrams. You can also add shade to text to make it stand out.

▲ Notice how the careful use of shading has made this heart look three dimensional.

Lines

Lines are drawn using a tool called the line tool. The line tool is used to draw straight lines on the canvas. It is pretty intuitive, you simply choose the line tool from the toolbox, click once on the canvas to specify the beginning point of your line and then drag the mouse to define the line extending from the starting point. As with the pencil and brush tools you can alter the thickness of the line and can choose, for example, if you want to end the line with an arrow head.

Another way to use the line tool is to click anywhere you want the line to start and then click anywhere you want the line to end. A line is automatically drawn between the two points.

Curves

You can draw curves freehand using tools such as the pencil or brush tool but it is very difficult to draw a smooth curve.

A better way to draw curves is to use the pen tool, which makes use of anchor points. This takes a bit of practice, but it is possible to produce smooth curves using this technique.

Layering

Layering is a very useful technique. If a graphic consists of lots of smaller graphics then you can draw each small graphic on its own layer. This is a bit like drawing the graphics on several sheets of glass, with each sheet being equivalent to a layer. When all the layers are placed over each other, the complete graphic is produced. It is easier to edit graphics and re-use them if they are in their own layer. Shapes on a layer will obscure shapes on layers below them if they overlap. This is useful in animation where you could have a walking person in one layer walking past a lamp post in a different layer.

Rotating

Occasionally to produce a more eye-catching display, you can rotate a graphic through a variety of angles. Rotating is often needed for photographs, which can be taken in either landscape or portrait.

Using a graphics package

London has been chosen as host for the 2012 Olympic Games. The Games are expected to attract more tourists, increase investment and create jobs as well as boost the profile of London and the UK.

You have been asked to produce some graphic designs for a number of products for the publicity campaign.

Here is what you need to produce:

- A series of designs for a logo to promote the London 2012 Olympic Games.
- There should be at least three designs and these should be saved and printed out so that a final one can be chosen.

Repeating pattern

A repeated pattern means a pattern that is repeated over and over; so, for example, a block can be repeated over and over to give the appearance of a wall. Repeated patterns can be used:

- for backgrounds (e.g., for slides, webpages, etc.)
- to fill shapes.

▲ With graphics software you are limited only by your imagination.

Specific features of basic graphics packages *continued*

Questions A

1 Which **three** important features would you expect to find in a graphics package? *(3 marks)*

	Tick **three** boxes only
Rotate an image	☐
Add shading	☐
Relative and absolute cell referencing	☐
Sort	☐
Choose the width of a brush	☐
Produce reports	☐

2 A graphic has been created using graphic design software.

Give the names of **two** ways a graphic can be edited. *(2 marks)*

3 Graphics software consists of a number of tools.

Explain the purpose of each of the following tools:
(a) Fill with colour *(2 marks)*
(b) Shade *(2 marks)*
(c) Layering *(2 marks)*

4 A graphics package is being used to create a new logo for a business. Give **two** advantages in using the graphics package to produce this logo rather than simply using a piece of clip art. *(2 marks)*

Extension activity

In this topic you learnt about some of the tools that are available in graphics packages and some of things you can do with them.

For this activity you should investigate the tools available in a graphics package that your school/college has.

Give the name of each tool and state its purpose.

Extension activity

Graphics software can be used to alter digital photographic images. There are many tools that can be used for this.

For this activity you have to list each tool and explain how it can be used to alter the image.

The first one has been done for you:

- Cropping – remove an unwanted part of an image or change the shape of the image that is left.

EXAM TIPS

Always be guided by the mark scheme to decide how much to write. For example, if you are asked to describe an advantage or disadvantage for one mark, then just a brief statement would be enough. If two marks were allocated, then you would be required to supplement this with further detail or an appropriate example.

Always think out your answer before you start writing it. You need to ensure you make your answer clear, so you need a little time to think about it.

Advantages (sometimes called benefits) and disadvantages are very popular questions. When covering a topic for revision it is a good idea to list advantages and disadvantages where appropriate.

Tasks that can be carried out using graphics packages

▷ **About the tasks that can be carried out using graphics packages**

In this section you will be looking at the sorts of tasks that can be carried out using graphics software. For example, graphics software can be used to create images from scratch or it can be used to edit or modify existing images. These images can be drawings produced using software, or scanned images or photographic images taken using a digital camera.

Tasks that can be carried out using graphics packages

Graphics software is quite varied and like most software differs in how complex it is and the number of features it has. Professional graphics designers and artists require software that has many complex ways of producing eye-catching images.

There are a number of ways you can produce an image and they are:

- Draw/paint it using graphics design software.
- Scan a photograph or picture using a scanner and then import the file.
- Obtain a photographic image using a digital camera and load/import it into a document.

Once an image has been produced, it may not look as good as it could do. All graphics packages allow you

to edit or manipulate an image in a number of ways in order to improve its appearance.

Imaging effects

Graphics editing software has many useful imaging effects and some are detailed here:

- **Altering the pixels in a photographic image/air brushing** – it is possible to zoom into a bitmap image until you can see the individual pixels. It is then possible to edit the pixels by changing their colour. You can therefore remove skin blemishes, unwanted objects and even people from an image.
- **Removing red eye from a photograph** – this is a common problem in photographs taken using a flash. It is easily removed using graphics software.
- **Morphing** – is a special effect where one image changes into another. You may have seen this with faces where an image of a person's face changes into a different person's face. You need two images for morphing: the image you start with and the image you want to end up with. Normally you then mark key points that need to maintain their position in the image such as the eyes and nose and the computer software then alters the

▲ You could change the colour of the red part to the colour blue or you can simply press a button to get rid of the red.

image keeping the position of the eyes and nose the same.

- **Warping** – involves changing the position of pixels in an image in some way using special software. This means the image can be distorted in lots of different ways. Warping is mainly used creatively for producing eye-catching images.
- **Applying filters** – filters allow you to apply an effect to an image or part of an image. You can, for example, turn a colour photograph into a black and white one. You can also make it look old by applying a sepia filter.

Cropping an image

When people take photographs they tend to take photographs a certain way. For example, if they are taking a photograph of a person, they usually either include the whole person or just their head and shoulders.

Sometimes you have to take a photograph in a hurry and don't have time to check the composition of the image. Cropping involves hiding part of the image. You can also use cropping to change a landscape image into a portrait image.

Adjusting colours in scanned, drawn or photographic images

Photographs cannot always be taken in ideal light conditions. Sometimes the colours do not come out as expected. Luckily there are ways you can edit the colour in any bitmapped image. For example, you may increase the amount of red, green or blue in an image. You can increase or decrease the brightness of the image and also increase the contrast, which is the difference between the bright and dark parts of an image.

Tasks that can be carried out using graphics packages *continued*

KEY WORD

Cropping only using part of an image.

Questions B

1 Give **one** reason why an image might need to be cropped. *(1 mark)*

2 Which **three** of the following are features you would find useful when trying to improve the appearance of a digital photograph using graphics software? *(3 marks)*

A Using filters
B Mail merging
C Insertion and deletion of fields
D Sorting
E Cropping
F Removal of red eye

3 Graphics software can be used to edit or manipulate digital photographic images.

By giving **two** suitable examples, explain why a digital photographic image might need editing or manipulating. *(4 marks)*

Extension activity

Using graphics software to manipulate digital images

For this activity you need a few digital photograph images. You can take these yourself or find them on the Internet and then save them to disk.

Load each photograph into the graphics software and experiment by altering the photographs. Try using as many of the graphics features that your graphics software has and try to be as creative as you can.

Save and print any of the images you particularly like and write on the images the features of the software you have used.

Extension activity

Producing a logo using graphics software

A new organization has been set up to make children more aware of the effects of global warming and to encourage them to help reduce its effects.

This new organization needs a logo and you have been asked to use graphics software to produce this logo.

1 Produce several initial designs initially on paper.

2 Use the graphics software to produce at least two possible logos for the organization to choose between.

Remember that the logo needs to be aimed at children, so it needs to be simple and eye-catching.

Questions

✔ Test yourself

The following notes summarize this topic. The notes are incomplete because they have words missing. Using the words in the list below, copy out and complete sentences A to G, underlining the words that you have inserted. Each word may be used more than once.

edit   morphing   rotate   airbrush

fill   red   cropping

A Graphics packages can be used to create graphic images as well as _____ existing images.

B In most graphics packages to _____ an enclosed shape with colour you use the paint bucket/pot tool.

C The _____ tool gives a soft-edge stroke similar to one you would get when using a can of spray paint.

D _____ is a special effect where one image changes into another.

E It is often necessary to _____ an image taken using a digital camera so that it can be viewed the right way around.

F _____ an image involves removing some of the image so that only part of the image is used.

G _____ eye often occurs in digital images of people when a flash is used. Luckily the graphics software can easily correct this.

Examination style questions

1 An artist uses a computer with graphics software for the production of graphics for teenage magazines.

   Which **three** important features would you expect to find in a graphics package? *(3 marks)*

	Tick **three** boxes only
Airbrush	☐
Mail merge	☐
Layering	☐
Recalculation	☐
Fill with colour	☐
Headers and footers	☐

2 Give **two** ways in which an image can be manipulated using graphics software. *(2 marks)*

3 Photographic images taken using a digital camera can be edited using graphics software.

   Describe **two** ways in which a photographic image can be edited. *(2 marks)*

END-OF-TOPIC REVIEW

Exam support

Worked example

Once a graphic has been obtained, it may need adjusting in some way. Graphics software is available that allows you to alter (i.e., manipulate) images.

(a) Give **two** different ways in which a graphic can be obtained. *(2 marks)*

(b) Describe **two** ways in which a graphic can be edited/manipulated using graphics software. *(2 marks)*

Student answer 1

(a) You can get one off the Internet and you can get one from a clip art library.

(b) You can change the colours in a graphic by editing it. You can also enlarge or reduce the size of an image so that it will fit in the space you have allowed for it.

▲ Examiner's comment

(a) The question asks for the different ways in which a graphic can be obtained. The student has answered a different question, which is the different places that a graphic can be obtained from. There is a difference between these questions.

If the student had said that 'you can copy an image off a website and paste it into your own document' then this would have been a suitable answer for one of the marks.

The student is not awarded any marks for their answer.

(b) Both of these answers are acceptable, so two marks are awarded here.

(2 marks out of 4)

Student answer 2

(a) *You can create the graphic yourself from scratch using graphics software and import it into your document.*

You can drag and drop a piece of clip art from a clip art library into place in your document.

(b) *A graphic can be cropped so that only part of the image is used. For example, a photograph of two people could be cropped so that only the part of the image with one of the people is shown.*

You can edit the image by removing the red eye in a photographic image. This can be done automatically using the editing facilities in the graphics software.

▲ **Examiner's comment**

(a) Notice that in both these answers the student has clearly identified the way the graphic is brought into the document they are working on. Both of these answers are good and are awarded marks.

(b) This is a very good answer. The student has offered clear explanations of how the graphic is edited/manipulated and they have offered examples for further clarification.

(4 marks out of 4)

Examiner's answers

(a) One mark each for the 'way' the graphic is obtained to a maximum of two marks.

Suitable answers include:

- Copy an image from a website/webpage and then paste into the document.
- Copy an image from a website and then save to disk and then open the image file in the document.
- Import a clip art file from a clip art library on disk/on the Internet, etc.
- Create a graphic from scratch using graphics software and load/import into the document.

(b) One mark each for two types of editing/manipulation such as:

- It can be resized (i.e., made bigger or smaller).
- It can be rotated through a certain angle.
- It can be mirror imaged (i.e., like reflecting the image in a mirror).
- Part of the image can be cropped (this is just like cutting the part you want out of the picture).
- The image can be morphed using special morphing software.
- The graphic can be repeated over and over.
- Red eye can be removed from a photographic image.
- The shape of an image can be changed (e.g., portrait to landscape and vice versa).
- You can change the colours in an image.
- You can airbrush out unwanted items such as skin blemishes.
- You can alter the brightness/contrast of an image.

Summary mind map

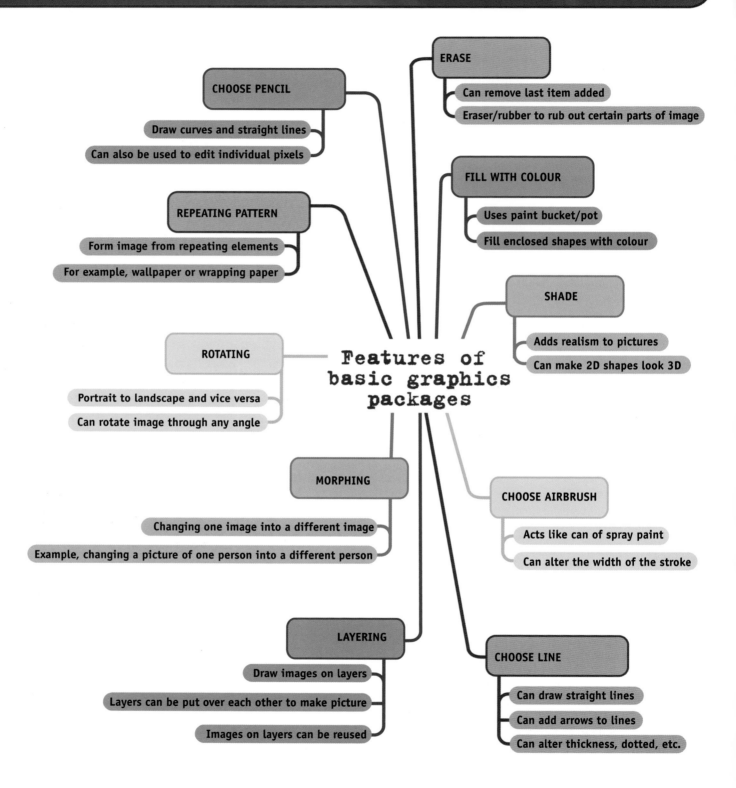

CHOOSE PENCIL
- Draw curves and straight lines
- Can also be used to edit individual pixels

REPEATING PATTERN
- Form image from repeating elements
- For example, wallpaper or wrapping paper

ROTATING
- Portrait to landscape and vice versa
- Can rotate image through any angle

MORPHING
- Changing one image into a different image
- Example, changing a picture of one person into a different person

LAYERING
- Draw images on layers
- Layers can be put over each other to make picture
- Images on layers can be reused

ERASE
- Can remove last item added
- Eraser/rubber to rub out certain parts of image

FILL WITH COLOUR
- Uses paint bucket/pot
- Fill enclosed shapes with colour

SHADE
- Adds realism to pictures
- Can make 2D shapes look 3D

Features of basic graphics packages

CHOOSE AIRBRUSH
- Acts like can of spray paint
- Can alter the width of the stroke

CHOOSE LINE
- Can draw straight lines
- Can add arrows to lines
- Can alter thickness, dotted, etc.

Spreadsheets and modelling software

The key concepts covered in this topic are:

- **Types of data (common to spreadsheets and databases)**
- **Specific features of a spreadsheet**
- **Formulae and functions**
- **Modelling**

You will have used spreadsheet software before as part of your Key Stage 3 studies. Spreadsheets are ideal if you are dealing with numerical data or need to produce graphs and charts. In this topic you will be building on your knowledge of spreadsheets.

You will also have covered computer modelling as part of your Key Stage 3 studies and in this topic you will be looking in detail at how models can be created using spreadsheet software.

Contents

Types of data (common to spreadsheets and databases)

You will find out

▷ **About the types of data and the facilities for entering data**

▷ **About the formatting that can be applied to cells**

There are many different types of data that can be entered into a database or spreadsheet. Both databases and spreadsheets need to be set up so that they are capable of holding this data and are able to do some processing using the data.

In order to validate the data, the structure of the spreadsheet or database can be used to help format the data that is entered into certain cells. This means, for example, that the spreadsheet would not allow you to enter a letter of the alphabet into a cell that had been formatted to hold a number.

Types of data

There are many different types of data that can be put into a spreadsheet or database.

Numerical/number formats

There are various different formats that you can have for numbers.

These are:

- Integers – these are positive and negative whole numbers (e.g. 1, 23, -9, -90).
- Percentages – these have a percentage sign shown next to them and can be used in formulae to find percentages of other numbers.
- Decimal places – you can specify the number of decimal places you want in a number.
- Currency – this is expressed to two decimal places and has a sign attached to the number (e.g. £23.97).
- Fractions – you can perform calculations involving fractions using a spreadsheet.

Text

Text can consist of letters of the alphabet, numbers and other characters on the keyboard.

Date/time

There are many different ways in which dates and times can be stored by a spreadsheet or database (e.g., 1 July 2011, 01/07/11, etc.).

Logical/Boolean

Logical/Boolean data can have only one of two values. Examples include yes/no, male/female, etc.

Facilities for data entry – spinners, list boxes and combo boxes

The main requirements for data entry into a spreadsheet model are that:
- It should be made as easy as possible for the user.
- It will reduce the likelihood of incorrect data being entered.

Other than just typing you can use the following facilities to enter data:

- **Spinners** – these let you alter the value in a cell by clicking on an up or down arrow.

  Here is a spinner used in a worksheet to alter the number of years:

- **List boxes** – list boxes present a choice of data to be entered into a spreadsheet cell. All the items in the list are shown in the box unless the list is too long in which case the scroll bar is used to make them visible.

- **Combo boxes** – these allow you to choose an entry from a list which only appears when you click on the arrow to drop it down. They are useful because they can be used to enter more than one piece of data from a table of data.

  Combo boxes are used when you have a fixed number of choices (e.g., days of the week, months of the year, certain sizes (S, M, L, XL), certain colours, etc.).

- **Logical/Boolean (True or False) boxes** – these are sometimes called check boxes or tick boxes and they return a true or false depending on whether they are selected or cleared.

They are useful when there are only two possible settings such as on/off, male/female, or true/false. Here is one where express delivery can be chosen by putting a tick in the check box.

- **Option buttons** – used when the user has to select between alternatives. Here is one where the user has to choose their age range:

Your age is?	
16 to 21	⦿
Over 21	○

- **Forms toolbar** – contains lots of ideas for making it easier to add data as well as making data entry more accurate by restricting choices.

Adding objects

You can insert an object in a spreadsheet. Examples of objects include:

- pictures (e.g., drawings, clip art, photographs, etc.)
- word-processing document
- media such as sound, video, etc.

Formatting
Aligning cells

When you enter data into a cell, the spreadsheet automatically aligns (i.e. positions) the cells according to the following:

- Numbers are aligned to the right.
- Text is aligned to the left.

Do not put any spaces in front of numbers in order to align them as this will make it impossible for the spreadsheet to use the numbers in calculations.

If you want to align the data differently, you can use the special buttons for alignment on the formatting toolbar. Using this

method, you can align them to the left, right or centre.

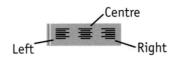

Formatting fonts to make text stand out

Text can be made to stand out by formatting it in a number of ways:

- Font type – changes the shapes of letters and numbers.
- Font size – used to make headings, subheadings, etc., stand out.
- Font style - Bold, Italics, Underline – used to draw attention to text.

Text alignment

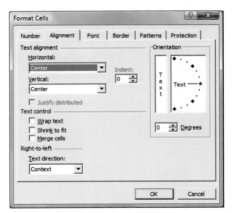

▲ Text can be aligned in the cells using Format Cells.

▲ This text has been aligned centrally in both the horizontal and vertical directions.

Sometimes a label may be too big to fit into a single cell and when this happens it can be made to overflow into the other cells. This is called cell merging.

Notice also that you can wrap text in cells. This means that instead of the cell width getting bigger or the text overflowing into the next cell, the cell width is kept the same and the text flows onto the next line thus making the vertical height of the cell bigger.

Borders and rotating text

Using borders you can: put a border around cells or groups of cells, shade in certain cells or groups of cells.

Rotating text is useful when you want a narrow column but the column heading is wide.

Adding colour/shading

Colour/shading may be added to:

- text
- borders
- background colours for cells.

Notice that you can also format the font, border and alignment as well as the patterns.

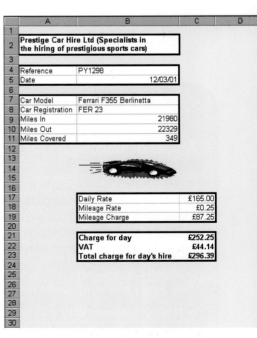

▲ The Format Cells menu allows choices of colours and patterns for cell shading.

▲ By adding borders, colour and a graphic, you can improve the presentation of the spreadsheet.

Types of data (common to spreadsheets and databases)
continued

Questions A

1 (a) Tick **one** box to show which one is not a type of cell format. *(1 mark)*

Tick one box only

Shading ☐
Centre ☐
Save ☐
Border ☐

(b) Tick **one** box to show which one of the following cannot be put into a spreadsheet cell. *(1 mark)*

Tick one box only

Formula ☐
Number ☐
Text ☐
Database ☐

2 (a) A title of a spreadsheet has been put into a spreadsheet cell like this.

This title needs to stand out.

	A	B
1	Ace Computer Supplies	
2		
3		
4		

Give **three** ways this cell could be formatted to make the text stand out. *(3 marks)*

(b) The following number is entered into a spreadsheet cell:

	A	B
1		
2		122.1219
3		
4		
5		

Numbers can be formatted. For example they can be formatted to integer.

Give **two** different formats for this number. *(2 marks)*

3 Explain the meaning of each of the following types of formatting for cells:
(a) Text alignment *(1 mark)*
(b) Text wrap *(1 mark)*
(c) Merging cells *(1 mark)*

Extension activity

A school barbeque for charity

Year 11 classes in a school want to raise some money for charity, so they decide to hold a barbeque. They intend to hire a large barbeque, some party lights and a disco unit from a local hire firm. They need to be sure that they will make a profit as well as enjoy themselves, so before they go ahead with the project, they have produced a spreadsheet. The spreadsheet will enable them to see how much profit they will make.

In this spreadsheet they will have:

Expenditure: things they have to pay out money for (hiring equipment, food, drink, etc.)

Income: money coming in from the sale of tickets, drinks, etc.

Tickets will cost £5 each and this includes admission and also the cost of the food.

It is up to you to provide sensible amounts for all the expenses (i.e., the money going out).

Although the pupils think that this is quite expensive, they reckon that people will be prepared to spend this much if it goes to a good cause.

You task is to produce a spreadsheet that will outline the income, expenditure and profit they expect to make.

Specific features of a spreadsheet

▷ **About a range of specific features of spreadsheet software**

You will already be familiar with many features and functions of spreadsheet software. This section seeks to revise some of the basics of spreadsheets but also to let you know what other features are available in spreadsheet software and how they are used.

You will, of course, have to develop spreadsheets and build up your practical skills in using some of the techniques and knowledge covered in this topic.

Spreadsheet basics

Just as a reminder, here are the basics of spreadsheets.

The concept of rows, columns, cells and cell references

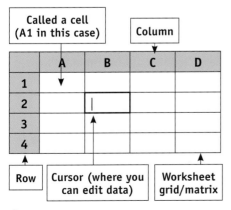

▲ Rows, columns, cells and cell references.

Labels

Labels are used for titles, headings, names, and for identifying columns or rows of data. You should never have values on a spreadsheet without labels, as a user will be left wondering what they represent.

Data

Data are the values (text or numbers) that you enter into the spreadsheet. It is the data that will be used for calculations or for producing graphs and charts.

Formatting cells

There are many different types of data and some of these are shown in the following table:

Type of data	Example of data
Date	12/12/10
Integer (a whole number)	34
Decimal number	3.14
Percentage	4%
Currency	£3.45
Text	Jenny Hayter

If the general number format is used (which it will be unless you tell the software otherwise) the numbers will be shown with up to eleven digits (including all the numbers up to and after the decimal point). A cell that has a formula typed in will show the results of the formula rather than the formula itself.

Cells need to be able to hold the data you want to put into them. The spreadsheet will interpret the data you put into the cell. What is displayed in a cell depends on the cell format. Although each cell is set to the general number format, it can change

automatically depending on the data you type in. If you type in a pound sign followed by a number, the spreadsheet will assume that you are dealing with currency and will format the cell to currency automatically. It will only show the currency to two decimal places, so if you typed in £1.349, '£1.35' would be shown.

For large numbers you often use a comma to make them easier to read (e.g. 3,000,000). As soon as such a number is entered with the commas, the spreadsheet will apply the number format with the thousands separator and use a maximum of two decimal places.

If a number is entered ending in a % sign (e.g. 4%), then the spreadsheet will set the cell automatically to the percent format with two decimal places.

Cell presentation formats

Data can be presented in cells in a variety of different ways. We will look at these in this section.

Printing formulae

When you print out a spreadsheet, it will always print out the results of any formulae along with any text or numbers. In order to check the spreadsheet it is useful to be able to see these formulae so that they can be checked. The activity on the next page will show you how to display the formulae on the screen.

Layout of worksheets

It is a good idea to sketch out the design of your worksheet before you start using the software. It is much easier to get the design right using pencil and paper rather than having to start moving items when you realize they are in the wrong place.

Specific features of a spreadsheet *continued*

◀ Tools Options menu (see below).

Cell gridlines

Cell gridlines are the feint lines used to mark the cells. You can remove the gridlines in the following way:

1 Click on the Tools menu and then click on Options.
2 Click on the View tab.
3 In the windows option of the screen click Gridlines to remove the tick.
4 Click on OK and the gridlines will be removed.

Linked sheets

When you look at a spreadsheet you will see that it contains three worksheets called Sheet 1, Sheet 2 and Sheet 3. There are many occasions when data on more than one worksheet needs to be used. To

do this, the worksheets need to be linked. You can link cells from one worksheet to another or even from a worksheet in one workbook to a worksheet in a different workbook. A link to more than one worksheet is called a 3D reference.

Suppose there is a total in Sheet 1 in cell F6 and this total needs to be displayed in Sheet 2 in cell B2.

You would first click cell B2 in Sheet 2 (i.e., where you want the results to appear) and enter the formula =Sheet1!F6.

Automatic recalculation

If a value in a cell is altered, and that cell is used in a formula, then the formula will automatically recalculate the result of the formula and display it.

Sorting rows/columns

Spreadsheets are often used to create simple databases called flat file databases. In these databases the column headings are the fields and the rows are the records (apart from the first row containing the column titles). You can sort on as many as three fields (i.e. columns) and this is particularly useful if the amount of data is very large and a search on just one field would retrieve lots of records. When the data is sorted all the records are kept together.

There are several orders you can sort on:

- Ascending order (A to Z for letters and 0 to 9 for numbers).

Ascending order

Descending order

- Descending order (Z to A for letters and 9 to 0 for numbers).

The icons for sorting appear in the toolbar and are shown here:

Graphs and charts

To make the results/output from a spreadsheet easy to understand you can present them as graphs and charts. Graphs and charts can be produced using the spreadsheet software on the same worksheet or on a different worksheet. If there is a lot of data, then it would be better to produce the graphs or charts on a different worksheet.

Data is often imported from other software such as database software into spreadsheet software because spreadsheets are ideal for analysing numerical data and for the production of graphs and charts.

You must make sure that you choose the most appropriate graphs or charts to display the results. If you are unsure about this, then ask a mathematics teacher or consult a GCSE mathematics textbook.

Some of the graphs and charts you may consider producing include:

- line graphs
- bar charts
- pie charts
- scatter graphs (sometimes called scattergrams)

When producing graphs or charts remember to:

- include a title for the graph/chart that explains its purpose clearly
- label each axis (adding units if appropriate)
- add a legend (a legend explains what each section of the graph shows)
- use appropriate colours and shading.

Activity

Copying formulae relatively and showing the formulae for a spreadsheet

1. Load the spreadsheet software and enter the following data exactly as it is shown here:

	A	B	C	D	E	F	G
1	Product	Sept	Oct	Nov	Dec	Total	
2	Lawn rake	121	56	23	12		
3	Spade (Large)	243	233	298	288		
4	Spade (Medium)	292	272	211	190		
5	Spade (Small)	131	176	149	200		
6	Fork (Large)	208	322	178	129		
7	Fork (Small)	109	106	166	184		
8	Trowel	231	423	311	219		
9	Totals						

2. Enter the formula =sum(b2:e2) in cell F2.

3. Copy the formula in cell F2 down the column to cell F8. You do this by moving the cursor to cell F2 containing the formula. Now click on the bottom right-hand corner of the cell and you should get a black cross shape. Hold the left mouse button down and move the mouse down the column until you reach cell F8. You will see a dotted rectangle around the area where the copied formula is to be inserted. Now take your finger off the button and all the results of the calculation will appear. This is called relative copying because the formula is changed slightly to take account of the altered positions of the two numbers which are to be added together.

4. Enter the formula =sum(b2:b8) into cell B9.

5. Copy the formula in cell B9 relatively across the row until cell F9. Check your worksheet looks the same as this:

	A	B	C	D	E	F	G
1	Product	Sept	Oct	Nov	Dec	Total	
2	Lawn rake	121	56	23	12	212	
3	Spade (Large)	243	233	298	288	1062	
4	Spade (Medium)	292	272	211	190	965	
5	Spade (Small)	131	176	149	200	656	
6	Fork (Large)	208	322	178	129	837	
7	Fork (Small)	109	106	166	184	565	
8	Trowel	231	423	311	219	1184	
9	Totals	1335	1588	1336	1222	5481	
10							
11							
12							

6. You are now going to display the formulae used rather than the values wherever there are calculations.
   Select the Tools menu and then click on Options.
   The screen on the right will appear:

7. In the bottom part of this screen you will see a box marked Formulas. Click on this box and a tick will appear indicating that the formulae will be displayed. The following screen containing the formulae now appears.

	A	B	C	D	E	F
1	Product	Sept	Oct	Nov	Dec	Total
2	Lawn rake	121	56	23	12	=SUM(B2:E2)
3	Spade (Large)	243	233	298	288	=SUM(B3:E3)
4	Spade (Medium)	292	272	211	190	=SUM(B4:E4)
5	Spade (Small)	131	176	149	200	=SUM(B5:E5)
6	Fork (Large)	208	322	178	129	=SUM(B6:E6)
7	Fork (Small)	109	106	166	184	=SUM(B7:E7)
8	Trowel	231	423	311	219	=SUM(B8:E8)
9	Totals	=SUM(B2:B8)	=SUM(C2:C8)	=SUM(D2:D8)	=SUM(E2:E8)	=SUM(F2:F8)
10						

8. Save this spreadsheet using the filename 'Product sales'.

Specific features of a spreadsheet *continued*

Activity

Producing a scattergraph

A driving school advertises for pupils and they would like to answer the following what if question: What if we spend more on advertising? Will we get more pupils?

They have collected the following data and put it into a table.

Amount spent on advertising per week (£)	Number of new pupils per week from adverts
20	1
30	2
40	4
50	4
60	5
70	6
80	6
120	9
150	10
160	12

This data is quite hard to interpret so they have decided to present it as a scattergraph. This will enable them to see the relationship (if there is one) more clearly.

1 Firstly enter the data into the worksheet like this: Check that you have centred the data in both columns.

	A	B	C
1	Amount spent on advertising per week (£)	Number of new pupils per week from adverts	
2	20	1	
3	30	2	
4	40	4	
5	50	4	
6	60	5	
7	70	6	
8	80	6	
9	120	9	
10	150	10	
11	160	12	
12			

2 Select the data by clicking and dragging the mouse from cells A1 to B11. The selected area will be shaded.

3 Click on the chart icon in the standard toolbar (it is the button with the picture of a bar graph on it).

4 Step 1 of the chart wizard appears. Select the **Chart type XY (Scatter)** and the **Chart sub-type** as shown here:

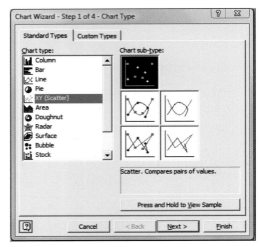

5 Click on **Next >**. Step 2 of the chart wizard appears. Check that Series in Columns is selected. The screen should be the same as this one.

6 Click on **Next >.** Step 3 of the chart wizard is shown.
In the Chart title box enter:
Graph to see any correlation between the amount spent on advertising per week and the number of new pupils per week
In the 'Value (X) axis' box type in **Amount spent on advertising.**
In the 'Value (Y) axis' box type in **No. of new pupils booked**
The screen in Step 3 of the chart wizard should now look like this:

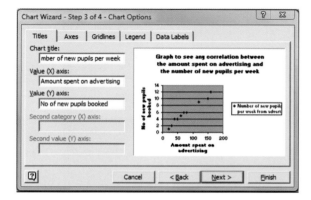

7 In Step 3 of the chart wizard click on the tab for Legend. The screen will change.
Here you can position the legend (this is the box next to the graph that explains the data). In this case we will remove the legend. To do this, make sure that the box Show legend is left blank. The legend now disappears.

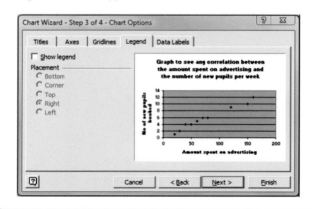

8 Click on **Next >** to go on to the next step of the chart wizard. Step 4 asks you if you want the chart with the data, or to put it into its own worksheet. Click on 'As new sheet' to put it into its own worksheet.

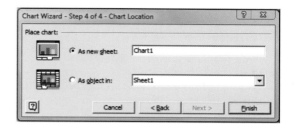

Click on **Finish.** The chart is now displayed.

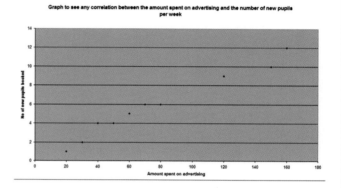

9 Look at the graph carefully. You can see that it shows positive correlation. This means that as the amount spent on advertising increases then so does the number of new pupils booked.

Specific features of a spreadsheet *continued*

Activity

Producing graphs/charts

1 The holiday destinations of 40 students are recorded in the following table.

Destination	Greece	Turkey	Spain	America
No of students	8	4	15	13

Produce a pie chart showing this information. Ensure that you:
- have a title to your chart
- include a suitably labelled legend.

2 Here is a table showing shoe sizes for 20 pupils in a school.

Shoe size	Frequency
5	1
6	5
7	6
8	3
9	2
10	3

Produce a fully labelled bar chart showing this information.

Questions B

1 Cells can contain labels, data or formulae.
   (a) Explain what is meant by labels. *(1 mark)*
   (b) Explain what is meant by data. *(1 mark)*
   (c) Explain what is meant by a formula. *(1 mark)*

2 There are **two** different types of cell reference. Give the names of both of them. *(2 marks)*

Extension activity

There are many ways you can improve the appearance of a graph/chart.

For this extension activity you are required to find out ways of improving the appearance of the graphs/charts you have drawn in the activities.

▼ You will probably need a tape measure to measure your classmates' height, and remember you will need to use the same units throughout.

Extension activity

Someone in your class states that taller people have bigger feet. Your class decides to test this hypothesis by asking everyone in the class to record their shoe size and height.

Using the class data that has been collected, enter the data into a spreadsheet.

Produce a scatter graph to show the data.

Save and print a copy of your work and on the copy write a short conclusion of what you have found.

Is the hypothesis true or false? Explain your answer in the conclusion.

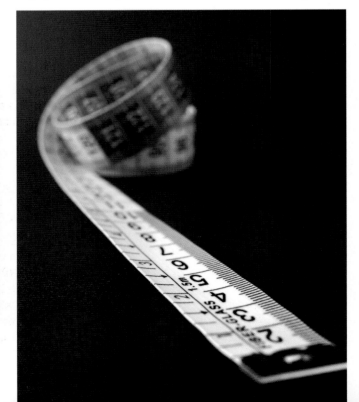

Formulae and functions

You will find out

▷ **About the use of common formulae**

▷ **About the use of functions**

You will have used some formulae and functions as part of your Key Stage 3 study. In this section you will be revising the simple formulae you will have already come across and also be learning about some new functions.

Formulae

Formulae are used to perform calculations on the cell contents. In order to distinguish between text and formulae a symbol, =, needs to be typed in first, like this =B3+B4.

Here are some calculations and what they do. Notice that you can use upper or lower case letters (i.e., capital or small letters).

=C3+C4 (adds the numbers in cells C3 and C4 together)

=A1*B4 (multiplies the numbers in cells A1 and B4 together)

=3*G4 (multiplies the number in cell G4 by 3)

=sum(b3:b10) (adds up all the cells from b3 to b10 inclusive)

=C4/D1 (divides the number in cell C4 by the number in cell D1)

=30/100*A2 (finds 30% of the number in cell A2)

Functions

A function is a specialized calculation that the spreadsheet software has memorized. There are many of these functions, some of which are very specialized. A function must start with an equals sign (=) and it must have a range of cells to which it applies in brackets after it.

Average: For example, to find the average of the numbers in a range of cells from A3 to A10 you would use: =AVERAGE(A3:A10)

Maximum: =MAX(D3:J3) displays the largest number in all the cells from D3 to J3 inclusive.

Minimum: =MIN(D3:J3) displays the smallest number in all the cells from D3 to J3 inclusive.

Mode: =MODE(A3:A15) displays the mode (i.e., the most frequent number) in the cells from A3 to A15 inclusive.

Median: =MEDIAN(B2:W2) displays the median of the cells from cells B2 to W2 inclusive.

Sum: =SUM(E3:P3) displays the total of all the cells from cells E3 to P3 inclusive.

Round: The ROUND function rounds a number correct to a number of digits that you specify. ROUND is used in the following way:

ROUND(number, number of digits) where number is the number you want rounded off and number of digits is the number of decimal places.

Here are some examples:
=ROUND(3.56678, 2) will return the number 3.57
=ROUND(5.43,1) will return the number 5.4

Roundup: ROUNDUP(number, number of digits) always rounds the number up. For example ROUNDUP(3.1, 1) will round the number 3.1 up to 4.

Rank: =RANK(A3,A1:A10) gives the rank of the number in cell A3 for all the numbers in cells from A1 to A10.

The rank is the position of the number if the numbers in the range A1 to A10 had been sorted into descending order.

COUNT: Suppose we want to count the number of numeric entries in the range C3 to C30. We can use =COUNT(C3:C30). Any blank lines or text entries in the range will not be counted.

COUNTA: To count a number of items or names of people we need to be able to count text entries. To do this we can use =COUNTA(C3:C30). You need to make sure that headings are not included in the range so that they are not counted as well. Again blank lines are not counted.

▲ Formulae end functions are fundamental to all spreadsheets.

Formulae and functions *continued*

IF: The IF function is called a logical function because it makes the decision to do one of two things based on the value it is testing. The IF function is very useful because you can use it to test a condition and then choose between two actions based on whether the condition is true or false.

The IF function makes use of something called relational operators. You may have come across these in your mathematics lessons but it is worth going through what they mean.

Symbol	Meaning	Examples
=	equals	5 + 5 = 10
>	greater than	5*3 > 2*3
<	less than	-6 < -1 or 100 < 200
<>	not equal to	"Red" <> "White" or 20/4 <> 6*4
<=	less than or equal to	"Adam" <= "Eve"
>=	greater than or equal to	400 >= 200

▲ **Relational operators.**

Activity

Using a LOOKUP function

In this activity you will learn how to create a lookup table using the VLOOKUP function. In the worksheet shown below the data have the headings above the columns so a VLOOKUP table is used.

	A	B	C	D	E	F
1	The Lookup function being used to return product information when a product code is entered					
2						
3						
4	Product Number		1023			
5	Product Description	HB pencils				
6	Product Price		0.04			
7						
8						
9						
10	**Product Number**	**Product Description**	**Product Price**			
11	1021	A4 paper	£5.45			
12	1022	Paper clips	£0.23			
13	1023	HB pencils	£0.04			
14	1024	Red pens	£0.28			
15	1025	Black pens	£0.28			
16						
17						

1 Key in the data exactly as it is shown in the screenshot. Do not type in the values for the cells B5 and B6 as these are to contain formulae that will be entered later.

2 Check that all the data is in the same position as the screenshot shown and that all the values are the same.

3 Cells B5 and B6 contain formulae. In cell B5 type the following formula:

• =VLOOKUP(B4,A11:C15,2,FALSE)

and in cell B6 type the following formula:

• =VLOOKUP(B4,A11:C15,3,FALSE)

In order to use the LOOKUP function we have to understand how it works.

Looking at the formula in cell B5, =VLOOKUP(B4,A11:C15,2,FALSE).

B4 is where the data is entered to match a value held in the table of data. In this case we are matching product number 1023. A11:C15 is the range of cells where the table of data is located. The number '2' then tells the computer it has to look at the second column in this table to find the data it needs to put into the cell where the formula is.

In cell B6 we have the formula =VLOOKUP(B4,A11:C15,3,FALSE) which is the same as the formula in B5 except for the '3' since the data for the product description is in the third column of the table.

Notice that as soon as the formulae are typed in, the data appears automatically.

4 You should now test your worksheet fully. Test this by entering other values for the product number and see if it produces the correct results. Also you should test it by entering a product number that is not in the table. What happens?

Here are some examples of the use of a single IF function:

$$=IF(B3>=50,"Pass","Fail")$$

This function tests to see if the number in cell B3 is greater than or equal to 50. If the answer is true, Pass is displayed and if the answer is false, Fail is displayed.

$$=IF(A2>=500,A2*0.5,A2)$$

This tests to see if the number in cell A2 is greater than or equal to 500. If true, the number in cell A2 will be multiplied by 0.5 and the answer displayed (i.e. 250 will be displayed). If false, the number in cell A2 will be displayed.

Lookup: LOOKUP functions are very useful. When you type in a number such as pupil number, NHS number, product number, the spreadsheet looks through a table until it finds this number along with other important data. For example, if each different product in a shop is given a unique number, then we can store this number along with a description of the product, price, etc., in a table in another part of the spreadsheet. If we type in a product number in another part of the spreadsheet, the spreadsheet will search through the table until it locates the product number and related details.

The two types of LOOKUP function

There are two types of LOOKUP function: VLOOKUP and HLOOKUP. The one to use depends on whether the data in the table is arranged vertically or horizontally. In the activity opposite the data to look up is contained in a vertical table with the headings at the top of the columns so the VLOOKUP function is used.

The HLOOKUP function is used when the data in the table to look up looks like that below.

Level	KS3	GCSE	AS-Level	A-Level	Degree
Rate per hr	£25.60	£27.50	£29.00	£30.00	£41.00

Absolute and relative cell referencing

There are two ways in which you can make a reference to another cell and it is important to know the difference if you want to copy or move cells. An absolute reference always refers to the same cell. The other type of reference, called a relative reference, refers to a cell that is a certain number of rows and columns away. When the current cell is copied or moved to a new position, the cell to which the reference is made will also change position.

To understand the difference we will look at two examples. The first example shows relative referencing with cell B4 containing a relative reference to cell A1. This reference tells the spreadsheet that the cell to which it refers is 3 cells up and one cell to the left of cell B4. If cell B4 is copied to another position, say E5, then the reference will still be to the same number of cells up and to the left, so the reference will now be to cell D2.

With absolute cell referencing, if cell B4 contains a reference to cell A1, then if the contents of B4 are copied to a new position, the reference will not be adjusted and it will still refer to cell A1.

In most cases we will want to use relative cell references and the spreadsheet will assume that ordinary cell references are relative cell references. Sometimes we want to refer to the same cell, even when the formula referring to the cell is copied to a new position. We therefore need to make sure that the formula contains an absolute cell reference. To do this, a dollar sign is placed in front of the column and row number.

Cell B6 is a relative cell reference. To change it to an absolute cell reference we would add the dollar signs like this: B6.

	A	B	C	D	E
1		←			
2					←
3					
4		=A1			
5					
6					

▲ Absolute cell referencing.

	A	B	C	D	E
1		←			
2					
3					
4		=A1			
5					
6					

▲ Relative cell referencing.

KEY WORDS

Absolute reference a reference to a cell used in a formula where, when the formula is copied to a new address, the cell address does not change.

Relative reference when a cell is used in a formula and the formula is copied to a new address, the cell address changes to take account of the formula's new position.

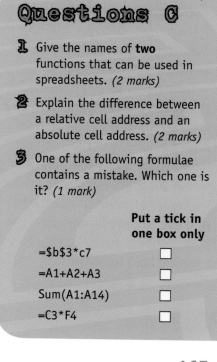

Questions C

1. Give the names of **two** functions that can be used in spreadsheets. *(2 marks)*

2. Explain the difference between a relative cell address and an absolute cell address. *(2 marks)*

3. One of the following formulae contains a mistake. Which one is it? *(1 mark)*

Put a tick in one box only

=b3*c7	☐
=A1+A2+A3	☐
Sum(A1:A14)	☐
=C3*F4	☐

167

Modelling

Modelling means producing a series of mathematical equations that can be used to simulate a real situation. For example, it might predict the likely sales for a new product that is being developed or you could use it for showing the likely flow of money in and out of your bank account when you start work.

In this section you will be looking at how simple models can be created using spreadsheet software and how these models can be used to answer certain questions.

For a personal finances model this could be: Can I afford to buy and run a car? Will I be able to afford a holiday in the summer if I do three hours overtime a week? All these questions are examples of 'what if' questions and you will see how useful spreadsheets are to be able to answer these questions.

The components of a simple model

Models consist of the following components:

Input values

These are the values that are not preset within the model. Input values are usually entered by the user using keyboard entry. It is important that these input values are validated so that only valid data is processed.

Variables

Variables are those items of data that we are likely to change in the model. For example, in a model to show the effect of inflation on someone's savings, the amount they have saved, the interest rate they are getting and the rate of inflation are all variables. Variables should never be put directly into formulae, since for a user to change their value they would have to understand formulae.

Constants

These are those numbers that do not change or that you want to keep the same. Be careful with constants because many quantities stay constant over a short period but not a longer period.

Constraints

A constraint is something that is imposed on a model. For example, you could have a credit limit imposed on you by the bank and your spending cannot go over it.

Rules (i.e. calculations and other operators)

Once data has been entered it can be subject to a range of operators:

> Arithmetic (+, −, ÷, √, etc.)
> Relational (=, <, >)
> Logical (IF, AND, OR, NOT).

Sometimes these calculations and logical operators are referred to as rules.

Benefits of being able to answer 'what if' questions

Spreadsheet models are created so that you can see the effect of changing certain of the quantities. They can be used to provide answers to 'what if' questions. For example, in a model of the economy, the model could be used to answer a question such as: What if we raised interest rates, what would be the likely effect on the economy? For a personal finance model you could use the model to answer a question such as: 'What if I lost my job? For how many months would I be able to manage?'

The person who creates a model can use it to get answers to such questions so that they can better consider any alternatives as to what they should do.

KEY WORDS

Constants those values in a model that do not change in the short term.

Constraint a limit that is imposed on a model.

Model a series of mathematical equations that can be used to simulate a real situation, such as the stopping distance of a car driven at different speeds in different road conditions.

Rules calculations and operators used when making a model.

Variables values in a model that are likely to be changed.

Activity

1 Setting up a simple model

A university student is living away from home for the first time and they want to make sure that they budget the limited amount of money they will have. They are going to create a spreadsheet model. You are going to follow their steps.

1 Load the spreadsheet software Excel.

2 Enter the details shown on the following spreadsheet exactly as they appear on the right.

   Note: You will need to format the text in some of the cells. You will need to format cells D3 and D10 so that the text is wrapped in the cell. (This keeps the cell width the same by moving text so that it fits the width.)

3 In cell D4 enter the following formula to work out the amount the student gets per week from the student loan.
   =b4/c4

4 In cell D5 enter the following formula to work out the amount of money the student gets each week from their part-time job.
   =b5/c5

5 In cell D7 enter the formula =d4+d5 This works out the total weekly income.

6 Enter a formula that will work out the weekly spending on rent and put the answer in cell D11.

7 Copy the formula you have entered in D11 relatively down the column as far as cell D16.

8 Put a formula in cell D18 to add up the spending from cells D11 to D16.

9 Enter a formula in cell D20 that will subtract the total spending from the total income.

10 Your completed spreadsheet should now look like that on the right.

11 Save your spreadsheet using the filename 'Budget model'.

	A	B	C	D	E
1	**Weekly budget**				
2					
3	**Income**	**Amount**	**Weeks**	**Income per week**	
4	Student loan (per term)	£2,250	12		
5	Weekly wage from part-time job	£105	1		
6					
7	**Total income per week**				
8					
9					
10	**Spending**	**Amount**	**Weeks**	**Spending per week**	
11	Monthly rent	£250	4		
12	Books (per term)	£210	12		
13	Food (per term)	£280	4		
14	Clothes (per term)	£240	12		
15	Entertainment (per term)	£50	1		
16	Travel (per term)	£145	12		
17					
18	**Total spending per week**				
19					
20	**Balance left/owed at end of week**				
21					

	A	B	C	D	E
1	**Weekly budget**				
2					
3	**Income**	**Amount**	**Weeks**	**Income per week**	
4	Student loan (per term)	£2,250	12	£187.50	
5	Weekly wage from part-time job	£105	1	£105	
6					
7	**Total income per week**			£292.50	
8					
9					
10	**Spending**	**Amount**	**Weeks**	**Spending per week**	
11	Monthly rent	£250	4	£62.50	
12	Books (per term)	£210	12	£17.50	
13	Food (per term)	£280	4	£70.00	
14	Clothes (per term)	£240	12	£20.00	
15	Entertainment (per term)	£50	1	£50.00	
16	Travel (per term)	£145	12	£12.08	
17					
18	**Total spending per week**			£232.08	
19					
20	**Balance left/owed at end of week**			£60.42	
21					

Modelling *continued*

Activity

2 Using the spreadsheet model to find the answers to 'what if' questions

1 Load the spreadsheet called 'Budget model' if it is not already loaded.

2 You are going to make some changes to the spreadsheet. It is important that you do **not** save any of these changes.

3 The monthly rent has been increased to £275 per month and his employers have reduced his hours for the part-time job, which means he now only earns £50 per week. Will he now be spending more money than he receives? Make these alterations to the spreadsheet to find out.
How much does he have left at the end of the week?

4 His grandparents decide they can give him £50 per week to help him.
Add this amount to the spreadsheet in a suitable place and using a suitable label.
Make any necessary changes to formulae.
How much does he now have at the end of the month?

5 Save your spreadsheet using the filename 'Revised budget model'.

6 Print a copy of this spreadsheet on a single page.

7 Print a copy of this spreadsheet showing all the formulae used.

Activity

3 Improving the appearance of the model

You are now free to develop this model to improve its appearance.
Here are some of the things you might consider:

- Using cell borders and shading to bring attention to the information in the main cells.
- Can you use an IF function to display different messages depending on whether there is a balance left or owed at the end of the week?
- Save the model using the filename 'Final budget model'.

Activity

4 Producing graphs and charts

For this activity you have to use the data from the spreadsheet 'Final budget model' to produce a couple of graphs/charts to show relevant data in the spreadsheet. It is up to you to produce the most appropriate graph/chart.
Ensure that your graphs/charts have:

- a title
- each axis clearly marked or a legend used.

Questions D

1 Many computer models are created using spreadsheet software.
   (a) Explain what is meant by a computer model. *(3 marks)*
   (b) Describe a model you have used that has been created using spreadsheet software. *(2 marks)*

2 A spreadsheet model is used to show the money coming into and going out of a personal bank account.
   (a) Give **two** advantages in using a spreadsheet model to help model personal finances. *(2 marks)*
   (b) Give **one** disadvantage in using a spreadsheet model to help model personal finances. *(2 marks)*

3 Here is a formula that performs a calculation in a spreadsheet:
   =B7*B3
   The above formula contains two cell references. Cell references may be either absolute or relative.
   (a) Write down the relative cell reference in the above formula. *(1 mark)*
   (b) Write down the absolute cell reference in the above formula. *(1 mark)*

   The formula is used in the following worksheet:

	A	B	C	D
1	Ace Computer Supplies			
2				
3	Rate of VAT	17.50%		
4				
5				
6	Item	Price excluding VAT	VAT	Price including VAT
7	16GB Pen drive	£24.99		
8	XD Media card (4GB)	£16.99		
9	SD Media card (8GB)	£32.99		
10	DVD-RW (6 pack)	£10.99		
11	DVD-R (6 pack)	£8.99		
12				
13				
14				
15				

   (c) The formula =B7*B3 is entered into cell C7. It is then copied down column C from cells C7 to C11.
   Explain with reference to this spreadsheet why the formula contains both absolute and relative cell references. *(2 marks)*
   (d) Write down the formula that would need to be entered into cell D7 in order to work out the Price including VAT. *(1 mark)*

Extension activity

Use spreadsheet software to create the model in question 3.

171

Questions

☑ Test yourself

The following notes summarize this topic. The notes are incomplete because they have words missing. Using the words in the list below, copy out and complete the sentences A to J, underlining the words that you have inserted. Each word may be used more than once.

> predictions   data   specialist
>
> formulae   labels   absolute
>
> relative   recalculation

A _____ are the text and numbers that are entered into the spreadsheet.

B _____ are used for titles, headings, names and for identifying rows or columns of data.

C _____ are used for performing calculations on the contents of cells.

D Functions are _____ calculations.

E There are two ways in which a cell in a formula can be referenced; relative cell referencing and _____ cell referencing.

F Unless you tell it otherwise, a formula in a spreadsheet will always use _____ cell referencing.

G A reference to a cell in a formula where, when the formula is copied to a new address, the cell address does not change, is called _____ cell referencing.

H When a cell is used in a formula and the formula is copied to a new address and the cell address changes to take account of the formula's new position this is called _____ cell referencing.

I One advantage of a spreadsheet is that you can change information/data in a spreadsheet model to make and test _____.

J When a value in a spreadsheet changes, then all those cells that depend on that and are linked with a formula will also change. This is called auto _____.

1   Explain the meaning of the following mathematical operators that are used in spreadsheets. *(4 marks)*
    (a) /
    (b) +
    (c) *
    (d) –

2   The diagram shows a simple spreadsheet that a student uses to help budget her money.
    (a) Write down the contents of cell A4. *(1 mark)*
    (b) Write down the contents of cell B7. *(1 mark)*
    (c) Put a tick in the boxes next to those formulae that would correctly work out the total of her expenditure when placed in cell B8. *(2 marks)*

Formula	Tick if formula gives correct total
=B2+B3+B4+B5+B6+B7+B8	
+A2+A3+A4+A5+A6+A7	
=sum(B2:B7)	
=sum(A2:A7)	
=B2+B3+B4+B5+B6+B7	

	A	B	C
1			
2	Rent	£32.50	
3	Food	£13.00	
4	Electricity	£2.50	
5	Phone	£1.50	
6	Gas	£4.00	
7	Entertainment	£15.00	
8	Total		
9			
10			
11			

3   A teacher has produced the following spreadsheet that records the marks in four examinations and works out the total mark.

	A	B	C	D	E	F	G	H
1	Forename	Surname	Exam 1	Exam 2	Exam 3	Exam 4	Total	
2	Amy	Hughes	56	34	67	78	235	
3	Jack	Danniels	56	58	45	56	215	
4	John	Harris	77	89	77	89	332	
5	Asif	Khan	57	79	75	78	289	
6	Ian	Handley	33	75	85	88	281	
7	Daisy	Doyle	74	45	88	90	297	
8	Jane	Adams	90	89	55	87	321	
9	Danielle	Prescott	87	90	77	77	331	
10	Harry	Sumner	99	100	88	90	377	
11	Jane	Hughes	45	56	65	66	232	
12	Adam	Jackson	55	50	45	54	204	
13								
14								
15	Average mark for all pupils							
16								
17								

(a) Which of the following formulae would correctly give the total in cell G2? *(1 mark)*
    A   =SUM(C2:C12)
    B   =C2+D2+E2+F2+G2
    C   =SUM(C2:F2)
    D   =SUM(C2*F2)

(b) Give a suitable formula to put into cell D15 to calculate the average of the numbers in column G. *(1 mark)*

(c) Which cell formatting feature has been used in column A? *(1 mark)*

(d) The text 'Average mark for all pupils' has cell formatting applied to it. Give the name of the cell formatting used. *(1 mark)*

(e) Give **two** advantages of using spreadsheet software rather than working out the totals using pen, paper and a calculator. *(2 marks)*

Worked example

Yasmin has started work after leaving university and has to live away from home. She has recorded her wages and costs in a spreadsheet and this is shown here.

	A	B	C	D	E	F	G	H	I	J
1	Month	Wages	Electricity	Gas	Phone	Rent	Clothes	Food	Total costs	Money left over
2	Jan	£1,500	£60	£55	£62	£210	£40	£600	£1,027	£473
3	Feb	£1,520	£60	£55	£65	£210	£40	£600	£1,030	£490
4	Mar	£1,550	£60	£55	£64	£210	£40	£600	£1,029	£521
5	Apr	£1,550	£60	£55	£50	£210	£40	£600	£1,015	£535
6	May	£1,680	£60	£55	£47	£210	£40	£600	£1,012	£668
7	Jun	£1,690	£60	£55	£47	£210	£40	£600	£1,012	£678
8	Jul	£1,730	£60	£55	£53	£210	£40	£600	£1,018	£712
9	Aug	£1,742	£60	£55	£54	£210	£40	£600	£1,019	£723
10	Sep	£1,800	£60	£55	£62	£210	£40	£600	£1,027	£773
11	Oct	£1,800	£60	£55	£44	£210	£40	£600	£1,009	£791
12	Nov	£1,800	£60	£55	£39	£210	£40	£600	£1,004	£796
13	Dec	£1,745	£60	£55	£53	£210	£40	£600	£1,018	£727
14										

(a) Which one of the following formulae could be used to work out the **Total costs** in cell **I2**? *(1 mark)*

A =SUM(I2:I13)
B =I2+I3+I4+I6+I7+I8
C =SUM(B2:H2)
D =B2+C2+D2+E2+F2+H2+I2

(b) Give a suitable formula that could be entered into cell J2 to work out the money Yasmin has over at the end of the month. *(1 mark)*

(c) The cells apart from cells in column A and row 1 have been formatted.

Which of the following types of cell formatting have been used for these cells? *(1 mark)*

A Euros
B Calculation
C Currency
D Right align

(d) Labels are important in spreadsheets. Give the cell reference of a cell containing a label. *(1 mark)*

(e) Give two advantages of Yasmin using a spreadsheet such as this to help her budget her money. *(2 marks)*

Student answer 1

(a) D

(b) B2−I2

(c) C

(d) A1

(e) It is quicker

It is more efficient

◀ **Examiner's comment**

(a) When adding up cells you do not include the cell where the answer is to be put so this answer is wrong.

(b) The student has forgotten to put the equals sign in front of this formula (i.e. =B2-I2). This small point has cost this student a mark here.

(c) This is correct so one mark here.

(d) A label is any cell that describes data on the spreadsheet so this is correct and gains one mark.

(e) This is a typical answer given by a weak student. The student needs to say in what way is it quicker and in what way is it more efficient. No marks for either of these answers.

(2 marks out of 6)

Student answer 2

(a) C=SUM(B2:H2)

(b) =B2−I2

(c) C Currency

(d) Row 1

(e) Provided the calculations have been set up correctly and tested, the formulae will always produce a correct calculation.

When one of the numbers in the spreadsheet is changed, the cells that depend on the changed cell will recalculate automatically.

◀ **Examiner's comment**

(a) This is correct so one mark here.

(b) This is correct so one mark here.

(c) This is correct so one mark here.

(d) All the cells in row 1 do contain labels but the question asks for a cell reference so this is an incorrect answer so no marks.

(e) These are both very good answers and worth a mark each.

(5 marks out of 6)

Examiner's answers

(a) One mark for the letter, formula or both (i.e. C = SUM(B2:H2)).

(b) One mark for a correct formula, which must include the equals sign

(i.e. =B2−I2).

(c) One mark for C Currency.

(d) One mark for any cell reference in row 1 or column A. It must be a cell reference and not a column letter or row number.

(e) One mark for each of two advantages of a spreadsheet such as:

- If set up correctly, the formulae will always produce a correct calculation.
- Automatic recalculation when numbers are changed in the spreadsheet.
- Once the spreadsheet has been set up it can be reused for different years by putting in different data.
- The data can easily be represented pictorially by getting the spreadsheet to produce graphs and charts.
- You can change the information in the spreadsheet in order to make and test 'what if' scenarios.

Summary mind map

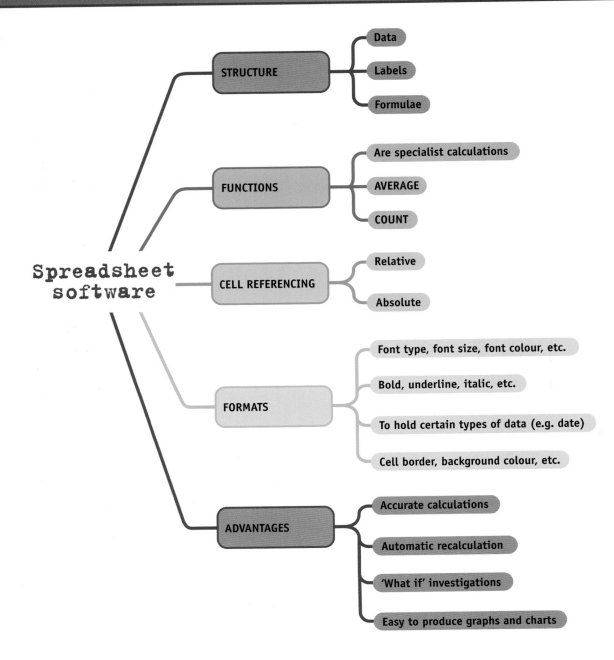

Topic 12

Databases

The key concepts covered in this topic are:

- Data structures and specific features of a database
- Collect/enter data into a database
- Everyday tasks for databases
- Data redundancy
- Outputs
- Mail merging

Database software is software that is able to store the data in a structure that allows the processing of that data to produce meaningful information. As well as using specialist database software, it is also possible to create simple databases using spreadsheet software. There are two types of database called a flat file database and a relational database. You will learn about the important differences between the two types and also the way data is held more efficiently using a relational database.

Contents

Data structures and specific features

You will find out

▷ **About fields, records and files**

Database software is used to put data into a certain structure. Once the data is put into this structure it can be manipulated and output in lots of different ways.

In this section you will learn about the structure of databases and the concept of a key field. You will also be looking at the two different types of database: the flat file and the relational database.

KEY WORDS

Relational database a database where the data is held in two or more tables with relationships (links) established between them. The software is used to set up and hold the data as well as to extract and manipulate the stored data.

Relationship the way tables are related or linked to each other. Relationships can be one-to-one, one-to-many or many-to-many.

Fields, records and files

An organized store of data on a computer is called a database.

Choosing the software to create a database structure

There are two types of software you could use to produce a database:

- spreadsheet software
- database software.

You can build a simple database by organizing the data in rows and columns in a table. In the database shown opposite, the columns represent each of the fields and the rows are the records.

Fields, records and files: what do they all mean?

There are some database terms you will need to familiarize yourselves with. These are:

Data: These are facts about a specific person, place or thing.

Information: Information is data that has been processed into a form that is useful to the user.

Field: A field is an item of data. In other words it is a fact. A Surname would be an example of a field.

Record: The detail relating to a single thing or person is called a record. A record consists of fields.

File: A collection of related records is called a file. The group of records for all the pupils in the school is called the pupil file. Often a simple file holding a single database is called a table.

Table: In databases a table is used to store data with each row in the table being a record and the whole table being a file. When only one table is used, it is a very simple database and it is called a flat file database.

For more complex databases created using specialist database software, lots of tables can be used and such a database is called a relational database.

Key fields

A key field is a field in a database that is unique to a particular record. For example, in a file of all the children in a school a record would be the details about a particular pupil. The key field would be Pupil Number, which would be a number set up so that each pupil is allocated a different number when they join the school. No two pupils would have the same number. Surname would not be unique and so is unsuitable for a key field. It is possible to have more than one key field in a record.

Flat files and relational databases

Computerized databases may be divided into two types: the limited flat file database suitable for only a few applications, and the much more comprehensive and flexible relational database.

Flat file databases

Flat file databases for storing data are little more than a computerized card box file where a single card is used to store one record. A record is simply the complete information about a product, employee, student, order, etc. An item of information such as surname, date of birth, product number, product name, in a record is called a field.

Flat files only contain one table of data. This limits their use to simple data storage and retrieval systems such as storing a list of names, addresses, phone numbers, etc. Flat files are unsuited to business applications where much more flexibility is needed.

QNo	Title	Initial	Surname	Street	Postcode	No_in_house	Type	Garden	Paper	Bottles	Cans	Shoes	Carriers	Compost	Junk_mail
1	Mr	A	Ahmed	18 Rycroft Road	L12 5DR	1	S	S	Y	Y	Y	Y	Y	Y	
2	Miss	R	Lee	1 Woodend Drive	L35 8RW	4	D	M	Y	Y	Y	N	N	Y	10
3	Mr	W	Johnson	42 Lawson Drive	L12 3SA	2	S	S	Y	Y	Y	N	N	Y	4
4	Mrs	D	Gower	12 Coronation Street	L13 8JH	3	T	Y	Y	N	N	N	N	N	0
5	Dr	E	Fodder	124 Inkerman Street	L13 5RT	5	T	Y	N	N	N	N	N	N	9
6	Miss	R	Fowler	109 Pagemoss Lane	L13 4ED	3	S	S	N	N	N	N	N	N	12
7	Ms	V	Green	34 Austin Close	L24 8UH	2	D	S	N	N	N	N	N	N	5
8	Mr	K	Power	66 Clough Road	L35 6GH	1	T	Y	Y	Y	Y	N	N	N	7
9	Mrs	M	Roth	43 Fort Avenue	L12 7YH	3	S	M	N	N	Y	N	N	N	7
10	Mrs	O	Crowther	111 Elmshouse Road	L24 7FT	3	S	M	N	Y	Y	N	N	N	7
11	Mrs	O	Low	93 Aspes Road	L12 6FG	1	T	Y	Y	Y	Y	Y	N	N	8
12	Mrs	P	Crowley	98 Forgate Street	L12 6TY	5	T	Y	Y	Y	Y	N	N	N	11
13	Mr	J	Preston	123 Edgehill Road	L12 6TH	6	T	Y	Y	Y	N	N	N	N	15
14	Mr	J	Quirk	12 Leopold Drive	L24 6ER	4	S	M	Y	Y	N	N	N	Y	2
15	Mr	H	Etheridge	13 Cambridge Avenue	L12 5RE	2	S	L	Y	N	Y	N	N	Y	2
16	Miss	E	James	35 Speke Hall Road	L24 5VF	2	S	L	Y	N	Y	N	N	Y	5
17	Mrs	W	Jones	49 Abbeyfield Drive	L13 7FR	1	D	M	N	N	N	N	N	Y	5

A flat file uses a single table of data set up like this.

This flat file has been set up using spreadsheet software to analyse answers to questionnaires about recycling. Each row represents a record (i.e., the recycling details for one household, and the column headings (in bold) represent the field names with the data in column below.

Simple flat files, which are the same as databases with only one table, can be set up in either specialist database or spreadsheet software. If the data needs a lot of further analysis, then it is easier to set it up using spreadsheet software.

The problems with flat file systems

Flat files store all the data in a single table. The disadvantages of using a flat file are:

- Data redundancy. There is often a lot of duplicate data needed in the table. Time is wasted re-typing the same data and more data is stored than needs to be, making the whole database larger.
- When a record is deleted a lot of data that is still useful, may be deleted.

Relational databases

In a relational database, we do not store all the data in a single file or table. Instead the data is stored in several tables with links between the tables to enable the data in the separate tables to be combined together if needed.

To understand this look at the following example:

A tool hire business hires tools such as ladders, cement mixers, scaffolding, chain saws, etc., to tradesmen. The following would need to be stored:

- data about the tools
- data about the customers
- data about the rentals.

Three tables are needed to store this data and these can be called:

- Tools
- Customers
- Rentals

If the above were stored in a single table, in other words using a flat file, there would be a problem. As all the details of tools, customers and rentals are stored together there would be no record of a tool unless it had been hired by a customer. There would be no record of a customer unless they had hired a tool at the time.

In the flat file there would be data redundancy because customer address details are stored many times for each time they hire a tool. This means the same data appears more than once in the one table.

Hence there are serious limitations in using flat files and this is why data is best stored in a relational database where the data is held in several tables with links between the tables.

Tables consist of columns and rows organized in the following way:

- The rows apart from the first row represent the records in the database.
- The columns contain the database fields.
- The first row contains the field names.

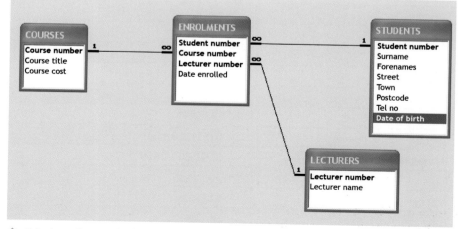

This shows the way the data is stored in a relational database. There are four tables in this database (represented by the boxes) and the links (correctly called relationships) are drawn as lines between the tables.

Data structures and specific features *continued*

Important note

- Records are always rows.
- Fields are always columns.

Each column represents a field of the table

Sex	Year	Form Teacher
M	7	Miss Hughes
M	7	Mr Thomas
F	8	Dr Hick
F	7	Mrs Standford
M	7	Miss Taylor
F	8	Mr Smith

This row contains the set of fields. Each row is a record.

Creating a database

Before you create a structure for a database it is important to look at a sample of the data that needs to be stored.

A school keeps details of all its pupils in a database. As well as personal details (name, address, etc.), the school also holds details of the forms and form teachers.

The person who is developing the database asks the headteacher for a sample of the data (shown below).

It is better to develop a relational database with more than one table. If you look carefully at the set of data you can see that it is basically about three things; Pupils, Forms and Teachers.

Description of data stored	Sample data
Pupil number	76434
Surname	Harris
Forename	Amy
Date of birth	15/03/98
Street	323 Leeward Road
Town	Waterloo
Postcode	L22 3PP
Contact phone number	0151-200-8899
Home phone number	0151-200-1410
Form	7G
Teacher number	112
Form teacher title	Mr
Form teacher surname	Harrison
Form teacher initial	K

Three tables are used with the names: Pupils, Forms and Teachers. The fields in each table are as follows:

Pupils

Pupil number

Surname

Forename

Date of birth

Street

Town

Postcode

Contact phone number

Home phone number

Form

Forms

Form

Teacher number

Teachers

Teacher number

Teacher title

Teacher surname

Teacher initial

The data is put into three tables rather than one because it saves time having to type the same details over and over about the teacher for each pupil. In other words it reduces data redundancy. If there are 25 pupils in each form, the teacher's details (i.e., Teacher number, Teacher title, Teacher surname, etc.) would need to be entered 25 times. If instead we put these details in their own table, we can access them from the Form field and we only need to type in the form details once.

Linking files or tables (i.e. forming relationships)

To link two tables together there needs to be the same field in each table. For example, to link the Pupils table to the Forms table we can use the Form field as it is in both tables. Similarly, the Forms table and the Teachers table can be linked through the Teacher number field.

Pupils

Pupil number
Surname
Forename
Date of birth
Street
Town
Postcode
Contact phone number
Home phone number
Form

Forms

Form
Teacher number

Teachers

Teacher number
Teacher title
Teacher surname
Teacher initial

Creation and development of graphs/charts

Data from a database can be imported into the spreadsheet software for the production of graphs and charts. If the database is fairly simple, such as a database of the replies to a questionnaire, then it would make sense to use a flat file, in which case the data can be analysed using the software the data is already in.

Data from a database can be imported into spreadsheet software to produce graphs and charts.

181

Data structures and specific features *continued*

Questions A

1 A luxury car rental firm keeps the details of the cars it rents out in a table. The structure and contents of this table are shown below.

Reg-number	Make	Model	Year
DB51 AML	Aston Martin	DB7	2009
CAB 360M	Ferrari	360 Modena	2008
P 762 GT	Ferrari	355 Spider	2000
MAS 12	Maserati	3200 GTA	2001
FG09 FRT	Porsche	911 Turbo	2009
M3 MMM	BMW	M3 Conv	2010
T433 YTH	Jaguar	XK8	2009

(a) Give the names of **two** fields shown in the above table. *(2 marks)*

(b) Give the name of the field that should be chosen as the key field. *(1 mark)*

(c) Explain why the field you have chosen for your answer to part (b) should be chosen as the key field. *(1 mark)*

(d) The highlighted details are an example of which one of these? *(1 mark)*

a record   a table
a field   a file.

(e) How many records are there in the above table? *(1 mark)*

2 Here is a sample of the data that is to be stored in an employee database. The data items shown are the employee's surname, initial, street, postcode and telephone number.

Adams, V, 123 The High Street, L23 6DE, 0151-264-1112

Dolan, N, 64 North Way, L9 8SS, 0151-267-0011

Doyle, B, 12 Crosby Road, L23 2DF, 0151-264-1212

Carrol, A, 15 Barkfield Drive, L23 7YH, 0151-261-0899

Conway, T, 6 Windle Hey, L23 6ER, 0151-289-0899

Harvey, J, 4 Empress Road, L22 7ED, 0151-340-9090

Harvey, J, 4 Empress Road, L22 7ED, 0151-340-9090

(a) A table is to be set up with four fields. Give suitable names for the four fields that would be suitable for the above set of data items. *(4 marks)*

(b) The person who is designing the database looks at the sample of data above and notices that there are two people with the same surname and initial who live at the same address.

(i) Explain why the surname would be an unsuitable key field. *(1 mark)*

(ii) It is decided that each employee should be given a unique number. What would be a suitable field name for this field? *(1 mark)*

(iii) Rather than have to keep remembering the last number used, it is decided that it would be better if this number were given automatically by the computer. What type of field should be given to this field from this list: Text, Numeric, AutoNumber or Boolean? *(1 mark)*

Extension activity

Access specialist database software and use it to create a database of your friends and their contact details (e.g., addresses, telephone numbers, email addresses, etc.).

Collect/enter data and everyday tasks

Once the structure of the database has been created it is then necessary to enter the data into the database. Forms are created that are then used to enter the data into one or more tables. After data has been entered into the database, the database will need to be maintained. Data will need to be amended on a regular basis. For example, old data that is no longer needed will need to be deleted. Some data will need to be updated (e.g., a change of address).

There are other everyday tasks that need to be performed such as searching for specific data, producing sorts of data and merging sets of data together.

Collect/enter data in a database

Once the tables have been created, it is necessary to put data into them. Data can be put straight into the tables but it is better to use input forms.

Input forms

Input forms are the electronic version of paper forms and they enable data to be entered directly into the computer via the keyboard. The form is similar to a form on paper and has on it boxes that need to be filled in by the user. The screen design will usually incorporate a title for the form and have prompts (usually the names of the fields) for the data that the user has to type in. Database packages allow you to enter data directly into the tables but it is usually better to create special forms to allow entry into the tables, one record at a time.

Most database software allows you to use text, data, pictures, lines and colour to improve the appearance of the form and this is particularly important if the screen faces the customer. As well as their use for entering the data, the form may also be used as an easy way to view the data on the screen. The data for such a form can come from a table or a query and some information, such as company logos, titles, etc., is stored in the form design itself. Forms can be used to see a single record or all the records for that form.

Forms can be used to:
- enter new records
- view records
- browse records
- add new records
- delete records
- edit records.

Amending data

Amending data means altering the set of data in some way. Amending data can involve:
- updating
- deleting redundant data (i.e., data no longer needed)
- modifying existing data.

Updating

Updating means bringing data up-to-date because of changes that may have occurred since the data was originally input. There are many situations that result in the data needing to be changed and here are just a few of them:

- A woman changing her surname when she gets married.
- A person changing their credit card (i.e., different credit card company, different credit card number, different start and expiry dates).
- A person changing their address.
- A person changing their car.
- A person paying a bill.

◀ **Data should be updated regularly.**

Collect/enter data and everyday tasks *continued*

Deleting

Some of the data stored in a database will become redundant. This means the data is no longer needed and therefore should be deleted. Deleting means removing some of the data from a database. For example, a person may no longer want to receive mail from a certain company, so they will need to be removed from their mailing database.

Here are some other situations where data needs to be deleted:

- Where personal information is wrong and a data subject has asked for it to be deleted.
- When a person dies.
- When a customer has not placed an order for a certain period of time.

It is important to delete data for the following reasons:

- You can waste money sending mail shots and other correspondence to people who have moved.
- It is a requirement under the Data Protection Act that personal information that is incorrect should be either corrected or deleted.

Sorting

Sorting means putting the data into order. Data can be sorted into ascending or descending order and it can be sorted on one or more fields.

Ascending order: in the case of numbers the smallest number is first and the largest number is last. In the case of text the letter A is first and the letter Z is last.

Descending order: in the case of numbers the largest number is first and the smallest number is last. In the case of text the letter Z is first and the letter A is last.

Reasons for sorting data include:

- If lists are printed, then it is easier to find a particular person if they are ordered according to surname.

- You can identify who your best customers are by the amount they have spent in a year. To do this you can sort them according to the total amount they have spent.

Searching/selecting/filtering

In order to narrow down information we can restrict it by asking only for data satisfying certain criteria. For example, in a list of all the pupils in a school, we might only want a list of boys. This is classed as searching using a single criterion. The single search criterion could be: Sex = Boys. Searches can also be performed using multiple criteria. This means that data is being searched for using more than one criterion. For example, we could search for all the boys in a school born before a certain date. The search criteria might be set up something like this:

Sex = Boys AND Date of Birth `< 01/09/99

Sorting techniques

Using spreadsheet software, you can produce a flat file containing data. The data in this file can be sorted according to any of the fields.

Filtering is also useful where only specific information is obtained.

Search for specific criteria

You can search for a record using a single field or a number of fields in a flat file. For example, here the record for the person with the surname 'Harman' is being searched for.

You can also add operators to your search criteria:

Operator	Meaning
=	Equal to
>	Greater than
<	Less than
<=	Less than or equal to
>=	Greater than or equal to
<>	Is not equal to

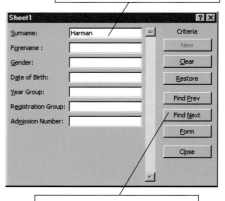

Enter one or more search criteria in these boxes.

Click on Find Next to display the whole record

Merging

Merging means combining two files to form the one file. This means that a file with 100 records could be merged with a file with 50 records to give a new file consisting of 150 records. This could be what happens if two people are inputting data into a database and need to combine both files at the end of the day.

Questions B

1 In order to maintain the integrity of data in a database, data must be updated on a regular basis. Using an example, explain what updating means. *(2 marks)*

2 Explain the difference between sorting and searching data. *(2 marks)*

3 A list of pupil details in a school is sorted into order. It can be sorted into order according to pupil surname in ascending order or descending order. Explain the difference between ascending and descending order. *(2 marks)*

Outputs from a database and mail merging

You will find out

▷ **About the outputs from a database**

▷ **About mail merging**

The outputs from the database are the results after processing the data in some way. For example, a list of data meeting certain criteria might be produced. Data from a database is usually produced in report format. Report format gives more flexibility as to how the information appears on the page. Reports are normally printed out. In this section you will learn about reports.

Some of the fields in databases can be used along with other types of software such as word-processing software to produce a mail merge. A mail merge is where a document is prepared containing blank fields. The mail merge is then performed, which takes the variable data (i.e. some of the fields from the database) and inserts it automatically in each document. In this way variable data from the database can be placed into documents such as letters, business cards, invoices, etc.

Outputs

Reports are used to present the output from a database system. Reports are used to present the data in such a way that it is more suited to printing, although you can view a report on the screen. If there is a lot of detail in a report then it may be better to print it out so that it can be taken away and studied.

Here are some points about reports:

- Reports should have a relevant title.
- The report should contain a date. Information changes, so the person looking at the information needs to know that it is the latest version.
- Only data or information that is important should be included.
- The details of the report should be clearly laid out.
- The report should present the information in the clearest way possible (in some cases this will be using a graph or chart).
- The pages of the report should be suitably numbered (NB you can use headers and footers).

Footers

A footer appears at the bottom of each page in a report and would contain the page number in the case of a multi-page report.

Headers

The header appears at the beginning of a report and usually contains such things as logos, a title for the report and the date when the report was produced.

The contents of a report

In a relational database, if data is stored in the tables it can be output in a report. The data in several tables can be combined to produce a report. It does not matter that the data is held in different tables. Data can also be calculated from the values that are stored and the results of these calculations can be shown in a report.

What is involved in mail merging?

Mail merging involves combining a list of, say, names and addresses with a standard letter, so that a series of similar letters is produced, each addressed to a different person. The list is created either by using the word-processor or by importing data from a database of names and addresses. The letter is typed using the word-processor, with blanks where the data from the list will be inserted.

The steps involved in mail merging are outlined below:

- Create a letter to be sent to different people.
- Create a name and address list for the recipients of the letter.
- Insert the variable fields into the letter.
- Merge the names and address details with the letter to produce the personalized letters.

Outputs from a database and mail merging *continued*

<<Forename>> <<Surname>>
<<Street>>
<<Town>>
<<Postcode>>

Dear <<Forename>>

As you know you will soon be taking your end of year examinations. For those of you in year 11, these will be your GCSE exams. We will be holding a revision club on Mondays and Wednesdays from 4 p.m. to 6 p.m. A variety of staff will be on hand to help you with your revision questions. You should take advantage of this as it is completely free.

There will be a meeting on Wednesday 3rd May at 4 p.m. in the hall for any of you interested in taking up the offer.

Happy revision and good luck.

▲ **Part of a letter, showing the variable fields.**

Kerry Jones
3 Grove Street
Liverpool
L7 6TT

Dear Kerry

As you know you will soon be taking your end of year examinations. For those of you in year 11, these will be your GCSE exams. We will be holding a revision club on Mondays and Wednesdays from 4 p.m. to 6 p.m. A variety of staff will be on hand to help you with your revision questions. You should take advantage of this as it is completely free.

There will be a meeting on Wednesday 3rd May at 4 p.m. in the hall for any of you interested in taking up the offer.

Happy revision and good luck.

▲ **The letter with the variable information added.**

Mail merging is not confined to letters. You can produce any document that needs variable data inserting. For example, each of the following could have the variable data inserted from fields of a database:

- invoice
- payslip
- membership card
- name badge.

◄ **Name tags can be printed using fields from a database and word-processing software to perform a mail merge.**

Activity

Producing a mail merge for name tags for all your friends

Create a database that will hold the forename and surname and form for the names of everyone in your ICT class. This database can be created using spreadsheet software. Now create a name badge using word-processing software and set up fields where the variable information is to be put. Use the mail merge facility of the word-processing software to merge the data in the spreadsheet file to produce the name badges for the class members.

Questions C

1 A new car dealership keeps in contact with their past customers by sending them information about new models. A personalized letter is sent to them with the brochures of the new models.

(a) Describe the processes involved in mail merging. *(4 marks)*

(b) The car dealership holds data about its customers in a database. Explain how this data can be used as a source of data for the mail merge. *(2 marks)*

(c) As well as the production of personalized letters, mail merge can be used for other purposes. Other than the production of letters, give one document that could be produced using a mail merge and describe why mail merge is appropriate. *(2 marks)*

2 Mail merge is often used to produce personalized letters to lots of different people.

(a) Explain what is meant by a personalized letter. *(2 marks)*

(b) Give **one** advantage in using a mail merge to produce personalized letters rather than typing each one individually. *(1 mark)*

Questions

✓ Test yourself

The following notes summarize this topic. The notes are incomplete because they have words missing. Using the words in the list below, copy out and complete the sentences A to H, underlining the words that you have inserted. Each word may be used more than once.

relational database   file   record

key field   sorted   fields   table

A A _____ _____ is a field in a database system that is unique to a particular record.

B The detail relating to a single thing or person is called a _____.

C A record consists of many _____ .

D A collection of records is called a _____ .

E Data can be _____ into ascending or descending order.

F _____ picks out data matching one or more _____.

G A database where the data is held in two or more tables with relationships (links) established between them is called a _____ _____.

H Flat file databases only contain one _____ of data.

Examination style questions

1 Most schools now use databases to store details about each pupil. The table shows some of the fieldnames and data types stored in one pupil database.

Fieldname	Data Type
UniquePupilNumber	Number
Firstname	
Surname	Text
FirstLineAddress	Text
SecondLineAddress	Text
Postcode	
LandlineNo	Text
DateOfBirth	Date
FreeSchoolMeals(Y/N)	

   (a) Give the most appropriate data types for the fields *(1 mark)*:
       (i)   Firstname
       (ii) Postcode
       (iii) FreeSchoolMeals(Y/N)
   (b) Give the names of **three** other fields that are likely to be used in this database. *(3 marks)*
   (c) Explain which field is used as the key field in the database and why such a field is necessary. *(2 marks)*
   (d) It is important that the data contained in this database is accurate. Describe how **two** different errors could occur when data is entered into this database. *(2 marks)*
   (e) Explain how the errors you have mentioned in part (d) could be detected or prevented. *(2 marks)*

2 Explain **one** difference between the database terms 'search' and 'sort'. *(2 marks)*

3 Security is improved with an information handling system compared with a manual system. Give **one** example of how security is improved. *(2 marks)*

Exam support

Worked example

The manager of a tool hire company wishes to use a relational database to help keep track of the business. The databases stores the data in three tables, called: Tools, Customers and Rentals.

(a) Explain what a relational database is and what its main features are.
(5 marks)

(b) What are the main advantages to **this** manager in storing the data in a relational database rather than a flat file database? *(3 marks)*

Student answer 1

(a) *A relational database is a database that has relationships between it. The relationships mean that you can get all the data out of the database in whatever order you want. Relational databases are proper databases and are good for businesses who use them a lot.*

(b) *The manager will be able to access the data from lots of different places.*

To put the data into the relational database requires less typing as you only need to put the data in one file.

The manager will be able to find out information such as which customer has which tool.

▲ **Examiner's comment**

(a) The first sentence could be thought up by anyone using the term 'relational database' so it gets no marks. To obtain the marks, they would need to mention that the relationships are links formed between tables.

The other sentences are vague statements and this student obviously knows little about these databases. No marks are awarded for this part of the answer.

(b) In the first sentence the student looks as though they are getting mixed up with distributed databases.

The second sentence is a main advantage in using relational databases and therefore gets one mark. The third sentence is not specific and is awarded no marks.

(1 mark out of 8)

Student answer 2

(a) A relational database consists of a collection of data organized into different tables with each table containing a set of data that is relevant to the organization. Three tables would be used here; a customer table, a tool table and a rentals table.

The data is put into the separate tables but the tables are linked together so it is possible to combine the information from data in all the tables.

(b) He won't have to type as much in as there is not as much duplication of data as there would be with a flat file.

If a customer changed their address then with a flat file the manager would have to change the address in each current record where a piece of equipment has been hired. This means that if a customer has hired five different pieces of equipment the address would need changing five times.

◄ **Examiner's comment**

(a) There are three separate points made here so three marks.

(b) This student has mentioned duplication of data and easier updating process and has explained each of these well. Two marks are given here.

(5 marks out of 8)

Examiner's answers

(a) One mark each for five features of a relational database.

Note they must be features and not advantages.

- Databases that do not store all the data in a single table.
- They use several tables.
- Tables are linked together (or mention of relationships).
- Data in one table can be combined with data in any of the other tables.
- Minimal duplication of data.

(b) One mark each for three distinctly different advantages that must be relevant to this application.

- Full customer details do not need to be entered when a customer who has rented before, rents again.
- If a mail shot needs to go out to customers, the manager will not need to go through all the orders extracting names and addresses as he can use the Customer table.
- An update is easier to make as the manager will only need to alter the data the once in one of the tables.
- The data is stored more efficiently so it will be faster to do searches and sorts.
- There will be fewer data errors since the data is only entered once, which means the manager can rely on the information produced.

Summary mind map

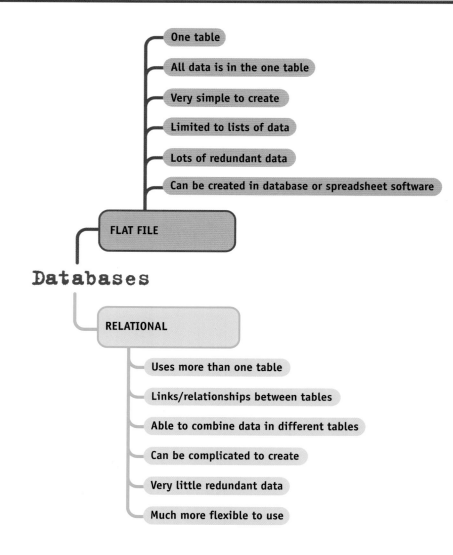

One table

All data is in the one table

Very simple to create

Limited to lists of data

Lots of redundant data

Can be created in database or spreadsheet software

FLAT FILE

Databases

RELATIONAL

Uses more than one table

Links/relationships between tables

Able to combine data in different tables

Can be complicated to create

Very little redundant data

Much more flexible to use

Topic 13

Web browsing and email

The key concepts covered in this topic are:

- Web browser and search engine software

- Email

In order to access, navigate and search the Internet, special software is needed called web browser software and search engine software. Both web browser and search engine software have a number of features and in this topic you will be looking at them.

You will also be looking at email software and its features.

Contents

Web browser and search engine software

▷ **About the features of web browser and search engine software**

▷ **About the role of the Internet service provider (ISP)**

In this section you will be looking at web browser software and search engine software and how is it used to access the Internet and search for and view webpages. This section also covers the role of the Internet service provider (ISP).

Accessing information using the Internet

Web browser software is a program that allows access to webpages stored on the Internet. A web browser allows the user to find information on websites and webpages quickly and it does this through:

- entering a web address (i.e. URL)
- a web/internet portal
- key word searches
- links
- menus.

Entering a web address

One of the ways of accessing a website is to type the website address (i.e. the URL) into a web browser. URL stands for Uniform Resource Locator, which is a complicated way of saying a website address.

Web/Internet portal

Web portals are pages that allow users to access lots of different webpages using the links on the page. Web portals usually contain a search engine, email facilities as well as all the links.

Examples of web portals include:

- Yahoo
- MSN
- AOL.

All of these portals provide links to news, weather, TV, financial information, entertainment, sport, etc.

The role of the Internet service provider (ISP)

Connecting directly to the Internet is very expensive and only suitable for large companies and organizations. Computers used to supply an Internet connection for other computers are called web servers. Most people connect to the Internet via an organization called an Internet service provider, or ISP for short. This is an organization that supplies the connection to the Internet as well as providing services including:

- storage on their server, where you can store your website
- email facilities
- instant messages where you can send short messages to your friends when they are online
- access to online shopping
- access to news, sport, weather, financial pages, etc.

Examples of Internet service providers include:

- AOL
- BT Broadband
- Virgin Media
- Tiscali.

KEY WORD

ISP (Internet service provider) a company that provides a connection to the Internet.

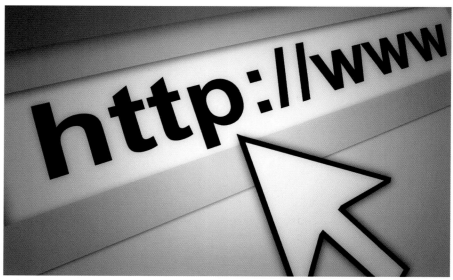

▲ Many URLs start this way.

Key word searches

If you want information about a certain topic but do not have the web addresses of any websites, then you can simply type some key words into the search box on the web browser or search engine.

Links

Links are sometimes called hyperlinks and by clicking on them the user moves to another place on the same webpage, a different webpage on the same site or a webpage on a completely different site. You can also link to files such as a presentation file.

Menus

Menus offer the user a series of selections that they make by clicking on one of them. The menus can use text or images, usually with some explanation on them.

Using search engines

Search engines are programs that you use for searching for information using the Internet. Examples of search engines are Google and Yahoo. The search results are displayed on the basis of relevance or who has paid the most money to get in the top results. Clicking on a search result takes you to a website and may take you straight to the information you want or you may go to the home page of the website. It may then be necessary to perform a search of the content of the website. This is done by entering key words into a search box.

▲ A key word search on a website.

Other features of web browser and search engine software

Home page

The home page is the webpage that shows when the web browser software has loaded. This means it is the first page shown when you log onto the Internet.

▲ A sitemap for a website.

In many cases this is the home page of the Internet service provider but you can change this to another. All you have to do is specify the web address of the webpage you want to use as your home page.

Rollover buttons/images

A rollover button/image is a button/image that changes its appearance when a cursor is moved over it.

Polygon links

These are links that are formed using various shapes.

Overviews and sitemaps

Overviews and sitemaps are forms of navigation. They allow a user to see exactly what is included on the site and to move around the site without having to use the normal navigation on the webpages.

Sitemaps can be a graphical map or text-based. A text-based sitemap is sometimes called a table of contents.

Bookmarks (also called favourites)

When you surf the Internet, you quickly move from one webpage to another. You often find interesting webpages that you would like to revisit in the future. To keep a record of the webpage you can use a bookmark. The bookmark records the web address with a title in a list that you can display at any time. All you need to do to go back to the webpage is to click on the name of the site in the list that is displayed.

Anchor links

If a webpage is long, you can use an anchor link that allows a user to jump to the section of content they are interested in. This saves a user having to read all the content they are not interested in to get to the part they want.

Web browser and search engine software *continued*

Navigation bars

A navigational bar is a bar containing buttons and a search box that appears when a webpage is accessed. The purpose of the navigational bar is to allow the user to move around the site, update the content and find things. The main components of the navigation bar are:

- **Key word search** – the site is searched for one or two key words.
- **Forward** – move forward to the next web page.
- **Back** – go back to the previous page.
- **Home** – return to page you use as your home page.
- **Refresh** – this reloads the webpage being viewed to show any changes since it was last loaded into the computer. This is important for constantly varying information such as share prices or online auction prices.
- **Stop** – this stops loading the current page.

Refresh

Many webpages contain information that changes fairly quickly. This means that if you load a page and the detail on the page changes, you will not see the changes. An example of this is when you are bidding on an item on eBay and it is near the time when the auction ends. You will not see the increases in the prices as more bids come in.

The way to see the changed information is to refresh the page. Refreshing the webpage loads the page again and this new page will contain any changes that have occurred. To refresh a webpage you click on the refresh button in the toolbar of the browser. In most browsers, pressing the function key F5 does the same.

▲ The refresh button on a web browser looks similar to this.

Stop

The stop button is used to stop a webpage from loading if it is taking too long.

▲ The stop button used to stop a webpage from loading.

Block

If you had young children, you would not want them to have full access to the Internet. If they had full access, they could see pornographic images and talk to adults (who could be paedophiles). All web browsers have parental controls that restrict a child's access to parts of the Internet.

The parental controls can be used to block certain things such as:

- access to certain websites
- access to certain email addresses
- instant messaging and chat
- email – you can decide who can send you email
- emails containing file attachments.

Of course as adults you can also use blocks as well.

Pop-ups

Pop-ups are windows that pop-up in front of the window you are looking at to conceal its contents. You then have to click on the cross to make it disappear. Pop-ups windows usually advertise something and they can be very annoying as they waste your time. You can disable pop-ups using the browser software.

KEY WORDS

Hotspot an image or piece of text used as a link. When you click on the image or text, you are taken to another part of the same page, a different page or a different site, or it may open a new file or a new window.

Hyperlink a feature of a website that allows a user to jump to another webpage, to jump to part of the same webpage or to send an email message.

Image map an image that contains more than one hotspot.

Rollover button/image a button/image that changes its appearance when a cursor is moved over it.

URL Uniform Resource Locator, a web address.

Phishing

Phishing is where fraudsters send random emails asking people who are using the online banking system to update their account details. When the user clicks on the link in the email or copies the URL into their browser, they are taken to a fake website that looks similar to the proper bank site. The user is then asked to type in personal information such as name, address, credit or bank details and password. Once this has been done, the fraudster has access to the bank and credit card details.

Phishing filters can be used to filter out these emails so that they end up in your spam folder ready to be deleted.

Commonly used Internet protocols

Internet protocols are methods by which data is sent from one computer to another on the Internet. Two commonly used Internet protocols you need to know about are:

- **POP (Post Office Protocol)** – this protocol is used when you retrieve your email from a mail server (i.e. a special server dedicated to dealing with email). It is designed to be used when you want to store email on your own computer.
- **SMTP (Simple Mail Transfer Protocol)** – this is the protocol used when email is transmitted across the Internet. SMTP is used for outgoing email.

Extension activity

Investigating web portals

Use the Internet to access the following portals:

- Yahoo
- MSN
- AOL

Write a list of the facilities that each portal offers.

Dear Valued Client

Due to a recent security check on Co-operative online banking, we require you to confirm your details by clicking on the logon link below

LOGON

Failure to do this within 24hrs will lead to access suspension

Sorry for the inconvenience

Regards

Co-operative Online Banking

▲ This is a phishing email – there are a few things that may make you suspicious, can you spot them?

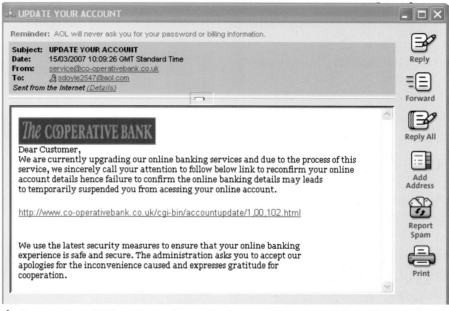

▲ If you used the link from the email it would take you to this website. It looks like a real one – but it isn't. If you entered your banking details now they would be stolen and used to commit fraud.

Questions A

1. There are millions of websites on the Internet.
   (a) Describe **two** ways in which a user can find a specific piece of information using the Internet. *(2 marks)*
   (b) Give the names of **two** interactive features that can be used on a website. *(2 marks)*

2. (a) Give the meaning of the term ISP. *(1 mark)*
   (b) Give **one** purpose of an ISP. *(1 mark)*

3. The Internet is a very useful source of information. Special software called web browser software is used to access information on the Internet.
   (a) Give **three** ways you can access information on the Internet using a web browser. *(3 marks)*
   (b) Explain what is meant by the home page. *(1 mark)*

4. Many people worry about their banking details being stolen and used to commit fraud. One way this could happen is by phishing.
   (a) Explain what is meant by phishing. *(3 marks)*
   (b) Give the name of the feature in web browser software that can help prevent phishing. *(1 mark)*

Email

▷ **About the features of email software**

▷ **About managing the efficient storage of ICT-based communications, attachments and contact addresses**

Email has become as familiar to most people as receiving their normal post through the letter box. It is a service we all use and, like mobile phones, it would be difficult to do without. Much of the material in this section will be familiar to you, as you will likely use email on a day-to-day basis. There will be some things that will be new to you.

An email is an electronic message sent from one communication device (computer, telephone, mobile phone, or portable digital assistant) to another. All web browser software has email facilities.

Email features

Creating a signature

Email signatures allow you to add a personal touch to your email by adding some or all of the following:

- name
- screen name
- address
- phone number
- job title
- a brief message
- favourite quote.

Signatures can be added after you have composed your email by clicking on the signature button. You then get a window where you can enter the details for your signature. The email program will remember this for next time so you only have to enter it the once. You can have lots of signatures depending on who you are sending the email to and each signature can be given a name.

There are many email facilities but those shown here are the main time-saving ones.

Search: Search allows you to find an email using keywords in the title or you can search for all the emails from or to a certain email address.

Reply: This allows you to read an email and then write the reply without having to enter the recipient's email address. As the recipient is sent both the original email and your reply they can save time because they know what your email is about.

Forward: If you are sent an email that you think others should see, you can forward it to them. An email, for example sent to you by your boss, could be forwarded to everyone who works with you in a team.

Looking for online quotes

Some people put interesting quotes in their email signature.

Use the following to find a suitable quote for use in the next activity:
http://www.wisdomquotes.com/

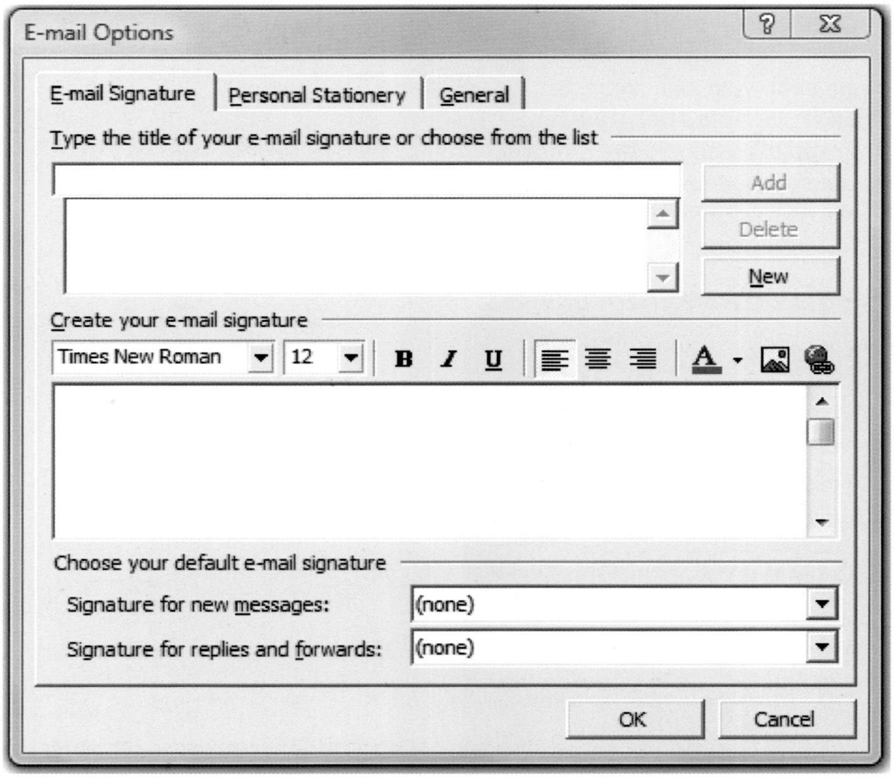

When you set up a signature, a window appears where you type in the information for your signature.

Creating a signature

For this activity you have to find out how email signatures work for the email software you use. If you get stuck remember that you will be able to get online help about this.

Send the email containing the signature to yourself (i.e., the sent to address will be your own email address).

Address book: In the address book are the names and email addresses of all the people to whom you are likely to send email. Instead of having to type in the address when writing an email, you just click on the email address or addresses in the address book.

You can get the email software to automatically add people to your address book if they have sent you or you have sent them email.

▲ The screenshot shows an address book. Rather than type in the email address of the recipients and maybe make mistakes, you can simply click on their address. Notice the facility to create groups.

Using appropriate language to suit audience

Sending an email is no different from producing any other document. The language used must be appropriate to the person who is to receive the email.

Here are a few things you should think about when deciding what to write in an email:

- No need for the formality of a letter.
- Email is meant to be quick and to the point.
- You do not need to worry about the odd typing or spelling mistake.
- Anything you say in an email is as legally binding as if you had written it in a more formal document such as a letter or a contract.
- Emails containing swearing or other inappropriate language may be intercepted by the network manager and read.

Groups

Groups are lists of people and their email addresses. They are used when an email needs to be distributed to people in a particular group. For example, if you were working as part of a team and needed to send each member the same email, then you would set up a group. Every time you needed to send the members of the group email, you could then just send the one email to the group thus saving time.

Manage Group

1. Create a name for your group. | Wonderland
2. Select from the Contact List and use the Add and Remove buttons to create or edit the group.

Contact List:
- Blogs,Fred
- dickens,charles
- mouse,michael
- vader,darth

Group:
- Hatter,Mad
- Wonderland,Alice

[Add ►] [◄ Remove]

3. Optional - To add contacts that are not currently in your Contact List, type the email addresses here. The email addresses must be separated by commas.

Additional Contacts in Group

4. Do you want to share this group? ○ Yes ⦿ No

[Save] [Cancel] [Help]

▲ Using the advanced features of email, you can create groups.

Creating and sending an email to a group

For this activity you are required to produce a distribution list so that the same email can be sent to a group of people. You will need to find out how to do this yourself.

Send the same email to four of your friends and check that they all received it.

Using cc (carbon copy) and bcc (blind carbon copy)

cc means carbon copy and it is used when you want to send an email to one person but you also want others to see the email you are sending. To do this you enter the email address of the main person you are sending it to and in the box marked cc you enter all the email addresses, separated by commas, of all the people you wish to receive a copy.

bcc means blind carbon copy and this is where you want to send an email to one person and others but you do not want the others to see each other's email addresses.

To...	email adress of the person to which you want to send the original email
Cc...	email address 1, email address 2, email address 2
Subject:	Re: School bullying

▲ The cc section contains the email addresses of all the people to be sent a copy of the original email.

197

Email *continued*

For example, a form teacher may send an email to a student about their bullying and send copies of the same email to the students and parents of the children who had been bullied. It makes sense not to allow the person doing the bullying to see the email addresses of all the people sent copies.

File attachments

You can attach files to emails. For example, you could attach a file containing a photograph of yourself obtained from a digital camera, a piece of clip art, a picture that you have scanned in, a long document, etc. Basically, if you can store it as a file, then you can attach it to an email.

You can attach more than one file to email, so if you had six photographs to send, then you could attach and send all of them together.

Before you attach a file you must first prepare an email message to send, explaining the purpose of your email and also giving some information about the files that you are sending (what their purpose is, what file format they are in, etc.). Once the email message has been completed, you click on the file attachment button and select the file you want to send. A box will appear to allow you to select the drive, folder and eventually the file that you want to send.

If you want to send more than one file, you can select a group of files and attach them. Usually, if there are lots of files to send, the files will be compressed to reduce the time taken to send them.

Create and manage an address book

An address book is part of an email package and it is here you can enter all your contacts' details such as names, addresses, telephone numbers and email addresses. Setting this up takes a little time but once it is set up it is easy to send emails because you only have to click on the name and the email address is automatically entered.

You can also set the address book up so that everyone who sends you an email has their address automatically added to your address book.

> **KEY WORD**
>
> **File attachment** a file that is attached to an email.

Organize and name email groups and folders

Rather than keep all the emails together it is better to be organized and set up folders. The way this is done depends on the email package you are using. When sending emails you can organize them in a similar way. For example, you could keep your personal emails in a separate folder to school/college-related work.

▲ Organization of emails is important.

It is important to remember to back up emails, as people tend to forget to do this.

Spam and spam filters

Spam (unsolicited/unasked for email) and often also called junk mail – use software called a spam filter that will remove spam automatically. The emails are not deleted automatically so they are put into a spam folder. You have to briefly check that no email sent by people you know has ended up there and then delete it all in one go.

▲ Spam filters trap spam email but sometimes emails you actually want can end up there.

Questions B

1 Most schools email as a method of communication between staff and students.
  (a) Define what is meant by email. *(2 marks)*
  (b) Teachers often use carbon copy (cc) emails. Explain what is meant by a carbon copy email and give **one** example of how a teacher might use the facility. *(3 marks)*
  (c) Teachers also make use of a facility of email called groups. Explain the purpose of this facility and give **one** example of how a teacher might use groups. *(3 marks)*

2 There are a number of facilities that help a user of email. Give **one** way in which each of the following can help a user of email:
  (a) Address book. *(1 mark)*
  (b) Groups. *(1 mark)*
  (c) File attachments. *(1 mark)*

Extension activity

Practise the use of some of the techniques covered in this chapter. Although all email software is slightly different, they all include the facilities covered here.

You should check that you can create an address book and set up groups.

Also try attaching files so that you can send them to yourself at your home email address. This is a good way of backing up your work.

Extension activity

Imagine you are the owner of a firm that employs a number of people. All of your employees need to use email as part of their job. There have been a number of incidents where the email system has been abused and you want to make sure that it does not happen again.

Write a list of rules that your employees must follow when using the email facilities.

Here is a diagram that will help you with some of your answers:

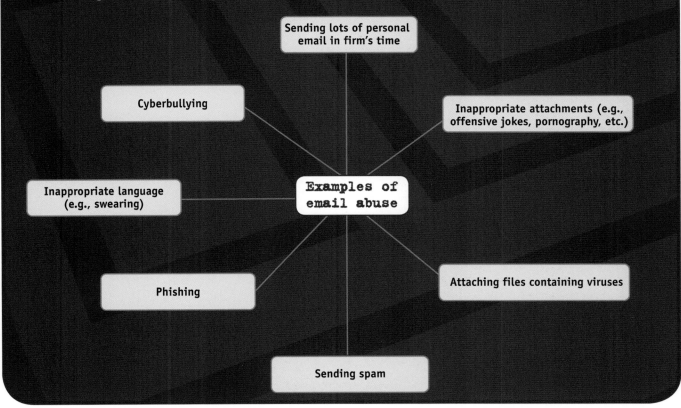

Questions

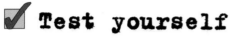 **Test yourself**

The following notes summarize this topic. The notes are incomplete because they have words missing. Using the words in the list below, copy out and complete the sentences A to L, underlining the words that you have inserted. Each word may be used more than once.

address   bcc   forward   spam   cc

web browser   attachment

web servers   signature   hyperlinks

A _____ _____ software is software that is used to gain access to the Internet.

B A URL is used to identify a website on the Internet. Another name for a URL is a web _____.

C _____ allow you to jump from one part of website to another or even to a completely different website.

D Some computers are permanently connected to the Internet and you can connect to the Internet via them. These computers are called _____ _____.

E In order to send an email you need the other person's email _____ .

F You can add an email _____ at the end of an email that can include your name, phone number, your job and even a fun quotation.

G The names and email addresses of all the people to whom you are likely to send email are stored in an email _____ book.

H If you are sent an email that you think others should see, you can _____ it to them.

I When you want to send the one email to a person and then send copies to other people you can use _____.

J If you want to send copies of an email to others but you do not want them to see all the other recipients' email addresses then you can use _____.

K A file that is attached to an email is called a file _____ .

L It is possible to use special software to filter out emails that are unasked for, which are popularly called _____.

Examination style questions

1 A teacher at a school likes students to word-process their homework and submit it to her by email.
   (a) Define what is meant by email. *(2 marks)*
   (b) Give **one** advantage in a student sending their homework to their teacher by email. *(1 mark)*
   (c) In order to send the homework to the teacher the student uses a file attachment. Explain what is meant by a file attachment. *(1 mark)*
   (d) When the file attached to the email is large, the email says that the file is being compressed. Give **one** reason why the email package compresses the file before sending. *(1 mark)*

2 A health centre has lots of people working there such as doctors, nurses, midwives, physiotherapists, etc., who work together as a team. They need to pass messages to each other. As the staff work different hours and in different parts of the building, communicating with each other can be difficult.
   (a) Explain **three** advantages of the staff contacting each other by email rather than by phone. *(6 marks)*
   (b) Describe **two** facilities provided by email software that will make it a lot easier to work as a team. *(4 marks)*

3 Many people now use email to communicate with each other.
   (a) Explain what is meant by email. *(1 mark)*
   (b) When people work together they often make use of cc when using email.
       (i) What do the initials cc stand for? *(1 mark)*
       (ii) Explain why the email facility cc is useful. *(2 marks)*

4 Some people misuse email by sending spam or sending phishing emails.
   (a) Explain what is meant by spam. *(2 marks)*
   (b) Describe what phishing is and explain why Internet users should be wary of it. *(3 marks)*

Exam support

Worked example

A software developer is working as part of a team of ten developers who are developing new software for an online loans company. The team members work in different parts of the country.

The developers need to keep in touch with each other and need to pass work (mainly programs, screen designs, etc.) to each other.

(a) Explain **three** advantages of the developers contacting each other by email rather than by post. *(6 marks)*

(b) Describe **two** facilities provided by email software that will make it a lot easier to work as a team. *(4 marks)*

Student answer 1

(a) Cheaper
Faster
Better

(b) Being able to send the email to more than one person.

Being able to attach a file to an email.

▲ Examiner's comment

(a) The word 'explain' means that a one word answer is not enough. There are 6 marks allocated here. One mark will be allocated to the clear explanation of the advantage with the other mark for the brief explanation of how it relates to working in teams.

Avoid general words like 'better'. You need to be specific. General words such as faster, cheaper, better gain no marks. *(0 marks out of 6)*

(b) 'Being able to send the email to more than one person' is a facility of email software but there needs to be a fuller explanation as to how this facility will make things easier when working as a team.

It is important to tailor answers to the information given in the question.

Again 'Being able to attach a file to an email' is a facility provided by email software. There needs to be further elaboration on why this is an advantage. *(2 marks out of 4)*

Student answer 2

(a) Sending emails speeds things up. An email can be sent and replied to in seconds, whereas a letter sent and replied to takes several days.

It is cheaper, as there is no cost for paper, printing, envelopes and stamps.

It is faster to send an email and get a reply.

(b) It is possible to create groups and send the same email to all the members of the group rather than send each email separately.

They can attach other files to the email such as programs and screen designs and this avoids them having to save them onto removable media such as CD.

▲ Examiner's comment

(a) The first two answers are good answers and would get full marks.

The third answer is almost a repeat of the first answer. It is always important to check your answer is not similar to an answer already given. *(4 marks out of 6)*

(b) Both answers are good and gain full marks. *(4 marks out of 4)*

Examiner's answers

(a) Any three advantages (2 marks each) such as:

- Email is cheaper than a letter. No stamp, envelope or paper is needed. There is also a time saving so this makes email cheaper. Even if the email is sent across the world, it will not cost any more than a local email.
- Quick to write. They are informal, meaning that people do not spend time on the layout, and the odd spelling mistake is acceptable.
- Ideal if there is a time difference. The reader can check email when they are ready.
- Inexpensive and easy to send the same email message to lots of different people.
- You can attach a copy of the sender's email with your reply, so this saves them having to search for the original message.
- You do not have to go out to a post box, so it saves time.
- You do not have to waste time shopping for stamps, envelopes and paper.
- Fast. It takes seconds to send and receive email. If the person at the other end checks their email regularly, then a reply can be sent very quickly.

(b) Two facilities (2 marks each) such as:

- Groups/distribution lists – allowing you to send the same email to a group of people without having to select individual email addresses.
- File attachments – being able to attach files to an email so others can download the work onto their own computers and can comment on it.

EXAM TIPS

If you are asked to 'explain' something then giving a one or two word example is not sufficient. You must include a sentence.

If you are asked to 'give' an answer, then a one or two word answer is ok.

The word 'describe' means that you must give your answer in sentences. Be guided by the mark scheme as to how much you need to write. If there are two marks then the minimum you need is two clearly different points. It is important to note that you are never penalized for writing too much, although you may waste some time.

Be careful about being too creative in your English. You are always limited by the number of lines given for your answer on the paper. Most students get to the end of the number of lines and stop. You need to work out your answer and try to convey it with the minimum number of words. This gives you plenty of room for making more points.

Summary mind maps

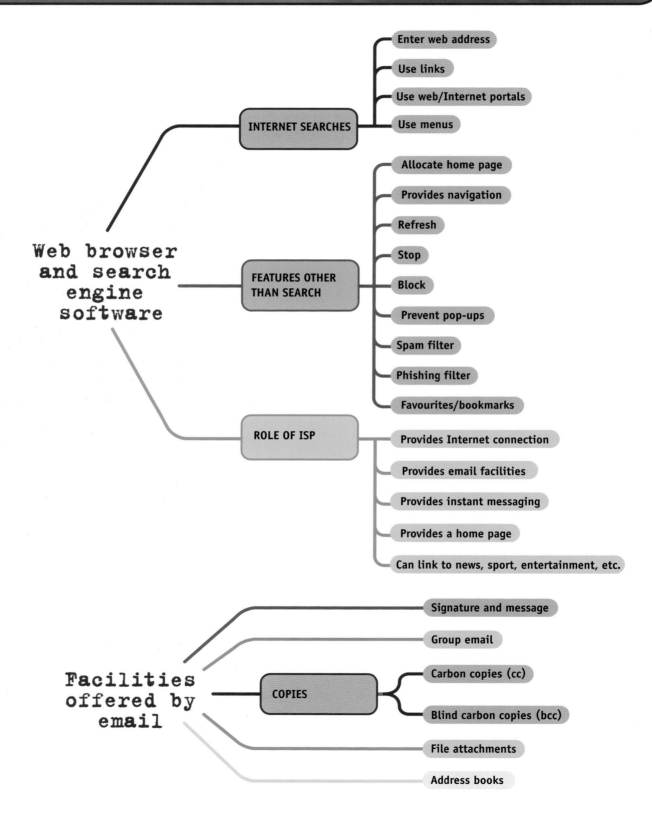

Web logs and social networking

The key concepts covered in this topic are:

- **Understand the use of web logs (blogs)**
- **Understand the use of social networking sites**
- **Explain the advantages and disadvantages of using web logs and social networking sites**

Web logs, commonly called blogs, have become very popular in recent years. They are websites that are created by an individual to tell others, who are interested, about their lives. They are very popular, especially with celebrities and other well-known people, who are keen to keep their fans interested in their work.

Social networking sites are also ways of keeping in touch with friends and they also offer the opportunity to meet new people. Social networking sites are not without their problems and critics and they need to be used with care.

In this topic the features of web logs and social networking sites will be looked at along with their advantages and disadvantages.

Contents

Contents

Web logs (blogs) and social networking sites

You will find out

▷ **About the use of web logs (blogs)**

▷ **About the use of social networking sites**

▷ **About the advantages and disadvantages of using web logs and social networking sites**

Blogs are a great place to talk about yourself or your thoughts and, even if they are viewed by only a few people, they allow you to reflect on your life so far.

Social networking sites have become very popular lately. They have become popular with many famous people such as musicians, film stars and world leaders. In this section you will be looking at the range of social networking services that are available and their uses. You will also look at the dangers that are connected with blogs and social networking sites.

Blogs allow people to read your thoughts, opinions and news.

What is a web log (blog)?

A web log (called a blog for short) is a website providing commentary, personal thoughts or news on a particular subject. It is written in chronological order and can include text, images and links to other blogs and websites. Blogs can be stored on a server with a connection to the Internet or more usually on a server owned by someone else.

Here are some facts about blogs:

- Blogs enable other people to comment on the material posted and often this means that these comments are vetted or moderated by the owner of the blog.
- Blogs can be created quickly by anyone with an Internet connection.
- Blogs can be considered to be online journals.

The use of web logs (blogs)

Blogs are used by anyone who wants to get a message across. There are blogs about all sorts of things but the most popular ones are:

- Personal online diaries – lets people know what you are up to.
- News – this can be the news from ordinary people or from professional journalists.
- Entertainment – here you can post information about good and bad concerts, films, books, etc.
- Food – here people can let others know about good and bad restaurants they have been to, exchange recipes, etc.
- Politics – many politicians have their own blogs. Here you can let them know whether they are doing a good job or not.

KEY WORDS

Blogger a person who posts their comments to a blog.

Web log/blog a website providing commentary, personal thoughts or news on a particular subject. It is written in chronological order and can include text, images and links to other blogs and websites.

The use of social networking

Social networking is a very popular use of computers connected to the Internet. Here are some of the main social networking sites and the services they offer.

Facebook

Facebook offers a way of keeping up-to-date with your friends online. You set up a profile of yourself and you then decide what about you is displayed if someone else also on Facebook types your name. You can see small pictures of other people in their profile along with a list of the people they are friends with. You can send alerts out to all your friends about what you are up to. For example, if you decide to go away to university then everyone can be notified easily.

Facebook offers a great way of getting in touch with people you have lost touch with.

MySpace

MySpace is a social networking site with a music connection holding the site together. Many bands and artists have chosen to have their own pages on the site along with the pages of millions of other ordinary people. MySpace has provided a way for artists to reach their audiences. The site allows direct communication between famous artists and their fans. As well as musicians other celebrities have their own MySpace pages.

When you sign up for MySpace you have to design a Profile page by adding a picture, making a quote and giving some information about your favourite music. You can also add information about your hobbies, the films and books you like, who you would like to meet, and choose your top friends.

◄ Add me as a friend.

"I do all of my tweeting on Twitter now."

The site has a range of services such as:

- email
- bulletins
- blogs
- friend comments
- photographs
- groups
- videos
- music.

Many people put personal details up on this website and although some settings allow anyone to view them, you can set your profiles to private so you can select who sees them.

Bebo

Bebo is a popular social networking site with mainly younger users. There is a whiteboard feature where you can detail what your friends got up to the night before.

There are plans for users to be able to share and download their favourite tracks using the site.

Twitter

Twitter is the simplest of all the social networking sites. All it asks is 'what are you doing now' and you can reply using your computer or your mobile phone. Twitter then sends your reply to all your friends, so they can then repeat the process the other way around. If you are interested in the minute detail of other people's lives then Twitter is the social networking site for you.

The above explanations of some of the main social networking sites give you some of the advantages of these sites but there are some disadvantages.

Advantages and disadvantages of web logs and social networking sites

Web logs (blogs) and social networking sites have their advantages and disadvantages and here are some of them.

Advantages

- Helps build online communities – this is important if you are lonely, disabled, etc.
- Allows you to make friends, with friends of your friends.
- Useful place for expressing your opinion on matters.
- Allows you to find out what your friends and family are up to.
- Useful place to exchange photographs with other family members and friends.
- Students can access blogs so that they can chat about their learning and help each other.

KEY WORD

Social networking site a website that is used to communicate with friends, family and to make new friends and contacts.

Web logs (blogs) and social networking sites *continued*

Disadvantages

- Your image might be posted on an inappropriate website.
- Paedophiles use blogs and social networking sites to obtain images. Again these images can be edited and put onto pornographic websites.
- Your image might be edited using image editing software. For example, an innocent image of a person's face could be put on someone else's body. You can imagine what images could be produced.
- You may be identified from your image even though there are no other contact details.
- You may encounter stalkers or be pestered by email, or worse still they may find where you live and your phone numbers.

- It is very easy to copy an image off a website or social networking site. Images sent to one person can be passed to others without their permission.
- Employers sometimes look at profiles of job applicants on social networking sites to see if they are suitable for a job.
- Starting rumours on the Internet. You only have to start a rumour in a chat room, a blog or on a social networking site and it soon spreads.
- Addiction to social networking sites. Some people cannot go for more than a few minutes before the need to check the sites.
- Social networking sites get users to reveal lots of personal information about themselves and their friends, which is an invasion of privacy.

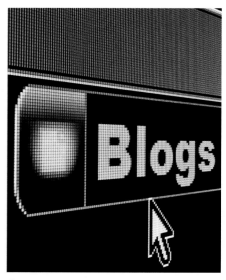

▲ The use of blogs (web logs) is not without its problems.

Questions A

1 Many people have joined social networking sites.
Explain what a social networking site is and give **two** things you might do using the site. *(4 marks)*

2 Social networking sites are not without their dangers.
Give **two** dangers in using social networking sites. *(2 marks)*

3 Social networking sites enable new friends to be made and old friends you have lost touch with to be found again.
Explain **two** different things you can do using social networking sites. *(2 marks)*

4 (a) Explain what is meant by a web log (blog). *(3 marks)*
(b) Give **one** example of the use of a blog. *(1 mark)*

5 Blogs and social networking sites have to be used with care. Give **three** precautions you should take when posting information onto a blog or social networking site. *(3 marks)*

6 Social networking sites are very popular and there are many examples of them.
(a) Give **two** advantages in using a social networking site. *(2 marks)*
(b) Explain why some people do not like these sites. *(3 marks)*

Extension activity

You have been asked to write an article about social networking sites and web logs (blogs) for a local community newspaper. The article is aimed at the older generation who have little knowledge of these things.

You will need to explain what social networking sites and blogs are and the sorts of things that can be done with them and also how they might be able to make use of them.

To make the article more interesting you have been asked to illustrate the article using two or three carefully chosen images.

You are free to choose appropriate software for the production of this article.

Questions

✔ Test yourself

The following notes summarize this topic. The notes are incomplete because they have words missing. Using the words in the list below, copy out and complete the sentences A to I, underlining the words that you have inserted. Each word may be used more than once.

personal   Facebook   photo editing

paedophiles   inappropriate   blog

website   social networking site

A You should never ever give out _____ information when you are online.

B _____ often lurk in chat rooms and social networking sites and are looking for their next victim to abuse.

C _____ is an example of a social networking site.

D You should avoid posting images of yourself on the Internet as they might be misused by posting them on an inappropriate _____.

E Images can be misused by others using _____ _____ software to distort what the original image showed.

F _____ use school and athletic club websites to obtain images.

G When using a service that can be viewed by others, you need to make sure that you do not use any _____ language such as swear words or threats to others.

H A website providing commentary, personal thoughts or news on a particular subject written in date/time order is called a _____.

I A website which allows you to find out what your friends are up to and allows you to make new friends is called a _____ _____ _____.

Questions *continued*

Examination style questions

1 Many people are using social networking sites.
   (a) Explain what is meant by social networking. *(2 marks)*
   (b) Describe **two** different things you can do using a social networking site. *(2 marks)*
   (c) Look carefully at the following list:
         MySpace
         Lots of space
         YourSpace
         Netbook
         Facebook
         Write down the names of **two** popular social networking sites in this list. *(2 marks)*

2 Social networking sites have become very popular especially with younger people.
   (a) Give **two** reasons why social networking sites have become so popular. *(2 marks)*
   (b) Give **two** advantages in using social networking sites. *(2 marks)*

3 Blogs and social networking sites are popular uses of the Internet.
   (a) Explain the differences between a social networking site and a blog. *(2 marks)*
   (b) Explain why a parent might be worried about their children using blogs and social networking sites. *(3 marks)*

4 There are many different ways to meet people using ICT.
   (a) Give the names of **two** ICT facilities that would enable you to meet new friends. *(2 marks)*
   (b) Describe **two** possible dangers in meeting people in real life whom you have communicated with online. *(4 marks)*

5 The growth of social networking sites has meant people can find out a lot about you.
   (a) By giving a suitable example, explain an advantage of them being able to do this. *(2 marks)*
   (b) It is important not to divulge personal data on social networking sites. Explain **two** reasons why not. *(2 marks)*

Exam support

Worked example

Many people spend time and have fun setting up and visiting social networking sites.

(a) Which **one** of these is a popular social networking site? *(1 mark)*

Tick one box only

MyFace	☐
Facebook	☐
Laptop	☐
Netbook	☐

(b) Explain what is meant by social networking. *(2 marks)*

(c) There are a number of problems with social networking sites. Explain **two** of these disadvantages. *(2 marks)*

(d) Give **two** reasons why social networking sites have become so popular. *(2 marks)*

(e) A person is thinking of using either a social networking site or a web log (blog). Explain what advantages there are in using the social networking site rather than the web log (blog). *(4 marks)*

Student answer 1

(a)

Tick one box only

MyFace	☐
Facebook	☐
Laptop	☐
Netbook	☑

(b) It is a site where you can keep in touch with others. You can exchange photos and discuss your interests.

(c) You can meet people thinking they are a fit 17 year old and they turn out to be a fat old man who has sent someone else's picture.

There are loads of them and you have to be on the same one as your mates so it is hard to know which one to use.

(d) You post an online diary of events in time order.

Other people can reply to your posts.

(e) With a blog you need to find an audience as they visit the website.

With social networking sites you can start up with all your friends and family.

Blogs are usually personal diaries, whereas social networking sites are used to keep in touch with old friends and even meet new ones.

◀ Examiner's comment

(a) A netbook is a smaller laptop computer that is lighter and used to access the Internet. Facebook is the correct answer, so no marks here.

(b) Both these points are valid answers so two marks here.

(c) Again two good disadvantages of social networking sites so two marks here.

(d) The student is getting mixed up between social networking and blogs. Both of these descriptions relate to blogs so no marks for this part.

(e) There are three valid and correct points made. The student should have seen that because there are four marks allocated, they are expected to make four points. Three marks are awarded for this part.

(7 marks out of 11)

END-OF-TOPIC REVIEW

Exam support *continued*

Student answer 2

(a)

	Tick one box only
MyFace	☐
Facebook	☑
Laptop	☐
Netbook	☐

(b) They are sites set up on the Internet where you can go to find out what your friends and family are up to. You can exchange files such as digital photographs and can contact others with the same interests as you.

(c) There have been people murdered by people they met off social networking sites.

Many of the profiles that people set up on the site are false, which means you never really know who you are contacting.

(d) You can keep in contact with friends and family if they do not live near.

It is easy to meet people who have identical interests to you.

(e) Blogs are more formal and famous people have them because they are a diary of events of their lives and people will find them interesting.

You have to find a person's blog. If you create one yourself you have to advertise it in order to get people to read it.

Social networks are less formal and more suited to younger people who want to keep in contact with their mates.

Social networks can be used to expand your circle of friends.

Social networking allow lots of interaction, whereas with blogs they are limited to comments.

Social networking can build online communities where people can help each other.

▲ Examiner's comment

(a) This is the correct answer so one mark.

(b) There are three answers worthy of a mark here so the maximum of two marks are awarded.

(c) Two very good and correct answers so two marks are awarded.

(d) Again two good answers so two marks.

(e) The first answer gains two marks because the student has correctly made a comparison between a social networking site and a blog.

For the second answer there is no clear comparison so only one mark is awarded.

For the third answer there is a slight comparison so two marks are awarded.

The fourth answer is just a statement so no marks.

The fifth answer has a clear comparison and is correct so two marks are given.

No marks for the last answer.

There are only four marks maximum for the whole of this part so the student has gained these early on in their answer. In a way they have penalized themselves by writing too much and therefore wasting time.

(11 marks out of 11)

Examiner's answers

(a)

	Tick one box only
MyFace	☐
Facebook	☑
Laptop	☐
Netbook	☐

(b) One mark for each point to a maximum of two marks.

- It is a website that is used to keep in touch with friends and family *(1)*.
- You can meet new people with similar interests *(1)*.
- You can use contacts your friends have made *(1)*.
- You can exchange files such as digital photograph images *(1)*.

(c) One mark for each of two disadvantages such as:

- Paedophiles use social networking sites to obtain images. Again these images can be edited and put on pornographic websites.
- Your image might be edited using image editing software. For example, an innocent image of a person's face could be put on someone else's body. You can imagine what images could be produced.
- You may be identified from your image even though there are no other contact details.

- You may encounter stalkers or be pestered by email, or worse still they may find where you live and your phone numbers.
- People have been raped or murdered by people that have made contact through social networking sites.

(d) One mark each for two reasons such as:

- You can find interesting personal details about people.
- You can find out what friends who have moved away are doing.
- You can meet people with the same interests as you.

(e) Two marks for a comparative reason of why a social networking site might be better × 2.

- Blogs are more formal than social networking sites and they appear in the same format.
- Social networking sites have an immediate audience, which is all the people you know, whereas you have to wait for people to use a blog.
- Blogs offer a diary type of posts where people can comment, whereas social networking sites offer a much greater range of interaction.
- A web log has to keep people coming back by making the content interesting but with a social networking site new users are asked to let others know that they are on the site.

EXAM TIPS

Always use ICT terminology in your answers. Try to always use the correct words to describe an answer.

If you are asked for two things for an answer, make sure that the two you supply are distinctly different and not simply the same thing explained in a different way.

You are almost certain to be asked about the problems of social networking sites, so make sure you can recite at least four problems.

Do not write too much. There is a lot to be said about social networking, so you need to keep it brief. If a sentence does not explain a point to gain a mark then you are wasting your time writing it.

As always, be guided by the marks when deciding what you need to write.

Short snappy sentences making one point are more appropriate than long rambling sentences.

Summary mind maps

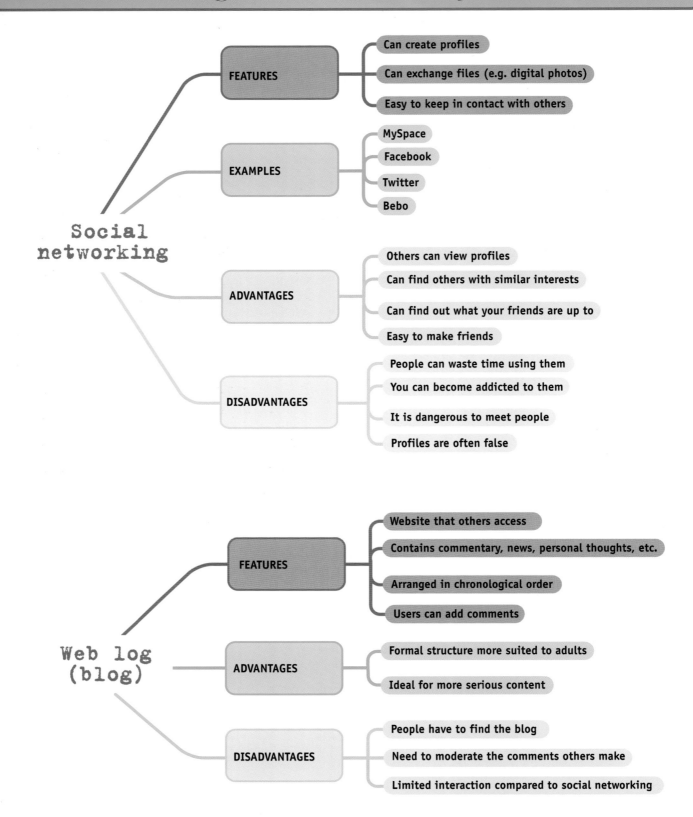

Social networking

- **FEATURES**
  - Can create profiles
  - Can exchange files (e.g. digital photos)
  - Easy to keep in contact with others
- **EXAMPLES**
  - MySpace
  - Facebook
  - Twitter
  - Bebo
- **ADVANTAGES**
  - Others can view profiles
  - Can find others with similar interests
  - Can find out what your friends are up to
  - Easy to make friends
- **DISADVANTAGES**
  - People can waste time using them
  - You can become addicted to them
  - It is dangerous to meet people
  - Profiles are often false

Web log (blog)

- **FEATURES**
  - Website that others access
  - Contains commentary, news, personal thoughts, etc.
  - Arranged in chronological order
  - Users can add comments
- **ADVANTAGES**
  - Formal structure more suited to adults
  - Ideal for more serious content
- **DISADVANTAGES**
  - People have to find the blog
  - Need to moderate the comments others make
  - Limited interaction compared to social networking

Data logging and control software

The key concepts covered in this topic are:

- Data logging
- Controlling devices
- Control–feedback loop

Data logging involves collecting data automatically from sensors over a certain period of time, called the logging period. Data logging can be used in science lessons for monitoring temperature, light, force, etc. In geography lessons data logging can be used to record the weather.

Contents

Data logging

You will find out

▷ **About sensors**

▷ **About data logging**

▷ **About the advantages and disadvantages of data logging**

Data logging means taking measurements automatically using sensors that are able to measure physical quantities such as temperature, pressure, sound, etc.

In this section you will learn about the available sensors, data logging and the advantages and disadvantages data logging offers.

▲ This data logger contains built-in light sensor, sound sensor, temperature sensor, barometric pressure sensor and two inputs where you can attach a whole range of sensors.

Sensors

Sensors are used to detect and measure physical quantities. Here are some examples of sensors:

- Temperature/heat sensors – can be used in school experiments such as investigating the cooling of a hot drink in different thicknesses of cardboard cup. Heat sensors can be used to control a heating system in a home or classroom.
- Light sensors – detect the brightness of light. Can be used to see how light levels affect the growth of a plant. They can be used to control lights that come on automatically when it goes dark.
- Sound sensors – measure the loudness of a sound. Can be used in noise disputes.

- Pressure sensors – barometric pressure sensors measure air pressure; other pressure sensors measure depth of liquid or something pressing on them.
- Humidity sensors – these measure the moisture in the air.
- Passive infrared sensors (PIRs) – these are the sensors used in schools and homes to detect movement. They can be used in burglar alarms and also to turn lights on/off automatically in rooms when a person walks in/out.

Data logging

Data logging is where readings are taken regularly over a period of time using sensors.

The main features of data logging are:

- The readings are taken automatically – there is no need for a human to be present. This means that it is much cheaper than employing a person to do this.
- You can set the logging period – this is the total time over which the readings will be collected.

- You can set the logging rate (also called the logging interval) – this determines how often the readings are taken. For example, in an experiment to investigate the cooling of boiling water, you might decide to set the logging rate to be every minute.
- The sensors can be put in remote locations – you can put them anywhere in the world and the data can be sent back wirelessly and even using satellites.
- The data sent can be stored and processed by a computer.
- The data can be analysed (you can do calculations such as work on the mean, mode, median, range, etc.) and graphs and charts can be drawn. The data can be processed using a spreadsheet package.

Sending data to a computer

The data from a data logger can be sent to a computer. There are two ways to do this:

- Use wires to connect the data logger to the computer.
- Use wireless (usually Bluetooth).

216

Advantages and disadvantages of data logging

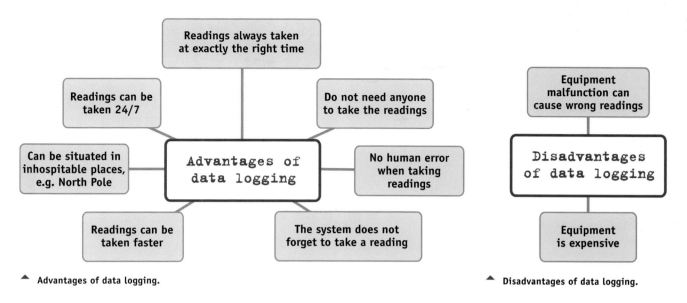

Advantages of data logging.

Disadvantages of data logging.

Data logger a device that collects readings from one or more sensors. The time interval between each reading can be varied (called the logging rate) and the total time over which the data is logged (called the logging period) can also be varied.

Data logging the process of using an ICT system to collect data from sensors at a certain rate over a certain period of time. Remote weather stations use data logging.

Sensors devices that measure physical quantities such as temperature, pressure, humidity, etc.

Activity

Which sensor?

A hot drink vending company wants to perform an experiment to see which cardboard cup is best at keeping hot drinks hot. They need to investigate how the temperature falls in each cup from the temperature at which the hot drinks are produced, which is about 90°C. They decide to use data logging for this.

1. Give the name of the sensor that is needed for this experiment. *(1 mark)*
2. A logging rate needs to be chosen for the data logger. Give the meaning of the term logging rate. *(2 marks)*
3. Out of the following, which logging rate should be chosen? Per second, per minute or per hour. *(1 mark)*
4. Explain what is meant by the logging period. *(2 marks)*
5. Out of the following, which logging period should be chosen? 30 seconds, 1 hour or 24 hours. *(1 mark)*
6. Explain your choice of answer for question 5. *(1 mark)*

Questions A

1. A sensor is used in a geography lesson to investigate how the outside temperature varies over the course of 24 hours. A data logger is used to collect the data from sensors.
   (a) What kind of sensor should be used with this system? *(1 mark)*
   (b) Explain why the sensor you have named in (a) is needed. *(1 mark)*
   (c) What is the logging period for this investigation? *(1 mark)*
   (d) Explain what is meant by a logging interval and suggest a suitable logging interval for this investigation. *(2 marks)*

2. Computer control is used to control growing conditions in a greenhouse. For example, a temperature sensor will turn on a heater if the temperature inside the greenhouse gets too cold.
   (a) Give the names of **two** other sensors that could be used in the greenhouse and for each one describe why it is needed. *(4 marks)*
   (b) Give **two** advantages in using ICT to monitor and control the growing conditions in the greenhouse. *(2 marks)*
   (c) Describe **one** disadvantage in using monitoring and control to control the growing conditions in the greenhouse. *(1 mark)*

Controlling devices

▷ **About using a sequence of instructions to control a screen image or an external device**

▷ **About controlling a range of devices**

The data from sensors can be used to control devices such as a lights, sirens, motors, etc. The data from the sensors is sent to a computer (in most cases a very simple one), where the computer decides what control signal to issue to an output device such as a light.

In this spread you will be looking at control systems.

Using a sequence of instructions to control devices

In control systems it is necessary to give a series of commands for the system to obey. For example, the following set of commands can be used to move an arrow on the screen of a computer. When the arrow moves, it leaves a line.

FD distance
LT angle
RT angle

Hence, using the commands FD 5 would move the arrow forward 5 units and LT 90 would turn the arrow left through an angle of 90°.

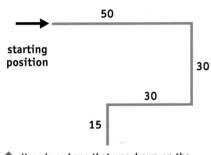

▲ Here is a shape that was drawn on the screen with the numbers representing the lengths of the lines.

The list of instructions that would draw this shape is as follows:

FD 50
RT 90
FD 30
RT 90
FD 30
LT 90
FD 15

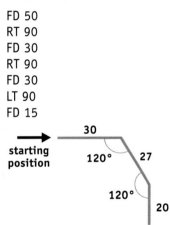

▲ Here is a more complex shape that makes use of angles other than right angles.

The set of instructions to draw this shape on the screen are:

FD 30
RT 60
FD 27
RT 60
FD 20

▲ Most household electrical appliances use computer control.

The main components of a control system

The main components of a control system are:

- **Sensors** – which are the input devices that send data to the computer/processor.
- **Computer/processor** – uses a control program to decide what action to take when it receives data from the sensors. Once the decision has been made, a control signal is sent to the output device.
- **Output devices** – such as lights, heaters, motors, etc., that are controlled by the control signals.

Non-feedback control systems

If you are writing a simple program to control a robot arm by rotating it, you can issue instructions to a stepper motor. A stepper motor rotates in short steps and you can determine how many steps you need. This will determine the angle it moves through.

▲ Stepper motors turn through set angles. This makes them ideal output devices for turning a tap so as to control how much water is released.

The motor will rotate through an angle and then stop. This is a non-feedback system because there is no way of detecting whether it has actually moved through the correct angle. If there was an obstacle in the way of the arm, it may not have been able to move the correct angle. If another instruction was issued then it will simply move from its incorrect starting point.

▲ This security light system uses a PIR sensor to detect a person, so the security lights are turned on.

Simple control systems

Security light system – uses a PIR sensor to sense movement. As soon as the sensor detects movement the system turns the light on. After a period of time the system turns the light off.

A burglar alarm – works in a similar way to the security light using PIRs as the input into the system. This time the output device is a bell or siren that sounds when the alarm is on and movement is detected.

▲ PIR sensors are used to detect intruders and sound an alarm siren in a burglar alarm system.

Electronic toys and games

Many children's toys and games use computer control. Instructions are issued in the form of a stored program and the device then obeys them.

Automatic doors

Automatic doors use motion sensors to detect someone walking towards the door. A signal is sent to an actuator (electric motor) to open the door. The door will only close if the system detects that there is no-one in the vicinity.

▲ Automatic doors use motion sensors to detect people walking towards them.

Burglar alarms and security systems

Modern burglar alarms are quite complex. They use computer control to enable people to set up zones. For example, when they are sleeping upstairs in a house they may want the downstairs alarmed but not the upstairs. Burglar alarms use motion detectors in each room and other detectors on windows and doors to detect people trying to break in.

Smart meters

Smart meters are small devices that all households will have that will give them instant information about the amount of gas and electricity they are using. The sensors will send information about the consumption to the meters, which can be placed in any room. The household can see the amount of power being used and its cost, so this will encourage them to switch lights off, turn off computers, TVs, etc. The system is also able to send the information back to the supplier, so there will be no need to read the meters anymore. This means that the people who read the meters will need to be trained to do a different job.

Car parking systems

Car park management systems provide a means of directing vehicles around a network to car parks with available spaces. Special signs indicating how many spaces are left are controlled by a central computer that uses data from how many cars have entered the car park and how many have left. Computer control is also used to control the barriers in a car park.

▲ A computer-controlled car park barrier – the system has to count the cars coming in and going out to know how many spaces are left.

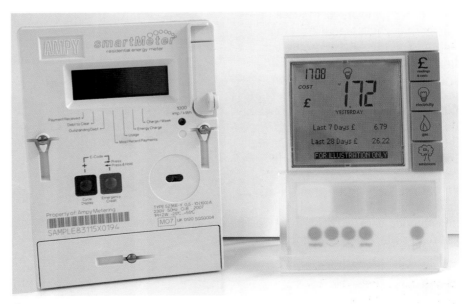

▲ A smart meter.

Controlling devices *continued*

Traffic control systems

Traffic control systems are found in all towns and cities and they ensure that the traffic runs fairly smoothly during the morning and evening rush hours and at other times during the day.

The aims of the traffic control system are:

- To improve the traffic flow.
- To improve driver and pedestrian safety by reducing frustration.
- To make sure that any delays in a journey are kept to a minimum.
- To reduce the risk to the environment caused by fumes from waiting traffic.
- To reduce the use of fossil fuels.

Town traffic systems need to be able to cope with a huge increase in traffic flow from the suburbs into a town centre in the morning and the corresponding reversed flow during the early evening. Setting the traffic lights on a set sequence would not be able to cope with this and serious delays would be the result.

In a traffic control system, the traffic flow is assessed on the basis of the quantity of vehicles around the whole area. Using this information the system can detect in which direction the majority of the traffic is flowing. It can then make sure that cars on main routes into a town will be given more green lights than usual so that the traffic in this direction runs more smoothly. In the evening this situation will be reversed.

Data concerning the number of cars passing is measured using an underground detector cable set into the road surface before a junction.

▲ Traffic control systems help keep traffic moving thus reducing pollution.

▶ The sequence of traffic lights.

Output devices controlled by control systems

The input signals from sensors are passed to the computer, where control signals are passed to output devices to control them. These output devices include the following:

- **Actuators** – devices such as motors that react according to signals given to them by the computers. An actuator can be used to open a window in a greenhouse.
- **Stepper motor** – a motor that turns in a series of small steps. The control signals tell the stepper motor how many steps and in which direction it should move. You can therefore control the angle through which the motor rotates. Stepper motors are found in robot arms.
- **Bells/sirens** – these are used in control systems where an alarm signal needs to be sounded. Burglar alarms use bells/sirens.
- **Heaters/coolers** – are used for controlling the temperature of an environment. Central heating/air conditioning systems use heaters/coolers as the output device.
- **Light** – floodlights or flashing lights are often used in control systems. For example, as well as sounding an alarm, a fire or burglar alarm system will also flash a warning light.

How control systems work

Input bits (0s or 1s) are detected by the sensors. For example, the input bit for a temperature sensor might be set to 1 if the temperature is too high. Otherwise it will be set to zero.

Output bits (0s and 1s) control the output devices. For example, if an output bit is set to 1, a heater could be turned on and if it is 0 it will be switched off.

The control program deals with the input bits and applies rules to it in order to set each of the output bits.

Example

In the heating system in a school, if the temperature gets too high, the heater is switched off and a fan is turned on. If it gets too cold, the fan turns off and the heater comes on.

The input bits and the output bits can be put into a table like this. The first row in the table shows the way the inputs and outputs are numbered.

Input bits	Output bits	
1	2	3
0	0	0

Input bit
    1 = a temperature sensor
Output bits
    2 = heater on/off control
    3 = fan on/off control

The bit pattern for the inputs and outputs is initially: 000

This means the temperature sensor records that the temperature is not too high and that the heater and fan are off.

Here are some bit patterns and what they mean:

1	2	3
0	1	0

The input temperature is 0, which means it is too cold, so this produces a 1 for bit 2 which means the heater is switched on. Bit 3, which is the bit for the fan, is 0 which means it is off.

If the temperature goes too high, bit 1 changes to a 1 and bit 2 (the heater) is switched off (i.e. it is a 0) and bit 3 (the fan) is turned on (i.e. it is a 1).

The bit pattern for this situation would be:

1	2	3
1	0	1

Robotics

Robots have been widely used in manufacturing for years, especially for painting and welding in car factories. Robots are also used for picking and packing goods in large warehouses.

Robots have been developed that will do some of the tasks humans hate to do such as mowing the lawn or vacuuming the floors.

▲ **Robots have been developed for use on farms and these robots can perform a variety of farm tasks such as planting, weeding in-between crops, crop spraying and picking crops.**

▲ **Robots will eventually be seen in all homes. This vacuuming robot is already in the shops.**

There are robots available for the home that will wash floors, clean gutters and clean swimming pools.

The robots that are available at the moment in the home are usually capable of performing one task. In the future you will probably buy a single multifunctional robot capable of carrying out a range of different tasks.

▲ **Mowing the lawn is a chore for many people, so this robot lawnmower is a useful device.**

Controlling devices *continued*

Questions B

1 A turtle that draws on paper uses the following instructions.

FORWARD *n*	Move *n* cm forward
BACKWARD *n*	Move *n* cm backwards
LEFT *t*	Turn left *t* degrees
RIGHT *t*	Turn right *t* degrees
PEN UP	Lift the pen off the paper
PEN DOWN	Place the pen on the paper

Write a set of instructions that makes the turtle draw the following shape.
Assume that the pen is down at the start.
(4 marks)

2 A particular control system controls the conditions in a greenhouse. Sensors for temperature, light, humidity and soil moisture send data to the computer.

If a sensor has detected that a value is too high, it sends a value of 1 to the computer otherwise it sends a 0.

The 4 bits (one for each sensor) are sent in the following order:

Temperature	Light	Humidity	Moisture (soil)

For each of the following, describe the conditions in the greenhouse when the following combination of bits are received *(4 marks)*

(a) 0000
(b) 1100
(c) 0011
(d) 1010

3 Give an example of how a digital pressure sensor could sensibly be used in a school. *(2 marks)*

Extension activity

Use the Internet to research examples of children's toys that use computer control.

Produce some notes explaining how the toys use control for their operation.

Control–feedback loop

Control systems are all around us and we could hardly do without them. We have many control systems in the home controlling the heating, washing machines, dishwashers, showers, burglar alarms and so on. Once you are in a car the number of control systems shoots up. There are control systems to control the management of the engine, the braking system, the airbags and so on. You will also learn what feedback is and how it makes a control system more useful.

Control systems

Here you will be looking at control systems that incorporate something called feedback. Basically, having feedback makes the control system more intelligent and more useful.

The main components of the control–feedback loop

The following diagram shows the three stages of control: input, process and output. It also uses feedback.

Inputs to a control system can come in different ways. They can be:

- given by the user as an instruction (e.g., press a button)

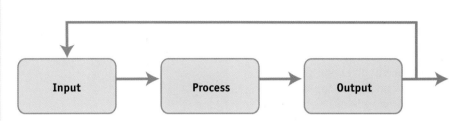

▲ Three stages of control; input, process and output with the feedback loop.

- sensed by sensors that send signals to the computer (e.g., a light sensor senses that a person has walked through a door).

Input data is gathered by an input device and sent to the processor for processing. The processor works with the data and a stored program to work out what it needs to output. Some of the output is fed back to the input using the feedback loop.

The importance of feedback

A computer can be used to control a robot arm. If we want the robot arm to move through a certain angle, we can give an instruction to a special motor that moves small steps at a time. When the command has been issued, the arm will move to the required position. If there is an object in the way of the arm, it will stop. The problem is that if this happens, it will assume that it has reached its desired position. The computer can no longer be sure of its position.

What is needed is a way for the arm to relay its actual position back to the computer. It can do this by making use of sensors. The sensors continually send data about the position of the arm back to the computer. If the robot arm is not in the correct position then remedial action can be taken to put it in the correct position. Here, output from the system directly affects the input. Such a system is said to use 'feedback'.

Example of process control making use of feedback

Here is a simple example of process control.

In a chemical process a container is filled with water to a certain level and heated up to a temperature of 80°C.

1 The computer issues a control signal to the motorized tap instructing it to turn the tap on and let the water into the container.
2 As the water enters and the level rises, the water pressure is continually fed back to the computer.
3 As soon as the pressure reaches a certain value the water is up to the correct level. A control signal is sent back to the tap to turn the water off. At the same time a signal is fed back to the computer from the temperature sensor. If the temperature of the water is less than 80°C, a control signal is sent to the heater to turn it on.
4 The temperature is continually measured and sent back to the computer, which compares the temperature with its set level (i.e. 80°C). As soon as the temperature reaches this level, a control is issued to the heater to turn it off. At any time the temperature drops below 80°C, the heater is switched on again so that the temperature remains constant at 80°C.

Control-feedback loop *continued*

In order to grow plants successfully they need perfect growing conditions. Computer control can be used to monitor the conditions and keep these conditions constant.

Greenhouses have sensors that collect data and this data is sent to the computer which controls the various output devices.

The sensors used to collect the input data include:

- light
- moisture
- temperature.

The output devices that are controlled by the computer include:

- lamps (to make the plants grow faster)
- heater
- motor to turn the sprinkler on/off to water the plants
- motor to open or close the windows (to cool the greenhouse down if it gets too hot).

A control program is written that is used to control the outputs using the inputs it obtains from the sensors. For example, the moisture sensor continually measures the amount of moisture in the soil. If the soil gets too dry, a signal is sent to the motor that turns the sprinkler on. Once the soil is wet enough, it is turned off.

KEY WORDS

Control getting the computer to operate devices automatically.

Control program the step-by-step instructions that control the output devices.

Feedback where the output from a system directly affects the input.

▲ Computer control is used to grow crops in greenhouses.

▲ Lamps, heaters, motors that open/close windows and sprinkler systems are controlled automatically by computers.

Questions C

1 The following diagram shows the input devices and output devices used in a control system.

Write the names of four input devices and three output devices in the boxes. (7 marks)

Input devices	→	Processor	→	Output devices

2 (a) Many control systems make use of feedback.
Explain what is meant by feedback. *(2 marks)*

(b) Explain how feedback is used to control a heater to keep the temperature of a room constant. *(4 marks)*

3 Give the names of **three** different output devices that can be controlled by a computer. *(3 marks)*

END-OF-TOPIC REVIEW

Questions

✔ Test yourself

The following notes summarize this topic. The notes are incomplete because they have words missing. Using the words in the list below, copy out and complete the sentences A to J, underlining the words that you have inserted. Each word may be used more than once.

data logging   frequency   automatically   period   physical

feedback   process control   sensors   humidity

A Data logging involves automatically collecting data from _____.

B The time over which the whole of the data is collected is called the logging _____.

C The process of using an ICT system to collect data from sensors at a certain rate over a certain period of time is called _____ _____.

D In data logging, the logging rate, or logging interval, is the _____ at which the readings are taken.

E The main advantage with data logging is that the readings can be taken _____.

F A sensor that measures the amount of moisture in the air or soil is called a _____ sensor.

G Sensors are devices that measure _____ quantities such as temperature, pressure, etc.

H Control often makes use of _____ where the output has some influence on the input.

I The input to control systems is usually obtained from _____.

J Computers are often used to control a process in a factory. This is called _____ _____.

Examination style questions

1 A home weather station consists of a base station that contains the processor and the display. Sensors are also included that are placed outside the house. Readings from the sensors are relayed back to the base station, which processes the data and produces weather information that is displayed on the screen.

(a) Give the names of **two** different types of sensor that could be used with this system. *(2 marks)*

(b) Describe **one** method by which the data can get from the remote sensors to the base unit that is situated inside the house. *(2 marks)*

(c) Once the data has been sent to the base unit it is processed and the information is output. Describe **one** way that the weather information is output from the system. *(2 marks)*

2 (a) Give the name of a household device that uses a control system. *(1 mark)*

(b) Explain how the control system controls the device you have named in part (a). *(3 marks)*

225

Exam support

Worked example

A cutter in a clothing manufacturing company is controlled by a computer. The cutter is used to cut various patterns in cloth automatically using the following instructions.

START   means start program

CU   means raise the cutter up

CD   means lower the cutter down

FD 10   means forward 10

BK 5   means backward 5

RT 90   means right turn 90 degrees

LT 45   means left turn 45 degrees

CS   means clear screen

END   means end program

The cutter always starts with the cutter up so that it does not start cutting. When the END command is used the cutter will automatically return to its starting position.

(a) Write a program using instructions similar to the above that will cut out the shape shown here. *(3 marks)*

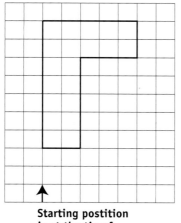

Starting postition is at the tip of the arow

(b) On the blank grid drawn below draw the shape that the cutter will cut out when carrying out the following program. *(2 marks)*

START

FD 6

CD

FD 3

RT 90

FD 7

RT 90

FD 7

RT 90

FD 2

RT 90

FD 4

LT 90

FD 5

CU

END

(c) Give **two** reasons why it would be difficult for the cutter to cut out a complex shape using only those commands given above. *(2 marks)*

Student answer 1

(a) FD 7

RT 90

FD 5

RT 90

FD 2

RT 90

FD 3

LT 90

FD 5

RT 90

FD 2

END

(b)

(c) You can't go diagonally because the diagonal distances are more than one square.

You can only go in straight lines.

▲ **Examiner's comment**

(a) There is no start command instructing the computer to start obeying the set of instructions. Also the student has started from where the shape starts and not from where the tip of the arrow is. There is also no instruction CD telling the cutter to go down and start cutting. The middle section of commands are correct but the student has failed to raise the cutter before the END command.

Only one mark is given for the middle section of correct commands.

(b) The student has drawn the correct shape for the instructions so full marks (i.e. 2 marks) are given.

(c) These are both valid reasons so two marks here.

(5 marks out of 7)

Exam support *continued*

Student answer 2

(a) FD 2

CD

RT 90

FD 2

LT 90

FD 5

RT 90

FD 3

LT 90

FD 2

LT 90

FD 5

LT 90

FD 7

CU

END

(b)

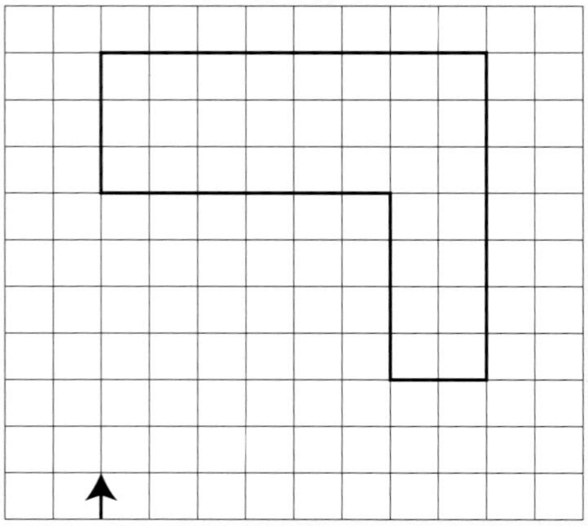

(c) You cannot give the instructions for curves.

Although you can move through angles it would be hard to know what distances to choose.

▲ **Examiner's comment**

(a) Most people would take a clockwise path around the shape but this student has decided to go anticlockwise. This is perfectly OK and these instructions will correctly cut the shape so three marks are given.

(b) The shape drawn on the gird is correct, so a full two marks here.

(c) Both reasons are correct so two marks are awarded.

(7 marks out of 7)

Examiner's answers

(a) One mark for all red steps correct.

One mark for all green steps correct.

One mark for all black steps correct.

NB This is only one of the many possible answers.

There is another correct answer given by a student in Student answer 2.

START

FD 2

CD

FD 7

RT 90

FD 5

RT 90

FD 2

RT 90

FD 3

LT 90

FD 5

RT 90

FD 2

CU

END

(b)

One mark for this section correctly drawn

START

FD 6

CD

FD 3

RT 90

FD 7

RT 90

One mark for this section correctly drawn

FD 7

RT 90

FD 2

RT 90

FD 4

LT 90

FD 5

CU

(c) One mark for each one to a maximum of two marks.

- The cutter can only travel in straight lines/You cannot cut a smooth curve
- The diagonal distances are not known so it is hard to move the cutter accurately through an angle

229

Summary mind map

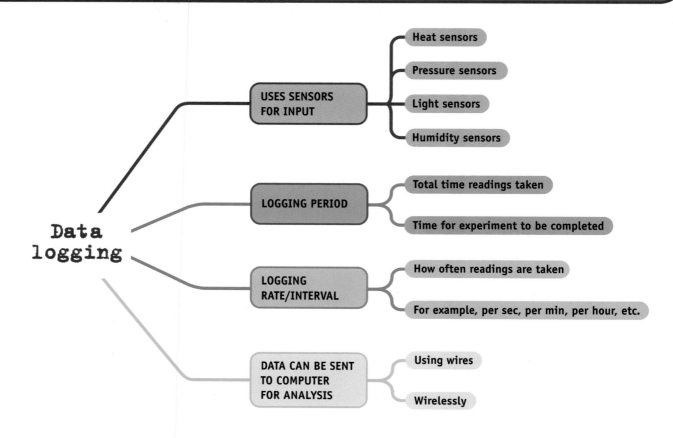

Data logging

USES SENSORS FOR INPUT
- Heat sensors
- Pressure sensors
- Light sensors
- Humidity sensors

LOGGING PERIOD
- Total time readings taken
- Time for experiment to be completed

LOGGING RATE/INTERVAL
- How often readings are taken
- For example, per sec, per min, per hour, etc.

DATA CAN BE SENT TO COMPUTER FOR ANALYSIS
- Using wires
- Wirelessly

Legal issues relating to the use of ICT, including issues of safety and security

The key concepts covered in this topic are:

- **The Data Protection Act 1998**
- **The Computer Misuse Act 1990**
- **Copyright law**
- **Health and safety issues at work**

There are lots of legal requirements when working with ICT and you need to know about all of them. Some of these laws relate to what you can and cannot do using computers and software, while others are concerned with keeping you safe when using ICT.

In this topic you will be looking at the laws that relate to protecting data from misuse, the misuse of computers, and copyright. You will also be looking at the health problems that can develop through the use of ICT equipment and what can be done to reduce the likelihood of them happening.

Contents

The Data Protection Act 1998

It is hard to keep information about yourself private. Everyone seems to want to store it and process it on ICT systems. Each time you fill in a form or complete a questionnaire you are supplying data about you which can then be processed by organizations. Finding out as much as they can about you enables companies to target their marketing. Privacy is a term used to describe keeping your personal details private.

The Data Protection Act (DPA) concerns personal data, which means data:

- about an identifiable person (i.e., the data must be about someone who can be identified by name, address, etc.)
- about someone who is living
- that is more personal than name and address (e.g., medical records, criminal record, credit history, religious or political beliefs, etc.).

There are a number of problems with organizations holding personal data:

- The personal data might be wrong, which means wrong decisions could be made.
- The organization may not take care of the personal data it holds, so others may find out about it.

Examples of the effect of wrong information:

- Your medical details could be wrong, meaning you get the wrong treatment – which could be life threatening.
- Wrong decisions might be made. For example, you could be refused a loan.
- Wrong exam results could affect you getting a job.

The provisions of the Data Protection Act 1998

ICT makes it easy for organizations and businesses to store and process information about individuals. This processing can build up a complete profile about someone. Much of this is done without the person being aware it is done.

To protect individuals against the misuse of personal data, in 1998 the government brought out a law called the Data Protection Act.

Rights of the data subject and the data holder

The person about whom the personal details are held is called the data subject by the Act. The person in the organization who is responsible for the personal data held is called the data holder.

The Data Protection Act 1998 protects individuals by placing obligations on the organizations who collect and process the data (i.e. the data holders) in the following ways.

Registration (also called notification)

It requires anyone who uses personal data to register with the Information Commissioner, who is the person who is in charge of the Act/Law. They must say what data they intend to hold and what they intend to do with it.

Individuals can see their own personal data

Anyone can apply to see the personal data held about them. Organizations have to show it and if there is any wrong information, then it must be corrected.

Data must be kept secure and up-to-date

Data subjects (the people the data is about) can sue an organization that does not keep their personal data secure.

The right for a person to claim compensation

If data is processed unlawfully by an organization then the person can take them to court and claim compensation.

The Data Protection Principles

The holder of the information has eight obligations (called Principles) placed on them by the Data Protection Act and these are summarized below.

The Data Protection Principles state that personal data should be:

1 processed fairly and lawfully
2 obtained only for specified purposes
3 adequate, relevant and not excessive
4 accurate and kept up-to-date
5 not kept any longer than is necessary

6 processed in accordance with the rights of the data subject
7 kept secure
8 not transferred to a country outside the EU unless they have a comparable data protection law.

Exemptions from the DPA

There are a number of exemptions:

- When the data is used for personal, family, household affairs or recreational use.
- Where the data is being used for preparing the text of documents (e.g., the writing of references using a word-processor).
- Where the data is used for producing accounts, wages and pensions.
- Where data is used for mail shots.
- Where the data is used by a sports or recreational club that is not a limited company.
- Where the data is used for the prevention or detection of crimes.
- Where the data is used for catching or prosecuting offenders.
- Collecting taxes or duty.
- Medical records or social worker reports.

KEY WORDS

Personal data data about a living identifiable person that is specific to that person.

Data Protection Act 1998 a law that restricts the way personal information is stored and processed on a computer.

Data holder/controller the person in the organization who is responsible for the personal data. They are responsible for making sure that the organization meets all the requirements of the Data Protection Act.

Data subject the person the personal data is about.

▲ **Biometric methods, such as fingerprinting and retinal scanning, can be used to gain access to computer rooms.**

The personal data guardianship code

The personal data guardianship code is a code to enable organizations and the people who work in them who handle personal data to understand their individual responsibilities. The idea is that the code will cover the law and in a more commonsense way.

The code is made up of the following parts:

Accountability – there must be clear management responsibility, authority and process for dealing with personal data. They must take charge of all aspects of collecting the information, using it, looking after it and the disposal of it when the information is no longer needed.

Visibility – data subjects must have the right to access their personal data and have it corrected should it be wrong.

Consent – the use of the personal data has to be fair and lawful and in accordance with the eight data protection principles. The people who the data is about (i.e. the data subjects) should be given more information on how the information is used and how it is disclosed to others. They can then decide in many

cases not to have the information used a certain way or disclosed.

Access – everyone should have the right to know the roles and groups of people within an organization who have access to their personal data. There should be an audit trail so that it is possible to identify the person who has accessed the information.

Stewardship – organizations collecting personal data should protect it throughout its life span. They need to ensure that the people using the data understand the risks to it, the purposes for which the data was obtained and the need for accuracy.

Responsibilities – all organizations should have a privacy policy that contains details of what they do to ensure they obey the Data Protection Act. It must be clear who is responsible for the protection of all personal data collected.

EXAM TIP

Many questions ask you about the Data Protection Principles, so you should try to remember them off by heart.

The Data Protection Act 1998 *continued*

Physical methods to prevent unauthorized access to computer systems

Physical security is all the sorts of security that prevent physical access by unauthorized people to the buildings, rooms the computers are in and the computers themselves. Good physical security will prevent theft of computers and data and some illegal access to computers.

Here are some things that can be considered:

- Locks – if entry to the building and computer rooms is restricted then it is much easier to secure the computers. Rooms should be locked with keypads, swipe cards and biometric methods (fingerprinting, retinal scanning and voice recognition).
- Clamps – these attach the computers to the desk. They will not stop a determined thief but will stop many others.
- Alarms – these include burglar alarms and alarms that are activated if a cable securing the computers is cut.
- Surveillance – CCTV cameras are positioned around the buildings and inside computer rooms to deter thieves and staff who might misuse computers.
- Location – it makes sense not to have lots of computers in public areas unless necessary. It also makes sense not to locate computer rooms on the ground floor where equipment can be seen by passers by and easily stolen at night.

Questions A

1. Some people are not happy about organizations storing and processing personal information about them.
   (a) Explain, by giving **two** examples, what is meant by personal information. *(3 marks)*
   (b) Give **one** reason why a person might object to an organization storing personal information about them. *(2 marks)*

2. All schools use computer systems to store details about past and present students.
   Schools are required to notify the use of the personal data they hold under the terms of the Data Protection Act 1998.
   (a) Give **three** items of personal information the school is likely to store about their students. *(3 marks)*
   (b) Students in the school are given certain rights under the Data Protection Act.
   Explain **two** of these rights. *(2 marks)*
   (c) One student is worried that the personal information the school holds about them might be incorrect. Explain, with an example, how incorrect information could affect a student. *(2 marks)*

3. Physical security is needed to keep computers safe.
   (a) Explain what is meant by physical security. *(2 marks)*
   (b) Give **two** things an organization could do to ensure the physical security of its computers. *(2 marks)*

4. Many organizations adopt a code called the Personal data guardianship code.
   (a) Explain the purpose of this code. *(2 marks)*
   (b) One of the code's principles is accountability. Explain what this means. *(1 mark)*
   (c) Another of the code's principles is consent. Explain what this means. *(1 mark)*

Extension activity

Find out more about the DPA by accessing the Information Commissioner's Office website at http://www.ico.gov.uk/

Find out more about the Personal data guardianship code by accessing the website at: http://www.bcs.org//upload/pdf/pdgc.pdf

Pay particular attention to the examples that help explain the code.

The Computer Misuse Act 1990 and copyright law

You will find out

▷ **About the purpose of the Computer Misuse Act 1990**

▷ **About the meaning of hacking**

▷ **About the measures that must be taken to avoid hacking**

▷ **About what computer viruses are and the dangers they present**

▷ **About the measures that must be taken in order to protect against viruses**

▷ **About copyright**

▷ **About plagiarism**

▷ **About the moral and ethical implications of illegal downloads and file sharing**

▷ **About the denial of Internet connection by ISPs**

There are a number of different misuses that arose as ICT systems became widespread. For example, hacking and the spreading of viruses became more of a problem. New laws such as the Computer Misuse Act 1990 and laws to deal with copyright theft needed to be introduced to deal with some of the misuses.

"For security purposes, the information should make no sense at all to spies and hackers. We'll bring in someone later to figure out what you meant."

The purpose of the Computer Misuse Act 1990

The Computer Misuse Act 1990 was passed to deal with a number of misuses as the use of computers became widespread.

The Computer Misuse Act makes it an offence to:

- deliberately plant or transfer viruses to a computer system to cause damage to programs and data
- use an organization's computers to carry out unauthorized work
- hack into someone else's computer system with a view to seeing the information or altering it
- use computers to commit various frauds.

Hacking

Hacking is the process of deliberately attempting to or actually gaining access to an ICT system without permission. Most hackers use the Internet to gain illegal access to other computers connected to the Internet. Hacking could also be where an employee gains access to their manager's computer without their permission, for example to see a confidential job reference written about them.

Once a hacker has gained access to a system, they may:

- do nothing and be content that they have gained access
- gain access to sensitive or personal data
- use personal data to commit blackmail
- cause damage to data
- deliberately alter data to commit fraud.

◁ Laws need to be introduced or changed regularly to cope with new misuses or crimes brought about by developments in ICT.

The Computer Misuse Act 1990 and copyright law *continued*

Protecting against hacking

There are a number of things that can be done to protect against hackers and these are outlined here.

Firewalls

Firewalls are software, hardware or both used to filter out unauthorized requests from outside users to gain access to a network. This keeps hackers out. Firewalls also filter data so that only allowable data is allowed into the system.

All networks that have access to the Internet should have a firewall.

Intrusion detection

An intrusion detection system is hardware or software that is used to detect unwanted attempts at accessing a computer system. Usually these attempts will be made by hackers using the Internet. Alarms can be sounded to alert the network manager that someone is trying to access their network illegally. Intrusion detection will also detect any unauthorized log-ins.

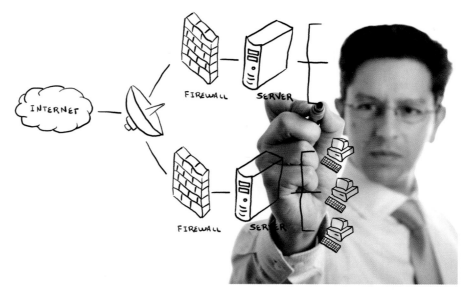

▲ Firewalls are used to protect networks from hackers.

Computer viruses

Viruses pose a major threat to ICT systems. A virus is a program that replicates (i.e., copies) itself automatically and usually carries with it some payload that may cause damage. Once a computer or media has a virus copied onto it, it is said to be infected. Most viruses are designed to do something apart from copying themselves. For example, they can:

- display annoying messages on the screen
- delete programs or data
- use up resources, making your computer run more slowly
- spy on your online use – for example, they can collect usernames and passwords and card numbers used to make online purchases.

One of the main problems is that viruses are being created all the time and that when you get a virus infection it is not always clear what a new virus will do to the ICT system. Apart from the dangerous payload many viruses carry, one of the problems with viruses is the amount of time that needs to be spent sorting out the problems that they create. All computers should be equipped with a virus checker/scanner, which is a program that is able to detect and delete these viruses. These virus checkers need to be updated regularly, as new viruses are continually being developed and would not always be detected by older versions of virus checkers.

Copyright 2002 by Randy Glasbergen.   www.glasbergen.com

"I know a lot of highly-confidential company secrets, so my boss made me get a firewall installed."

What can be done to help prevent a virus attack?

Here are the main things that can be done to help prevent a virus attack:

- install virus checking software
- perform virus scans regularly (can timetable them automatically)
- do not open file attachments to emails unless you know who they are from
- train staff on the problems caused by viruses
- do not allow staff to attach portable drives or memory sticks unless they are scanned first
- do not allow employees to download games and other unauthorized software onto their computers, as these are frequently sources of viruses
- treat all files with suspicion as they may contain viruses.

Copyright law

Issues concerning copyright misuse

Many people spend a lot of time and money creating original work such as a piece of music, a picture, a piece of software, a photograph, a newspaper article, etc. Many of these people do it for a living, so it is only fair that their work should not be copied without permission.

The Copyright, Designs and Patents Act 1988 protects intellectual property from being copied such as:

- software
- text (e.g., books, magazine articles, etc.)
- a new innovative human–computer interface
- hardware (e.g., a flexible screen, the design of a power-saving chip, etc.)
- books and manuals
- images on websites.

KEY WORD

Virus a program that replicates (i.e. copies) itself automatically and usually carries with it some payload that causes damage.

Here are some actions that are illegal:

- copying software and music illegally
- copying images or text without permission
- copying sections of websites without permission
- sharing digital music illegally using peer-to-peer file sharing software
- running more copies of software than is allowed by the site licence.

Avoiding plagiarism

Plagiarism is passing off someone else's work as your own. For example, cutting and pasting an article off the Internet and handing it in as an essay would be plagiarism.

In order to avoid plagiarism:

- Use several articles and put them into your own words.
- If you do use sections of someone else's work you must acknowledge them by stating the source of the material, the date and the name of the author.

▲ Copyright law protects products from being copied.

"You caught a virus from your computer and we had to erase your brain. I hope you've got a back-up copy!"

The Computer Misuse Act 1990 and copyright law *continued*

The moral and ethical implications of illegal downloads and file sharing

You may think that illegal downloads and file sharing do not really hurt anyone as it is only the record companies, software companies and famous stars that have lots of money that are affected. The truth is it affects everyone and here is how:

- It is against the law and is a crime so it is not OK to commit crimes.
- It is theft, as it deprives someone of some money and it is no different from shoplifting.
- The money from illegal copying is bad because much of the money is used to fund other illegal activities such as drug dealing, people trafficking, etc.

- Not everyone who produces copyright material is wealthy and many rely on this income for their everyday living expenses.
- Companies will not invest in new music, software, etc., if they think they will lose most of the income from illegal file sharing and copying.

ISP (Internet service provider) denying service

If you are caught illegally downloading music, video and other files then your Internet service provider (ISP) could deny you the facility of connecting to the Internet. The aim of this is to prevent persistent offenders from gaining Internet access.

Questions B

1. Give the name of the Act that is designed to allow organizations to prosecute anyone accessing their ICT systems illegally. *(1 mark)*

2. Explain, by giving an example, what is covered by the Computer Misuse Act 1990. *(2 marks)*

3. Passwords are one method used to protect against unauthorized access to ICT systems. Give **one** other way in which unauthorized access can be prevented. *(2 marks)*

4. Briefly explain the term software piracy. *(2 marks)*

Extension activity

Someone has said to you that as many people copy software and music illegally, it is morally OK even though it is illegal. Produce a word-processed magazine article putting both sides of the argument. You can use the Internet to provide you with information for this article.

▼ ISPs provide an Internet connection as well as email.

▲ Many people are guilty of copying copyrighted material without permission.

Health and safety issues at work

You will find out

▷ **About the potential health hazards when using computers**

▷ **About the methods of preventing or reducing the risks of health hazards**

As there are potential hazards when using computers and other ICT equipment, you need to be aware of what the hazards are. You also need to be aware of the symptoms of the medical conditions they cause. In this section you will be looking at both of these aspects.

As you will be using computers throughout your life, you need to ensure that you do as much as possible to avoid health problems. In this topic you will looking at the causes of the health problems and what you can do to prevent or reduce the risk of them occurring.

The potential health hazards when using computers

The main health hazards are:

- Repetitive strain injury (RSI) – this is caused by typing at high speed or using a mouse over a long period of time. RSI

is a painful illness that causes swelling of the joints and is similar to arthritis. It can get so bad that many sufferers are unable to use their hands.
- Eye strain – looking at the screen all day can give you eye strain. Many of the people who use computer screens for long periods have to wear glasses or contact lenses. The symptoms of eye strain include blurred vision and headaches.
- Back ache – is a painful condition that prevents you from sleeping properly and doing many activities such as playing sport.
- Stress – computers can cause situations that are very stressful, such as losing your work, getting a virus, being unable to connect to the Internet and so on. All these things tend to go wrong at the worst possible time; for example, when you have an important piece of work to hand in. Stress is also caused by too much work to complete in too little time. Stress can produce headaches and can affect a person's behaviour towards others. Stress can cause depression and mental illness.

Methods of preventing or reducing the risks of health hazards

Back ache

The following can cause back ache:

- Not sitting up straight in your chair (i.e. incorrect posture).
- Using a laptop on your knee for long periods.
- Working in cramped conditions.

RSI repetitive strain injury. A painful muscular condition caused by repeatedly using certain muscles in the same way.

▲ **Back ache is a common ailment in computer users.**

To help prevent back problems:

- Use an adjustable chair (NB in workplaces this is a legal requirement but you need to ensure that the chair you use at home is adjustable).
- Always check the adjustment of the chair to make sure it is suitable for your height. Use a foot support, called a footrest, if necessary.
- Sit up straight on the chair with your feet flat on the floor.
- Make sure the screen is lined up and tilted at an appropriate angle.

Health and safety issues at work *continued*

Repetitive strain injury (RSI)

The following can cause RSI:

- Typing at high speed.
- Using a mouse for long periods.
- Not adopting correct posture for use of mouse and keyboard.
- Not having properly arranged equipment (e.g., keyboard, mouse, screen, etc.).

To help prevent RSI:

- Adjust your chair to the correct seating position for you.
- Make sure there is enough space to work comfortably.
- Use a document holder.
- Use an ergonomic keyboard/mouse.
- Use a wrist rest.
- Keep your wrists straight when keying in.
- Position the mouse so that it can be used keeping the wrist straight.
- Learn how to type properly – two finger typing has been found to be much worse for RSI.

Eye strain

The following can cause eye strain:

- Using the screen for long periods.
- Working without the best lighting conditions.
- Glare on the screen.
- Dirt on the screen.

To help avoid eye strain:

- Keep the screen clean, so it is easy to see characters on the screen.
- Use appropriate lighting (fluorescent tubes with diffusers).
- Use blinds to avoid glare.
- Give your eyes a rest by focusing on distant objects.
- Have regular eye-tests (NB if you use a screen in your work, then your employer is required by law to pay for regular eye-tests and glasses if they are needed).

Stress

The following can cause stress:

- The pace of work (e.g., too much to do in too little time).
- Worry about using the new technology – older people may feel they cannot cope.
- Software that is frustrating to use because it has not been designed properly.
- Losing work, problems with viruses and technical problems.

To help prevent stress:

- Have a help-desk to help with user problems.
- Train users fully in all the ICT systems they use so they do not get stuck.
- Ensure that all software is thoroughly tested so that it does not crash.
- Design the software so that it is easy to use.
- Ensure that users do not have an unreasonable workload.
- Take regular breaks to avoid stress.

Safety issues

There are a number of other safety issues related to using computers and these include the following:

- **Excessive heat/temperatures** – computers give out large amounts of heat and rooms containing them can become unbearably hot in the summer. It is for this reason that most computer rooms are air conditioned.

Air conditioning allows you to adjust the temperature in a room.

- Management of electrical systems/computers – computers need lots of power sockets. Computer equipment uses a lot of power and if multi sockets are used then it is easy to overload the mains circuit. This is dangerous and could cause a fire. Computer rooms should be wired specially.

Electrical circuits should not be overloaded as it can cause fires.

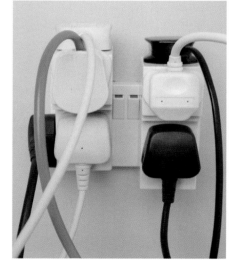

Circuits should not be overloaded like this.

- The cables need to be managed. The cables are of two types: electrical, which carry the power to the components of computer systems, and the cables such as network cables, which carry the data around. There should be no trailing wires that are likely to cause a tripping hazard.

- Any malfunctioning equipment must not be used and should be reported to the technician.
- Lighting is important in computer rooms. There needs to be sufficient light, yet the light should not be so powerful that it produces glare on the screen. Normally lights in computer rooms have diffusers that throw the light out evenly and prevent reflections on the screen.
- Sunlight can be a problem. Apart from heating up the room, it makes the screens difficult to see. Computer rooms should have adjustable blinds to control the amount of light. Screens should also be positioned so they are not in full sun.
- Fire prevention is important. Fire extinguishers should be provided and many large organizations use sprinkler systems that activate automatically. Smoke detectors should also be used.
- Food and drink should be kept away from computers. A drink spill over a computer or keyboard is very dangerous.
- UPS (uninterruptible power supplies) and surge protectors should be used. A power failure can be dangerous. Apart from the damage it can cause to the computers, all the lights go out, which is dangerous. A UPS is used to ensure the power is switched over to a generator or battery supply if the mains fails.
- Surges in power are also dangerous and a surge protector prevents this happening.

KEY WORD

Ergonomics an applied science concerned with designing and arranging things people use so that the people and things interact most efficiently and safely.

▲ A spacious office with diffused lighting.

Activity

Investigating the equipment available to reduce health risks in using ICT

Computer equipment manufacturers and office equipment manufacturers produce many different pieces of equipment to minimize health risks in using ICT.

For this activity you have to produce a handout on the equipment available and how it reduces certain health risks. In this handout you will need to:

- find pictures of the piece of equipment/furniture
- identify which health problem(s) the piece of equipment reduces
- explain how it reduces the health problem
- list the web address(es) where you found the picture and information.

Extension activity

The Health and Safety Executive (HSE) is a government body responsible for enforcing health and safety in the workplace. Further information about health and safety aspects of using computer screens can be found at:

- http://www.hse.gov.uk/pubns/indg36.pdf
- http://www.direct.gov.uk/en/Employment/HealthAndSafetyAtWork/DG_10026668

Use both these sites for information in order to produce a short leaflet (you decide which software to use), outlining the health and safety issues, to be given to Year 7 students when they start senior school.

Health and safety issues at work *continued*

Questions C

1. The use of ICT systems has been associated with a number of health problems.
   (a) State **three** health problems that have been associated with the prolonged use of ICT systems. *(3 marks)*
   (b) In order to avoid computer-related health problems certain preventative actions can be taken. Describe **six** such preventative actions that can be taken to alleviate the health problems you have identified in part (a). *(6 marks)*

2. An employee who spends much of their time at a keyboard typing in orders at high speed is worried about RSI.
   (a) What do the initials RSI stand for? *(1 mark)*
   (b) Give **one** of the symptoms of RSI. *(1 mark)*
   (c) Write down two precautions that the employee can take to minimize the chance of contracting RSI. *(2 marks)*

3. Copy the table and tick (✓) the correct column to show whether each of the following statements about health risks in using ICT is true or false. *(5 marks)*

	True	False
The continual use of keyboards over a long period can give rise to aches and pains in the hands, arms and wrists		
RSI stands for repeated stress injury		
Wrist rests and ergonomic keyboards can help prevent RSI		
Back ache can be caused by slouching in your chair when using a computer		
Glare on the screen can cause RSI		

4. A computer worker said that using computers can be stressful. Describe **one** situation in which using a computer is stressful. *(1 mark)*

EXAM TIP

Always be guided by the mark scheme to decide how much to write. For example, if you are asked to describe an advantage or disadvantage for one mark, then just a brief statement would be enough. If two marks were allocated, then you would be required to supplement this with further detail or an appropriate example.

Always think out your answer before you start writing it. You need to ensure you make your answer clear, so you need a little time to think about it.

Advantages (sometimes called benefits) and disadvantages are very popular questions. When covering a topic for revision, it is a good idea to list advantages and disadvantages where appropriate.

You need to be clear about the health problems (i.e., what they are called), the symptoms (i.e., how they affect your body) and what can be done to help to prevent them.

Extension activity

Repetitive strain injury (RSI) has become a major worry for those people who use computers continually throughout their working day.

You are required to use the Internet to find out more about this condition. You need to find out:

- What are the symptoms?
- Can you make it better?
- What is the likelihood of getting it?
- What can you do to prevent it?

Questions

✓ Test yourself

The following notes summarize this topic. The notes are incomplete because they have words missing. Using the words in the list below, copy out and complete the sentences A to M, underlining the words that you have inserted. Each word may be used more than once.

headaches	eye-tests	RSI	Data Protection	blinds
	viruses	eye strain	deleted	hacking
		Computer Misuse	back ache	

A _____ is caused by typing at high speed or using a mouse over a long period of time.

B Looking at the screen all day can give you _____.

C The symptoms of eye strain include blurred vision and _____.

D Working in cramped conditions and not adopting the correct posture when using a computer can lead to _____.

E An adjustable chair should be used in order to prevent _____.

F Working in poor lighting conditions can lead to _____.

G Adjustable _____ should be used on windows to prevent glare on the screen and the screen should also be kept free from dirt.

H It is important to have regular _____ and use glasses or contact lenses when working with computers if needed.

I The _____ _____ Act 1998 was passed to protect individuals from the misuse of personal data.

J Anyone can apply to see the data held about them and if the information is wrong then they can have it corrected or _____.

K The Computer Misuse Act makes it an offence to deliberately plant or transfer _____ to a computer system to cause damage to programs and data.

L Unauthorized use of an ICT system with a view to seeing or altering the data is called _____.

M Hacking is made a criminal offence under the _____ _____ Act 1990.

END-OF-TOPIC REVIEW

Questions *continued*

Examination style questions

1 (a) What do the initials RSI stand for? *(1 mark)*

(b) RSI is a health problem that may be caused by prolonged computer use.
Write a sentence to show how RSI is caused. *(2 marks)*

(c) Write down **one** precaution that a computer user can take to minimize the chance of contracting RSI. *(1 mark)*

2 Here is a list of health problems. Write down the names of those that can be caused by prolonged computer use: *(4 marks)*

Back ache
Toothache
Stress
Sprained ankle
RSI
Eye strain

3 People who work with computers for long periods may experience some health problems. These health problems include eye strain and RSI.

(a) Give the names of **two** health problems other than eye strain and RSI that a user may experience. *(2 marks)*

(b) Explain **two** things a user should do when sitting in a chair at a desk and using a computer in order to prevent future health problems. *(2 marks)*

4 Put a tick if the statement is one of the Principles of the Data Protection Act 1998. *(4 marks)*

Statement	Tick
Data is adequate, relevant and not excessive	☐
Personal data should be adequate and kept up-to-date	☐
Software should not be copied	☐
Personal data should only be used for one or more specified and lawful purposes	☐
There must be sufficient security to cover the personal data	☐
Hacking is illegal	☐

5 The Data Protection Act 1998 protects people from having their personal data misused.

There are eight Data Protection Principles that are regulations that an organization must adhere to when collecting, storing and processing personal information.

(a) State **three** of the Data Protection Principles. *(3 marks)*

(b) Tick **two** boxes to show which of the following have partial exemption from the Data Protection Act 1998. *(2 marks)*

	Tick *two* boxes
Word-processed documents	☐
Insurance company data	☐
A database of friends' names and addresses	☐
A database of doctors' patients	☐
Files stored on paper	☐

(c) The Data Protection Act 1998 gives certain rights to data subjects.

(i) Explain what is meant by a data subject. *(2 marks)*

(ii) Give **two** rights that are given to data subjects under the Act. *(2 marks)*

6 Protection of your privacy is essential if you bank or shop online.

(a) Give the names of **three** different pieces of personal information you would need to supply in order to complete an online purchase. *(3 marks)*

(b) Give **one** item of personal information (that you would not want others to know) that you need to supply in order to complete an online purchase. *(1 mark)*

(c) Give **one** method by which the item of personal information in your answer to (b) can be kept private. *(1 mark)*

Case studies

Case study 1

Cyber warfare

Most developed countries are totally dependent on their ICT systems and the loss of such systems could do serious damage to the infrastructure of countries.

For example, could you imagine the loss of the Internet for a lengthy period or the loss of the entire mobile phone network. What about the erasure of all the health information on the NHS computers or the erasure of tax information, so that the government could not collect money to pay for schools, hospitals, the police, etc.

In many ways damage to ICT systems could do a lot more damage than a series of terrorist bombs or even a war using conventional weapons.

Many terrorist groups use the Internet for recruitment, propaganda and communication purposes. They may also conduct cyber attacks against their enemies.

Some countries have started to investigate the use of the Internet to cause damage to the infrastructure of other countries. Targets would typically involve key businesses, the national power grid (for electricity supply), financial markets and government departments. The government has decided to set up a new office for cyber security. This department will monitor, analyse and counter any cyber attacks.

It is interesting to note that as well as protecting against cyber warfare, Britain is investigating the potential of using cyber warfare itself should the need arise.

The government has turned to hackers who have the experience to know how to get past security methods and break into networks.

Cyber attacks from other countries have already occurred. For example, there was an attack on the Foreign Office's computer from China and also an attack on the House of Common's computer system that temporarily closed it down.

Questions

1 **(a)** Explain what hacking is and why it is so important to keep hackers out of key networks. *(3 marks)*

(b) Networks can be protected using firewalls. Explain how a firewall can be used to prevent unauthorized access. *(2 marks)*

2 Give **two** examples of systems that could be hacked into and deliberately damaged as part of a cyber attack. *(2 marks)*

3 Some people think it is morally wrong to give good well-paid jobs to hackers who have deliberately broken the law. State, with reasons, whether you agree or disagree with this. *(2 marks)*

4 Hacking is made illegal under a law. Give the full name of the law. *(1 mark)*

5 Terrorists use encryption to ensure the privacy of communication and to avoid being detected and caught.

(a) Explain what encryption is and how it ensures the privacy of communication. *(2 marks)*

(b) Some countries are worried that encryption of data causes as many problems as it solves. Explain why a country might ban encryption. *(2 marks)*

END-OF-TOPIC REVIEW

Case studies *continued*

Case study 2

Hackers destroy a flight simulation site

Many people are interested in flying a plane but do not have the money to do this in reality. Instead they fly the planes virtually using flight simulation software.

A very popular website that covered all aspects of flight simulation has been destroyed by hackers. The hackers took down the site's two servers. The problem was that there was no external backup system. This meant that each server was used to back up the files on the other server. This meant that because both servers were affected, all the data was lost.

The person who founded the site said that the site would be down for the foreseeable future and that it might not be possible to set the site up again. One user of the site was really annoyed and said, 'there's a special place in hell for hackers who pull stunts like this'.

Questions

1 (a) Explain what is meant by the word 'hacker'. *(2 marks)*

  (b) There is a law that makes hacking illegal. Give the name of this law. *(1 mark)*

2 It is essential for security purposes that all files are properly backed up.
  (a) Give the names of **two** different media on which files can be backed up. *(2 marks)*

  (b) It is important that data is backed up off site. Give **one** reason why data should be kept off site. *(1 mark)*

3 One or more servers are used in networks. Explain the purpose of a server. *(2 marks)*

Case study 3

The NHS losing patient medical records

You would think that your personal medical details are safe in the hands of the NHS, but they are not. The Information Commissioner, the person who is in charge of the Data Protection Act, has been forced to take action against the NHS many times for breaching data protection regulations.

Here are some of the things they did:

- One GP downloaded a complete patient database containing medical histories of 10,000 patients onto an unsecured laptop. The laptop was then stolen and never recovered.
- A memory stick containing around 6000 patient details was lost. Although the details were encrypted, the password was written on a piece of paper attached to the memory stick.

The Assistant Information Commissioner said that procedures were laid out by the NHS but were not being followed. He also commented that 'medical history is very sensitive personal information which is likely to cause harm and distress'. He went on to say that 'the law dictates that they must keep this information confidential'.

◀ **Medical details are personal data and need to be protected.**

Questions

1 What could a person do who has suffered harm and distress when their medical details were revealed through negligence? *(1 mark)*

2 One data protection regulation (called Data Protection Principles in the Data Protection Act) is that 'Personal data shall be accurate, and where necessary, kept up-to-date'. Give another **two** of the Data Protection Principles. *(2 marks)*

3 The Deputy Information Commissioner mentioned 'sensitive personal information'.
Give **three** items of sensitive personal information that you might find as part of a medical record. *(3 marks)*

4 All disks containing personal information should be encrypted.
  (a) Explain what is meant by encrypted. *(2 marks)*

  (b) If a laptop is stolen and the laptop has stored personal information that is encrypted on its hard drive, explain how this protects the information. *(1 mark)*

  (c) Describe **two** ways in which medical details could be misused. *(2 marks)*

Exam support

Worked example

There are a number of health hazards associated with the use of computers.

(a) Give the names of **three** health hazards, outlining the health problems they create. *(6 marks)*

(b) For each of the health hazards described in part (a) describe what a user can do to help reduce the risk of their occurrence. *(3 marks)*

Student answer 1

(a) People who use computers a lot get fat and this can cause a heart attack.

You can get eye strain when using computers.

You can get repetitive strain injury which causes aches in your hands and wrists.

(b) Fatness – do not snack while you are using your computer.

Eye strain – have regular eye-tests.

Repetitive strain injury – use a wrist rest when using a keyboard or mouse.

◀ Examiner's comment

(a) Getting fat is not really directly caused by computers because this is caused by overeating or lack of exercise so no mark is awarded here.

The second answer is OK but it fails to explain what the symptoms of eye strain are (i.e., headaches, tiredness, etc.). Only one mark for this.

The third answer is fine and both the health hazard and the symptoms are made clear. Three marks are given for part (a).

(b) The answer about 'Fatness' gains no marks but the other answers are good and gain full marks. Two marks for this part.

(5 marks out of 9)

Student answer 2

(a) Back ache which causes aches and pain in the lower back and meaning you cannot get a good night's sleep.

Too much change in the workplace causing stress, meaning you cannot sleep because you are worried all the time.

Incorrect lighting causing headaches which give migraine and blurred vision.

(b) Back ache – use an adjustable chair and make sure you adjust it to suit your height. You can use a footrest if there is one.

Stress – make sure that users get good training so they are not stressed by the changes they have to cope with.

Headaches – make sure that fluorescent tubes are used with diffusers on them to spread out the light.

◀ Examiner's comment

(a) Here the hazard has been identified and it is clear what discomfort this causes the user. Full marks so six marks for this part.

(b) Again an excellent answer. Notice how it is clear which health hazard is being referred to. Full marks again for this section so three marks.

(9 marks out of 9)

END-OF-TOPIC REVIEW

Exam support *continued*

Examiner's answers

(a) One mark for the health hazard and one mark for an explanation of how it affects the user.

- Eye strain – causing headaches, migraines, blurred vision.
- Back ache – pain in back or shoulders.
- Stress – loss of sleep, tiredness, changes in personality, etc.
- RSI – pains in fingers, hands, wrists, etc.
- Neck strain – unable to move head without it hurting.
- DVT (deep vein thrombosis) – can cause a stroke or heart attack.

(b) One mark for each prevention method. For the mark it should be clear which health problem the prevention refers to.

Here are some of the many possible answers:

- Eye strain – have regular eye-tests/focus on distant objects/keep screen clean/eliminate glare on screen.
- Back ache – use adjustable chair/sit upright using correct posture.
- Stress – employers to provide adequate training on new systems/have regular breaks/employers to give reasonable workload.
- RSI – use wrist rests or supports; use systems that minimize keyboard and mouse use; use an ergonomic keyboard.
- Neck strain – use a copy holder; ensure the screen is level with your eyes.
- DVT (deep vein thrombosis) – do not sit in the same position; get up and walk around every now and again.

EXAM TIP

The Data Protection Act is very important and you need to know it in detail. Make sure you understand the reasons for the Act and the rights it gives, particularly to the person the data is about (i.e., the data subject).

There are a number of exemptions to the Data Protection Act. Make sure you can remember them.

The personal guardianship code is fairly new and you are sure to be asked about it.

Under the Data Protection Act, organizations must ensure the privacy and security of the personal data held. Make sure you understand all the methods that can be used to prevent unauthorized access.

Summary mind maps

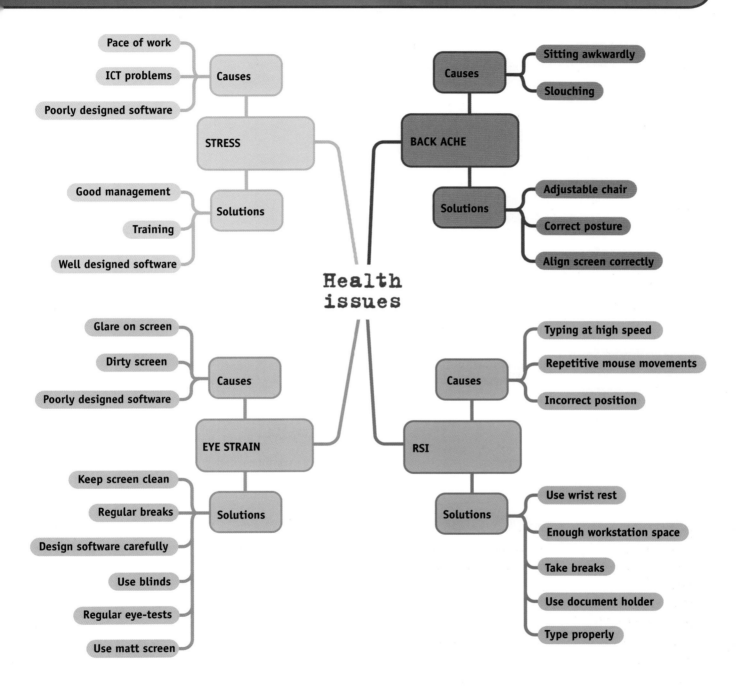

STRESS

Causes
- Pace of work
- ICT problems
- Poorly designed software

Solutions
- Good management
- Training
- Well designed software

BACK ACHE

Causes
- Sitting awkwardly
- Slouching

Solutions
- Adjustable chair
- Correct posture
- Align screen correctly

Health issues

EYE STRAIN

Causes
- Glare on screen
- Dirty screen
- Poorly designed software

Solutions
- Keep screen clean
- Regular breaks
- Design software carefully
- Use blinds
- Regular eye-tests
- Use matt screen

RSI

Causes
- Typing at high speed
- Repetitive mouse movements
- Incorrect position

Solutions
- Use wrist rest
- Enough workstation space
- Take breaks
- Use document holder
- Type properly

Summary mind maps *continued*

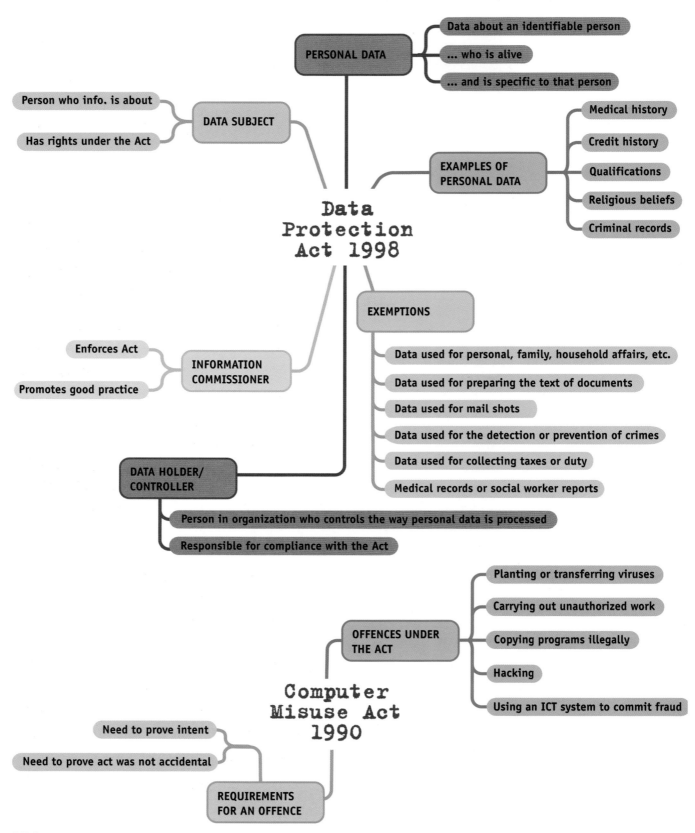

Social and economic issues relating to the use of ICT, including responsible use

The key concepts covered in this topic are:

- Changing pattern of commerce and industry due to increased use of ICT
- Changing pattern of employment due to increased use of ICT
- Acceptable ICT use
- Responsible behaviour online
- Social and personal effects of ICT
- Accessibility
- Sustainability and recycling

The use of ICT has changed life in a number of ways. For example, industry and commerce use ICT extensively, enabling people to do business globally, automating production lines and allowing many people to work from home. ICT has also changed the way people work. More people have to work flexibly and on the move and many jobs have disappeared or been created.

The use of ICT places responsibilities on the people who use it and these people must ensure that they do not do anything that will cause harm or annoyance to other ICT users.

Contents

Changing pattern of commerce, industry and employment due to increased use of ICT

You will find out

▷ **About the changing pattern of commerce and industry due to increased use of ICT**

▷ **About the changing pattern of employment due to increased use of ICT**

Commerce and industry have changed a lot due to the introduction of ICT. Much of the routine administration is now performed by computers, and in factories it is common to see completely automated production lines without a human in sight. These changes to commerce and industry have resulted in changes to employment patterns with some types of job being lost while others have been created. In this section you will be looking at all of these changes.

▲   This automated production line fills plastic bottles with water and puts the caps on them.

The changing pattern of commerce and industry due to increased use of ICT

Industry and commerce has changed due to the introduction of ICT in the following ways:

Automated production lines – production lines are heavily computer controlled resulting in fewer manual jobs. Robots are used to assemble components, weld panels of cars together, spray paint and so on. Factories employ fewer people than they used to and the people they employ are more highly skilled.

More standard products – it takes time and is quite expensive to reconfigure robots to assemble different products. This means most manufacturing companies make standard products.

Automated stock control – computers know how much stock is left because they know what stock has been used to up orders. As soon as items of stock fall below a certain limit they are automatically re-ordered from the suppliers.

Internet shopping – reduces the need for some stores to have an expensive high street presence. Fewer staff are needed and the costs of electricity, gas, etc., are a lot lower. Customers who are busy or who are housebound find it much easier to spend time Internet shopping than visiting traditional stores.

Creation of new industries – a whole new variety of jobs has been created by the introduction of ICT. Call centres, online stores, web design companies, online content providers (people who provide material for websites), people who produce new equipment, staff who program robots in factories, etc., have replaced many of the industries that have disappeared.

Globalization – wherever you go in the world people seem to eat the same food, drink the same brands of drink, wear the same designer clothes, have the same high street stores, etc. Globalization means that the social and cultural barriers that make countries different are being removed and the world is becoming more the same. Some people think this is good but others feel that some countries are losing their identities. Globalization has been helped by ICT because it is much easier for organizations to operate in other countries and transfer data using networks and the Internet. The rise in low cost airlines has meant that people travel to countries they would not have thought of going to in the past.

Changing pattern of employment due to increased use of ICT

Increased use of ICT in the workplace has meant that many businesses and organizations are different than they used to be. If you worked for these businesses or organizations you would notice a difference in the way people now work and the types of job they now do.

There are many changes to the workplace brought about by the use of ICT.

Size of the business and workforce

As so many of the manufacturing processes and also the administrative procedures are automated, it means that businesses do not need to be as large. They still manufacture the goods but they are more efficient at getting them to the customers, so they do not need as much space. Office space is not taken up with filing cabinets and desks as a lot more of the administration, such as ordering stock and paying for it, is

done automatically. This also affects the workforce as the same amount of business can be conducted with fewer employees.

Type of workforce

The days are gone where thousands of people performed routine tasks day after day assembling goods in factories. Also there are fewer people performing routine, tedious tasks such as paying invoices, checking stock, etc. All these can be done automatically using ICT. Instead fewer but much more interesting and more skilled jobs are left. There has therefore been a shift from a less skilled to a more skilled workforce.

Location of offices/manufacturing plant

Working together (called collaborative working) is easy due to networks and other communications systems. This means that many organizations can have branches in many places. Many people now telework, so fewer staff need to work from an office, which means the offices can be smaller and located anywhere in the country.

Manufacturing plants can be located where there is an abundance of skilled labour and in many cases this will be abroad because of the lower labour costs. Because of the use of ICT there is no problem in coordinating organizations situated in different countries.

Different ways of working

With ICT the way of doing things changes as new technologies are developed. This means employees have to adapt quickly to cope with the changes and this means continual training and skills updating.

Different capabilities of people and computers

New ICT systems are being created all the time and people need to develop these. Highly skilled people are needed to create and use these systems so that everyone benefits from the changes.

▲ With Internet shopping and international delivery companies you can buy goods from anywhere in the world and have them delivered to your door.

Changes in employment due to the introduction of ICT and networking technology

The use of ICT has produced many changes in the way people work. Here are some of them.

Training and retraining

In the past the pace of change was slow. When you started a job, you tended to do more or less the same thing throughout your working life. Things are very different in the workplace now. The pace of change is rapid and the workforce has to adapt to new ICT systems, new ways of working, new codes of practice and new laws.

In order to equip employees with new knowledge and skills, employers need to continually train and retrain staff.

Changes to ICT systems that result in retraining include:

- New software – for example, a new database package is being used.
- New hardware – for example, a new printer that can print on both sides of the page is being introduced.
- New laws – these could be introduced to cope with misuses of new technology.
- New ways of working (i.e. procedures) – for example, the use of email rather than letters to communicate with customers.

Changing pattern of comerce, industry and employment due to increased use of ICT *continued*

Different ways of working

The way people work has changed in the following ways:

- Greater collaboration – it is much easier for people to work collectively on a project and transfer work between team members using networks. They no longer have to be in the same place to work together.
- Blurring of boundaries between work and play – people can do work at home because it is easy to access the data they need using the Internet.
- They are also contactable at any time – using mobile phones, PDAs and laptops with wireless Internet access.
- Fewer journeys to meetings – as meetings can be conducted at a distance using videoconferencing technology.

Homeworking/teleworking

With the use of telecommunications and the Internet in particular, many people can now work from home. Working from home by making use of computers and telecommunications equipment is called teleworking. This increased use of teleworking has benefits for everyone and these are covered in detail in Topic 19.

▶ Homeworking/teleworking is ideal for people with limited mobility.

Teleworking has meant people are not as restricted to where they live and organizations benefit, too, with the reduction in costs resulting from smaller offices.

Mobile computing

More people are working whilst they are travelling and are doing work while they are waiting in train stations, airports, etc. Many business people use laptops, mobile phones, PDAs whilst they travel so they can be more productive.

▲ PDAs and some computers can be used on the move.

Flexible hours

Businesses have to be staffed 24/7 – because business is often done globally (i.e., all over the world). People do not work 9–5 like they used to and many people work more flexibly.

Job satisfaction

Many employers do not mind where and when the work gets done as long as it gets done. This enables employees to plan their own time and work, which gives them greater job satisfaction. Also, many of the boring repetitive tasks are now carried out by computers or robots, leaving the more interesting jobs for humans to perform.

Ease of tasks

With the use of ICT, tasks that would have taken hours to complete can be accomplished very quickly. Examples of this include sending personalized letters to lots of people using mail merge. Finding information can be very quick by making use of the latest search engines.

Increased unemployment

Because of ICT, some jobs have been created and some have disappeared. Jobs that have disappeared include:

- Filing clerks – many organizations use computer databases, so no paper files are kept. Records can be obtained easily by anyone connected to the network, so there is no need for filing clerks.
- Factory workers such as welders, paint sprayers, fabricators (who assemble products) – most of these boring repetitive jobs have been replaced by robots. It is safer to use robots in some environments.
- Packers – many large mail order/e-commerce organizations use automated picking and packing machines to select items off shelves and pack them ready for delivery to customers.
- Typists – most people choose to type their own correspondence. Much of the routine correspondence is automated. Many people use voice

recognition systems that allow a user to dictate letters, etc., into a word-processor.

- Stock takers in shops/till staff – fewer staff are needed in supermarkets as more of the tasks are automated. There is no need to price individual articles as the bar code along with a database can give all the information needed such as price, description, etc.
- Bank employees – many customers now bank online and use cash dispensers to take cash out. Also many more people use debit and credit cards to pay for goods.
- Call centre staff – these people provide support for customers and many of these jobs have been lost abroad because of the lower wage costs there.

New jobs that have been created through ICT include:

- Network managers/administrators – these are the people who keep the networks running for all the users, see to the taking of backup copies kept for security purposes, etc.
- Website designers – these are the people who design and create websites for others, as well as keep them up-to-date by adding new and deleting old material. The work involves design skills as well as programming and other technical skills.
- Development staff – these include systems analysts (who design new ICT systems) and programmers who write the step-by-step instructions (i.e. the programs) that instruct the computers what to do.

Monitoring employees at work

Employers often monitor the use of the Internet by their staff and they may read their emails and check what they have been looking at. You may think that this sounds fine but many people have to do some personal business at work such as check their bank accounts, contact friends, arrange doctor's appointments and so on. Much of this is private and personal, so you can see there is a problem.

Emails can be monitored by the network manager.

Questions A

1. ICT has replaced or changed many jobs.
   (a) Give the names of **two** types of job that have been replaced by ICT. *(2 marks)*
   (b) Some jobs have changed their nature due to the introduction of ICT. Name **two** jobs where this has happened. *(2 marks)*
   (c) The increase in high speed broadband links has led to cheaper international telephone calls using the Internet. Name **one** job that has been lost from this country to abroad as a result of this. *(1 mark)*

2. The widespread use of ICT has had a huge impact on society. One benefit that it has brought is the creation of new and interesting jobs.
   (a) Give **three** examples of jobs that have been created through the introduction of ICT. *(3 marks)*
   (b) Many people have had to be retrained to cope with the introduction of new ICT systems. Explain why regular retraining is needed in the workplace. *(2 marks)*

3. ICT systems and facilities mean that many employees can telework.
   (a) Explain what is meant by 'telework'. *(3 marks)*
   (b) Describe **two** advantages to the employer of teleworking. *(2 marks)*
   (c) Describe **two** disadvantages to the employer of teleworking. *(2 marks)*

4. Many organizations monitor their employees at work.
   Explain what this would involve and the reasons why employers do it. *(4 marks)*

Extension activity

Use the Internet to find out about automation in factories.

Find out about the types of tasks that are being automated and find out about the use of robots in manufacturing.

Write a few short lines about each different use you have found.

Acceptable ICT use and responsible behaviour online

You will find out

▷ **About acceptable and unacceptable use of ICT**

▷ **About responsible behaviour online**

ICT makes it easy to get things done and this is why ICT is used so much. It also makes unacceptable use more of a problem. ICT can magnify the impact of actions. For example, you can collect millions of email addresses and then send spam email to every one. Once the addresses have been collected, you can go on and on sending more and more spam emails. If you had to send each individual email separately, you would soon get fed up. Unfortunately, ICT is easy to use in an unacceptable way.

In this section you will look at aspects of acceptable use while online. The section also looks at responsible behaviour while online and the various problems the use of the Internet causes as well as how to stay safe online.

Unacceptable use of ICT

Here are some of the ways ICT can be used in an unacceptable way.

Email flaming

Email flaming means communicating emotionally using email. Often it means sending email messages that are rude or impolite. Flaming can offend others and should therefore be avoided.

Spam

Spam is unwanted emails that are usually advertising things you have no interest in. The main problem with spam is that it has to be deleted and there is always the danger that you delete some important email mixed in with it. Also it takes time to delete spam. You can of course get a spam filter that will trap most spam but you may find that it also traps the odd legitimate email, so you still have to look carefully at who it is from or the subject of the email before you delete it.

▲ Spam email is added to a special folder by a spam filter. This allows you to look at it briefly before deleting it.

▲ Spam is a nuisance to all Internet users.

Intentional theft

Data can have considerable value. For example, a database of customers and their orders would be of real value to a competitor. Databases can be copied onto a memory stick in minutes but this is theft just the same as if a car had been stolen.

Copyright theft is also a problem because music and video are so easily stolen when in digital form. Internet service providers have now started to take action against anyone who steals music and video and the penalty is to lose the Internet connection.

Plagiarism

Plagiarism means taking other people's work (usually off the Internet) and then passing it off as your own. If you use a small amount of someone else's work then this is ok provided you acknowledge the person who produced the work. You must not simply copy sections off the Internet and use that to produce coursework or essays as this is plagiarism.

Essay banks good or bad?

John is under pressure because he has an essay to write. He heard from a friend that there is a site where people submit essays and coursework that they have done to help others. It is free to use the site.

Take a look at the site at:
www.essaybank.co.uk

Discuss with your friends and your teacher the moral implications of such a site. Is it a good or a bad thing? Think about the following issues:

- What are the dangers if John simply copies one of the examples on the site and passes it off as his own work?
- What would be the likely consequences if the work is submitted as coursework and it is spotted by the assessment board?

Corruption of information

Sometimes people may feel disgruntled by their school or employer or other organization and they may seek revenge. They may decide to deliberately damage the data/information held. This is illegal and you would be prosecuted for doing this damage and, if found guilty, you would end up with a criminal record.

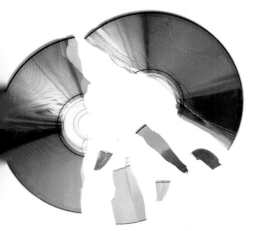

▲ Corrupting or destroying data intentionally is criminal damage.

Responsible behaviour online

The Internet is a great thing and brings tremendous benefits to us all. It is not, however, without its dangers. In this section you will be looking at the dangers lurking in many corners of the Internet. If you are aware of the dangers then at least you can take precautions to ensure that you are not put at risk.

The dangers of disclosing personal information

You should never ever give out personal information when you are online. You may be chatting to someone who seems genuine but you could be chatting to anyone. If you reveal your personal information or even worse meet them then you could meet someone who wants to do you harm. There are lots of weird people out there, and they may try to contact you.

Not opening or forwarding emails/ files from unknown sources

Attachments to emails should not be opened unless you know who they are from or they are from a trusted source. The latest virus scanning software should be used to ensure any viruses that enter are discovered and removed. Files on media should not be opened unless you are sure you can trust the source of them.

Inappropriate use of a webcam

It can be good to see the person you are chatting to, but the use of webcams is not without some dangers such as:

- Sometimes webcam sites show inappropriate content (e.g., pornography, torture, etc.).
- Webcams in combination with chat rooms have been used by paedophiles.
- Terrorists have used webcam services to promote terrorism.

Not physically meeting people from chat rooms

You frequently read in newspapers about young people going missing after meeting someone in a chat room. Unfortunately not all of these stories have happy endings, so everyone needs to be aware of the dangers that lurk in cyberspace. You should therefore not meet anyone from a chat room – they could be anyone!

Copyright 2000 by Randy Glasbergen.
www.glasbergen.com

"I MET SOMEONE WONDERFUL IN A CHAT ROOM. . . AND THEN I FOUND OUT SHE'S A CAT!"

Acceptable ICT use and responsible behaviour online *continued*

Prevention of cyberbullying

Cyberbullying means using the Internet or mobile phones to harass or intimidate another person. You must ensure that you are not a victim of this by letting adults know immediately this starts to happen, even if it seems to start off as a joke. Luckily, as it is easy to trace the origin of messages, this makes it easy for the culprit to be identified.

Not accessing pornography

Your Internet use is monitored by your network manager (in the case of school and work). Accessing pornography will be against the acceptable use policy of the organization and you will get into trouble. In addition, your Internet service provider (ISP) may identify that you have accessed sites which contain illegal images which can land you in trouble with the police.

Using copy lists with discrimination

Many people use copy lists to send the same email to a group of people such as work colleagues or friends. Using copy lists indiscriminately means people who have no real interest in the subject matter, end up with a copy of the email. This means that they have to waste time reading them and deleting them.

Checking websites have the correct URL

The URL is the website address. It is important to always keep an eye on the website address when you follow a link, especially using a link in an email. If you see the website address change then you need to be suspicious and not enter any personal information asked for. Also there are websites that have web addresses very similar to one you want, which means when you make a mistake you are directed to these sites and not the site you wanted.

Ethical guidelines

Ethics is about your behaviour towards others. There are a number of things that you need to bear in mind regarding ethics.

The misuse of images

It is very easy to copy an image off a website or social networking site. Images sent to one person can be passed to others without their permission. It is very easy to misuse an image, so you need to be very careful where you put your images online and what sort of images you send.

Here are some ways in which an image can be misused:

- Some people may spot you from your image and this could lead to problems like you being stalked by them.
- They may recognize someone else in the picture with you and ask them for your details such as address and phone number.
- Your image might be added to a dating website without your knowledge.
- You image could be distorted in some way using image editing software causing ridicule and embarrassment to you.
- Paedophiles may see your image and post it on their own websites.

Making defamatory statements

Many people think that you can say what you like about people on the Internet as it offers free speech. They may also think that what they say cannot be traced back to them. Both of these are untrue.

You have to be careful what you say because if you cannot prove that what you say is true, you can be sued by the person who you are saying these things against. They can claim compensation from you for any harm you have caused them.

Defamatory statements can be libel, which would be via a written statement or a false image, or slander, which is via the spoken word. You have to be careful in posting opinions about others in public places such as blogs, chat rooms, message boards and social networking sites.

Phishing

Be very suspicious of any emails sent to you. The Internet email system is very insecure and you should never divulge personal information in an email or follow a link to a site from an email and divulge personal information.

Always view official-looking emails with scepticism despite them having the right logos and using official language. Do not be tricked into inputting the details even if they say things like 'your account will be suspended unless you enter these details'. If necessary, send the bank a copy of the email. These emails are called 'phishing' because they are emails that fish for people who will respond to them. You need to make sure you are not one of them!

The emails often contain links and if you clicked on the link you would be taken to a fake site that looks like the official bank website. The URL is different though, and this is the reason why you must always look at the URL. If you then entered your bank details, your identity would be stolen and someone would use it to commit fraud.

▲ Fraudsters send thousands of emails hoping a few people are foolish enough to send them their bank details.

Scamming/fake websites

Fake websites are websites that look authentic but are not the real website. In some cases, if you make payments into such sites, you may lose your money. Scamming websites are deliberately set up to part you from your money.

Avoiding accidentally sending viruses

When you receive an email that has been sent to lots of others from an unknown source, be careful about forwarding it to others. It may contain a virus. Viruses are distributed by their writers using files such as videos, pictures and games.

Online bank card readers

Some programs are able to store your bank card details as you enter them to pay for goods that you have ordered online. These programs then send the details back to the person who wrote the program. They may then use the details to commit fraud. This type of program can usually be picked up by virus checking software.

Use of financial security procedures

There are a number of procedures banks and building societies use to help prevent fraud and these include:

- Monitoring unusual activity in accounts – for example, if a large transaction were to take place on your account to pay for goods abroad they may suspend the transaction until they have spoken to you.
- Use of encryption – any financial/ personal data sent over the Internet will be encrypted.
- Use of user-IDs and passwords and security questions to verify the user.

Questions B

1 Some people misuse email facilities. For example, spam is an annoyance for many computer users.
   (a) Explain what is meant by spam. *(1 mark)*
   (b) Describe how it is possible to reduce the amount of time dealing with spam. *(2 marks)*

2 It is important to adopt responsible behaviour when online.
   Give **three** things you should do when using the Internet in order to stay safe. *(3 marks)*

3 Many people get sent phishing emails.
   (a) What is meant by phishing emails? *(2 marks)*
   (b) Explain the dangers in these phishing emails. *(2 marks)*

Extension activity

Use the Internet to do some investigation on the following:

- Fake websites
- Scamming websites
- Phishing
- Identity theft

Produce a poster to outline the dangers in using the Internet to make online purchases or for online banking.

Effects of ICT, accessibility, sustainability and recycling

You will find out

▷ **About social and personal effects of ICT**

▷ **About accessibility (e.g., features of hardware and software to aid people with disabilities)**

▷ **About sustainability and recycling**

There has been a huge increase in the use of personal websites, web logs (blogs) and social networking sites. Many people spend lots of their leisure time creating profiles on these sites, sending messages/files to others and making new friends.

In order to reap the benefits of ICT you need to be able to access it. It is easy for us in this country but in other countries it is not as easy. ICT is for everyone and ICT can be tailored to help people with disabilities use it. ICT can also be used to help monitor and manage sustainable resources.

Social and personal effects of ICT

There has recently been a big interest in personal websites, web logs (blogs) and social networking sites. Many people use these and they

have had quite an impact in a short amount of time. In this section you will be looking at the effect that these have all had on individuals, organizations and society.

Effects on individuals

Social networking sites can be good fun and they allow you to keep in touch with old friends and also make new ones. They can be used for networking where you can be put in touch with others who may have the same interests or be able to put some work your way.

Effects on organizations

Employees might spend large amounts of time on social networking sites and this is why most organizations either block access to the sites or forbid employees from accessing the sites. The network manager can always check up on the sites being visited, so there is a way of monitoring user activity.

Effects on society

There is a danger than people will develop an online 'life' at the expense of their real life. Spending too much time in front of a computer is not good for you and many people may have health problems in the future owing to too little physical activity. There have been many problems with people meeting up after forming online relationships and this is a real danger.

The variations in computer access and ICT skills

There is a huge difference in the wealth of some countries in the world. The wealthier countries can use ICT to become wealthier and

their whole population benefits. The poorer countries stay still and the gap between them widens.

Here are some of the many problems poorer countries have with access to ICT:

- Low levels of education and poor literacy make it hard for them to learn.
- Lack of money.
- Lack of English skills as much of ICT especially the Internet is in English.
- Restricted access to the Internet. Some countries have poor infrastructure and many do not even have a reliable electricity supply.

Accessibility

ICT developments have helped people with disabilities gain employment and do many of the things they could not do without the use of ICT. Above all ICT has allowed people with disabilities to remain independent. In this section you will be looking at learning devices to support disabilities. There are a number of ways ICT can help people with disabilities and these are outlined below.

The use of specialist input devices

There is a huge range of specialist input devices that can be used by people with disabilities to help them learn.

Braille keyboards are used to enter text into a computer and are used by blind or partially sighted people.

Voice recognition systems can be used that enable people to issue commands and use speech to enter data into a word-processing document.

Computer-controlled engine management in cars reduces fuel consumption.

This keyboard can be used by sighted or sight-impaired people.

Features of software that allow it to be used by people with disabilities

When designing websites and presentations you must be aware that users with a range of disabilities will also be using your products.

You will need to consider people who are visually impaired (i.e., blind or partially sighted) by:

- having a facility to speak words on the screen
- having a facility to zoom in so that the page is magnified
- increasing the font size
- choosing those font types that are easy to read
- using plenty of contrast between the text and the background
- allowing the user to change the colour scheme.

You will need to consider people who have a hearing impairment (i.e., are completely or partially deaf) by:

- using visual warnings rather than sound warnings
- using typed versions of any speech used
- using subtitles for any video used.

Sustainability and recycling

Humans are placing more and more demands on the planet. The world's population is increasing and our need for new homes and power is increasing all the time. This means we are using more and more resources and this cannot carry on.

Sustainability means only taking out of the planet what we can without having any adverse environmental effect.

ICT can be used to help with sustainability in a number of ways:

- In supermarkets, more efficient stock control has mean that food is not thrown away.
- ICT can be used to control central heating systems. It can be used to set temperatures of each room individually thus reducing fuel consumption.
- Engine management systems in cars help decrease fuel consumption.
- Smart meters show householders how much electricity they are using thus encouraging them to turn off devices they are not using.
- Teleworking means that commuting is not needed thus reducing fuel consumption.
- Many ICT systems deal with administration and do this electronically without the need for paperwork. This saves trees as well as the energy needed to produce the paper.

ICT can be used to manage recycling. For example, rubbish can be sorted using robots that are able to pick out certain pieces of rubbish that can be recycled.

There are also websites where you can recycle mobile phones as your old phone can be someone's new phone.

Smart waste bins

Hewlett Packard make printers and their ink refill/toner cartridges. Rather than throw the empty cartridges in the general rubbish, they should be recycled. The company has produced a smart waste bin into which the empty cartridges are placed and when the bin is full, a radio signal is sent to an office to inform them that the cartridges are ready for recycling.

There is also a scheme where chips are put into wheelie bins to record the amount of rubbish a householder is throwing away. The less they throw away the less they have to pay for their council tax. This encourages householders to recycle more.

The use of ICT systems reduces the need for printouts on paper.

Questions

☑ Test yourself

The following notes summarize this topic. The notes are incomplete because they have words missing. Using the words in the list below, copy out and complete sentences A to I, underlining the words that you have inserted. Each word may be used more than once.

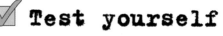

manual	globalization	cyberbullying	spam
smaller	phishing	URL	skilled	teleworking

A Automated production lines means fewer _____ jobs in factories.

B Offices are often much _____ than they used to be because fewer people are needed and computers take up less space than filing cabinets.

C Owing to the introduction of ICT there are fewer employees in factories and offices but the remaining staff are more highly _____.

D _____ is where all the countries become very similar owing to the use of ICT systems.

E _____ means sending emails that falsely say they are from banks or other organizations in order to trick people into revealing their banking or credit card details.

F Bullying using the Internet and mobile phones is often called _____.

G _____ means working from home by making use of computers and communications equipment.

H It is possible to use special software to filter out emails that are unasked for, which are popularly called _____.

I It is important to check the _____ of any website you are using before you enter any personal or financial information into it to check that it is the correct site.

Examination style questions

1 There have been a lot of changes in the pattern of employment due to the increased use of ICT.

   Tick **three** boxes that give sensible reasons why the pattern of employment has changed with increased use of ICT. *(3 marks)*

   Tick three boxes only

   Homeworking/teleworking is more popular ☐

   Employees are more likely to work more flexibly ☐

   It has brought about a huge rise in employment especially among factory workers ☐

   Training and retraining are needed regularly ☐

   Workers are generally less skilled than they were ☐

2 The pattern of commerce and industry has changed due to the increased use of ICT. One way it has changed is that it is much easier to order goods and do business with companies anywhere in the world.

   Give **two** different ways in which the pattern of commerce and industry has changed. *(2 marks)*

3 Describe **one** way in which ICT is used in manufacturing in order to reduce the number of people needed to produce goods. *(3 marks)*

4 The widespread use of ICT has had a huge impact on society. One benefit that it has brought is the creation of new and interesting jobs.
   - **(a)** Give **three** examples of jobs that have been created through the introduction of ICT. *(3 marks)*
   - **(b)** Many people have had to be retrained to cope with the introduction of new ICT systems. Explain why regular retraining is needed in the workplace. *(2 marks)*

5 ICT developments in organizations have caused changes to working practices.

   Describe **three** changes that might be needed. *(3 marks)*

6 ICT systems and facilities mean that many employees can telework.
   - **(a)** Explain what is meant by 'telework'. *(3 marks)*
   - **(b)** Describe **two** benefits to the employee of teleworking. *(2 marks)*
   - **(c)** Describe **two** disadvantages to the employee of teleworking. *(2 marks)*

Exam support

Worked example

Parents of young children are worried about them using the Internet.

(a) Explain, by giving examples, why their fears are justified. *(4 marks)*

(b) Explain **two** things a parent can do to protect their children from harm when using the Internet. *(2 marks)*

Student answer 1

(a) *Their child may reveal a lot about where they live, where they go to school, their phone number.*

They may go into a chat room and a stranger might ask them to meet up and this is really dangerous.

(b) *They can make sure their child only uses the Internet when they are sitting with them.*

They can use a special function of the software called parental controls that will only allow them access to certain parts of the Internet.

◀ **Examiner's comment**

(a) These are two good answers, but the student should have looked at the marks allocated. It is always a good idea to work on one point is worth one mark unless the question indicates otherwise. Only two marks are given here.

(b) Two good answers get both of the marks. *(4 marks out of 6)*

Student answer 2

(a) *They might access inappropriate material such as violent video or pornography by accident.*

They may chat to someone in a chat room and arrange to meet them without their parents' knowledge.

The images they send to a stranger could be misused.

They may reveal information in a chat room that could be used by a stalker to harass them.

(b) *They can ban the child from using the Internet.*

They can tell them that they must not ever go into a chat room.

◀ **Examiner's comment**

(a) Four points well explained get four marks here.

(b) Banning the child from using the Internet may seriously hinder their education as the Internet for the most part is a good thing. No marks for this answer even though it might be the choice of some parents. The second answer gains a mark.

(5 marks out of 6)

Examiner's answers

(a) One mark for each point to a maximum of four marks.

- They could reveal personal details such as name, address, school, age, phone number, etc., to a stranger.
- They could arrange to meet a stranger without their parents' knowledge.
- They may access unsuitable content (e.g. pornography).
- They may take part in or be a victim of cyberbullying.

(b) One mark for each point to a maximum of two marks.

- Only allow them to access the Internet at home when they are present.
- Do not allow Internet access in a bedroom.
- Set the parental controls so they can only access suitable material and enter certain sites.
- Ask them to report anything they are not happy with to their parents.
- Examine favourites, email, etc., to check there is no abuse.

Summary mind maps

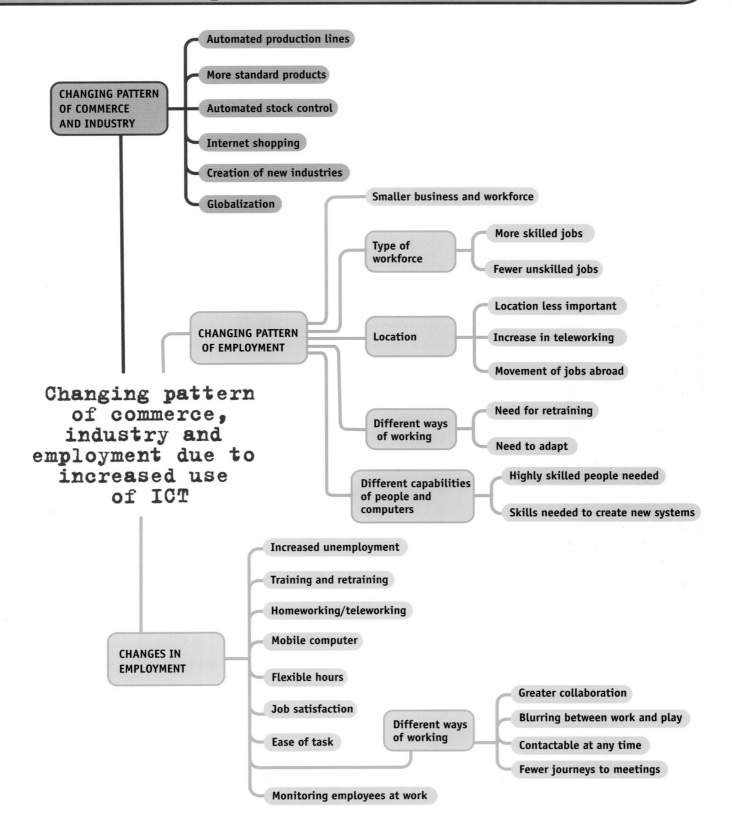

CHANGING PATTERN OF COMMERCE AND INDUSTRY
- Automated production lines
- More standard products
- Automated stock control
- Internet shopping
- Creation of new industries
- Globalization

Changing pattern of commerce, industry and employment due to increased use of ICT

CHANGING PATTERN OF EMPLOYMENT
- Smaller business and workforce
- Type of workforce
  - More skilled jobs
  - Fewer unskilled jobs
- Location
  - Location less important
  - Increase in teleworking
  - Movement of jobs abroad
- Different ways of working
  - Need for retraining
  - Need to adapt
- Different capabilities of people and computers
  - Highly skilled people needed
  - Skills needed to create new systems

CHANGES IN EMPLOYMENT
- Increased unemployment
- Training and retraining
- Homeworking/teleworking
- Mobile computer
- Flexible hours
- Job satisfaction
- Ease of task
- Different ways of working
  - Greater collaboration
  - Blurring between work and play
  - Contactable at any time
  - Fewer journeys to meetings
- Monitoring employees at work

Summary mind maps *continued*

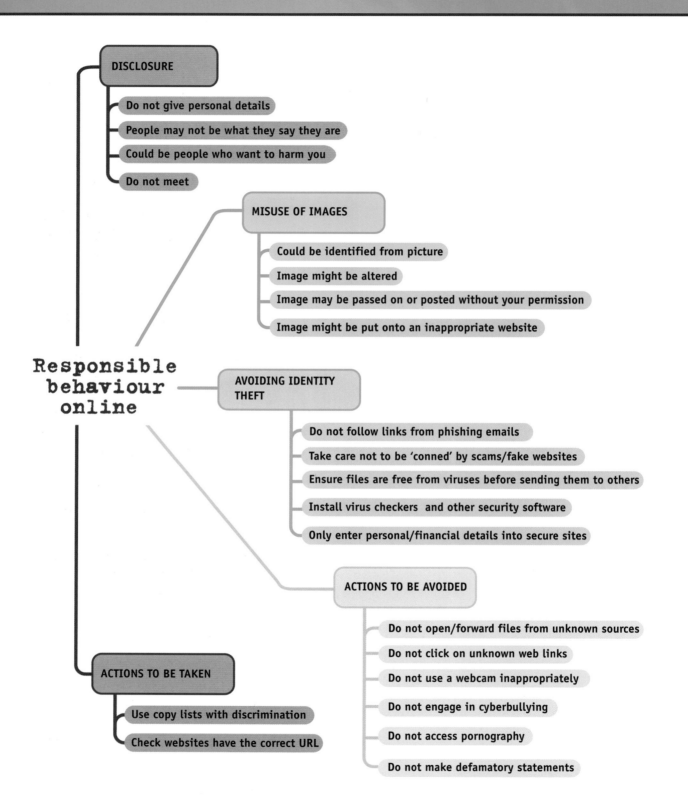

DISCLOSURE
- Do not give personal details
- People may not be what they say they are
- Could be people who want to harm you
- Do not meet

MISUSE OF IMAGES
- Could be identified from picture
- Image might be altered
- Image may be passed on or posted without your permission
- Image might be put onto an inappropriate website

Responsible behaviour online

AVOIDING IDENTITY THEFT
- Do not follow links from phishing emails
- Take care not to be 'conned' by scams/fake websites
- Ensure files are free from viruses before sending them to others
- Install virus checkers and other security software
- Only enter personal/financial details into secure sites

ACTIONS TO BE AVOIDED
- Do not open/forward files from unknown sources
- Do not click on unknown web links
- Do not use a webcam inappropriately
- Do not engage in cyberbullying
- Do not access pornography
- Do not make defamatory statements

ACTIONS TO BE TAKEN
- Use copy lists with discrimination
- Check websites have the correct URL

Topic 18

Political, ethical and environmental issues relating to the use of ICT

The key concepts covered in this topic are:

- Political and ethical issues
- Using ICT to monitor and minimize the effects on the environment
- Impact of ICT on different people

The use of ICT raises a lot of political and ethical issues and in this topic you will be looking at issues such as the introduction of national databases and the problems they can create. Many people are worried that there is far too much state involvement in people's lives and that there is too much monitoring and surveillance.

There are other ways that ICT can impact on our lives. For example, the use of ICT can reduce energy consumption. Smart meters, which will be in every home soon, will make people aware of the amount of energy they are using and will also give them some idea of the cost of this energy. ICT also has a global effect by widening the gap between the technologically advanced and less advanced countries.

Contents

Political and ethical issues

The public are very worried about the large amount of data stored about them by public and private organizations. There have been many stories in the press about the surveillance by the state and the huge rise in the number of CCTV cameras. In this section you will be looking at the political and ethical issues of these and other ICT systems.

◀ DNA can be used to identify people.

Purpose and costing of national databases

There are many large national databases that have been set up by organizations such as the police, NHS, etc. Here are some of the main ones:

National DNA database – DNA uniquely identifies a particular person. It is used by police forces in the fight against crime. Anyone who is arrested will have details of their DNA added to the database. The main concern people have is that the samples are taken after arrest, so if the person is not charged then their DNA details are not deleted from the database. Some people argue that everyone's DNA details should be put on this database as this would make fighting crime much easier.

The Police National Computer (PNC) – this is a national police system that can be accessed by anyone who has authority to access it. It contains details of crimes and criminals. It allows the police to search on criminals and vehicles when they only have a small amount of information. For example, they could search for all the Ford Mondeos with a registration YY04 _ _ T, where the dashes are unknown letters.

The Passport Agency – anyone who has a passport will be on their database. The database is used to identify criminals who are entering or leaving the country. It can also prevent people entering the country using forged passports.

The NHS national database – this database contains medical details for everyone who is able to access NHS services. Keeping this data centrally, means that if you were involved in an accident away from home, the doctors at the hospital would have access to your medical details.

These details could include details of allergies to certain drugs and this information could be life saving.

National identity cards

Many countries in the world have a national identity card that everyone has to carry. The UK was supposed to have had such a scheme for everyone but at present only foreign nationals have to have one. At the moment as a UK citizen you do not have to have one but you can buy one if you want one for £30.

Many people object to these cards for everyone because of the cost and because they interfere with civil liberties and also they feel that they do nothing to prevent terrorism and illegal immigration.

The costing of national databases

Large national databases are complex projects that are very expensive. Many of these projects go wildly out of control because the costs start to rise and some projects get abandoned halfway through. Some of these databases and other ICT systems are political issues. For example, the Labour Party favour the introduction of identity cards but the Conservative Party said that they are not in favour of them.

The security of public data

One of the problems with national databases is that they are accessed by lots of different people from lots of different locations. Trying to ensure the privacy and the security of this data is not easy. Much of this information would be difficult to re-create. For example, if all the tax files for everyone who pays tax in the country were lost, then it would cause havoc because the government would not have the money coming in to pay for public services.

Here are some of the things that can be done to ensure the security of public data:

- Regular backups taken with the copies of the original data kept off site.
- Training of all personnel who use data on such topics as not leaving computer unattended whilst logged on, viruses, data protection, etc.
- Use of firewalls to prevent hackers accessing data.
- Virus checkers to prevent the introduction of viruses.
- Physical security (e.g., access restriction on rooms, access restrictions to computers, etc.).

Links between public and private databases

There are often links between information held by private companies and public organizations. Many people are concerned that some private organizations are using information that was given to councils and government departments.

Here are some of the links:

- Building societies and banks sending information about interest to HM Revenue and Customs (i.e., about tax that should be paid).
- Insurance companies sending data about car insurance so that people can tax their cars online.
- The police and MI5 can gain access to databases of Internet service providers (ISPs) who keep details of all their customers' Internet use (e.g., emails sent and received, searches made, etc.).

CCTV

CCTV stands for closed circuit television and these are the cameras you see just about everywhere. Some of these cameras can be used with sophisticated software to actually recognize a person and others can recognize a car registration plate and find the name and address of the registered owner.

▲ Here CCTV is being used to detect illegal rubbish tipping.

Government access to personal data

Many people are worried about the government holding so much personal data about all of us. The government say that they need this information for planning purposes. For example, they need to know about the nation's health in order to plan for hospitals, old people's homes, etc. Some people are worried that their right to privacy is being eroded.

The surveillance society

More and more government departments and councils are undertaking surveillance. Some of the surveillance is done to detect and prosecute criminals and some is done to protect us against terrorist attacks. Most people would agree that this is a good thing but some people are worried that surveillance is being directed at ordinary people.

For example, a local authority used surveillance to check whether parents whose child attended a popular school actually lived in the catchment area or just said they did to gain their child's admission.

Some people think the Act is a 'snoopers' charter for public bodies to check up on us all. Under an act of parliament the police, MI5, councils and other government departments can:

- demand access to your emails, instant messages, etc., from your Internet service provider without you knowing
- listen in secret to phone calls and see all your text messages
- monitor all your searches made on the Internet.

Questions A

1 (a) Give the meaning of the term CCTV. *(1 mark)*
(b) People are worried about the huge rise in the use of CCTV. Give **one** reason why they are worried. *(1 mark)*

2 Public organizations set up national databases and they store lots of personal information about individuals.
(a) Give **two** reasons why an individual might worry about these huge stores of information about them. *(2 marks)*
(b) Give **one** example of a national database that stores personal information and is set up by an organization run by the government. *(1 mark)*

3 There have been many stories in the press about government and local councils snooping. Snooping involves using surveillance to find out about people and what they are up to.
(a) Describe **two** ways ICT can be used for surveillance. *(2 marks)*
(b) Explain, by giving an example, why the government or council might want to conduct surveillance on a person. *(2 marks)*

Impact of ICT

In Topic 15 you learnt about the use of data logging and how it can be used to take readings of such quantities as temperature, pressure, light, etc., automatically. ICT can be used to monitor climate change and also monitor other environmental changes.

In this section you will learn about the things that can be done using ICT to help the environment. This section also looks at the impact of ICT on different people, such as how ICT can widen the gap between rich and poor countries.

Monitoring climate change

The increased amount of carbon dioxide in the atmosphere, due mainly to the burning of fossil fuels such as oil, coal and natural gas, is reckoned by most scientists to cause global warming. In order to get a complete picture for the whole world, it is necessary to take accurate environmental measurements regularly over a long period of time. ICT is suited for this because the readings can be taken automatically and then sent wirelessly to the main computer system for processing.

The way ICT helps the environment

Many ICT systems help the environment in some way. Here are some examples:

- Environmental control systems – here the heating can be controlled accurately in each room in a building. If a room is not being used, then the heating can be turned off. This helps reduce fuel bills as well as carbon dioxide emissions.
- Satellite navigation systems – ensure people do not get lost and therefore use more fuel and create more pollution.

▼ Paper should be kept separate from rubbish and recycled, saving trees and energy.

- Traffic management systems – these coordinate traffic lights, which ensures that the main body of traffic keeps moving.
- Pollution monitoring systems – monitor the environmental conditions in rivers and lakes and produce alerts if there are problems.

The effects that low energy use and recycling have on the environment

The production of ICT equipment produces lots of carbon dioxide and the use of the equipment produces lots as well. Carbon dioxide is a greenhouse gas and causes global warming, which is bad for all of us.

In order to help the environment there are a number of actions we can all take:

- Recycle hardware, as this reduces the greenhouses gases.
- Reduce the amount of printouts you make. Use print preview so you only print your final copy.

- Recycle paper – printouts and other paper documents should not be thrown away with general rubbish. Instead it should be collected for recycling.
- Switch off computer equipment rather than leave it on stand-by.
- Teleworking or working from home – this will reduce congestion and pollution and cut down on greenhouse gas emissions.
- Recycle printer cartridges by having them re-filled with ink.
- Recycle mobile phones as your old phone can be someone's new phone.

Ozone layer

The ozone layer is a layer of gas which is important to us all because it filters out some of the harmful rays from the sun that can cause some cancers. Some manufacturing processes produce gases that destroy this layer. Computer models have been created to give scientists an idea of how the layer is being destroyed and what we can do to stop it.

Landfill sites

Recycling reduces the amount of rubbish dumped in landfill sites. Landfill sites reduce the land available for housing or for growing crops.

The impact on rich and poor communities

The use of ICT is essential if a country is to remain or become prosperous in the world. Here are some of the impacts on rich and poor communities:

- Widening the gap between rich and poor countries – the use of ICT makes already rich countries richer. As many poorer countries do not have reliable electricity or telecommunications, they cannot take advantage of the financial benefits of ICT.
- ICT widens the gap between the 'haves' and the 'have nots' – there are large savings to be made on the Internet. You can buy cars, CDs, books, electrical goods, take part in online auctions and so on. All

this is fine, but you need one thing to take part; a valid credit/debit card. This credit card gives you an electronic identity. If you do not have a credit/debit card, then it is hard to take advantage of Internet savings. Getting a credit/debit card is not that easy if you do not have a job or have a bad credit history.

Changes in culture

There are a number of changes to culture due to ICT and here are some of them:

- The way we buy and listen to music has changed – downloads are more popular and people listen to music more on the move.
- TV is watched on the Internet – people are not restricted to the times they watch programmes.
- Viewing figures for TV are getting smaller – many more people are using the Internet in their leisure time.
- The use of ICT encourages globalization – countries can lose their identity and culture.
- Many people use ICT for entertainment – playing games (not just the arcade type but games such as Scrabble, chess, etc.).
- Social networking sites/chat rooms, etc. – people can chat with anyone in the world.

▲ Internet access is a low priority in some countries where there is no stable government and poor access to an electricity supply.

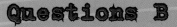

Questions

✓ Test yourself

The following notes summarize this topic. The notes are incomplete because they have words missing. Using the words in the list below, copy out and complete the sentences A to I, underlining the words that you have inserted. Each word may be used more than once.

private	matched	CCTV	identity cards	manufacture

surveillance	privacy	crimes	rich

A The National DNA database contains DNA data that can be _____ with samples taken at the scene of a crime.

B The PNC contains details about _____ and it is the main database used by all the police forces.

C Because national databases are used by thousands of different people in thousands of different places, many people are worried about the _____ of their personal data.

D Many countries have _____ _____ that their citizens must carry with them and the details on the card can be used to check that the person is who they say they are.

E Many public databases are linked to _____ databases and this allows the passage of information between the two.

F Government has been criticized for the amount of snooping on their citizens. This snooping is called _____.

G One method of surveillance makes use of _____ cameras.

H ICT can widen the gap between _____ and poor communities.

I ICT uses a lot of energy to make the equipment and also to _____ the computers.

Examination style questions

1 Data logging is used to monitor long-term environmental change.
   (a) Explain what is meant by the term 'data logging'. *(2 marks)*
   (b) Give **one** advantage of data logging for monitoring long-term environmental change. *(1 mark)*
   (c) Give the name of the sensor that would be used to monitor global warming. *(1 mark)*

2 ICT equipment should be recycled rather than added to landfill sites.
   Explain **two** reasons for this. *(2 marks)*

3 ICT can widen the gap between rich and poor people.
   Give **three** ways ICT can widen this gap. *(3 marks)*

4 In order to minimize the effect on the environment in using ICT there are a number of actions we can all take. Describe **three** actions we can take. *(3 marks)*

Exam support

Worked example

Discuss the political, ethical and environmental issues relating to the use of ICT. Your answer should refer to the concerns the public have about the use of personal data by the state. *(8 marks)*

Student answer 1

People are worried that the government knows too much about us. We cannot keep our life private any more. They know about your medical history, what car you drive, what your qualifications are. They know all about you.

There are lots of CCTV cameras checking up on you. They spy on you as you walk down the road. They are supposed to make you feel safer.

The state snoops on people such as finding out how much money they have in the bank so they can tax them more.

ICT can help the environment because it can be used to make central heating systems work more efficiently.

◀ Examiner's comment

There are three different issues that need to be discussed: political, ethical and environmental. All of these issues need to be discussed in order to gain the maximum marks.

The student has made four points worthy of marks but the answer could really have done with more structure.

(4 marks out of 8)

Student answer 2

Political issues

Large national databases have been created so that all the data about a person can be held centrally. This will make it easier to secure the data and keep it up-to-date. People worry that government does not look after personal data well and that the data will be misused.

Ethical issues

People are worried that too much personal data is held about them. They are also worried that there is too much surveillance. Their phone calls can be intercepted and all their email and searches are kept by the ISP they use.

They are worried that identity cards could mean that they have to produce them if asked for by the police.

Environmental issues

Data logging can be used to check up on pollution. It can also be used to monitor long-term temperature rises due to global warming. ICT is responsible for a lot of energy being used and this is why it is important to upgrade existing equipment rather than buy new equipment and recycle old equipment. Also computers should be switched off rather than put on stand-by to save power.

◀ Examiner's comment

The student has carefully structured their answer and it is clear to the examiner to which issue the points refer. This is good exam technique.

National databases have been discussed along with the problems that government's past record of ensuring the privacy of such data is not good.

Surveillance and identity cards have been discussed and several points have been made.

The environmental issues referring to monitoring of global warming, use of energy and the need for recycling have been discussed.

There are more than eight points made in the answer that could be awarded marks so the maximum marks are given for this question.

(8 marks out of 8)

Exam support *continued*

Examiner's answers

One mark for each point to a maximum of eight marks. In order to get over six marks, they must have covered political, ethical and environmental issues.

Political:

- National identity cards (1) – reduce civil liberties (1), people could be monitored (1), etc.
- National databases (1) – lots of personal data stored centrally (1), can be used by lots of government departments (1), exchange of data with private companies (1), examples of loss of data/loss of privacy.
- Examples of databases (PNC, DNA, etc.) (1).

Ethical:

- Surveillance (1) – by security services such as police/MI5 (1), use information about phone calls, emails, IMs, etc. (1).
- Use of CCTV (1) – to recognize faces (1), car registration plate recognition systems (1).

Other examples such as:

- Essay banks (1) – encourage young people to cheat (1).
- Google Earth (1) – destroys people's privacy by allowing people to view their house from the street or from above (1).

Environmental:

- Data logging (1) – helps monitor environmental quantities to research climate change/global warming.
- Heating control systems (1) – help reduce the energy required to heat buildings (1).
- Recycle (1) – don't put computer equipment in landfill as many components can be re-used (1).
- Reduce power consumption (1) – turn off computers rather than leave on stand-by (1).
- Upgrade existing computers (1) – new computers require a lot of power to make and this gives off greenhouse gases (1).

Summary mind maps

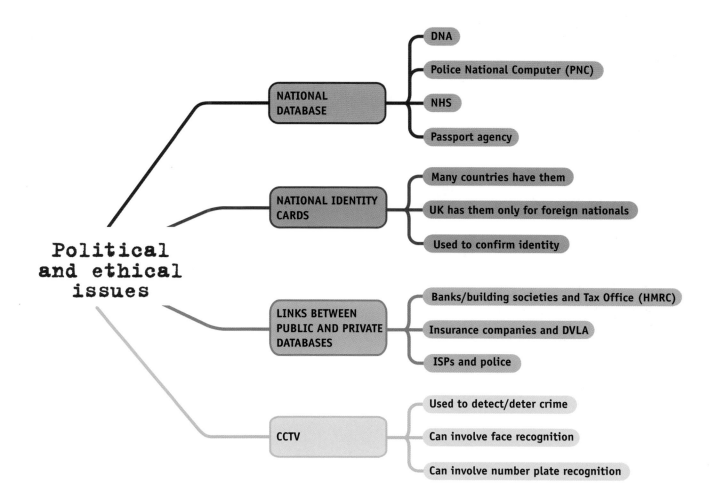

Political and ethical issues

- **NATIONAL DATABASE**
  - DNA
  - Police National Computer (PNC)
  - NHS
  - Passport agency
- **NATIONAL IDENTITY CARDS**
  - Many countries have them
  - UK has them only for foreign nationals
  - Used to confirm identity
- **LINKS BETWEEN PUBLIC AND PRIVATE DATABASES**
  - Banks/building societies and Tax Office (HMRC)
  - Insurance companies and DVLA
  - ISPs and police
- **CCTV**
  - Used to detect/deter crime
  - Can involve face recognition
  - Can involve number plate recognition

Summary mind maps *continued*

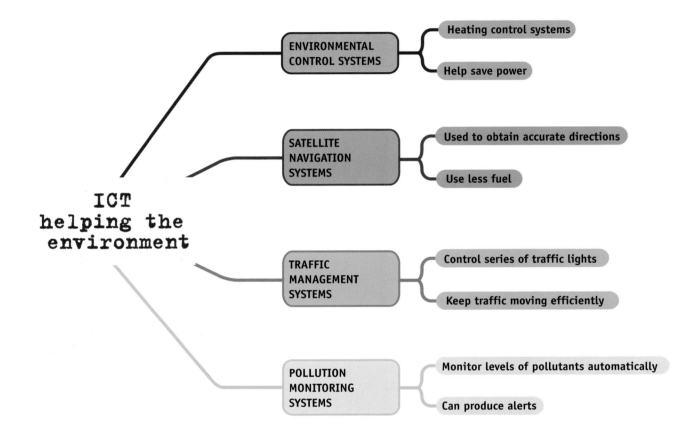

Collaborative working

The key concepts covered in this topic are:

- Collaboration
- Collaborative working processes
- Video/teleconferencing
- Collaborative situations and software
- Sharing information and online safety
- Advantages and disadvantages of collaborative home working

Many people work together when completing a common task and this is called collaborative working. The use of ICT means that collaborative working is made easier. For example, the use of networks such as the Internet makes it easy for people to transfer work to each other for comments. It also helps people communicate effectively with each other. The use of ICT has also meant that not all the people working on the same task need to be in the same place.

In this topic you will be looking at the impact of ICT on collaborative working for individuals, organizations and society.

Contents

Collaboration and collaborative working processes

You will find out

▷ **About what collaboration involves**

▷ **About collaborative working processes**

Many projects involve teams of people working together to get things done. The use of ICT makes this much easier. In this section you will be looking at collaborative working, what it is and what it involves.

▲ Collaboration involves teamwork.

Many tasks are completed by collaborative working. For example, a website may be created by several different people, with each person completing a certain series of tasks. Matching the task to the person is important because all team members will have their strengths and weaknesses. For example, one person may have good knowledge of web design software, another might be very good at English and another might have an artistic streak.

Collaborative working processes

When people work together they rely on each other to produce work of a suitable standard and complete it on time. If the project fails then they will all be judged as having failed. There are a number of processes that should take place in order that collaborative working is a success and these include the following.

Group plans

Before starting work on a project the group must plan the project by considering such things as who does what, establishing deadlines for tasks, planning how work will be reviewed, etc. They will also establish milestones, which are key points in

Collaboration

Collaboration means actively working together. In other words the people involved are working jointly together towards a common goal or target.

Collaboration involves two or more parties working together and these parties can be:

- people
- organizations
- countries.

Collaboration is a recursive process. This means that the work is continually refined and improved upon until everyone involved is satisfied with the results. Working as a team is ideal for this as they are able to review each other's work and suggest improvements.

▲ Collaborative working enables a team to do things it would be impossible for them to do on their own. These ants have formed a bridge for other ants to walk across.

the project where the progress of the project is assessed. Milestones are also stages where a particular part of the project is delivered.

Issues

A number of issues may arise before starting the project and these may include:

- Establishing exactly what it is the team have to produce.
- Deciding on the best solution.
- Appointing of someone to be in charge of the project (sometimes called the project manager).
- Establishing the strengths and weaknesses of each member of the team so they can be given the most appropriate task to do.
- Dividing the project into a series of smaller tasks.
- Dividing the work fairly and equally.
- Establishing dates for meetings at which progress will be assessed.
- Establishing methods by which team members communicate with each other.

Risks

Before starting a project it is important to assess the risks to the project. By knowing these risks you can do your best to reduce the likelihood of them happening.

Here are some of the risks and what might be done to minimize them:

- Costs escalating – using spreadsheet software, keep careful track of how the budget is being spent.
- The completion date of the project being delayed – use project management software to see the effect of any delays in tasks and help decide what can be done to get the project back on track.
- Loss of work – the use of virus checkers, firewalls, user-IDs and passwords and the regular taking of backups will minimize this risk.
- Work produced not being fit for purpose – the work being produced is not of satisfactory quality. Monitoring through regular reviews of progress and standards of work.

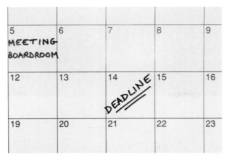

▲ Deadlines are dates by which part or all of a project must be completed.

Ensuring consistency

When more than one person works on a project it is important that everyone has a consistent approach. Without this, the work can look as though it has been produced by different people and will not look professional.

Here are some ways a project such as a book, presentation, website can be inconsistent:

- Layout appears different for each page – objects on the page are in different places from page to page. No consistency in headings with different font types and font sizes used.
- Style of writing can be different – the level and tone can change.
- Words can be spelt differently – for example, one person might use 'e-mail' where another uses 'email'.
- Buttons on a website might be different (e.g., sizes, appearance, etc.) depending on who produced the webpage.
- Colour schemes are different without reason – pages of the same document should look as though they belong together.

House style

To aid consistency a house style should be established. A meeting can be organized where members of the project team discuss issues that will make sure that problems with inconsistency do not arise. For example, they can agree a layout by producing a template for documents that everyone will adhere to. They can also agree on the spellings of certain words. Agreeing on these things before anyone produces anything will save time having to make changes later on.

Organizing work schedules and meetings

For a project to go smoothly it must be well planned as without such planning the project may not be completed in the time available or it may go over the budget allocated to it. To be able to plan the project successfully, it will be necessary to be able to break the project down into a series of smaller tasks and determine the order in which these smaller tasks need to take place.

Work schedules need to be planned showing what work is to be completed, who is going to complete it and the dates by which it must be completed (called deadlines).

Meetings should be planned at the start so everyone knows their dates and times in advance. Meetings will be used to assess progress at regular intervals and also for reviewing the work that has already been produced. Colleagues will be given each other's work to assess and work will also be given back for further refinement.

Project management

Someone has to be in charge of a project and take most of the responsibility for it and this person is called the project manager. A good project manager will ensure that:

- work is divided fairly among the team members
- each team member is given the most appropriate task for their skills and abilities
- conflicts/disagreements are sorted out
- the project does not go over budget
- the project's progress is reviewed regularly
- the work produced by team members is fit for purpose
- the deadlines are met.

KEY WORD

Templates Electronic files that hold standardized document layouts.

Collaboration and collaborative working processes *continued*

Questions A

1. Many people use ICT to help them work collaboratively.
   (a) Give **two** developments in ICT that help people work collaboratively. *(2 marks)*
   (b) By giving a suitable example, describe a situation where collaboration took place to complete a task using ICT. *(4 marks)*

2. A publisher is producing a book for schools for GCSE History. There are several authors who will write the book and several people at the publishers will be involved in its production.
   (a) The publishers have a house style and a document giving this is given to each of the writers. Explain what a house style is and why it is needed. *(2 marks)*
   (b) Give two things that would be specified as part of the house style. *(2 marks)*
   (c) The people involved in writing and producing the book will need to work collaboratively. Explain briefly what this means. *(3 marks)*

3. Collaboration is a recursive process.
   (a) Explain what is meant by collaboration. *(2 marks)*
   (b) Give **one** advantage in collaborative working. *(1 mark)*
   (c) Explain, by giving a suitable example, what recursive means. *(2 marks)*

Activity

Thinking about how to ensure consistency when working collaboratively

When working collaboratively, you need to ensure the consistency of the work produced by the team. Think about how you might go about ensuring this.

What can be done to make sure that none of the things in the list below occur?

- Layout appears different for each page – objects on the page are in different places from page to page. No consistency in headings with different font types and font sizes used.
- Style of writing can be different – the level and tone can change.
- Words can be spelt differently – for example, one person might use 'e-mail' where another uses 'email'.
- Buttons on a website might be different (e.g., sizes, appearance, etc.) depending on who produced the webpage.
- Colour schemes are different without reason – pages of the same document should look as though they belong together.

Write a list of the things you would do to ensure the consistency of the work produced by a team you have been put in charge of.

Video/teleconferencing and collaborative situations and software

You will find out

▷ **About what video/ teleconferencing is**

▷ **About the advantages and disadvantages of video/ teleconferencing**

▷ **About the range of situations where collaboration can take place**

▷ **About the software tools that aid collaborative working**

Videoconferencing or teleconferencing enables people to have virtual meetings, saving time and benefiting society in the process. It also facilitates collaborative working because people in different locations find it much easier to have meetings. ICT developments have led to people being able to conduct virtual meetings. In this section you will be looking at video/teleconferencing and the benefits it brings.

In this section you will also be looking at situations where collaborative work is appropriate and the software that can make collaborative working easier.

What is video/ teleconferencing?

Teleconferencing is a general term that is used to describe the communication between two people at remote sites using video and/or audio. Teleconferencing includes videoconferencing. Videoconferencing and teleconferencing are used in GCSE ICT to mean the same thing, so do not worry about the differences between them.

Video/teleconferencing is an example of a form of collaborative working. This means that people are able to work on a joint task together when they are not working in the same location. Video/teleconferencing is based on workers in two or more locations being able to interact with others via multi-way video/tele and audio transmission simultaneously.

Videoconferencing

Videoconferencing allows face-to-face meetings to be conducted without the participants being in the same room or even the same geographical area. You will probably have seen videoconferencing systems used to interview people in distant locations on the TV news.

Videoconferencing allows people to hold a 'virtual' meeting. The people at the meeting can see and speak to each other. They are also able to share documents, presentations, etc.

Advantages of using videoconferencing

There are many advantages in using videoconferencing and these include:

- Less stress as employees do not have to experience delays at airports, accidents, roadworks, etc.
- Improved family life, as less time spent away from home staying in hotels.
- They do not have to put in long working hours travelling to and from meetings.
- Saves money as business does not have to spend money on travelling expenses, hotel rooms, meals, etc.
- Improves productivity of employees, as they are not wasting time travelling.
- Meetings can be called at very short notice without too much planning.
- Greener, as there are fewer people flying to meetings. This cuts down on carbon dioxide emissions.
- Roads will not be clogged up with traffic and this will cause less stress and cut down on pollution.

KEY WORD

Videoconferencing ICT system that allows face-to-face meetings to be conducted without the participants being in the same room or even the same geographical area.

Video/teleconferencing and collaborative situations and software *continued*

Disadvantages of using videoconferencing

There are many disadvantages in using videoconferencing and these include:

- The cost of the equipment, as specialist videoconferencing equipment is expensive.
- Poor image and sound quality.
- People can feel very self-conscious when using videoconferencing and may fail to come across well.
- Although documents and diagrams in digital form can be passed around, an actual product or component cannot be passed around.
- Lack of face-to-face contact may mean a discussion may not be as effective.

Collaborative situations

There are many examples where people work collaboratively using ICT and here are some examples:

1 **The production of computer games** – there are many people involved in the production of computer games from start to finish. There are designers who design the animations, there are programmers who create the programming code, there are people who advertise and market the game, there are people who design the covers, there are the people who produce all the DVDs, etc. All these people have to work together and pass work to each other for review and comments.

2 **Business** – most people in business work as a team. For example, insurance companies have to process claims made for accidents. Workflow software is used to ensure that the different people are given the information at the correct time in order to process the claim. For example,

Videoconferencing allows virtual meetings where delegates are not at the same location.

there will be claims forms to be processed, witness statements to be obtained, photographs and images to be processed, documentation from solicitors, quotes from garages for the repairs and so on. By all working together and the efficient use of ICT it means that the claims can be processed in the least amount of time.

3 **Education** – the production of a school magazine involves collaboration. Staff and students submit artwork and text for inclusion. Staff and student editors receive much of the material by email and they can then plan what material to include and a template. Different people can then work on their part of the magazine. Having a template means that the layout and design will be consistent. Staff and students will use email with file attachments to pass work to and from each other for comments. They will proof read each other's work and mark up any alterations needed. Refining of the work will take place until everyone is happy with the final result.

4 **Cultural interaction** – many schools have an exchange programme where students go to live in another country for a few weeks. It is a reciprocal arrangement and the other students come to live in this country for a few weeks at a later date. There is a lot of planning and organization needed and ICT is used to facilitate this.

Collaborative software tools

There are many different software tools that make it easy for people to work together and produce work according to deadlines.

Shared workspaces

A shared workspace is an area on a network where files are kept that need to be used by different people working on the same project. Templates can be stored here so everyone can use them to ensure a consistent approach. Files of work in hand can be stored in this area for other people's comments. It is also easier to make sure that the work is regularly backed up if all the files are stored in one place.

Software tools to help with project management

A good project will normally be judged on the following:

- Did it produce a quality piece of work?
- Was it produced on time?
- Was it produced on budget or less than budget?
- Did the team work well together?
- There are software tools that help with project management.

Software for producing Gantt charts

Gantt charts are used to schedule jobs and to show when the tasks that make up the whole job start and finish. They have a timescale going across the page and a list of the activities to be done going vertically down the page. The blocks that show the duration of the activities are shaded to show the time taken on each task. They are used as a planning tool, since they can be used to determine which jobs are late and which jobs are running ahead of schedule.

Most project management software makes use of Gantt charts in some way.

	Tasks	Weeks 1–13 (shaded duration)
1	Investigate existing system	Weeks 1–2
2	Feasibility study	Weeks 2–3
3	Analysis	Weeks 3–5
4	Design	Weeks 6–7
5	Implementation	Weeks 7–10
6	System testing	Weeks 10–11
7	User training/documentation	Weeks 11–12
8	Evaluation and monitoring	Weeks 12–13
9	Maintenance	Week 13

▲ Here is a simple Gantt chart.

Project name:
Company name:

Project lead: John Smith
Today's date: 05/03/10
Viewing weeks: 01/01/10 – 26/11/10

WBS	Tasks	Start	End	Duration (days)	% Complete	Working dyas	Days complete	Days remaining
1	Category 1	03/01/10	20/01/10	76	85	55	65	11
1.1	Sub task	03/01/10	21/01/10	18	100	13	18	0
1.2	Sub task	22/01/10	21/02/10	30	95	23	29	2
1.3	Sub task	22/01/10	10/02/10	19	95	15	18	1
1.4	Sub task	11/02/10	20/03/10	37	50	27	19	19
2	Category 2	01/03/10	13/05/10	73	20	52	15	58
2.1	Sub task	01/03/10	18/03/10	17	50	12	9	9
2.2	Sub task	01/03/10	18/03/10	17	30	12	5	12
2.3	Sub task	19/03/10	27/04/10	39	0	30	0	39
2.4	Sub task	15/04/10	13/05/10	28	0	20	0	28
3	Category 3	27/04/10	08/08/10	103	0	74	0	103
3.1	Sub task	27/04/10	14/05/10	17	0	12	0	17
3.2	Sub task	15/05/10	01/06/10	17	0	14	0	17
3.3	Sub task	02/06/10	09/07/10	37	0	22	0	37
3.4	Sub task	10/07/10	08/08/10	39	0	26	0	39

▲ This Gantt chart has been produced using specialist software. The red line shows the date on which progress is being assessed.

Video/teleconferencing and collaborative situations and software *continued*

Workflow tools

Different people in an organization are responsible for different processes. For example, a person who is responsible for making orders with suppliers will not be the same person who is responsible for making the payments to the supplier. This means that work has to flow between different personnel in an organization.

Workflow tools provide automatic routing of work to the people responsible for working on them. This means each person responsible for completing each step is given access to the data at exactly the right time. Workflow tools are ideal for collaborative working, and because the work is routed using networks, the people can be situated anywhere.

KEY WORD

Workflow the scheduling of independent tasks using a manual or automatic system.

▲ **Different people in an organization are responsible for different functions.**

Questions B

1 **(a)** A company has decided to use videoconferencing. Explain what is meant by videoconferencing. *(2 marks)*

(b) Other than a computer, what equipment would the company need to supply to enable videoconferencing? *(2 marks)*

(c) Write down **one** advantage and **one** disadvantage of videoconferencing. *(2 marks)*

2 Software tools are available that help with collaborative working.

Give the names of **two** software tools and explain how they help people to work collaboratively. *(4 marks)*

3 Email is used to help people work together.

(a) Give the names of **two** features of email that help people to work collaboratively. *(2 marks)*

(b) Using **one** of your answers to part (a) describe how the feature would be used when working collaboratively. *(1 mark)*

Extension activity

For this activity you have to find out more about videoconferencing.

Use the Internet to find answers to the following and produce a brief set of notes for future reference:

- The benefits of videoconferencing to society.
- The hardware needed.
- The software needed.
- Some typical applications of videoconferencing.

Sharing information and online safety

You will find out

▷ **About sharing files and transferring data safely**

▷ **About the need to respect others and legal aspects**

▷ **About the systems that ensure the security of data**

One of the problems in working collaboratively is that it can expose the data held to be less secure. For example, people working remotely might work on the move or in public places on laptops that may be stolen. There are a few other problems that occur when people are working on files that are altered by lots of different people.

In this section you will be looking at the issues concerning the sharing of information and online safety.

Sharing files

When many people are working on the same project such as developing a new website, they often have to share files.

It is important to name files carefully. For example, it should be possible to know who created the file from its name. When working on multiple versions of a file, each version should have a different filename from the previous version. There is always a danger of saving an older version of a file using the same filename and losing work in the process. Saving using different version names helps avoid this. This is called version control.

Transferring files safely

Some organizations may have spent millions of pounds developing a new website, multimedia product, piece of software, etc. They need to protect this investment.

When transferring work between team members they must take steps to prevent the work being accessed by others. Encryption can be used, which scrambles files before sending over the Internet. Only the correct recipient will be able to unscramble it.

Team members must ensure that others cannot access the work from their computers. The use of user-IDs/usernames and passwords will help and also the use of firewalls will ensure that hackers cannot gain access using the Internet.

Access rights such as read only and read/write can be used to ensure that work is only amended by team members who are supposed to amend it.

▲ Firewalls stop hackers accessing computers using the Internet.

Other things to consider

Respecting others

When working collaboratively you must respect the opinions of others and put personalities aside and get on with the task.

As working collaboratively is a recursive process there will be times when you will have to comment on other people's work and they in turn will comment on your work. Comments about anyone's work can be a delicate subject and you are never quite sure about the way they will take them. Comments should always be constructive so as to not give the indication that they are serious criticisms. They should suggest how the work might be improved.

Complying with data protection regulations

When working on projects such as creating databases you may be using personal data.

If you are using personal data then you have to meet all the requirements of the Data Protection Act. This act controls what you can and cannot do with personal data.

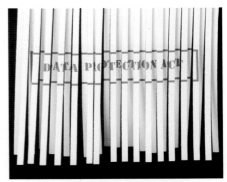

▲ If your project involves personal data, then you will need to comply with the Data Protection Act.

Sharing information and online safety *continued*

▲ This external hard disk drive is used to backup the data on the hard drive.

Systems that enable the security of data

Many collaborative workers work from remote locations and therefore the risks to data are greater. Here are the things that need to be put in place in order to ensure the security of data:

Firewalls – these must be installed to prevent hackers accessing files using the Internet.

Encryption – encryption can be used to protect personal information and financial details from being accessed illegally. Encryption can also be used to prevent access to files if a computer is stolen.

Backups – these are copies of the data and these should be taken at regular intervals and kept off-site. Secure sites – these are sites that are safe and use encryption.

Extension activity

Produce a mind map that covers all the things to do with security that would need to be considered when working collaboratively using ICT.

KEY WORDS

Data Protection Act 1998 A law that restricts the way personal information is stored and processed on a computer.

Encryption The process of coding files before they are sent over a network to protect them from hackers. Also the process of coding files stored on a computer/storage device so that if the computer/storage device is stolen, they cannot be read

Firewall A piece of software, hardware or both that is able to protect a network from hackers.

▲ Firewalls stop hackers accessing files stored on a network.

Questions C

1 (a) When sharing files you need to be careful with file naming conventions. Give **one** reason why it is important to be careful when naming files. *(2 marks)*

(b) When working collaboratively it is important to be careful about version control. Explain **one** way that getting confused with different versions of the same file can cause problems. *(1 mark)*

2 When working collaboratively, it is important to ensure the security of data.

(a) Describe **two** ways in which the security of data can be put at risk when working collaboratively. *(2 marks)*

(b) Explain **two** precautions that can be taken to ensure the security of data. *(2 marks)*

3 When working with personal data, the data is often encrypted. In most cases it is encrypted when transferred over the Internet. In some cases it is encrypted when it is stored on portable media and computers such as laptops and netbooks.

(a) Explain the meaning of 'encrypted'. *(2 marks)*

(b) Give **one** reason personal data being transferred using the Internet is often encrypted. *(1 mark)*

(c) Give **one** reason personal data being stored on portable media and computers is often encrypted. *(1 mark)*

Advantages and disadvantages of collaborative home working

You will find out

▷ **About the advantages of collaborative home working**

▷ **About the disadvantages of collaborative home working**

Many collaborative workers work from home and many of the developments in ICT enable them to do almost everything they could do if they were working in an office.

There are many advantages of working from home and most people would choose to do so given the chance. However, there are some disadvantages and in this section you will be looking at both the advantages and disadvantages of collaborative home working, which is more commonly known as teleworking.

Collaborative home working/teleworking

If you have an Internet connection then you can communicate easily with people all around the country or even the world. Many people who use computers for their work are able to do their work at home. Working from home using ICT equipment and telecommunications to do collaborative work is called home working or teleworking.

The advantages of teleworking to the employee:

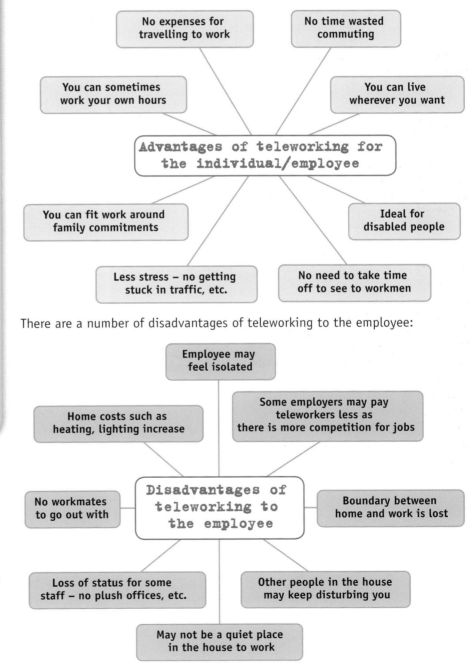

No expenses for travelling to work

No time wasted commuting

You can sometimes work your own hours

You can live wherever you want

Advantages of teleworking for the individual/employee

You can fit work around family commitments

Ideal for disabled people

Less stress – no getting stuck in traffic, etc.

No need to take time off to see to workmen

There are a number of disadvantages of teleworking to the employee:

Employee may feel isolated

Home costs such as heating, lighting increase

Some employers may pay teleworkers less as there is more competition for jobs

No workmates to go out with

Disadvantages of teleworking to the employee

Boundary between home and work is lost

Loss of status for some staff – no plush offices, etc.

Other people in the house may keep disturbing you

May not be a quiet place in the house to work

287

Advantages and disadvantages of collaborative home working *continued*

Why do employers allow staff to telework? You can see the advantages that teleworking offers to employers:

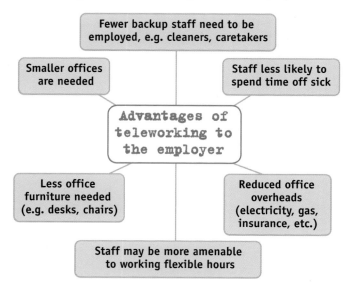

There are also a number of disadvantages of teleworking to employers:

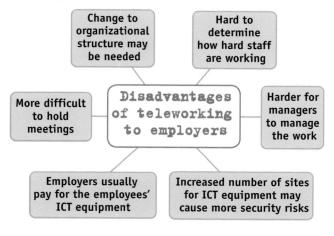

There are advantages to society in teleworking:

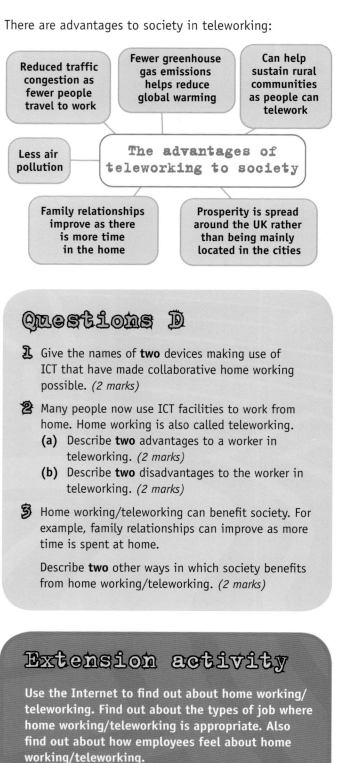

Questions D

1 Give the names of **two** devices making use of ICT that have made collaborative home working possible. *(2 marks)*

2 Many people now use ICT facilities to work from home. Home working is also called teleworking.
 (a) Describe **two** advantages to a worker in teleworking. *(2 marks)*
 (b) Describe **two** disadvantages to the worker in teleworking. *(2 marks)*

3 Home working/teleworking can benefit society. For example, family relationships can improve as more time is spent at home.

 Describe **two** other ways in which society benefits from home working/teleworking. *(2 marks)*

EXAM TIPS

You may simply be asked about the advantages or disadvantages of teleworking. You can therefore give a mixture of answers that relate to the employer, employee or society as a whole.

When asked to give a certain number of advantages/ disadvantages, always make sure that your answers are distinctly different.

Extension activity

Use the Internet to find out about home working/ teleworking. Find out about the types of job where home working/teleworking is appropriate. Also find out about how employees feel about home working/teleworking.

Produce a brief word-processed document explaining what you have found out.

Questions

☑ Test yourself

The following notes summarize this topic. The notes are incomplete because they have words missing. Using the words in the list below, copy out and complete the sentences A to I, underlining the words that you have inserted. Each word may be used more than once.

collaborative   home   working   collaboration

VoIP   distractions   family

home   recursive   project

videoconferencing

A _____ means two or more parties working together in order to meet a common target or goal.

B A _____ process is a process that is continually refined and improved upon until everyone involved is satisfied with the results.

C Many people who work collaboratively are able to work from _____.

D Videoconferencing is an example of collaborative working because many people can discuss a _____ at a virtual meeting.

E _____ _____ _____ means working on a joint project from home by making use of computers and networking equipment.

F One big advantage with home working is that you are able to work around _____ commitments.

G A disadvantage of home working is that there are many _____ at home.

H _____ uses cameras and microphones in addition to computers and special software in order to conduct a virtual meeting.

I _____ is a cheap method of making phone calls over the Internet and many home workers make use of it.

Questions *continued*

Examination style questions

1   Collaborative workers use ICT to help complete the work and communicate with each other.
    Match the letters A, B, C, D, E with the best descriptions in the table shown below. *(5 marks)*

A	Videoconferencing
B	Shared workspace
C	Firewall
D	House style
E	Template

Description	Letter
A style for documents that is agreed and aids consistency between documents produced by different people.	☐
A shared work area on the network where each person can access any files that are placed there.	☐
Software used to protect a network against hackers gaining illegal access.	☐
A file that contains the layout of a document such as positioning of items such as logos, font types and font sizes, etc.	☐
ICT system that allows collaborative workers to conduct face-to-face meetings without the participants being in the same room or area.	☐

2   Tick **two** boxes to show which of the following are advantages of collaborative home working. *(2 marks)*

	Tick two boxes only
It limits face-to-face contact	☐
It helps the environment owing to fewer carbon emissions	☐
Security of the data held is improved	☐
It removes regular social interaction	☐
It reduces travelling costs	☐
It leads to a feeling of isolation	☐

3   The use of ICT has enabled many staff to work from home. Working from home has both advantages and disadvantages. Give **two** advantages and **two** disadvantages to an employee in working from home. *(4 marks)*

4   Here are some descriptions of words or terms used when discussing collaborative working.
    Match the letters A, B, C, D with the best descriptions in the table shown below. *(4 marks)*

A	Videoconferencing
B	Firewall
C	Shared workspace
D	Version control

Description	Letter
Hardware or software used to prevent illegal access to networked computers using the Internet.	☐
Interaction with others via multi-way video/tele and audio transmission simultaneously.	☐
Ensuring that team members use the correct version of files when they are working together using ICT.	☐
An area on a network where files are kept that need to be used by different people working on the same project.	☐

5   Videoconferencing is used to help people work collaboratively.
    (a) Describe **two** advantages of using videoconferencing as a means of working collaboratively. *(2 marks)*
    (b) Describe **two** disadvantages of using videoconferencing as a means of working collaboratively. *(2 marks)*

Exam support

Worked example

There are many ways in which ICT has had an effect on the way people work. Two such ways are teleworking and videoconferencing. Describe the benefits that each of these technologies has brought to people. *(6 marks)*

Student answer 1

With videoconferencing you can see who you are talking to. People with relatives abroad can chat to them as if they were all together. They do not need to travel to see each other. Also meetings can be set up at the last minute, so everyone can meet. The people who are attending do not have to waste time travelling and there aren't the costs of travelling as well.

Teleworking is good because you can get to work at home. You have no boss standing over you telling you what to do and if you come in late no-one notices. You may be able to work your own hours, which is great if you need to take a holiday.

◀ Examiner's comment

In the part of the answer for videoconferencing the student seems to be confused between using webcams on home computers and professional videoconferencing. Videoconferencing equipment is expensive, which means its use is usually restricted to businesses, although it is sometimes used for distance learning in schools, colleges, etc. The part about meetings probably means businesses, so marks are given from here on.

The other parts were better and four points were awarded marks.

(4 marks out of 6)

Student answer 2

With teleworking there are lots of advantages such as:

- *You can work more flexibly, so by working harder you may be able to free up time to take time off later.*
- *As long as the work gets done, it does not matter when it is done. This means you can work at a time that suits you best.*
- *You do not have the time to spend commuting, which is unproductive and it can also be expensive in terms of petrol and car parking.*
- *It suits people who are self-motivated and like to work on their own.*

With videoconferencing there are lots of advantages such as:

- *You do not waste time driving to meetings and the company does not have the cost of this.*
- *You do not need to spend time away from your family, which is good for family life.*
- *There is also the environmental aspect to consider. Fewer journeys means less pollution and less global warming.*

◀ Examiner's comment

This is a well-structured and factually correct answer. The student has carefully explained many answers worthy of marks and there are more points made than were actually needed for this question. As six marks had been given the student needed to make six points but this is not a complaint because there is nothing wrong with writing more, because if one of the points is not quite right then the mark can be made up with one of the extra points.

(6 marks out of 6)

Examiner's answers

- One mark each for a benefit of teleworking to a maximum of three marks and the same for videoconferencing. Points should be made in complete sentences.

- Benefits of teleworking – no time spent travelling, greener/less pollution, can fit around family commitments, ideal for disabled/housebound, lower costs for teleworkers, etc.

- Benefits of videoconferencing – less time spent away from home, less cost as no travel and hotel costs, more productive as less time wasted on the move, greener as fewer journeys are made, etc.

Summary mind maps

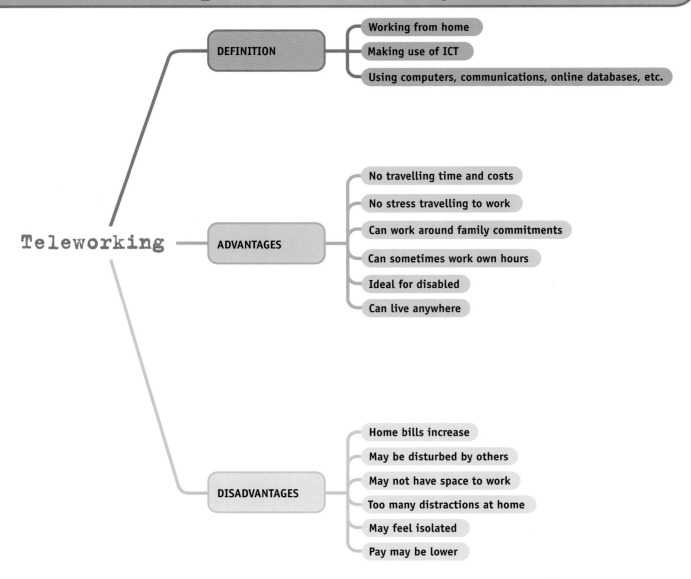

Teleworking

DEFINITION
- Working from home
- Making use of ICT
- Using computers, communications, online databases, etc.

ADVANTAGES
- No travelling time and costs
- No stress travelling to work
- Can work around family commitments
- Can sometimes work own hours
- Ideal for disabled
- Can live anywhere

DISADVANTAGES
- Home bills increase
- May be disturbed by others
- May not have space to work
- Too many distractions at home
- May feel isolated
- Pay may be lower

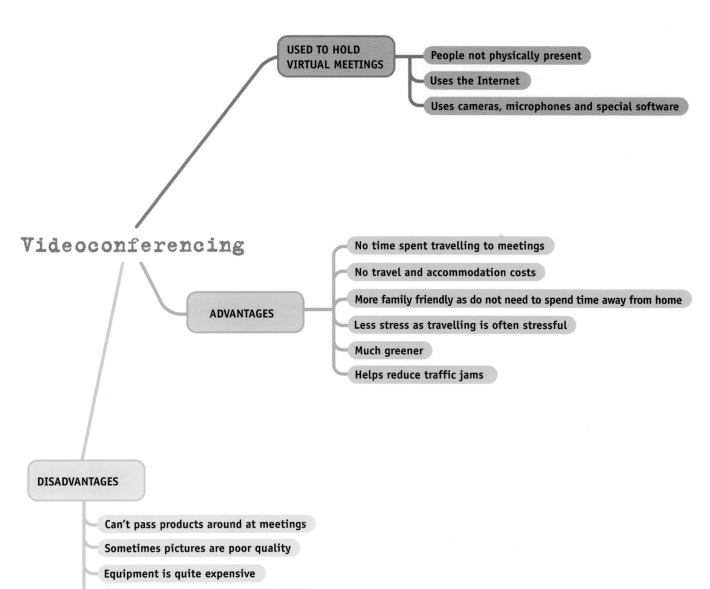

Videoconferencing

USED TO HOLD VIRTUAL MEETINGS
- People not physically present
- Uses the Internet
- Uses cameras, microphones and special software

ADVANTAGES
- No time spent travelling to meetings
- No travel and accommodation costs
- More family friendly as do not need to spend time away from home
- Less stress as travelling is often stressful
- Much greener
- Helps reduce traffic jams

DISADVANTAGES
- Can't pass products around at meetings
- Sometimes pictures are poor quality
- Equipment is quite expensive
- Some people like to travel to meetings

Topic 20
Case studies

The following case studies can be used to help consolidate the work you have studied in the topics. See if you can answer the questions that follow each case study.

Case study 1

Identity fraud

At a recent trial five people who had stolen the identities of the living and the dead were found guilty of fraud and were sentenced to between 4 and 8 years in prison.

The gang forged driving licences, pay slips and utility bills (e.g., gas and electricity bills) to steal the real identities of people who lived at properties that were now vacant.

The gang stole the identities of 60 people around the country and used them to take out bank loans, overdrafts and credit cards.

The money they made was huge and the ringleader drove a £160,000 sports car and wore a £30,000 watch.

When passing sentence the judge said that the crimes were complex and sophisticated.

Questions

1 Which one of the following laws covers identity theft/ fraud? *(1 mark)*

      The Computer Misuse Act 1990
      The Copyright, Designs and Patents Act 1988
      The Data Protection Act 1998

2 Identity theft has risen by a large amount over recent years.

Give **two** pieces of advice to a person who does not want to be a victim of identity theft/fraud. *(2 marks)*

3 Once a person's identity has been stolen, the thief can do several things with the new identity.

Describe **one** thing that the thief can do that will affect the victim. *(2 marks)*

Case study 2

Home copying

The music industry has been hit hard by Internet file sharing and CDs being copied. Over half of young people copy the music on their hard drives to friends and they also copy CDs. This deprives the music industry of a large amount of money and prevents them investing in new artists.

The music industry has tended to focus its attention on the file sharing sites that allow people to illegally copy music or video files between each other. Such sites allow use of peer-to-peer networking to transfer files.

It has been estimated that 95% of young people are illegally copying music and that only one in twenty downloads is legal. It is interesting to note that the average 18–24 year old keeps around £750 of unpaid for music on their MP3 player. Multiply this by the number in this age group and you have a massive amount of money being lost to the music industry.

The organization called the BMR (British Music Rights) helps the music industry take the owners of file sharing sites to court but it is worried that individuals who know that file copying is illegal still do it.

The worry is that professional musicians and songwriters will reach the point where they cannot make a living and they will have to give up. This will be to the detriment of everyone who enjoys listening to music.

Questions

1 Peer-to-peer networking is mentioned in the case study. Explain what the main features of peer-to-peer networking are. *(2 marks)*

2 Music can be downloaded legally or illegally.

   (a) Explain what the term 'downloading' means. *(2 marks)*

   (b) Describe **one** situation where music can be downloaded legally and **one** situation where music can be downloaded illegally. *(2 marks)*

3 Anyone who is involved in the music industry is affected by illegal downloads.

   (a) Explain **one** way in which a recording company would be affected by these illegal downloads. *(1 mark)*

   (b) Explain **one** way in which a musician, group or singer would be affected by these illegal downloads. *(1 mark)*

4 The Copyright, Designs and Patents Act 1988 makes it an offence to illegally download or copy music. It forbids the copying of other things as well.

   Give the names of **two** different things that could be copied illegally. *(2 marks)*

Case studies *continued*

Case study 3

How using Facebook might cause you health problems

You already know that using computers can cause a number of health problems such as back ache, repetitive strain injury (RSI), eye strain and stress. Some doctors think that the use of social networking sites such as Facebook could cause serious health problems.

Increased isolation from people could raise your risk of serious health problems because of lack of face-to-face contact. It may impair immune responses and alter hormones.

Social networking sites, such as MySpace and Facebook, allow people to keep in touch with friends over the web. But, although they are supposed to bring people together, they may be doing the reverse. The hours spent communicating with 'virtual' friends is reducing the amount of time spent with real people.

More people are also teleworking, which means that most of their communication with other workers is via email, VoIP and videoconferencing.

One doctor has stated that: 'Levels of hormones such as the "cuddle chemical" oxytocin, which promotes bonding, altered according to whether people were in close contact or not.' He went on to say that: 'There does seem to be a difference between "real presence" and the virtual variety.'

Questions

1 One health problem caused by the use of computers is RSI. Give the meaning of the term RSI. *(1 mark)*

2 Explain **two** things you can do using a social networking site. *(2 marks)*

3 Many teleworkers use ICT systems, which means they do not have to meet face-to-face (i.e. in person).

   (a) Explain what is meant by teleworking. *(2 marks)*

   (b) Many teleworkers make use of VoIP. Give the meaning of the abbreviation VoIP. *(1 mark)*

   (c) Explain one reason why many teleworkers choose to use VoIP. *(1 mark)*

   (d) Teleworkers often make use of a system that allows them to conduct 'virtual' face-to-face meetings. Give the name of this system and explain how it benefits teleworkers. *(3 marks)*

4 Explain why some doctors reckon that lack of social contact with real people might cause some health problems. *(2 marks)*

Case study 4

Wikipedia

Wikipedia was set up to empower and engage people around the world by collecting and offering free content that can be disseminated globally. It is a huge success story and has changed the way the Internet is used.

You will probably have already used Wikipedia but if not, take a look at it now on: www.wikipedia.com

Wikipedia is a charity, and unlike most other free providers of content, it does not contain adverts and therefore gets no money from these sources. Instead it relies mainly on asking you and me to donate money or on revenue from grants. The money it obtains is used to buy hardware and also for the website hosting and bandwidth costs. People are not paid to add content – they do it for free!

Wikipedia is best described as an online encyclopaedia but it is different from other encyclopaedias in so much as it is made up from contributions by ordinary people. You may think this is a bad thing. After all, what if the information is wrong? It is easy to put in bogus information or information that someone believes is true but isn't. Luckily, other people can add information that corrects the information that is already there.

The idea is that if enough people contribute, then the information is as good as that provided more traditionally.

Questions

1 Wikipedia is a good example of lots of people working collaboratively using ICT.

   (a) Explain what 'collaboratively' means. *(1 mark)*

   (b) Give **one** reason why some people like to contribute towards Wikipedia. *(1 mark)*

2 One commenter on Wikipedia said: 'There is plenty of bogus information on the Internet. What we don't want is non-experts making any old rubbish up on Wikipedia and then our children getting hold of it and believing it to be true.'

Give a reason why this is less likely to happen than the commenter thinks. *(2 marks)*

3 You have been asked to give a brief description of what Wikipedia is to someone who has little knowledge of ICT.

Describe Wikipedia in easy to understand non-technical language.

You should make at least **three** main points in your description. *(3 marks)*

Topic 21
Advice about Unit 2

Introduction to Unit 2: The Assignment: Applying ICT

Unit 2 consists of practical work (i.e. an Assignment) and for this work you have to solve problems like the ones you would come across in education, the community or the workplace. You have to use ICT in order to solve these problems.

The assignment for Unit 2 is:

- Set by AQA.
- Internally assessed (i.e., your teacher/lecturer will mark it).
- Externally moderated (your teacher/lecturer will have their marking checked by someone else).
- To be completed under controlled conditions.
- Worth 30% of the total marks for the GCSE in ICT.

Each year the assessment board (i.e. AQA) will produce a list of tasks from which your school or college will choose which ones it is appropriate for you to do. This will be provided in a candidate booklet and you will be given your own copy of this by your teacher/lecturer.

The task is to take around 25 hours of your time and it needs to be completed in controlled conditions. What this means is that you will have to complete the majority of the work in normal class time with your teacher/lecturer present.

The way your work will be marked

Your teacher/lecturer will be marking your work for Unit 2 and the detail and marks are shown below.

Here are the marks that are allocated for the assignment:

- Analysis (10 marks)
- Design (20 marks)
- Implementation (40 marks)
- Testing (10 marks)
- Self-evaluation (8 marks)
- Report (6 marks)
- Evaluation of others' use of ICT (6 marks)
- Total marks = 100

Here is what you have to produce under these headings in order to get the maximum marks:

Analysis

As the way the analysis is marked will change annually, it is impossible to say here what you have to do to get the maximum marks for this section. The marks for the analysis will depend on the nature and content of the tasks. Your teacher will have to give you information about the analysis.

Design

You need to develop a creative planned design that is appropriate to the needs of the user and fit for purpose, and show how the problem is to be solved.

Where there is a choice about a design, you need to explain clearly your choices and relate these to the needs of the user.

Implementation

There are three elements to the implementation: skill, understanding and efficiency; evidence of solution; changes required and annotation.

You must use the resources and techniques with a high level of skill and understanding.

You must have implemented all, or nearly all of the changes resulting from required judgement or testing and efficiency to produce the solution.

You must include all or nearly all of the evidence of a creative and high quality solution and include earlier stages of creation of the solution.

Testing

There are two elements to testing: testing plan and evidence.

You should design an effective testing plan that:

- identifies all or nearly all the data used to check the problem
- identifies all or nearly all expected results.

Test against a correct testing plan producing a full record of results that are clearly checked and explain the changes needed (if any).

Self-evaluation

You should present a high quality evaluation clearly discussing the effectiveness of the solution in some cases, with reference to the desired outcomes/performance criteria.

Report

You should produce a clearly presented and high quality report explaining issues involved and making suitable recommendations.

Evaluation of others' use of ICT

You should produce a high quality evaluation that makes effective comments about another student's ICT solution as a whole. Effective improvements are recommended to improve the quality of their own work in future.

Questions and answers on Unit 2

Here are some questions and answers to help you understand what is required:

Can I work with others?

In some cases, yes. However, group work is less appropriate for Unit 2 than it is for Unit 3. For any group work you do, it has to be clear what contribution you have made, so that your component can be accurately marked.

Is there any work I can do at home?

Yes there is. However, your teacher must authenticate your work as your own, so the majority of the work is expected to be done in the classroom. You can, however, do research at home and collect material, provided the material produced is not directly assessed.

Is there just one task or several to complete?

There may be one or more than one task to complete.

▲ Your teacher can give you limited feedback but they are not allowed to explain how to improve your work to get more marks.

Can my teacher/lecturer give me feedback on what I have produced?

Yes, they are able to give you limited feedback. This means that you are able to show your teacher a draft piece of work for their comments. However, their comments can only refer to the focus of the piece of work. Your teacher cannot give you detail as to how to improve your work or gain more marks for it.

Can I just submit a disk with my work on?

No. Your work must be submitted as a portfolio of work in hard copy (i.e., printed out on paper).

▲ You cannot submit your assignment work on disk – it must be printed out.

Advice about Unit 3

The Assignment: Practical Problem Solving in ICT

For Unit 3 you have to produce a piece of practical work called Practical Problem Solving in ICT.

This piece of work is completed under controlled conditions and is to take about 25 hours of your time. As with Unit 2, you will be given a candidate booklet that outlines exactly what you have to do.

The practical problem solving work for Unit 3 is:

- Set by AQA – your teacher/lecturer will give you the task or tasks from which to choose.
- Internally assessed (i.e. your teacher/lecturer will mark it).
- Externally moderated (your teacher/lecturer will have their marking checked by someone else).
- To be completed under controlled conditions.
- Worth 30% of the total marks for the GCSE in ICT.

You will have to produce a portfolio of work and a report that will demonstrate your ability to identify requirements and make appropriate use of ICT in providing solutions that you will analyse, design, implement, test and evaluate. You must also show that you can evaluate the work of others.

The way your work will be marked

Your teacher/lecturer will be marking your work for Unit 3 in two parts. The detail and marks for each part are shown in the following tables.

Part 1: Planning and managing the problem	
1a	Milestones
1b	Risk
1c	Progress
1d	Managing storage
Part 1 sub total = 27 marks	

Part 2: Independently using ICT to:	
2a	Collect information
2b	Select information
2c	Format information
2d	Modelling with data
2e	Develop information
2f	Produce a report
2g	Evaluate
2h	Evaluate others' use of ICT
Part 2 subtotal = 73 marks	

The total marks for Unit 3 (i.e. Parts 1 and 2) = 100 marks

Important note

Students often think that the practical coursework is in isolation of the theory.

Before you start on your tasks or assignment work, make sure you read again any of the theory chapters that apply to what you are doing.

For example, suppose you are producing work for the evaluation for the assignment. Make sure that you look back at Topic 5 on the systems life cycle, which will tell you about what is included in an evaluation.

Questions and answers on Unit 3

Here are some questions and answers to help you understand what is required.

Do I have a choice of which tasks I complete?

Yes there are six possible tasks but your teacher/lecturer may decide only to let you choose from some of them. You are only required to do one task.

Can I work with others?

Yes you can. Group work for Unit 3 can be undertaken but it must be clear to your teacher which part of the work you have produced so that it may be accurately assessed.

▲ Group work can be undertaken for Unit 3 – you need to speak with your teacher about this.

Can I take work home to complete?

You cannot do work that is directly assessed at home but you can do research using the Internet, books, etc., provided that whatever you produce is not directly assessed.

It is important that all the work is your own and that you do not spend more than the allocated time (i.e. 25–30 hours) on it.

Can my teacher/lecturer give me feedback/help on what I have produced?

Yes, they are able to give you limited feedback. This means that you are able to show your teacher a draft piece of work for their comments. However, their comments can only refer to the focus of the piece of work. Your teacher cannot give you detail as to how to improve your work or gain more marks for it.

Is there a candidate booklet for Unit 3?

Yes, as with Unit 2 a candidate booklet is provided that tells you exactly what you have to produce.

Do I do functional skills separate to this in ICT?

No. This is because the functional skills for ICT are part of this subject. This means you do not have to produce extra work.

What evidence do I need for my work?

Evidence should include legible printouts, screenshots or diagrams with annotation and be presented as hard copy.

Can I just submit a disk with my work on?

No. Your work must be submitted as a report in hard copy (i.e., printed out on paper).

Where can I find further information about Units 2 and 3?

You can find all information about these Units along with examples of specimen candidate booklets at the following website: www.aqa.org.uk/ictzone

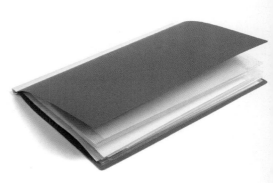

▷ Use thin folders like this to store your assignment work.

▲ Do not submit your assignment in folders like this – they are far too bulky.

▲ You cannot do work, that is directly assessed, at home but you can do research using the Internet, books, etc.

Glossary

Absolute reference A reference to a cell used in a formula where, when the formula is copied to a new address, the cell address does not change.

Access rights Restrictions of a user's access to only those files they need in order to perform their job.

Address book The names and email addresses of all the people to whom you are likely to send email, stored as a file.

Application software Software designed to do a particular job.

Artificial intelligence (AI) Creating computer programs or computers that behave in a similar way to the human brain by learning from experience.

ASCII A code for representing characters in binary.

Bandwidth A measure of the amount of data that can be transferred per second over the Internet or other network.

Batch processing All the inputs needed are batched together and processed in one go.

Batch total A meaningful total that is used to check that the computer has input all the data.

bcc (blind carbon copy) Copy of an email sent to lots of people who are unable to see the email addresses of the other people who have been sent the same email.

Biometric A property of the human body such as fingerprints or pattern on the retina that can be used to identify a person.

Bitmap graphic A graphic or image that is stored as a map showing the position and colour of individual dots of light called pixels.

Blog A website that allows comments to be posted.

Blogger A person who posts their comments to a blog.

Bluetooth A method used to transfer data wirelessly over short distances from fixed and mobile devices.

Bullet point A block or paragraph of text that has a symbol placed in front to make the section of text stand out.

cc (carbon copy) A copy of an email sent to more than one person.

CCTV Stands for closed circuit television.

Character Any symbol (letter, number, punctuation mark, etc.) that you can type from the keyboard.

Check digit A decimal number (or alphanumeric character) added to a number for the purpose of detecting the sorts of errors humans normally make on data entry.

Client–server A network where several computers are connected to a more powerful computer that controls the operation of the network.

Compression Storing data in a format that requires less space. Bitmapped graphics such as photographs are usually compressed to a fraction of their normal file size.

Computer Misuse Act 1990 An Act that makes illegal a number of activities such as deliberately planting viruses, hacking, using ICT equipment for fraud, etc.

Content The actual text, images, etc.

Control total A meaningful total (e.g., the total of a batch of invoices) that is entered to check that all the data has been entered/processed.

Copyright, Designs and Patents Act 1988 A law making it a criminal offence to copy or steal software.

Cropping Only using part of an image.

Data Raw facts and figures, e.g. readings from sensors, survey facts, etc.

Data capture Term for the various methods by which data can be entered into the computer so that it can be processed.

Data integrity The correctness of data stored.

Data logger A device that collects readings from one or more sensors. The time interval between each reading can be varied (called the logging rate) and the total time over which the data is logged (called the logging period) can also be varied.

Data logging The process of using an ICT system to collect data from sensors at a certain rate over a certain period of time. Remote weather stations use data logging.

Data Protection Act 1998 A law that restricts the way personal information is stored and processed on a computer.

Data redundancy Where the same data is stored more than once in a table or where the same data is stored in more than one table.

Digital signature A way of ensuring that an email or document sent electronically is authentic. It can be used to detect a forged document.

Download To copy files from a distant computer to the one you are working on.

Encryption The process of coding files before they are sent over a network to protect them from hackers. Also the process of coding files stored on a computer/storage device so that if the computer/storage device is stolen, they cannot be read.

Ergonomics An applied science concerned with designing and arranging things people use, so that the people and things interact most efficiently and safely.

Expert system An ICT system that mimics the decision-making ability of a human expert.

Export To take data from the package you are working on and save it. You can then view this exported file separately from the file it was created with or it can be imported into a different software package.

Extranet An external network that can be used by the customers, suppliers and partners of an organization as well as the organization itself.

Fact finding The investigation of a system to understand how it works or should work.

Favourites Storage area where the URL (i.e., the web address) of a website can be stored so that it can be accessed later using a link.

Fax A machine capable of sending and receiving text and pictures along telephone lines.

Feedback Where the output from the system directly affects the input.

Field A space in an information handling system or database used for inputting data. For instance, you could have fields for surname, date of birth, etc.

File attachment A file that is attached to an email.

File server A file server is a high-speed computer in a network that stores programs and data files shared by users.

Firewall A piece of software, hardware or both that is able to protect a network from hackers.

Footer Text placed at the bottom of a document.

Format checks Checks performed on codes to make sure that they conform to the correct combinations of characters.

Gateway The device/software that translates between two different kinds of computer networks (e.g., between a WAN and a LAN).

GIGO Abbreviation for garbage in garbage out. It means that if you put rubbish into the computer then you get rubbish out.

GIS An ICT system used to capture, manage, analyse and display geographically referenced information.

GPS (global positioning system) Another name for a satellite navigation system.

GUI (graphical user interface) Interface that allows users to communicate with the computer using icons and pull-down menus.

Hackers People who try to break into a computer/computer network.

Hardware The physical components of a computer system.

Hash total Meaningless total of numbers such as order numbers used to check that all the data has been entered.

Header Text placed at the top of a document.

Hotspot An image or piece of text used as a link. When you click on the image or text, you are taken to another part of the same page, a different page or a different site, or it may open a new file or a new window.

Hyperlink A feature of a website that allows a user to jump to another webpage, to jump to part of the same webpage or to send an email message.

HyperText Markup Language (HTML) A computer programming language used to create documents on the World Wide Web. You use it to specify the structure and layout of a web document.

Image map An image that contains more than one hotspot.

Import To bring data from outside the software you are using into the software. The software being used converts the incoming file so the user can see and use the data.

Information Data that has been processed by the computer.

Information Commissioner The person responsible for enforcing the Data Protection Act. They also promote good practice and make everyone aware of the implications of the Act.

Input device The hardware device used to feed the input data into an ICT system such as a keyboard or a scanner.

Instant messaging (IM) A method of two people using real-time text to conduct a conversation.

Interactive Where there is a constant dialogue between the user and the computer.

Internet A huge group of networks joined together.

Internet service provider (ISP) A company that provides users with an Internet connection.

Intranet A private network used within an organization that makes use of Internet technology.

Key field A field that is unique for a particular record in a database.

Knowledge Derived from information by applying rules to it.

LAN (local area network) A network of computers on one site.

Magnetic ink character recognition (MICR) Input method making use of numbers printed onto a document, such as a cheque, in a special magnetic ink that can be read by the magnetic ink character reader at very high speed.

Mail merge Combining a list of names and addresses with a standard letter so that a series of letters is produced with each letter being addressed to a different person.

Management information system (MIS) An ICT system that supplies information that helps give managers and others the information they need to make effective decisions.

Megapixel One million pixels (i.e. dots of light).

Memory cards Thin cards you see in digital cameras used to store photographs and can be used for other data.

Microprocessor The brain of the computer consisting of millions of tiny circuits on a silicon chip. It processes the input data to produce information.

MIDI (Musical Instrument Digital Interface) Used mainly to communicate between electronic keyboards, synthesizers and computers. MIDI files are compressed and the files are quite small.

Mind map A hierarchical diagram with a central idea or image at the centre of the map surrounded by branches that extend from the central idea.

Motherboard The central circuit board of the computer that contains all the electronic components such as the CPU and memory chips.

MP3 Music file format that uses compression to reduce the file size considerably, which is why the MP3 file format is popular with portable music players such as iPods and mobile phones.

Multimedia Making use of many media such as text, images, sound, animation and video.

Network A group of computers that are able to communicate with each other.

Networking software This is systems software that allows computers connected together to function as a network.

Notification The process of letting the Information Commissioner's Office know that an organization is storing and processing personal data.

OCR (optical character recognition) This is a combination of software and a scanner that is able to read characters into the computer.

OMR (optical mark reader/recognition) Reader that detects marks on a piece of paper. Shaded areas are detected and the computer can understand the information contained in them.

Online shopping Shopping over the Internet, as opposed to using traditional methods such as buying goods or services from shops or trading using the telephone.

Online tutorial Using ICT to help in the learning process.

Operating system software Software that controls the hardware of a computer and is used to run the applications software. Operating systems control the handling of input, output, etc.

Output The results from processing data.

Parity check Check to make sure that the data sent is the same as that received when data is transmitted from one computer to another.

Password A series of characters chosen by the user that are used to check the identity of the user when they require access to an ICT system.

PDA (personal digital assistant) A small hand-held computer.

Peer-to-peer network Arrangement where each computer is of equal status.

Personal data Data about a living identifiable person that is specific to that person.

Phishing Tricking people into revealing their banking or credit card details.

Piracy The process of illegally copying software.

Pixel A single point in a graphics element or the smallest dot of light that can appear on a computer screen.

Plagiarism Passing off someone else's work as your own.

Podcasts (personal on demand broadcast) Digital media files that can be audio or video that are released in episodes so that you can be fed them automatically when you connect to the service.

Print server A print server is a computer in a network that controls one or more printers.

Process Any operation that transfers data into information.

Processing Performing calculations or arranging the data into a meaningful order.

Program The set of step-by-step instructions that tell the computer hardware what to do.

RAM (random access memory) Fast temporary memory which loses its contents when the power is turned off.

Range check Data validation technique that checks that the data input to a computer is within a certain range.

Real-time processing Type of processing where data received by the system is processed immediately without any delay.

Relational database A database where the data is held in two or more tables with relationships (links) established between them. The software is used to set up and hold the data as well as to extract and manipulate the stored data.

Relationship The way tables are related to or linked to each other. Relationships can be one-to-one, one-to-many or many-to-many.

Relative reference When a cell is used in a formula and the formula is copied to a new address, the cell address changes to take account of the formula's new position.

Report The output from a database in which the results are presented in a way that is controlled by the user.

RFID (radio frequency identification) Obtains data stored on a tag (a small chip) using radio signals, which means that the reading device and tag do not have to come into contact with each other

Rollover button/image A button/image that changes its appearance when a cursor is moved over it.

ROM (read only memory) Memory stored on a chip which does not lose data when the power is turned off.

Router Hardware device that is able to make the decision about the path that an individual packet of data should take so that it arrives in the shortest possible time.

RSI (repetitive strain injury) A painful muscular condition caused by repeatedly using certain muscles in the same way.

RSS (Really Simple Syndication) A method of sending podcasts.

Sat nav Satellite navigation systems commonly just called sat nav enable maps to be displayed and show a location and guide the person to their destination.

Scams Setting up bogus companies with bogus websites and then making off with the money from customers' orders.

Sensors Devices that measure physical quantities such as temperature, pressure, humidity, etc.

SMS (short messaging service) or as most people know it texting, allows short low cost messages to be sent between phones. It is also possible to send text messages to phones using a computer or mobile device such as a PDA or palmtop.

Social networking site A website that is used to communicate with friends and family and to make new friends and contacts.

Software The programs used by computers.

Spam Unsolicited bulk email (i.e., email from people you do not know, sent to everyone in the hope that a small percentage may purchase the goods or services on offer).

Spellchecker Program usually found with a word-processor and most packages that make use of text, that checks the spelling in a document and suggests correct spellings.

Stand-alone computer If a computer is used on its own without any connection (wireless or wire) to a network, then it is a stand-alone computer.

Style sheets A document that sets out fonts and font sizes for headings and subheadings, etc., in a document. Changes to a heading need only be made in the style sheet and all the changes to headings in the document will be made automatically.

Swipe card Plastic card containing data stored in a magnetic strip on the card.

Tags Special markers used in HTML to tell the computer what to do with the text. A tag is needed at the start and end of the block of text to which the tag applies.

Templates Electronic files that hold standardized document layouts.

Thesaurus Software that suggests words with similar meanings to the word highlighted in a document.

Touch screen A special type of screen that is sensitive to touch. A selection is made from a menu on the screen by touching part of it.

Transaction A piece of business, e.g. an order, purchase, return, delivery, transfer of money, etc.

Transcription error Error made when typing data in using a document as the source of the data.

Transposition error Error made when characters are swapped around so they are in the wrong order.

Update The process of changing information in a file that has become out of date.

UPS (uninterruptible power supply) Alternative power supply in case the mains supply fails.

URL (uniform resource locator) A web address.

USB (universal serial bus) A connection to the computer, such as cameras, external hard drives etc., that allows many devices to be attached via a cable.

User A person who uses a computer.

Username or User-ID A name or number that is used to identify a certain user of the network or system.

Validation checks Checks a developer of a solution sets/creates, using the software, in order to restrict the data that a user can enter so as to reduce errors.

Vector graphic A graphic that is expressed mathematically as an equation and can be resized without loss in quality.

Verification Checking that the data being entered into the ICT system perfectly matches the source of the data.

Videoconferencing ICT system that allows face-to-face meetings to be conducted without the participants being in the same room or even the same geographical area.

Virus A program that copies itself automatically and can cause damage to data or cause the computer to run slowly.

Voice recognition The ability of a computer to 'understand' spoken words by comparing them with stored data.

VoIP (Voice over Internet Protocol) Enables cheap international phone calls to be made using the Internet.

WAN (wide area network) A network where the terminals/computers are remote from each other and telecommunications are used to communicate between them.

WAP (wireless application protocol) Offers a way for users of mobile phones to access the Internet.

Web browser Software program you use to access the Internet. Microsoft Internet Explorer is an example of a web browser.

Webcam A digital camera that is used to capture still images and video images (i.e. moving images).

Web logs (blogs) Websites that are created by an individual with information about events in their life, videos, photographs, etc.

Wi-Fi A trademark for the certification of products that meet certain standards for transmitting data over wireless networks.

Wiki (Wikipedia) The online encyclopaedia created by ordinary people and is a huge store of information on almost every subject.

WIMP (Windows Icons Menus Pointing devices) The graphical user interface (GUI) way of using a computer rather than typing in commands at the command line.

Index

Acknowledgements

Background – Coloured swirls © Bocos Benedict/Fotolia
Background – Question mark © Stephen Coburn/Fotolia

p.v © Nmedia/Fotolia; p.2 © Tinka/Fotolia; p.2 © Dasha Kalashnikova/ Fotolia; p.2 © Big Daddy/Fotolia; p.2 © Harris Shiffman/Fotolia; p.3 © Tan Kian Khoon/Fotolia; p.4 © 300dpi/Fotolia; p.5 © Marco Forante/Fotolia; p.5 © pshek/Fotolia; p.5 © pressmaster/Fotolia; p.5 © Rafa Irusta/Fotolia; p.6 © alphaspirit/Fotolia; p.7 © Helder Almeida/Fotolia; p.8 © Jens Ochlich/Fotolia; p.8 © Arpad Nagy-Bagoly/Fotolia; p.9 © Tyler Olson/Fotolia; p.16 © almagami/Fotolia; p.16 techno-vision.co.uk. p.16 Inclusive Technology p.17 Inclusive Technology p.17 © sasha/Fotolia; p.17 © Digital Photique/ Fotolia; p.17 © Albo/Fotolia; p.18 Glasbergen; p.18 © IKO/Fotolia; p.18 © Andres Rodrigo Gonzalez Buzzio/Fotolia; p.19 © GLUE STOCK/Fotolia; p.19 © Marek Tihelka/Fotolia; p.19 © io/Fotolia; p.20 GreenGate Publishing Services p.20 © Ronald V/Fotolia; p.20 © kmit/Fotolia; p.21 © Vieloryb/Fotolia; p.22 Glasbergen; p.23 © JackF/Fotolia; p.23 © luchsche/Fotolia; p.23 © charles taylor/Fotolia; p.24 © Small Town Studio/Fotolia; p.32 © Harris Shiffman/Fotolia; p.32 © BlueMiniu/Fotolia; p.34 © Kirsty Pargeter/Fotolia; p.35 © Andrzej Tokarski/Fotolia; p.35 © Yong Hian Lim/Fotolia; p.35 © Nikolai Sorokin/Fotolia; p.35 © Glenn Jenkinson/Fotolia; p.36 © Yuriy Zakharov/Fotolia; p.36 © Marlee/ Fotolia; p.36 © Carsten Reisinger/Fotolia; p.37 © aldorado/ Fotolia; p.37 © blake sandifur/Fotolia; p.44 © alphaspirit/ Fotolia; p.45 © titimel35/Fotolia p.46 © Hao Wang p.46 © Sean Gladwell/Fotolia; p.47 Glasbergen p.47 © Samuray/Fotolia; p.47 © Sean Gladwell/Fotolia; p.48 Glasbergen p.49 Glasbergen p.49 © Konstantin Shevtsov/Fotolia; p.50 © cristimatei/Fotolia; p.52 © sigitas1975/Fotolia; p.53 © kentoh/Fotolia; p.62 © Ewa Walicka/Fotolia; p.63 © Arrow Studio/Fotolia; p.64 © pressmaster/ Fotolia; p.66 © Sorin Popa/Fotolia; p.74 © Kheng Guan Toh/ Fotolia; p.75 © loutocky/Fotolia; p.77 © Photosani/Fotolia; p.79 © Leo Blanchette/Fotolia; p.82 © imagesab//Fotolia; p.82 www.chipandpin.co.uk; p.83 © Willee Cole/Fotolia; p.83 © picsfive/Fotolia; p.83 GreenGate Publishing Services; p.83 © Embosser/Fotolia; p.84 © Albert Lozano p.86 © Marc Dietrich/Fotolia; p.86 © M.Tomczak/Fotolia; p.89 © isdngirl/ Fotolia; p.91 Stephen Doyle p.91 WinZip Computing p.91 © Emin Ozkan/Fotolia; p.100 © Kheng Guan Toh/Fotolia; p.100 © Artyom Yefimov/Fotolia; p.104 © Sean Gladwell/Fotolia; p.105 © Mikhail Tolstoy/Fotolia; p.105 © Milan Surkala/Fotolia; p.115 © snoopdoug/ Fotolia; p.116 © Vanessa/Fotolia; p.119 © luchschen/Fotolia; p.130 © Sebastian Crocker/Fotolia; p.130 © hazel proudlove/Fotolia; p.131 © Maximo Sanz/Fotolia; p.134 © Piotr Marcinski/Fotolia; p.135 Glasbergen p.138 © Dan Marsh/Fotolia; p.139 © wayne ruston/Fotolia; p.147 © tdoes/Fotolia; p.147 © Maria Adelaide Silva/Fotolia; p.147 © Yuri Arcurs/Fotolia; p.149 GreenGate Publishing Services; p.164 © Djordje Korovljevic/Fotolia; p.165 GreenGate Publishing Services; p.181 © innershadows/Fotolia; p.183 © Bobby Deal/Fotolia; p.186 © klikk/Fotolia; p.192 © Guy Erwood p.194 © JJAVA/Fotolia; p.194 © BVI Media/Fotolia; p.195 Reproduced with kind permission from The Co-operative Financial Services p.198 qoqazian/Fotolia; p.198 © Yong Hian Lim/Fotolia; p.206 © MacX/Fotolia; p.207 © iQoncept/Fotolia; p.207 Glasbergen p.208 © PricelessPhotos/Fotolia; p.216 www.data-harvest.co.uk p.218 © Iglira/Fotolia; p.218 © Nivellen77/ Fotolia; p.219 © Arvind Balaraman/Fotolia: p.219 © kapp/Fotolia; p.219 © Arthur Eugene Preston/Shutterstock; p.219 © Michael Fritzen/Fotolia; p.219 Image supplied by the Energy Retail Association; p.220 © wrangler/Fotolia; p.220 © Andrey Khritin/Fotolia; p.221 www.hortibot.dk; p.221 © Baloncici/ Shutterstock p.221 wh@mowbot.com p.224 © b.neeser/Fotolia; p.224 © Pierre-Emmanuel Turcotte/Istock p.233 © doug Olson/ Fotolia; p.235 Glasbergen p.235 © khz/Fotolia; p.236 Glasbergen; p.236 © Helder Almeida/Fotolia; p.237 © kentoh/Fotolia; p.237 Glasbergen; p.238 © dundanim/Fotolia; p.238 © Attila Toro/Fotolia; p.239 © bilderbox/Fotolia; p.240 © daseaford/ Fotolia; p.240 © Vladimir Popovic/Fotolia; p.240 © Monkey Business/Fotolia; p.241 © victor zastol'skiy/Fotolia; p.246 © Sean Gladwell/Fotolia; p.246 © Sorin Popa/Fotolia; p.252 © TEA/ Fotolia; p.253 © juanjo tugores/Fotolia; p.254 © Ken Ng/ Fotolia; p.254 © Monkey Business/Fotolia; p.255 © Hedgehog/ Fotolia; p.256 © beaucroft/Fotolia; p.256 © Fredy Sujono/ Fotolia; p.257 © picsfive/Fotolia; p.257 Glasbergen; p.259 © DomLortha/Fotolia; p.261 © tlorna/Fotolia; p.261 Hooleon Corporation, Sales@hooleon.com p.261 © DX/ Fotolia; p.268 © Dmitry Sunagatov/Fotolia; p.269 © Stephen Finn/ Fotolia; p.270 © cs-photo/Fotolia; p.271 © Carla Marcellini/ Fotolia; p.278 © michanolimit/Fotolia; p.278 © che/Fotolia; p.279 GreenGate Publishing Services; p.282 © tetrex/Fotolia; p.284 © Philip Date/Fotolia; p.285 © Sebastian Kaulitzki/ Fotolia; p.285 © grandaded/Fotolia; p.286 © Alysta/Fotolia; p.286 © phecsone/Fotolia; p.299 © Monkey Business/Fotolia; p.299 © ioannis kounadeas/Fotolia; p.300 © Yuri Arcurs/Fotolia; p.301 © Lai Leng Yiap/Fotolia; p.301 © Eisenhans/Fotolia; p.301 © Julieann Krajci/Fotolia;

Adobe product screen shot(s) reprinted with permission from Adobe Systems Incorporated.

Microsoft product screenshots reprinted with permission from Microsoft Corporation.

Every effort has been made to contact copyright holders of material used in this publication. If any copyright holder has been overlooked, we should be pleased to make any necessary arrangements.